Veniselos (Prime Minister of Greece) in March 1921

DAVID WALDER

The Chanak Affair

THE MACMILLAN COMPANY

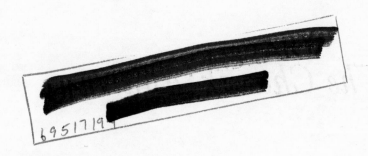

Library of Congress Catalog Card Number: 69-18248

First American Edition 1969

First published in Great Britain in 1969
by Hutchinson & Co. (Publishers) Ltd

THE MACMILLAN COMPANY

Printed in Great Britain

Contents

Illustrations

Lloyd George with Poincaré after lunch at 10 Downing Street, 19 June 1922   (*Press Association*)

Between pages 172 and 173

Mustapha Kemal inspects his troops in Anatolia, March 1922

General Papoulas and his staff in Anatolia, March 1922 (*both photographs by courtesy of Radio Times Hulton Picture Library*)

British and French warships at Constantinople, 1922   (*by courtesy of Captain A. B. C. Reynolds*)

Turkish infantry advancing on Smyrna, August 1922

Greek artillery prepare for attack, Anatolia, July 1922 (*both photographs by courtesy of Radio Times Hulton Picture Library*)

Between pages 284 and 285

Smyrna in flames, September 1922

Refugees on the quay at Smyrna, September 1922   (*both photographs by courtesy of Radio Times Hulton Picture Library*)

Chanak   (*Imperial War Museum*)

Ismet Pasha at Mudania   (*by courtesy of Major I. N. Tubbs*)

General Harington and Ismet Pasha at Mudania after the signing of the Armistice   (*by courtesy of Brigadier J. S. Blunt*)

General Harington about to inspect the last Allied parade in Constantinople, 2 October 1923   (*by courtesy of Captain A. B. C. Reynolds*)

MAPS

Acknowledgments

One of the most important sources for this book has been the recollections of a large number of the participants in the drama which took place in Greece and Turkey during the period 1919–23.

I should therefore like to thank all those who gave me assistance by interview and correspondence, or who lent me documents or photographs; in particular: Field Marshal Earl Alexander, Brigadier Sir Norman Gwatkin, Brigadier J. S. Blunt, Colonel J. Judge, Colonel W. A. Asher, Lieutenant-Colonel J. A. Codrington, Major J. B. Carmichael, Major L. Ridgway, Major I. N. Tubbs, Captain G. Whitaker, Mr. W. T. Henson and Mr. Harold Wykes.

I am grateful to Major F. C. Bedwell, who searched on my behalf among the remaining papers of General Sir Charles Harington, which are in the possession of his widow, Lady Harington.

Owing to periodic defence reorganisations, a number of regiments and units which served in Greece and Turkey have disappeared from the Army List, and in consequence many of their records of service and war diaries have been lost or discarded. Nevertheless a number of serving and retired officers entered into the spirit of my search for information, but for reasons of space I have been forced to list their names in my note on sources at the end of this book. I must, however, pay particular thanks to Major John Ainsworth, who unearthed a great deal of valuable material at the R.H.Q. of the Royal Sussex Regiment; and to Major P. R. Adair, Regimental Adjutant of the Coldstream Guards, who assisted me enormously in contacting retired officers of his regiment. To one of these, Captain A. B. C. Reynolds, I am indebted for many kindnesses and for the opportunity to inspect and use his splendid contemporary photographs.

Like many other writers on subjects involving military matters, I am obliged to Mr. D. W. King of the Ministry of Defence (War Office) Library for the unfailing help I received from him and his staff, in particular Mr. C. A. Potts, for whom no request was too much trouble. The assistance I received from the Royal United Services Institution Library also went a long way to make this book possible.

I should like to record my indebtedness to the Libraries of the House of Commons, *The Times* and the London Library.

Mr. G. Reynolds, M.P., then Minister of Defence for the Army, was most helpful in allowing me to see certain War Office papers, and I must thank the Rt. Hon. William Whitelaw, M.C., M.P. and Mr. Geoffrey Block of the Conservative Research Department for their guidance with regard to the first ' '22 Committee'.

No one would dare to write anything touching upon the life of Kemal Ataturk without constant recourse to Lord Kinross's definitive biography. I should also like to thank Lord Kinross for his advice on sources, as also Mr. John Terraine and the Hon. C. M. Woodhouse.

With regard to my documentary sources contained in the Public Record Office and previously unpublished, the mass of material only became coherent in the hands of Mrs. Joan St. George Saunders, who also stormed on my behalf the twin fortresses of the British Museum Reading Room and the Newspaper Library at Colindale. To Mr. A. J. P. Taylor, who presides benignly over the Beaverbrook

Library, I am much indebted for further unpublished material and background information from the Lloyd George papers, and I should like to thank him and the staff of the library for their kindness and efficiency.

Throughout the writing of this book I have been assisted by Lady Paulina Pepys, whose research, industry and enthusiasm have all been invaluable. Finally I should like to thank Mrs. Meriel Rebbeck, who, on this occasion as on others, has had the unenviable task of reading my handwriting.

Needless to say, all judgments, opinions and prejudices expressed are my own.

D.W.

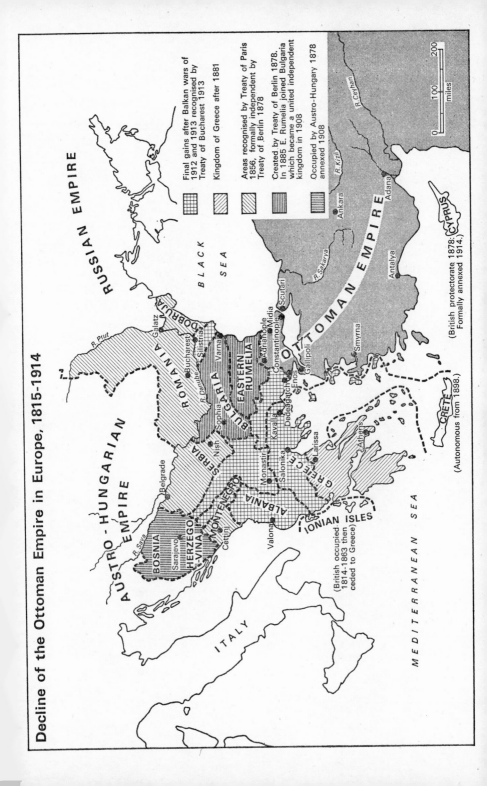

Decline of the Ottoman Empire in Europe, 1815-1914

Final gains after Balkan wars of 1912 and 1913 recognised by Treaty of Bucharest 1913

Kingdom of Greece after 1881

Areas recognised by Treaty of Paris 1856, formally independent by Treaty of Berlin 1878

Created by Treaty of Berlin 1878. In 1885 E. Rumelia joined Bulgaria which became a united independent kingdom in 1908

Occupied by Austro-Hungary 1878 annexed 1908

RUSSIAN EMPIRE

AUSTRO-HUNGARIAN EMPIRE

OTTOMAN EMPIRE

BLACK SEA

MEDITERRANEAN SEA

IONIAN ISLES

ITALY

BOSNIA
HERZEGOVINA
Sarajevo
R. Sava
Belgrade
MONTENEGRO
Cettini
SERBIA
Nish
Sophia
BULGARIA
Danube
Silistra
ROMANIA
Bucharest
DOBRUJA
Galatz
R. Prut
Varna
EASTERN RUMELIA
Adrianople
Midia
Constantinople
Scutari
Gallipoli
Enos
Dedeagatch
Kavalla
Salonika
Monastir
ALBANIA
Valona
GREECE
Larissa
Athens
CRETE
(Autonomous from 1898.)

Smyrna
Antalya
Adana
CYPRUS
Ankara
R. Kizil
R. Sakarya
R. Ceyhan

(British protectorate 1878. Formally annexed 1914.)

(British occupied 1814-1863 then ceded to Greece.)

200
100
0
miles

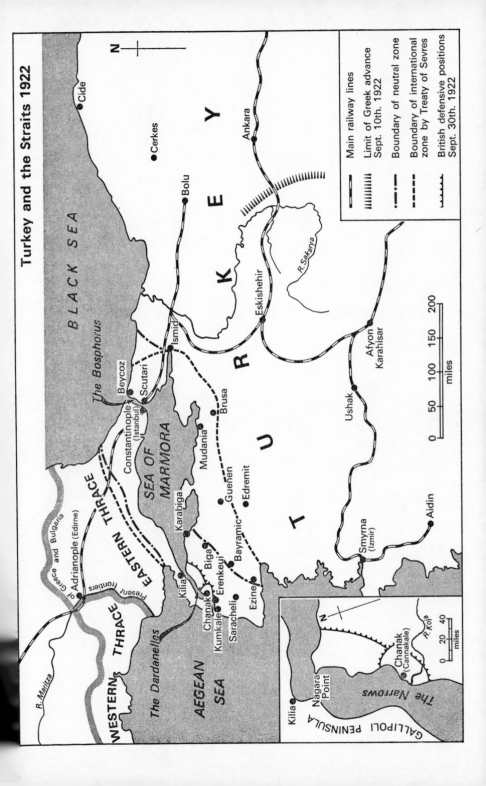

Turkey and the Straits 1922

KEY

Main railway lines	
Limit of Greek advance Sept. 10th. 1922	
Boundary of neutral zone	
Boundary of international zone by Treaty of Sevres	
British defensive positions Sept. 30th. 1922	

N

BLACK SEA

Cide

Cerkes

Bolu

Ankara

R. Sakarya

Eskishehir

TURKEY

Ismid

The Bosphorus

Beycoz

Scutari

Constantinople (Istanbul)

SEA OF MARMORA

Mudania

Brusa

Guenen

Edremit

Bayramic

Karabiga

Biga

Erenkeui

Kilia

Chanak

Kumkale

Saracheli

Ezine

EASTERN THRACE

WESTERN THRACE

Present frontiers of Greece and Bulgaria

Adrianople (Edirne)

R. Maritza

The Dardanelles

AEGEAN SEA

Ushak

Afyon Karahisar

Smyrna (Izmir)

Aidin

0   50   100   150   200
miles

Inset:

N

GALLIPOLI PENINSULA

The Narrows

Kilia

Nagara Point

Chanak (Cannakale)

R. Koja

0   20   40
miles

Prelude

'Who is to have Constantinople?'
Napoleon

September 1922.

The autumn of the first real year of peace after the Great War.

In the United States President Harding had coined the word 'normalcy', and it mirrored accurately what most people were seeking. In Britain war memorials were still being unveiled by the Royal Family and distinguished admirals and generals but unofficial Britain was trying to forget the war. The song of the moment on both sides of the Atlantic was 'Ain't we had fun'. It was more of a wish than a statement.

Still, in thousands of homes, pride of place was given to the photograph of the uniformed son, husband or brother who would not return; but now after four years, although the photograph was always dusted with a bit of extra care, the memories were fading. The British were beginning to feel that at last they were at peace. Not that peace had produced any of the results promised during the course of the war by the politicians. Lloyd George, he was still Prime Minister, had promised 'a land fit for heroes to live in', but it had not come to pass. There were still over a million unemployed, and whether in stagnant industry or depressed agriculture many men counted themselves lucky to have a job at all.

Abroad, too, the era of peace and plenty scheduled to follow 'the war to end wars' had somehow failed to materialise. The Germans and the French were uneasy, there was fighting on the Polish border and in Russia a civil war still raged. Since early 1919, too, Greeks and Turks had been killing each other on the dusty plains of Anatolia.

Yet 1922 had a different look from the years immediately after the war. The moustaches that so many had grown in the trenches were being shaved off. At the Universities of Oxford and Cambridge the serious young men in dyed army greatcoats had disappeared, to be replaced by a new generation with longer hair and consciously aesthetic manners. In London at the end of February the wedding of King George's only daughter Mary, the Princess Royal, to Viscount Lascelles had given society an opportunity to appear again in all its pre-war finery. Winston Churchill had been there, dressed in his uniform of an Elder Brother of Trinity House. With a dozen campaign medals, gold epaulettes, a cocked hat and a naval sword he looked more like an admiral than a civilian Cabinet Minister. There was a mood of escapism about, although that particular word had not yet been invented. In the London theatre that year there were some revivals but nearly all the new plays were light comedy. Only one serious play made any mark: *Loyalties*, by the established John Galsworthy. *The Last Waltz*, with music by Oscar Straus, and *Lilac Time*, which used Schubert's frothier melodies, were both performing to packed houses. At the 'picture theatres' *Nanook*, 'the life of an Eskimo 'mid Eternal Snow', was the great draw, and there was a newsreel of the Prince of Wales on his official visit to Japan. It was the year when the British Broadcasting Company was formed and those with £5 for a 'wireless receiving set' could enjoy a new form of entertainment.

Jack Hobbs scored his hundredth century.

Suddenly the headlines in all the newspapers announced the imminence of war. War with Turkey. For those who read them in Britain in that autumn of 1922 the crisis seemed to have blown up, incomprehensibly, overnight. Photographs appeared again of khaki-clad troops weighed down with Field Service Marching Order, the familiar F.S.M.O. to thousands in the war, embarking for active service. Regiments were being inspected by royal personages and marching to the stations, there to be waved away by wives, children and sweethearts. To many it seemed like 1914 again. The Guards had left Windsor, the Rifle Brigade had left Winchester. Battalions of infantry and batteries of artillery were being shipped from Egypt and Malta. The Mediterranean Fleet with reinforcements from the Atlantic was steaming eastwards.

To fight the Turks. The veterans of Gallipoli, Mesopotamia and Palestine shook their heads. They knew the Turkish soldier as a stubborn, doughty fighter and one for whom they had developed a kind of affection. 'Johnny Turk' was not a bad chap in their view. It had been a pity that his country had been dragged into the last war, and now apparently the British were going to fight him again, at a little town called Chanak, which one had never heard of a week ago. The more thoughtful attributed the situation to the aftermath of the war and the wrangling that had gone on over the peace treaties. In the immediate sense they were right but the British have traditionally short memories so far as their own history is concerned. In fact the crisis had a longer ancestry.

For two nations, both with much longer memories, the recent battles in Anatolia had been but the continuation of a conflict which seemed to have its roots almost as much in legend as history. For the Greeks it was 500 years old. Still, to the superstitious among them, Tuesday was a day of ill omen, in memory of that Tuesday, May 29th, 1453, when Constantinople, capital of the Byzantine Empire, fell at last to the conquering hordes of the Sultan Mehmed II. The Turks could point to the year 1683, when the army

3

of another Sultan had been driven back from the walls of Vienna by John Sobieski, King of Poland. A defeat which signalised the beginning of the slow decline of Turkish power in Europe, a process which had taken over two hundred years. Even the Turkey which had entered the war in 1914 had been a considerable empire, the Ottoman Sultan ruling, as well as the Turkish homeland, Syria, Mesopotamia, Lebanon, Jordan, Palestine and part of Saudi Arabia, and having a nominal suzerainty over Egypt as well. A hundred years before, at the conclusion of the Napoleonic wars, the Ottoman Empire had stretched from the Polish border to the valley of the Euphrates and had included the North African coastal lands and, in Europe, the whole of modern Greece, Bulgaria, Yugoslavia, Romania and Albania. In 1922 men in their seventies of all these nations had been born subjects of the Sultan, ruling his vast multi-racial conglomeration from Constantinople. Even the present Prime Minister of Greece, M. Veniselos, born in Crete in 1864, had started life not as a Greek but as a Turkish subject.

The history of Eastern Europe in the nineteenth century had been, simply, the waning of Turkish power in all these territories and the consequent creation of a number of independent nation states. The manner, however, in which the Balkans had achieved their independence had been far from simple. The removal of the Turks left as many if not more problems in their wake than had been generated by their presence. The filling of the vacuum by over a dozen rival races of diverse tongues and religions had finally made the very adjective 'Balkan' synonymous with double-dealing, conspiracy and violence. It would be unfair, however, to lay the blame entirely on the native peoples. Turkish rule, fantastically incompetent and unbelievably oppressive by turns, had over the centuries done little to improve the character of its subjects. Massacre or indifference, there had seemed to be no middle course, had not bred ready-made nations of democrats ripe for responsibility once the Turkish flag was lowered. Unfortunately, too, for the peoples of the Balkans, their struggles for independence were never a

4

matter entirely for themselves. For the core of the Ottoman Empire was Constantinople, on the most strategic waterway in the world, the Bosphorus, the Sea of Marmora and the Dardanelles, linking the Black Sea and the Mediterranean. Every move in the power complex in this sensitive area was in consequence of immediate concern to the Great Powers: the Russian and Austrian empires, France, Britain, and later the German Empire. The Balkan nations and Turkey herself became mere puppets but occasionally took revenge on their masters. From 1821 to 1922 crises in the Balkans twice involved the Great Powers in war and on countless other occasions brought them to its brink.

This whole mass of complicated actions, motives and issues, statesmen, diplomats and historians almost despairingly labelled 'the Eastern Question'.

The Greeks were the first to seek their independence. In 1821 they took up arms against their Turkish overlords. Curiously enough with little immediate reason, for among the Christian subjects of the Sultan they occupied almost a privileged position. The Turks recognised religious but not racial divisions in their empire, and though certain posts and professions were barred to non-Moslems, within those limits many Greeks of the Phanariot or official class had gained both power and wealth under the Crescent. All, of course, was subject—life, land and property—to the whim and caprice of the Sultan, who was truly absolute and irresponsible. The Greeks, perhaps because of their religious unity, perhaps because of their very power and prosperity, bore this yoke less willingly than the other subject races. The first revolutionary outbreak in the Peloponnese swiftly developed into a full-scale war of independence. Officially the Great Powers, still recovering from the French and Napoleon, were against revolutions. A mixture of self-interest and sentiment, however, drove them towards interference. Russia savoured the delightful combination of concern for fellow members of the Orthodox Church and the possibility of establishing in Greece a satellite state carved out of the territory of Turkey, her rival in the Black Sea. Britain and France were both concerned with their maritime and commercial interests in the eastern Mediterranean, while at the same time yielding to the pull of the classical association, of people called Greeks fighting for liberty. Only the Austrian Empire under its Chancellor, Metternich, with its own quota of subject nationalities and its trade from the Danube carried in Turkish ships, could remain aloof.

Unofficially, in Europe, sentiment was overwhelmingly on the side of the Greeks. For the literate and romantic there were the words of Schiller, Hugo, Pushkin, Byron and Shelley. For the religious the sense of kinship with fellow Christians fighting the infidel. Admittedly the language of Homer was as incomprehensible to a Morean peasant as Mandarin Chinese, and the conduct of the Greeks and their belligerent priests was indistinguishable from that of the Turks; nevertheless money poured into the funds of the Philhellenic societies and volunteers sped to Greece. From France, unemployed veterans of Napoleon's army; from Britain, Admiral Lord Cochrane to command the Greek navy and General Sir Richard Church to attempt to command the land forces. In April 1822 George Jarvis of New York, the first volunteer from the United States, celebrated Easter in Corinth. He was to be wounded and see much action and eventually rise to the rank of general, leaving behind him a journal which reveals his feelings, of alternating admiration and exasperation, for the Greeks he led. In January 1824 there arrived, wearing an Achilles helmet of his own design, the most famous volunteer of all, Lord Byron, whose death at Missolonghi crystallised the romantic view of the Greek cause.

It was not, however, this mixed crowd of adventurers and idealists, outcasts and eccentrics which struck the final blow for Greek freedom but three admirals, British, French and Russian. George Canning, British Foreign Secretary and then Prime Minister, had welded the three nations into an uneasy alliance. In 1825 the Sultan, losing to the Greeks, reluctantly sought the aid of his powerful vassal, Mehemet Ali, ruler of Egypt. Mehemet, not without ambitions of his own in Greece, sent his son, Ibrahim

6

Pasha, with a fleet of sixty ships and an army of 16,000 men to subdue the rebels. The rumour spread through Europe that Ibrahim intended to clear the whole of the Peloponnese of its native inhabitants and re-populate with Egyptian Arabs and Sudanese from his father's domains.

Britain, Russia and France determined to impose an armistice upon the belligerents. On October 20th, 1827, Vice-Admiral Sir Edward Codrington in H.M.S. *Asia* sailed into the Bay of Navarino where the Egyptian fleet was anchored. Behind him, Admiral Heiden and Admiral de Rigny led the Russian and French squadrons respectively. Ibrahim Pasha was ashore, encouraging his troops to further slaughter of the Greeks. Muharrem Bey, his naval commander, was a proud and obstinate man. An explosive situation exploded. The multi-coloured flags fluttered from the signal-yards of the *Asia*, 'prepare for action'. In a few hours the most formidable obstacle to Greek independence was reduced by gun-fire to a few burning hulks, some spars and driftwood, and a large number of corpses floating in Navarino Bay.

Soon after the battle the Allies disagreed. Canning was dead and with him his skill. The Duke of Wellington, now Prime Minister, fearful of Turkey's total collapse, back-pedalled so furiously that Greeks and Turks, French and Russians all believed he must be playing some deep double game. Russian armies threatened Constantinople and a French army cleared Greece of Ibrahim's Egyptians.

Finally, despite the *volte-face* of the British government, in 1832 the Greeks did achieve their independence as a constitutional monarchy, with Otto, second son of the philhellene King of Bavaria, as their first king. The guarantors of the new kingdom were Britain, Russia and France.

When Admiral Codrington died in 1851 the Greek Deputies decreed that his name, surmounted by a wreath of laurels, should be carved on a tablet in the Assembly Chamber. By his own countrymen he deserves to be better remembered, for his actions gave them a not untypical introduction to the problems that were to come.

*   *   *

In the 1830's and 40's the British had more trouble with Mehemet Ali, whose ambition overreached itself when he tried to extend his empire from Egypt both eastwards and westwards. Twice more, as he ruefully observed, he was to be thwarted in his aims by a British fleet, acting this time in support of the Sultan. It was in the 1850's, however, that Britain fought her only European war until 1914. In the Crimea, against the Russians, with the French and the Turks as allies.

The causes were footling, the conduct of the war deplorable; yet, certainly in its early stages, it was the most popular war the British ever fought. The Prime Minister, Lord Aberdeen, and Albert, Prince Consort, who were opposed to it, were vilified in both right and left wing press in terms which no modern journalist could hope to get past his sub-editor. At one time there was a hopeful rumour that Albert had been confined to the Tower as a traitor.

The cause of all this passion, surprising to those who think of the Victorians as staid and quiet, was that Britain had found a new enemy—the Tsar of Russia. Nicholas I, 'the Autocrat', the 'Cossack Tsar' of the British press, oppressor of the Poles, subjugator of the Hungarians, had plans to divide up the decaying Ottoman Empire. On at least three occasions the Tsar used his picturesque similes about the Turks, 'the sick man of Europe', 'the dying bear', to persuade British ambassadors or cabinet ministers that Britain might take Egypt and Cyprus or Crete while Russia would 'protect' Bulgaria and Serbia and the principalities of Moldavia and Wallachia (now modern Romania). Unfortunately the more Nicholas expounded his schemes the more frightened British officialdom became, for the same reasons as Wellington had recoiled from the victorious Greeks. Britain could not afford to allow the Ottoman Empire to collapse because Turkey sat astride the spinal column which linked Britain with her proudest possession, her Indian Empire.

Better a thousand times the corrupt incompetent Ottomans than the powerful Russians, the volatile Greeks, or some Slav nation controlled from St. Petersburg. The mutterings about Russian imperialism grew in the corridors of the Foreign Office and the British Embassy in Constantinople. The Black Sea would become 'a Russian lake', the Russian fleet would rival the British in the Mediterranean, the Tsar, master of a million men, would cut Britain's land communications with India. So Turkey had to be bolstered up against Russia. At the same time a dispute between Orthodox and Catholic clerics over the custody of the Holy Places in Jerusalem, in Turkish territory, became a matter of prestige between the two protecting Powers, Russia and France. In Paris there was what Alexander Kinglake, the historian, called 'a small knot of middle-aged men who were pushing their fortunes'. Their leader was the new Emperor Napoleon III, anxious to appear publicly patriotic, Catholic and respectable. So the second Bonaparte to rule France opposed himself to Russia and became the ally of Britain. At the last moment diplomacy failed to avert a war. Britain had as Ambassador in Constantinople, Stratford de Redcliffe, of immense prestige and admired by the Turks. The Russians sent Prince Menshikov, a blunt, short-tempered soldier. In the circumstances the Turks found it easy to reject Russian demands, confident of British help.

Soon the Russians had occupied Moldavia and Wallachia, notionally to extract terms for the welfare of the Sultan's Christian subjects. Turks and Russians fired on each other. In November 1854 Admiral Nakimov, commanding the Russian Black Sea Squadron, sank a complete Turkish fleet in the Bay of Sinope on the southern coast of the Black Sea. As Turks and Russians were already fighting on land it was a perfectly justifiable act of war. The British, however, called it 'a massacre'. Queen Victoria, a good barometer of her subjects' feelings, wrote of 'the selfishness and ambition of one man [the Tsar] and his servants'.

In March 1855 the British and French demanded the evacuation of Moldavia and Wallachia; on the 27th France declared war and on the 28th Britain followed suit. Soon the Queen, with Albert and the children, was waving farewell from the Buckingham Palace balcony to her guardsmen in scarlet and bearskins *en route* for the East. The

9

mood was still one of high optimism. The British had got their war with Browning's 'icy Muscovite', and the cheers of the London crowd literally drowned the band of the Scots Fusilier Guards as it led the regiment to Waterloo Station.

Two years later there were 21,000 British dead in the Crimea. Lord Raglan, the army commander, had died, of a broken heart, it was said. Lords Lucan and Cardigan, a pair of aristocratic, military maniacs, had between them perpetrated the military disaster known as the Charge of the Light Brigade. A large fleet had been taken off to the Baltic by Admiral Sir Charles Napier, who in better days had coerced Mehemet Ali, and had achieved nothing. At the battles of the Alma, Balaclava and Inkerman and the siege of Sebastopol, the courage of the British private soldier and regimental officer had just saved their elderly, incompetent commanders from defeat. The Tsar had died and in Britain the government had fallen. Queen Victoria was much concerned, the Turks had generally run away, the French were weary. Only two people, Florence Nightingale and William Howard Russell, *The Times* war correspondent, had made enviable reputations and they had fought not the enemy but fools and worse among their fellow countrymen.

Peace was signed in Paris in 1856 and Napoleon III had his brief moment of glory as host and victor. For fourteen years Russian naval and military power was excluded from the Black Sea. The Sultan gave bland assurances as to the future welfare of his Christian subjects. Moldavia and Wallachia combined to become the semi-autonomous state of Romania. Of the custody of the Holy Places in Jerusalem, officially the cause of the war, there was no mention whatsoever. The British, who had been forced by their losses to recruit a foreign legion of German volunteers, consoled themselves with the distribution of the newly instituted Victoria Cross and an orgy of street naming.

In London alone there are fifteen Almas, a Balaclava, an Inkerman, a Sebastopol, seven Raglans, seven Cardigans, a Lucan, a Napoleon and, with justice, nineteen Nightingales.

By contrast, there are only fourteen Waterloos, and
Waterloo was a great victory.

*   *   *

The private of the Royal Fusiliers who, on his way to
the Crimea, had described the preservation of the Ottoman
Empire as 'a rotten cause' would, twenty years later, have
had no reason to revise his opinion. Turkish promises of
reform remained what they had always been, mere paper
words to pacify allies in the West. The condition of the
Christian subjects of the Sublime Porte[1] did not change and
whether Russian statemen wished it or no Bulgars, Serbs,
Slovaks, Croats and Montenegrins looked to Russia, the
most powerful Slav state in the world, as their protector and
potential liberator.

Romania was virtually autonomous, Serbs and Montenegrins had never really been subdued, but only Greece
could call herself an independent state. Perhaps because they
were seafarers, perhaps because they were neither satellites
of Austria nor Russia, the Greeks alone enjoyed the interest
of Britain. Originally they had taken Otto as king 'so that
all division and rivalry for preference should cease among
us', but Otto had not been a success. The harshly bureau-
cratic rule of his Bavarian advisers grated upon his subjects.
In 1843, as a result of a totally bloodless revolution, he had
bound himself to choose his ministers only from Greeks.
During the Crimean War in a foolish venture he had attempted to regain the regard of his subjects by invading Thessaly
and the Epirus. He had been saved from his own mistake by
Britain and France, at the time the allies of Turkey. In
1863, with few regrets and without violence, Otto left his
troublesome kingdom for ever. The Greeks were again in the
market for a king. They organised a plebiscite and voted
overwhelmingly for Prince Alfred, Duke of Edinburgh,

[1] The Sublime Porte. Originally the gateway to the palace where the
Sultan or his Grand Vizier conducted official business. The metonymy
became official and the expression came to mean either the Ottoman
government itself or the empire. Frequently abbreviated to 'the Porte'.

Victoria's second son, and had begun to celebrate his victory when they were informed by Britain, France and Russia that Alfred, as a British prince, was, by the 1832 convention between the three guarantors, inelegible. The angry mob stormed the British legation in Athens, but finally Prince William George of Glucksberg, the second son of Prince Christian of Denmark, accepted the throne. With the Prince, whose sister was engaged to Edward, Prince of Wales, the British threw in the Ionian isles as a makeweight. Thus in 1863 an eighteen-year-old Danish prince, later to be the brother-in-law of Edward VII and the Tsar Alexander III, assumed the style of 'George I, King of the Hellenes', thereby accepting, with his title, his subjects' ambitions with regard to all those Greeks not yet included in the Greek kingdom.

In 1868 George's first son was born and named, by popular demand, Constantine, after the first Byzantine Emperor. Christened into the Orthodox faith, he became Prince of Sparta and the Diadoch (successor) and was Greece's first native-born prince. His father had rapidly made himself a model constitutional monarch and Constantine's future seemed assured. Greece was not, it was true, a settled nation; her politicians still entertained ambitions with regard to 'the unredeemed Greeks', those of their co-nationals under foreign rule. They formed sizable minorities throughout the Balkans and in Turkey itself. They dominated the trading population of Constantinople, and in Asia Minor the port of Smyrna was practically a Greek town. Greek-populated islands were also in the possession of the Turks, notably Crete and Cyprus. Nevertheless in the 1860's and 70's Greece stood out among the Balkan countries as being both relatively stable and free from interference by the Great Powers.

An uneasy quiet hung over the rest of the Balkans ruled by the Turks until 1875, when by a process of sympathetic combustion Bosnians, Serbs, Montenegrins and finally Bulgars in turn took up arms in revolt. Against the Bulgars the Turks moved with unaccustomed haste and more than usual savagery. Over sixty villages were razed to the ground by 'irregulars' and over 12,000 men, women and children were butchered. As news of the 'Bulgarian atrocities' filtered through the consulates to their home governments the Great Powers braced themselves for another Near Eastern crisis.

The Crimean alignments had shifted and changed and there was an important addition to the ranks of the great, Bismarck's five-year-old German Empire. France had been defeated by Germany and was now again a republic. The Austrian Empire had also gone down in battle and in consequence was forced to make terms with her most powerful minority, the Hungarians. Henceforth the Habsburg domains were Austro-Hungarian, the Dual Empire, and her ambitions Balkan rather than German. Bismarck had then created his Dreikaiserbund, his league of the three emperors, German, Austro-Hungarian and Russian, and hoped thereby to contain the ambitions of all three. In his view 'the Eastern Question was not worth the bones of a Pomeranian grenadier', but its complications were to defeat him in the end.

The reports from Bulgaria sent a wave of pan-Slav sentiment sweeping through Russia. Prayers for a Serbian victory were said in the churches, large sums of money were collected for the rebels, and volunteers, like Vronsky in *Anna Karenina*, left to aid the Serbian cause. In the most despotically ruled state in Europe its absolute ruler, the Tsar, had to bow to public opinion. As before, diplomacy was tried first and the Dreikaiserbund demanded of the Turks independence for Bosnia and Herzegovina and a minimum of rights for the Ottoman Christians. Disraeli, the British Prime Minister, not greatly concerned with 'Bulgarian horrors' and obsessed with Turkey's relationship to India, refused to add his weight to the protest. Queen Victoria wrote: '[The Queen] fears our refusal to join the other countries may have a serious effect and may encourage the Porte to refuse to listen to advice and to look to us for support in their difficulties.' The Queen, who did not often disagree with Disraeli, was right and her Prime Minister was wrong.

13

The Turks murdered one Sultan, deposed his subnormal successor, and produced within a year Abdul Hamid, who promised to rule according to a constitution and with the advice of a parliament. He was also determined to defeat the Serbs. When Turkish troops were within marching distance of Belgrade the Russians intervened and, using the mobilisation of six army corps as an argument, imposed an armistice. A conference in Constantinople failed because Britain was still lukewarm and Austria-Hungary feared Russian ambitions. Once more Russia was on her own and within weeks was again at war with Turkey. Russian troops by agreement moved through Romania, so Turkey declared war on Romania as well. The Russians were by no means as successful as had been expected, but by January 1878 they had captured Sofia and Adrianople. In Britain public opinion was divided between the opposing camps of Gladstone, violently anti-Turk, and Disraeli, the ever-sensitive Imperialist, but Disraeli was Prime Minister. It looked as if the Russians were about to occupy Constantinople. The Mediterranean Squadron sailed into the Sea of Marmora. The Russians reached San Stefano, eight miles from Constantinople, and there signed an armistice. The British ships moved to within sight of Constantinople, preparations were made to mount an expeditionary force, reserves were recalled and troops moved from India to Malta. Again the British Empire was coming to the rescue of the Turks.

The Russians yielded reluctantly and the terms of their armistice were submitted to a European conference to meet in Berlin. The Congress of Berlin was Disraeli's swan song. 'The old Jew, that is the man,' said Bismarck, who presided. Under pressure from Britain and, to their fury, their allies Germany and Austria-Hungary, the Russians gave up the 'big Bulgaria' they had hoped to create as a satellite, allowed Austria-Hungary to 'protect' Bosnia and Herzegovina and saw Disraeli rewarded by the Turks with Cyprus. The British Prime Minister, having confided to the Crown Princess of Prussia that he didn't think the settlement would last seven years, returned home to announce 'Peace with

Honour', and received the Order of the Garter from a now reconciled Victoria.

*   *   *

The Congress of Berlin was the end of an era and the settlement in the long run disastrous.

The three emperors' league was broken up and henceforth Austria-Hungary and Russia were to be rivals in the Balkans. Bulgaria, divided, was to unite, and to prove, after a number of vicissitudes, unwilling to be a Russian dependency. Abdul Hamid was to show himself to be the worst tyrant even in Turkish history, and became 'Abdul the Damned', 'the Red Sultan' and, in Anatole France's atrocious pun, 'Le Grand Saigneur'. Britain, involved in Egypt, was to make Alexandria her naval base in the eastern Mediterranean and not need Cyprus, which was to become a severe irritant in the twentieth century.

Overall, after Disraeli's death in 1881, Britain lost interest in both Turkey and the Balkans. The Suez Canal, although curiously Disraeli had not seemed to realise it, made Turkey unimportant as the guardian of the route to India. The British occupation of Egypt, technically a Turkish possession, destroyed the image of disinterested friend. For thirteen of the remaining twenty years of the century the Prime Minister was Gladstone, whose detestation of the Turk and all his works was only equalled by the feelings entertained at Constantinople for Mr. Gladstone. He was passionately concerned with the oppressed Christians in the Ottoman Empire, but ironically Gladstone, the anti-imperialist, was to have his hands full with Egypt, South Africa, Afghanistan and Ireland. The cause of the Balkan Christians, however worthy, had to be neglected.

In the mind of Lord Salisbury, Gladstone's Tory rival, there lingered no feeling of regard for the Sultan as Sultan or even as Caliph, spiritual head of the Moslem faith. Of Disraeli's championship of the Turks he admitted, 'We put our money on the wrong horse.'

In the Balkans, during the last twenty years of the nineteenth century, there were three springs of action: the rivalry of two Great Powers, Russia and Austria-Hungary, the activities of the Balkan nations, and those of Turkey itself. This was the period during which Bismarck's carefully preserved pattern of alliances shifted and re-formed. Austria-Hungary and Germany came closer together as partners and took in Italy as a half-hearted third. Russia, on her own, eventually came to an understanding with the other outcast, France. Britain stayed aloof for the moment. Bulgaria, Romania, Serbia and Montenegro went through their own internal troubles and tended to reproduce in microcosm the groupings of the larger Powers. Greece, secure in British friendship, by contrast enjoyed the most peaceful period of her existence. In the Ottoman Empire Abdul Hamid, cruel, calculating and cowardly, took advantage of European dissension to go his own way. Reactionary forces were encouraged; Westernisation was only tolerated in the army and the police so that they could be more efficient as instruments of repression. No power in Europe was prepared to risk a war with her rivals to put Turkey's internal affairs to rights, so the Armenian Christians were massacred in their thousands without redress. Germany and Austria-Hungary were indifferent. Russia would not interfere, as she had Armenians within her own borders and there were enough internal problems already. France and Britain were suspicious of each other's colonial ventures so would only make ineffective protests and hope that one day the Ottoman Empire would disintegrate of its own accord.

Then in the new century the unbelievable happened and there was a revolution in Turkey. In 1908 the hitherto secret Committee of Union and Progress declared itself in Macedonia, won over the army and prepared to march on Constantinople. The movement drew its strength from young army officers, one of them called Mustapha Kemal. Abdul Hamid's regime collapsed overnight, a constitution was accepted and a parliament summoned. When, characteristically, the Sultan attempted to go back on his word he was easily deposed and replaced by Mohammed V, a mere cypher in the hands of the revolutionaries. At first sight all was sweetness and light. Turks and Christians danced in the streets; even the surviving Armenians were given hope and in Europe 'the Young Turks' were hailed as idealists and liberators. Unfortunately, they were neither. Their leaders, Enver, Talaat and Djavid, were only determined that Turkey should be modernised in order to regain her former power. Fervent nationalists, there was no consideration in their programme for the lot of non-Turks. The Bulgars, Serbs and Greeks were further oppressed, more taxes were imposed on the Albanians, and the Greeks in Crete were given no hope of freedom. In less than two years the Young Turks proved that the force of nationalism, Turkish nationalism, could be invoked to hold an empire together as well as destroy it. Among the Balkan states the realisation quickly grew that to free their minorities they would have to resort to arms and for once agree among themselves. The Young Turks succeeded where Abdul Hamid had failed and united Greeks, Bulgars, Serbs and Romanians against them. The architect of the Balkan League, formed of these states, was Eleftherios Veniselos, first active in his native Crete, now Prime Minister of Greece.

When Italy, provoked to imperial ambition by German and French intentions in Morocco, declared war on Turkey and sent an army into Libya, Veniselos decided that the time to strike the Turks had come. Greeks, Serbians and Bulgarians attacked on all fronts. The Greeks took Salonika, the Serbs, Monastir and Macedonia; the Bulgarian army drove the Turks into the Chataldja lines, a stone's throw from Constantinople. Within six weeks European Turkey had ceased to exist outside Constantinople.

In 1912 the London Conference assembled to redraw the map of the Balkans, and by the creation of Albania managed to appease Austrian demands on behalf of Bulgaria and Russian demands on behalf of Serbia. While the Conference was still sitting, Enver, killing the War Minister with his own hand, carried out a coup in Constantinople and reopened the war. Again the League was successful, but dissent was growing among the victors. King George of

Greece was assassinated in Salonika, where he had accompanied his men to forestall the Bulgarians, who coveted Constantinople as well but realised that the Russians would deny them that prize. Resentment drove out reason and the Bulgarians turned on their allies, only to be defeated by Greeks and Serbs plus Romanians.

The peace treaty signed in Bucharest recognised the final military situation. The Bulgarians were cast down, the Turks in the confusion had taken back some territory, the Greeks were elated, and the Serbians were the most powerful nation in the Balkans. The Great Powers regarded these changes with apprehension. Austria-Hungary saw Bulgaria, her favoured friend, humiliated, and Serbia, patronised by Russia, raised up. Germany, who had been wooing the Turks, covered her disappointment by making the new Greek king, Constantine, now the Kaiser's brother-in-law, a German field marshal. No one thought of the settlement as permanent. The soldiers in Vienna were convinced that Serbia, now the focus of Slav ambitions in Austrian-ruled Bosnia and Herzogovina, must be cut down to size. The Germans were prepared to befriend the friendless Turks for their own advantage. Behind the Serbs stood their protector Russia, France's ally, in turn now allied to Britain.

On June 28th, 1914, Mr. Jones, the British Vice-Consul in Sarajevo, the capital of Bosnia, sent a telegram to Sir Edward Grey, the Foreign Secretary. 'According to news received here heir apparant and his consort assassinated this morning by means of an explosive nature.' Mr. Jones was wrong. The Archduke Franz Ferdinand, heir to the Austro-Hungarian Empire, had been killed not by a bomb but by bullets from an automatic supplied to a Bosnian youth by agents of the chief of Serbian military intelligence.

As Bismarck had prophesied, 'some damned foolish thing in the Balkans' had sparked off a European war.

I

'This damned system of alliances'
Gottlieb von Jagow,
German Foreign Minister

The causes of the 1914-18 War have been rehearsed and investigated too many times for another attempt. Sufficient is it here to echo the complaint of Gottlieb von Jagow, the German Foreign Minister, as he watched Europe divide itself in two in those fateful days of July. Conveniently forgetting the part his own country had played in their making, he laid the blame on 'this damned system of alliances, which were the curse of modern times'.

On July 28th Austria-Hungary declared war on Serbia. Russia, to lend support to her ally, began the slow ponderous process by which the Tsar's army was mobilised. The Germans, honouring their alliance with the Dual Empire, demanded that Russian mobilisation should cease. Russia refused, both unwilling and unable to sacrifice a potential advantage. Therefore on August 1st Germany declared war on Russia and two days later on Russia's ally France. In attacking France Germany invaded Belgium and so on August 4th Great Britain, pledged to defend Belgian neutrality, declared war on Germany. On August 6th Austria-Hungary declared war on Russia, and four days later on France, and Britain completed the circle by declaring war on Austria-Hungary. On August 11th the Austro-Hungarian army, leisurely to the last, when all the major European powers were at war, began in earnest its invasion of Serbia.

The 'ifs' and 'buts' of this incredible chain reaction have been posed and analysed countless times. The chief participants, the princes, the statesmen, the generals and the ambassadors, have all testified to the feelings of reluctance with which they signed their orders, delivered their ultimatums and asked for their passports.

The crowds gathered in the various capitals and cheered and sang their national anthems, but some were less enthusiastic. The Russian liberals had been hesitant, the German Social Democrats reluctant. Two members of the British Cabinet, Lord Morley and John Burns, had already resigned. David Lloyd George, then Chancellor of the Exchequer, was in two minds to the last, and talked of the German entry into Belgium as 'only a little violation'.

Yet despite the reluctance and the doubts, within little more than a month of an assassination in an obscure Bosnian town British troops were in France, ready to fight, as they sang ruefully, 'all because of a bounding Balkanite'.

Really the most fantastic feature was the speed and the efficacy with which von Jagow's system did work, and the reason for that lay not in the wishes of the statesmen but in the fears of the generals and the admirals who advised them. The pressure for speed was exerted by them, armed with their maps and charts, protractors, slide rules and compasses. For each one of the belligerents had a war plan, from the German, most exact and detailed, to the Russian, slipshod, vague and unpractised. Whatever the worth of the plan, each and all depended on the vital element of time and time was important because every nation thought in terms of a short war.

The Germans had to invade and conquer France as

quickly as possible, so as to be ready to transfer their forces to fight the slow-moving Russians. The whole of French military strategy was based upon an immediate invasion of Germany. The Commander of the British Grand Fleet, Admiral Jellicoe, expected action within days, perhaps hours, of the expiry of the British ultimatum to Germany.

At much lower levels, too, quick conquests were thought of as the essence of the coming war. An officer of the Russian Imperial Guard worried about his uniform for the ceremonial entry into Berlin. A German officer had named the restaurant for his first dinner in Paris. French reservists marching to the railway stations echoed the shouts of the crowds, '*à Berlin*'. All ranks in all armies agreed with the Kaiser's prophecy to one of his departing regiments: 'You will be home before the leaves fall from the trees.'

Only in England did anyone raise a dissident voice: the new Minister of War, Field Marshal Lord Kitchener of Khartoum, the victor of Omdurman, the conqueror of the Sudan and South Africa, Sirdar of the Egyptian army and Commander-in-Chief in India, and lately *de facto* ruler of Egypt. At his first Cabinet meeting in his new post he announced, in his oracular way, 'we must be prepared to put armies of millions in the field and maintain them for several years'. His hearers, his civilian Cabinet colleagues, who up to that moment had been thinking in terms of months, if not weeks, charitably assumed that the great proconsular figure had spent too much time in the sun.

Lloyd George said of Kitchener that he arrived at his conclusions by flashes of intuition rather than the slower processes of reasoning. What light illuminated the mind behind the enormous sweeping moustaches and the staring, almost hypnotic, eyes on that occasion is not known. The Field Marshal was to be drowned on his way to Russia in June 1916, so he did not live to see his prediction fulfilled in its entirety. Nevertheless he was to survive at the centre of affairs long enough to see the concepts of speed, quick victories and a war of movement disappear into the muddy trenches of France and Flanders, to see the efforts made by the Western Allies to escape that deadlock end in failure, and to see the war extended by one stroke to embrace another continent.

For a brief moment or two, however, in the autumn of 1914, it did appear as if the war would be a short one and confined to Europe. A vast stretch of Europe, admittedly: from the West, where obedient to the plan of the dead von Schlieffen the German armies endeavoured to encircle Paris, to the pine-covered desolations of the East, where the Czechs, Croats, Slovenes, Slavs, Austrians, Hungarians and Poles who made up the Habsburg army, with their German allies, held back the ill-armed and ill-led Russian hordes.

Britain and France, and to a lesser extent Germany, were all colonial Powers, of course, but it did seem as if the contribution of their overseas possessions was to be confined to the sending of troops to the Western Front. Consequently, in those early days, grave, bearded Sikhs, moustached Punjabis and cheerful Gurkhas came to suffer the mud and cold of that first winter for the King Emperor, regarded by and regarding the equally picturesque Moroccans, Algerians, Spahis and Foreign Legionaires of the French colonial army.

The concept of a European cockpit was to last for only a few more months; it was soon to be destroyed by the actions of a German admiral. Admiral Souchon, as the hours of the British ultimatum were running out, was in command of the new, fast battle cruiser *Goeben* and the light cruiser *Breslau*, steaming through the Mediterranean and anticipating in his mind that if war broke out his first task would be to intercept troop convoys from French North Africa. However, on the morning of August 4th he received new instructions from the German Admiralty: 'Proceed at once to Constantinople', the capital of a neutral state, indeed the only one of the Great Powers of the Balkan crises of the nineteenth and twentieth centuries not at war. Neutral at the moment but, as Admiral Souchon was informed by wireless, the Turks were a nation of whom the Germans had hopes. The system of alliances may have caused the war, but the search for allies was still to continue.

Turkey had been neglected in the last few years by those

nations previously most interested. The Young Turk revolution had come and gone, and apparently the Ottoman Empire, even under new direction, was not capable of reforming itself internally. Externally her defeats in the Balkan Wars had revealed her military incompetence and although her territories were still vast it was as if Britain, Russia and France had given up in disgust. Some day this decaying hulk would die, but at the moment it was best left to moulder on its own.

Britain, it is true, still had some contact with her old ally, and in 1914 a British Naval Mission under Admiral Limpus advised the Turks on their navy. Nevertheless under the Liberal government, which had succeeded to power in 1906, many of whose members had inherited Gladstone's view of the 'unspeakable Turk', any closer relationship between Britain and Turkey was unthinkable. So in 1911 tentative approaches put out by the Turks for a firm alliance with Britain had been rejected. What was the point, the Cabinet argued, of an alliance with an empire soon to decay, whose internal regime was anathema, and whose support would have meant the enmity of Greece and the Balkan states? In short, in the British view Turkey was not worth an alliance.

One nation in Europe, however, thought differently: the German Empire.

So Kaiser Wilhelm II, who in 1889 and 1898 had paid state visits to the Sultan, the only European monarch to do so, during his tour of the Near East postured on a white horse in Jerusalem, had himself photographed in Turkish uniform with a fez, and called upon the Sultan and his subjects to regard him as their friend. On a more practical level the Germans, under the direction of General Liman von Sanders, began to provide the Turkish army with arms, munitions, and an increasingly large number of officers and instructors. The Berlin–Baghdad railway too, which had caused so much disagreement with Britain, provided an easy introduction to the economic wooing of the Ottoman, and in the wake of the soldiers there followed the engineers, the bankers and the businessmen.

23

From 1908 to 1914 this process of military and economic advances continued with increasing momentum, and although many Turks were apprehensive of the embraces of their new and powerful friend, after the defeats of the Balkan Wars it seemed as if in Europe they had no one else to turn to but this beneficial provider of military advice and cheap goods. War clouds were gathering in Europe and many Turks had not relinquished the idea of an opportunity, in a general conflict, of revenge upon their late enemies, especially the Greeks.

In July 1914 Djemal Pasha, Minister of Marine and a powerful member of the Turkish Cabinet, had journeyed to Paris and raised there the question of the return of the Aegean islands, seized by Italy in the 1911–12 War. Both the British and French were unco-operative. The snubbing of Djemal, a staunch Anglophile, confirmed the view that in the event of a war Turkey had nothing to gain from an alliance with Britain.

This impression was underlined on the very eve of the war by a piece of incredible bungling on the part of the British government. In 1913 the Turks, still smarting from their defeat by the Greeks, Serbians and Bulgarians, were determined to equalise their naval position in the Aegean and had bought a far from modern battleship from Brazil. Despite the protests of Djemal Pasha to the U.S. Ambassador, Henry Morgenthau, a violent Philhellene who rejoiced in his discomfiture, the U.S.A. immediately sold two modern ships, the *Idaho* and the *Mississippi*, to the Greeks.

Turks who contemplated a renewal of their conflict with the Greeks now looked elsewhere, and their hopes were concentrated on two other battleships, the *Sultan Osman* and the *Reshadieh*. As part of British naval advice and assistance, apparently not open to the same moral objections as military or diplomatic help, these two first-class ships, modern and, in the case of the *Osman*, equipped with 13.5 inch guns, were nearing completion on the Tyne in the spring of 1914. The *Sultan Osman* was completed in May and the Turks had paid half of her purchase price; the *Reshadieh* was ready in early July and Turkish crews were ready to take over.

Their overall cost was £7,500,000, but it was not only their cash value that was important to the Turks. The money had been raised by popular, if not perhaps always voluntary, subscription, and every Anatolian peasant felt he had a share in these magnificent new ships which at one move would wipe out the effect of the Greeks' sharp deal over the *Idaho* and *Mississippi*.

The British, however, ignored all this, and in July began a process of delaying the departure of the ships, which they thought could be better employed by the Royal Navy. Accordingly, as soon as war seemed inevitable, Winston Churchill, the impetuous and bellicose First Lord of the Admiralty, ordered their seizure. The Turkish captain, with his 500 sailors already on board a transport in the Tyne, threatened to hoist the Turkish flag and take his ships away. Churchill, from the Admiralty, ordered the use of force if necessary and there was a clash, with a few casualties on both sides. The Turkish government was informed of the seizure in the bluntest possible terms and the question of compensation for the financial loss was not mentioned. Winston Churchill, in justification some years after the event, was to talk, in his *History of the Great War*, in a rather vague way of Turkey's plans to attack not Greece but Russia, as if Turkey intended to attack Russia before the two ships were seized. Such plans were known to Churchill, but strangely enough to no one else.

It was only on August 2nd that the Turkish government, succumbing to the blandishments of Baron Wangenheim, the German Ambassador, secretly promised to enter the conflict on the side of the Central Powers if Russia intervened in the Austro-Serbian War.

It was towards this situation in the Turkish capital that Admiral Souchon with his two battleships now steamed at full speed. After August 4th all other warships he would see would be enemies, as the British and French navies dominated the Mediterranean. The French, as Souchon had originally surmised, were occupied in convoying their troops from North Africa to France, so the task of intercepting the *Goeben* and *Breslau* fell to the British.

A number of factors unimagined by Souchon operated in his favour. No one, either at the Admiralty or in the British fleet, ever dreamed that the German ships were heading for Constantinople; presumably Churchill's fear of the Turks had evaporated once he had carried out his coup on the Tyne. So, although the *Goeben* and *Breslau* were followed by units of the Royal Navy, it was assumed, incredibly, that Souchon's course to the east was dictated by prudence not design.

Again, Churchill's instructions to the Admiral in the Mediterranean, Sir Archibald Berkeley Milne, were ambiguous to a degree. There was talk of avoiding superior force, which the First Lord much later on was to say referred to the Austro-Hungarian fleet of slow and superannuated vessels in the Adriatic. Milne and his second-in-command, Rear-Admiral Sir Ernest Troubridge, rather naturally assumed this to mean that their individual ships, unless stronger than the *Goeben*, were not to engage her. The Austro-Hungarian navy may have been in the First Lord's mind but not in that of the naval officers who had the two German warships and no others in their view. Nelson would have engaged, but years of peace and easily held supremacy had had its effect on the Royal Navy, and neither Milne nor Troubridge was a Nelson. So, aided as well by incredible luck, Souchon found himself, his ships untouched, on August 11th at the entrance to the Dardanelles, under the guns of the fortress of Chanak.

Now came the real crunch. Would the Turks, still outwardly neutral, allow the Germans to penetrate the Dardanelles? Souchon's telegraphic communications with his Ambassador in Constantinople produced a flurry of diplomatic activity. The Turkish Cabinet met hurriedly to consider the unwelcome news. Unwelcome, that is, to those Ministers like the Grand Vizier, Said Halim Pasha, who still hankered after neutrality, or to those like Djemal who still had a sentimental attachment to the British.

The decision was taken out of their hands by Enver Pasha, the Minister of War. A soldier trained at the military academy in Berlin, and retaining from that period the

waxed moustache with upturned points in flattering imitation of the Supreme War Lord himself, Enver had an
admiration for all things German, particularly military
efficiency. The most ruthless and determined member of the
Committee of Union and Progress which ruled Turkey,
never doubting that Germany would be victorious, he was
impatient to put his own country on the winning side.

Ignoring his Cabinet colleagues, on his own responsibility,
he ordered the commander at Chanak to allow the *Goeben*
and *Breslau* to steam up to Constantinople.

Still the British failed to grasp what was going on. When
the news reached the Admiralty Milne was ordered to
establish a blockade of the Dardanelles to prevent the
German ships coming out. The British Ambassador demanded that the ships be interned. Slowly it was realised
that the Turks welcomed the Germans, and that the arrival
of these two powerful ships was regarded as the most poetic
justice, rivalling as they did the two sold to the Greeks
and the two stolen by the British.

The proceedings soon entered the realm of farce. French,
British and Russian Ambassadors, in President Poincaré's
words, 'moved heaven and earth' to persuade Turkey back
to the side of the Entente. It was announced that the
Germans had, in fact, sold the battleships to the Turks.
The crews put aside their caps and donned the fez, the
Star and Crescent was hoisted, the *Goeben* became the
Sultan Yavuz Selim and the *Breslau* the *Midilli*, and in their
new guise they were solemnly inspected by the Sultan.
Souchon replaced Limpus in command of the Turkish
fleet and on the 9th September the British Naval Mission
was dismissed. The ambassadors still argued, bargained
and threatened, although their bargains were unco-ordina-
ted. The French, with their large economic interests,
would not resign the Capitulations whereby foreigners
enjoyed special rights in Turkey, while neither the British
nor the Russians would guarantee Turkish territory against
the Balkan nations but were prepared to let the Capitulations go.

The Turks wavered, but could not ignore the final

argument of kings: the guns of the still German-commanded ships anchored in the Sea of Marmora, threatening the iced-cake façade of the Dolma Bagtche Palace.

For three months the matter stayed suspended in the balance, the Turks were never speedy negotiators, and then on October 28th Souchon, with the connivance of Enver, acted. The *Sultan Yavuz Selim* and *Midilli*, still German-crewed, accompanied by some small Turkish vessels, entered the Black Sea and shelled the Russian ports of Odessa, Sebastopol and Theodosia.

The Ottoman Empire willy-nilly had been pushed into the war. Russia, in retaliation, declared war on November 4th, followed by Britain and France a day later. The voyage of the *Goeben* and the *Breslau* had come to an end.

The whole pattern and scope of the war had been changed. Russia, sensitive over the Straits for a century, had lost her exit to the Mediterranean; her only ports now were Archangel, ice-bound half the year, and distant Vladivostock, 8,000 miles from the battlefront. Her exports and imports reduced to almost nothing, from now on she was cut off from her allies. Equally important, by the addition of the Ottoman Empire to the ranks of the Central Powers the field of military action was spread into the Turkish dominions: Mesopotamia, Palestine and the Arab lands. Further, with Turkey a belligerent her neighbours in Europe, Bulgaria, Romania and Greece, became automatically desirable allies for both the Entente and the Central Powers.

The *Goeben* and the *Breslau*, which were to stay in the Sea of Marmora for the rest of the war little used, rusting and collecting barnacles, had extended the 'damned system' halfway round the world.

Winston Churchill remained as First Lord of the Admiralty, Admiral Milne had retired from the Navy on August 18th, but Rear-Admiral Troubridge was court martialled in November and, although acquitted, never held a sea command again.

2

*'The interests of Greece demand that she
should observe complete neutrality'*
King Constantine of the Hellenes

The manner in which Germany had succeeded in pushing
Turkey into the war occasioned many reflections in Britain
on the devilish cunning of her adversaries, the perfidy of
old friends and, to a lesser extent, the inadequacies of
British diplomacy. However, so far as actual military
operations were concerned, Germany's new ally at first gave
the British little trouble, mainly because the triumvirate
of 'Young Turks', Enver, Talaat and Djavid, curiously for
men who had begun their careers as modernisers, relied on a
very old-fashioned concept indeed: the dual position of
their Sultan as ruler of Turkey and also Caliph, Commander
of the Faithful, spiritual head of all Moslems.

Encouraged by the declaration of Abbas Ailmi, Khedive
of Egypt, of his loyalty to his titular overlord, an unimpressive decision as the Khedive was on a visit to Constantinople at the outbreak of war and it is difficult to see how
he might have returned to his British-occupied domains,
the Sultan was prevailed upon to declare a Jihad, a holy

war, to be fought by Moslems against the infidel. Thus fortified Enver adapted the aims of the Turkish war effort accordingly: the conquest of Egypt and the Suez Canal, the domination of Persia and Transcaucasia and, as he never lacked ambition, perhaps the eventual invasion of India through Afghanistan.

British statesmen, over-sensitive to the religious suscepti-bilities of subject races since the Indian Mutiny, had a moment of anxiety which disappeared quickly as all Enver's plans failed ignominiously. An attempted Turkish invasion of Egypt in February 1915 was repulsed with ease, and behind a screen of British and Indian troops the native population remained torpidly indifferent to the appeals of their co-religionists. Hussein Kamal, a benevolent elderly gentleman, became by edict of the British the successor of his deposed nephew, with the new title of Sultan, and Egypt apathetically became a British Protectorate.

Moslem Indian troops under their British officers, whether in India or elsewhere, remained loyal to 'Garge Panjam' (King George V), and showed no inclination to mutiny or desert for the sake of the Ottoman Sultan hoist-ing the banner of religious war in the rather curious com-pany of the Lutheran German and the Catholic Austrian emperors.

Both French and Russians had Moslems in their army and these, too, stayed true to their oath of allegiance. Indeed it was against the Russians, in an almost forgotten episode of the war, that Enver suffered the biggest setback of his career. At the end of the year he led an army of 95,000 German-trained Turks against the Russians in Caucasia. A final attempt at rousing a local Moslem popu-lation was to prove fruitless, and this time in conditions of overwhelming military disaster. At Sarakamish, in the bare freezing mountains, there perished of shell, bullet and frostbite more than 30,000 Turkish soldiers. Of the whole Turkish army engaged there survived some 18,000, and Enver Pasha, who fled from the scene of his defeat.

After Sarakamish, one of the simplest and most signal

defeats of the war, although Turkey's military fortunes fluctuated, the initiative was henceforth with her enemies. Of Sarakamish, a point on the map between Kars and Erzerum, the statesmen in the West heard and knew little. Their minds were concentrated upon the enormous casualty lists from the battlefields of northern France, an ever-mounting toll as both sides began to dig themselves in and war deteriorated into the sacrifice of hundreds of lives for a few yards of shell-torn mud.

The lists of names lengthened and with them the estimates of the war's duration. Soon the voices of those who favoured some attempt to break away from the deadlock of the Western Front were to be heard, if not necessarily heeded. Among them were Winston Churchill, the First Lord of the Admiralty, longing to employ Britain's greatest asset, command of the seas, and David Lloyd George, the energetic Minister of Munitions, who distrusted generals on principle and especially when they maintained that the only way to beat the Germans was by head-on, bloody collision.

This difference of opinion, 'Westerners' against 'Easterners', was exacerbated by the fact that on one side were arrayed the most controversial politicians of the day and on the other nearly all the generals. In the contemptuous terms of their rivals: 'the Frocks', the civilians, and the 'Brass Hats', the soldiers. Distrust was mutual and became a permanent feature of the War Cabinet and General Staff, and consequently of the conduct of the war.

Dislikes and personalities were both larger than life. Winston Churchill, in his time a flamboyant cavalry officer and war correspondent, the *enfant terrible* of pre-war politics, distrusted by those with more conventional careers and minds. Douglas Haig, the commander of the British armies in France, dour, Scots, uncommunicative, but possessed of an iron will and unshakeable faith in his own prescience. Lloyd George, like Churchill the terror of the British upper class before the war, long haired and with a fiery eloquence, soon to be called, with all his faults, to the supreme direction of the war. Haig's devoted admirer Sir William Robertson, the Chief of the Imperial General Staff, the only British soldier to rise from trooper to field marshal, and still unable in times of emotion to distribute correctly his aspirates. More outspoken than Haig he didn't even bother to conceal his contempt for those such as Lloyd George who, from his experience as a Welsh solicitor and a parliamentarian, presumed to argue with one who had been a soldier all his life. To Lloyd George when the latter was Prime Minister he said, 'It is a waste of time explaining strategy to you. To understand my explanation you would have had to have my experience.'

The arguments put by these and other advocates were to continue throughout the war. Was it only possible to win by defeating the German army in the field, by pouring men into the mincing machine of the Western Front, or were there any alternatives? Was Lloyd George's idea of 'knocking away the props' possible? Were the generals wrong to oppose his 'constant wish to strike the enemy where he was weakest'?

The argument could never be put to the test either way. It was never possible to use one strategy to the exclusion of all others, and in the event the war was eventually won for a combination of reasons, some not contained in either brief.

It is fair, however, to say that 'the sideshows', so described by their opponents, were only allowed to be staged in a half-hearted, necessarily ill-prepared manner, always subject to the superior demands for men and material on the Western Front. In the second and third years of the war two such operations, intended to outflank the enemy and at the same time give succour to a hard-pressed ally, were mounted. One, Gallipoli, is notorious; the other, Salonika, is less well known. With both were intertwined the fate of the Balkans and especially that of Turkey's age-old enemy, Greece.

The entry of Turkey into the war had placed before each Balkan nation an almost insoluble problem and at the same time a gambler's choice. As the Entente and the Central Powers sought allies, so Bulgaria, Romania and Greece strove to decide where the ultimate profit and loss of participation might lie. In short, the agonising unanswerable question: who would win? For no nation was this problem posed so acutely as for the Greeks.

Leaving aside any question of partiality or sentiment there were three possible courses open to Greece. The first, neutrality, was attractive to a nation whose armed forces and finances had not yet recovered from the Balkan Wars. Could such neutrality be preserved, however, in the face of Turkey's participation and possibly that of Bulgaria? The second was alliance with Germany and Austria-Hungary, seemingly in those early months possessed of overwhelming military might. Such an alliance, though, meant alliance with the traditional enemy, the Turk, and would expose the vulnerable Greek coastline to the British and French navies which, despite the *Goeben* fiasco, ruled the Mediterranean. The third course was alliance with the Entente, which appealed to many liberal-minded Greeks, who could not fail to observe at the same time that one partner in the Entente was Russia, extremely unlikely in the event of victory to allow Greece to reap much territorial advantage in an area where she regarded her own interests as paramount.

The view from London and Paris was somewhat different. As is the way of belligerents in times of war arguments by others in favour of neutrality were not well received, but were regarded as in some way despicable or, even worse, as cloaking some sinister intent to side with the enemy. Consequently a grossly over-simplified view was taken of the Greek problems, which had at its roots the attitude that those who were not for the Entente were against it. Unfortunately the situation in Greece tempted Allied statesmen to come to snap conclusions.

When Turkey entered the war it had been confidently assumed that Greece, who little more than twelve months before had been fighting Turkey, would happily move into the Allied camp. That she did not do so was a disappointment and one did not have to look far, it was thought, to find the reason: the man who ruled Greece, King Constantine. The man who had been educated at Heidelberg University and the Berlin Military Academy, who was married to the Kaiser's sister and had been created a German field marshal by his Imperial brother-in-law.

That Wilhelm II had not looked favourably on his sister Sophie's marriage, that he had objected to her having to change her religion, were forgotten. That German foreign policy had been consistently pro-Turk and therefore anti-Greek, particularly in the recent matter of Crete and the Aegean islands, was ignored. In their disappointment, too, the Allies forgot that dynastic relationships and military dignities had not prevented a war breaking out. Wilhelm II and George V were both grandsons of Victoria. The Colonel of the British Royal Dragoons was that same Wilhelm, old Franz Josef of Austria-Hungary was Colonel of another British regiment, the King's Dragoon Guards, just as George V himself was the Colonel of a Prussian regiment, an appointment which had caused his mother, formerly a Danish princess, to exclaim: 'Now our Georgy is a filthy pickelhaube blue-coated Prussian!'

To take the absurd argument about Constantine's honorary rank to its absurd limits, the British seemed to have forgotten that the Kaiser himself was an Admiral of the Fleet in the Royal Navy, and that when he first donned the uniform he had said that it was the proudest moment of his life to be thus honoured by the greatest navy in the world.

So much then for the platitudes of princes. More seriously the Allied statesmen chose to ignore the fact that at the beginning of the August crisis Wilhelm had formally asked Constantine for his help, and, as formally, Constantine had refused. Needless to say, the Greek King's letter to the Kaiser had contained in its first sentence some vague sentiments of personal sympathy, again the platitudes of princes, but the letter had been one of refusal. Its most important sentence, which infuriated the Kaiser, read as follows: 'It seems to me that the interests of Greece demand that she should observe strict neutrality and the maintenance of the *status quo* in the Balkans as created by the Treaty of Bucharest.' The letter was countersigned by the Greek Foreign Minister.

34

Constantine, then, favoured neutrality, but the Allies found it difficult to believe that he was sincere, for it was the King's fate always to be judged in contrast with his Prime Minister, Eleftherios Veniselos.

In 1914 Veniselos was fifty and had been Prime Minister for the last four years. Alone among Balkan statesmen of the period he was known and liked in the West. His political apprenticeship had been served in his native Crete. The only son of a family of small merchants, in 1887 he had qualified as a barrister, and within a few years had taken to the often related profession of politics. It was a career pattern familiar in England, but anything less like the gentle English political scene than Crete in the 80's and 90's it would have been difficult to imagine.

The island was still ruled by the Turks, but a minority of the Cretans were themselves Moslems, bitterly opposed to their Christian co-nationals. The young Veniselos, like most Cretan Christians, longed passionately for 'Enosis', union with Greece, but this could not be achieved by verbal argument. When Veniselos became leader of the Cretan Christian Defence Force in 1896, he and his followers were guerrillas, carrying on a war from their hiding places in the peninsula which separates Canae from Suda Bay.

Years later, at the Paris Peace Conference in 1919, the Greek Prime Minister was to enchant Lloyd George and Woodrow Wilson by telling of the manner in which he had perfected his English, sitting in the Cretan hills translating the reports in *The Times* of the international complications caused by his own rebellion, all the time with a loaded rifle across his knees.

In 1897 *The Times* certainly had a great deal to report, for the Cretan disturbances had produced all the elements in microcosm of the War of Independence of seventy years before. In February Britain, France and Russia had sent naval squadrons into Suda Bay to persuade the Cretans to accept autonomy but not independence. In April the Turks, typically losing patience, declared war on Greece. An army under Crown Prince Constantine was soundly defeated in Thessaly, but in September a mob of hysterical Cretan

Moslems massacred a small party of British blue-jackets at Candia. The admirals, in their turn, lost patience, and without consulting their governments bombarded Turkish fortresses and put ashore landing parties. There were excellent historical parallels and doubtless the shades of Codrington, de Rigny and Heiden approved. Eleftherios Veniselos was enabled to improve his English conversation with a number of naval officers. By the next year Prince George of Greece, the King's younger son, was High Commissioner of Crete, with Veniselos as his Councillor of Justice.

The subsequent progress of Crete to union with Greece was, however, not smooth but complicated, violent and passionate. Veniselos disagreed with Prince George, the prince resigned, and the conflict spilled over into Greece, where on occasions revolvers were brandished in the Assembly. In 1910, by a coup in Athens organised by the Military League, a body of disaffected officers, Veniselos was hoisted into power as Prime Minister of Greece.

Once there, it is true, he began his avowed task of reforming the chaos of Greek government. His ambitions were Western, but it would have been better if his admirers in the West had occasionally remembered that romantic as the apprenticeship of Veniselos had been compared with their own staid progress to office, something also might have been learnt from it of the nature of Greek politics.

Of admiration abroad Veniselos always had more than his fair share. In 1899 Clemenceau, on returning from Greece, had announced to the Comtesse de Noailles a discovery which he had placed higher than the architectural and archeological splendours: 'A young advocate, a M. Venezuelos or Venizelos. Frankly I cannot quite recall his name, but the whole of Europe will be speaking of him in a few years.'

The prophecy was to be proved true. As the architect of the Balkan League and the victor of the Balkan Wars Veniselos was to achieve an international reputation. At the London Conference in the winter of 1912-13 Prince Lichnowsky, the German Ambassador, described him as 'the most distinguished personality' present, and further:

'His prepossessing charm and ways of a man of the world secured him much sympathy.' This, then, was the man who stood against the stern brusque military figure of his King, who was advised by the undoubtedly pro-German Chief of Staff Colonel Metaxas.

The Allies in their disappointment came to an obvious conclusion, and in their desperation made a hasty choice. The actions of the two principals, Constantine and Veniselos, seemed to confirm their judgment.

As early as the autumn of 1914 Veniselos had been most attentive to the British, French and Russian ambassadors in Athens, throwing out suggestions as to how the Balkans might be divided after the war. Flatteringly, he always assumed that the Entente would be victorious, and by implication that Greece would be somehow, at some time, at their side. From the circle of army officers and courtiers who surrounded the King there came only prognostications of a German victory. So it was to Veniselos and not Constantine that on January 10th, 1915, the British, supported by the French and the Russians, offered their price for Greek participation.

In Sir Edward Grey's Note of that date the actual expression used was 'important territorial concessions on the coast of Asia Minor', and it included the town of Smyrna with its hinterland the vilayets (provinces) of Smyrna and Aidin. There is no evidence that Sir Edward Grey, the Foreign Secretary, or any other member of the War Cabinet, had thought deeply about the implications of the offer. Sir Edward Grey himself, who had held the direction of British foreign policy since 1906, was both ignorant of and curiously indifferent to anything that smacked of military as opposed to diplomatic considerations. Apparently no military opinion was taken as to how after the war the Greeks might take and hold this particular stretch of Anatolian territory, nor of the likely reaction of the native Turkish population.

This was a period when the Allies were very prodigal with territorial bribes to likely allies; bribes, of course, which could be taken up only after the war and at the expense of defeated enemies. At various times attractive offers were made to Bulgaria, Romania and Italy, and from these offers and counter proposals for participation or benevolent neutrality there were born the Secret Treaties, which with their extravagant and often mutually contradictory promises were to prove the bane of the Peace Conference. Ironically Greece was on more than one occasion offered Cyprus, a piece of rare generosity as it was the only such offer that was made at the expense of one of the allies herself, namely Britain. Such generosity, like the concessions in Anatolia, was normally limited to territories which at the time belonged to someone else.

So much for one party to the bargain. What of the other? To the Greeks it was not an entirely new idea. Smyrna, the prosperous, bustling seaport on the eastern shore of the Aegean, had been regarded covetously before. With a population of over 400,000 of whom well over half were Greek, it could not help but engage the attention of all patriots who wished to liberate the 'unredeemed Greeks', those thousands of their fellow countrymen still under foreign rule. Formerly a part of the Ionian Empire, the original city had been laid out at the command of Alexander the Great and completed by his generals Antigonus and Lysimachus. Substantial arguments could be advanced to show that this city had been the birthplace of Homer. More practically, from the present Greek population came the bankers, merchants and traders not only of Smyrna but of the whole coast and hinterland which it served. All this, the claims of Greeks to be added to the Hellenic Kingdom, the traditions of the glorious past, and the present opportunities for trade and commerce, made Smyrna a glittering prize to offer any Greek, even one less ambitious than Veniselos. Strangely enough, the Greek Prime Minister, unlike the British Foreign Secretary, had had an opportunity of considering the disadvantages. In 1913, at the time of the Balkan War, Colonel Metaxas, now the King's closest military adviser, had considered the possibility of taking and holding Smyrna. He had prepared a report, seen by Veniselos, in which for sober, well-argued reasons he came to the conclusion that in the long term it was a dangerous, if not an impossible, project.

In 1913 Metaxas had been examining the plan in terms of Greece acting on her own. Now, in 1915, Greece would not be on her own but would have the encouragement, if not the help, of Britain, France and Russia in taking for herself some of the territory of their joint enemy. Charitably one can only assume that this difference acted on Veniselos' mind, for seemingly with no sign of hesitation or reluctance he accepted. His acceptance was to change the history of his country. For the present he had the immediate task of fulfilling his part of the bargain and bringing his country into the war on the Allied side. Naturally, but unfortunately, his friends and admirers in London and Paris decided to help him.

3

*'I cannot refrain from expressing my
astonishment and regret'*
King George V

The period from Edward Grey's offer to Veniselos in
January 1915 until the actual Greek entry into the war in
July 1917 provides examples of some of the Allies' most
curious diplomatic and military actions of the whole war.

In January 1918 Sir Edward Grey, no longer in office
and suffering from increasing blindness, had a long after-
dinner talk with his old friend Professor Gilbert Murray
and rather sadly reviewed the part he had played in those
events. He had hoped, he said, to unite the Balkan countries
against the Turks despite what his own experience during
the Balkan Wars should have told him: that this was
virtually an impossibility.

The conflicting claims of Serbia, already engaged, and
Bulgaria, Romania and Greece, not yet committed to either
side, had been difficult enough to reconcile, but these
were not the only problems which had plagued the British
Foreign Secretary. Russia, already showing alarming signs
of her eventual military and economic collapse, had to be

kept in the war, and consequently her power of veto on any arrangements in the area had to be respected. France, too, proved a difficult ally, suspicious of what she thought were likely extensions of British influence abroad after the war. Sir Edward, apparently, always had at the back of his mind the fear that either or both of his allies might make a separate peace with Germany.

One is left with a very distinct impression of a kindly, peace-loving idealist, not really at ease in his wartime role, fearful of coercion, despising bribery and offended by the extortionate demands of would-be foreign allies. For one foreigner, however, Sir Edward had a very definite enthusiasm, the Prime Minister of Greece. He 'admired Veniselos more than any statesman in Europe', and this attitude was understandably common in English political circles, for seemingly alone in the Balkans Veniselos stood out as a genuinely disinterested friend.

So then, thus ran the simplified reasoning of wartime, Veniselos was a friend; therefore his opponent Constantine, who disagreed with him and thwarted his plans, must be an enemy, itching to join the ranks of his Imperial brother-in-law as soon as a favourable opportunity presented itself. It was with this convenient piece of logic in mind that both the British and French War Cabinets set about the task of influencing and persuading the Greeks.

In April 1915 the Allies embarked on their expedition to the Dardanelles, with the triple objects of knocking Turkey out of the war, bringing assistance to Russia by breaking through the Straits and turning the flank of the Austro-German bloc stretching across Central Europe. When the plans were first mooted Veniselos, always fertile with helpful suggestions, proposed an Anglo-French landing at Salonika to be combined with the entry of Romania into the war. Unfortunately the proposal fell to the ground because the Romanians were not prepared to move and their intervention was regarded as essential to prevent a Bulgarian attack on Greece's northern frontier.

So the plans for the Dardanelles expedition went forward alone. Still Veniselos remained helpful and on his own initiative offered to send a Greek division and the fleet to aid the British and the French. The proposal produced two typical reactions: the pro-Veniselos British Cabinet was delighted, but Sazonov, the Russian Foreign Minister, was horrified, and insisted that on no account must Greek troops be allowed into Constantinople and that Greece must receive no territory in the neighbourhood of the Straits. At home in Greece, on March 3rd and again on the 5th, a Crown Council met in Athens under King Constantine and forbade any such intervention. On March 6th Veniselos, never long-suffering with his fellow countrymen, resigned as Prime Minister.

In fact no Allied troops entered Constantinople. The initial impetus of the naval attack faded away when a few obsolescent battleships were sunk or damaged by mines. Admiral de Robeck, the British naval commander, became over apprehensive at the very moment when victory might have been his. On April 25th began the landing of British and Dominion troops on the inhospitable shore, which the Turks had been allowed time to fortify.

Soon another military stalemate developed as thousands of troops dug themselves in and began to die as their comrades in France died. The fresh divisions landed in August suffered 38,000 casualties in three weeks, without being able to improve their position one whit. By the autumn the whole enterprise was beginning to smell of failure.

Way back in April, when there had been hope of success, Rupert Brooke, the gilded young poet unromantically dead of a mosquito bite, had received a rather more civilised burial than most. Lieutenant Asquith, son of the Prime Minister, watched as a Greek interpreter wrote on the back of the cross at the head of the grave: 'Here lies the servant of God, sub-lieutenant in the English navy, who died for the deliverence of Constantinople from the Turk.' There were now 46,000 others, British, Australian, New Zealand and French, and nearly 220,000 wounded.

Only one man had made a reputation at Gallipoli, a Turkish general who had successfully disobeyed and overruled his German superiors, Mustapha Kemal Pasha.

In Athens Constantine could doubtless be forgiven for congratulating himself on having kept his subjects out of this holocaust. Elsewhere, too, the fortunes of the Allies looked grim. The Russians were retreating and dying in Poland; the French had recently lost 100,000 men in ten days in order to advance little more than two miles into the German lines. Paradoxically it was from this decline in the fortunes of the Entente that there arose the next clash between King and Prime Minister.

On June 13th there had been a general election in Greece which had given an overwhelming vote of confidence to Veniselos and his liberal party, 184 seats out of 310. Ten weeks later, the delay being caused by the King's illness, he was asked to form a government.

On September 22nd the King of Bulgaria, with justification known to contemporaries as 'Foxy Ferdinand', influenced by the Allies' failure at Gallipoli, signed the order of general mobilisation for the Bulgarian army. In one move he intended to join the Central Powers and, with the aid of the Austrian and German divisions now massing along the Danube and the Drave, pay off his old score against the Serbs. That tough, fighting race whose problems had sparked off the war, which had repulsed the first Austrian invasion at the bloody battle of the River Kolubara, and produced their proud communiqué: 'Having liberated Belgrade not one enemy soldier remains at liberty on the soil of the Serbian kingdom', were about to be swamped.

In London Lloyd George, lately Chancellor of the Exchequer in a Liberal government and since May 26th Minister of Munitions in the new Coalition government, his enthusiasm fired by the plight of a small nation and also the possible prospect of another way of shortening the war, devoted his thoughts to methods of aiding the Serbs.

Veniselos too, so very similar in his enthusiasms and his impatience with military advice, saw an opportunity and an excuse. The Serbs had asked for aid. By the Convention of June 1st, 1913, which arose out of the Balkan Wars, the Greeks had bound themselves to aid the Serbs if attacked by Bulgaria, each ally being bound to contribute 150,000 men to the joint war effort. Now the Serbs were to be attacked by Austrians, Germans and Bulgarians, and they could certainly not provide anything like 150,000 effectives. Veniselos, however, regarded Greece as being bound in honour to help her old ally; perhaps, too, the deficiency in men could be made up by Britain and France. As Serbia had no sea coast any help would have to be channelled through the largest port in Greek Macedonia, Salonika. The attractions of the plan for Veniselos were obvious. On September 23rd, armed with his arguments, the Prime Minister had an audience of his King, alone.

Both men have left differing accounts. Veniselos maintained that he told the King that by their decision in the general election the Greeks had shown their support for this policy, which meant not permitting Bulgaria to destroy Serbia and asking the British and French for assistance. 'Your Majesty,' he said, 'as representative of the sovereign people, I must tell you that you have no right on this occasion to differ from me.' To which the King is said to have replied: 'As long as it is a question of internal affairs, I must bow to the people's will, but in foreign affairs I must decide what shall or shall not be done, for I am answerable before God for my people.'

Whatever the exact words, undoubtedly some such exchange took place, and critics of Constantine, from Winston Churchill downwards, have poked fun at the King's rather pompous sentiments. Yet with the benefit of hindsight years later Churchill could write: 'King Constantine had been trained all his life as a soldier. The road to his heart was through a sound military plan, and this he was never offered.' What the Allies did offer and Veniselos advocated was very far from being a sound military plan.

The overall situation was fantastic. British and French troops in their tens of thousands were barely holding their own in the West. The British were committed in Egypt and were becoming increasingly involved in Mesopotamia. The evacuation of Gallipoli was fast becoming an obvious necessity. Not surprisingly the Coalition government was in woeful disagreement with its military advisers, with the French and within itself.

Now it was proposed to bring aid to Serbia, about to be invaded by an Austro-German army from the north and a Bulgarian from the east, by landing troops at Salonika, more than 300 miles from the Serbian capital, Belgrade; more than 300 miles as a very hardy crow might fly over some of the most mountainous and difficult country in Europe. It is small wonder that Constantine, faced with this proposal, thought that his primary duty was to his own people and not to the doomed Serbs and their desperate allies.

What followed as a result of the confrontation between these two irreconcilable men is even now a matter of controversy. Veniselos maintained that he again tendered his resignation; the King refused to accept it, but did agree to mobilise the army as a precautionary measure and in addition to seek the aid of the British and French. Constantine, on the other hand, claimed that though he agreed to call his army of 180,000 men to its war stations, he did not request any Allied military assistance, but was informed by letter from Veniselos that such a request had been made after the Prime Minister had seen the British and French Ministers in Athens.

Whatever the truth, and the King's story would seem more consistent with his own reluctance and his Prime Minister's enthusiasm, confusing telegrams reached London as to Veniselos' wishes and intentions, and on October 3rd in Athens the proceedings began to degenerate into farce. Veniselos summoned the British Minister, Sir Francis Elliott and his French colleague, M. Deville, to his office. There he first asked that Allied troops should be landed at Salonika and promised that all the port facilities would be put at their disposal. That done, he read out a formal protest at the breach of Greek neutrality which would be involved, which is strong evidence to suggest that the King had not agreed, and handed a written copy of this note to the French Minister. The Allies, confused but determined to read between the lines, decided that Veniselos would support them and gave orders for the landings to take place, the first British troops to be taken from Gallipoli for the purpose. They were to be joined by the French and Russians.

In the Greek Parliament Veniselos forcefully and successfully defended his actions, but on October 5th he was again summoned by the King, who told him bluntly that in his view, and that of the General Staff, participation would mean suicide for Greece. Again Veniselos offered his resignation which this time was accepted, and the King called on M. Zaimis to form a new government.

The mixed force of British, French and Russians disembarked on the quays of Salonika but precisely what their function was to be no one was quite clear. Much would depend on the character and actions of their commander, General Sarrail. Under the Second Republic there were two types of French general officer. The first, they were roughly in the majority, were aristocratic, Catholic and still with a vestige of sentimental royalism in their make-up. The second were avowed Republicans of middle-class origin, anti-clerical and ferociously liberal and great politicians. It was to the latter category that Maurice Sarrail belonged. Indeed, as in the French army a nice balance in preferment had to be preserved between the two types, it was for that reason rather than for any particularly outstanding military qualities that he had been chosen.

Such subtleties were lost on the British, but of the man himself General Sir William Robertson, the C.I.G.S., had this to say: 'He was a fine-looking handsome man of the swashbuckler type, he completely captivated the Prime Minister who has formed the opinion that he is an exceptionally good man. In my opinion he is a man who will one day pull off a good coup, but he is quite as likely, perhaps even more so, to do the reverse and land us in difficulties. I am quite sure that he means to have trouble with Greece if he can possibly create it and I do not think that he would regret having a few troops cut up it that would suffice to bring about a row. We do not want a war with Greece if we can possibly avoid it, it would be as bad as going into Afghanistan. It would be like attacking a swarm of wasps.'

The judgment was correct. Sarrail had no objection to having trouble with Greece nor to attacking wasps. In Salonika he soon began to stir up the swarm. The foreign consuls, German, Austrian, Bulgarian and Turkish, who were undoubtedly sending military information home, were arrested and shipped off to France. He then persuaded the reluctant British commander, General Mahon, to assist him in taking the Greek fort of Karaburun, which covered the estuary of the Vardar. King Constantine, when asked for its surrender in peremptory terms, said that he would not be treated by the Allies like a native chieftain. His officers on the spot did not share his indignation, however, and Karaburun was handed over without a shot being fired.

Sarrail was elated, and even more so when the Germans carried out an air raid and dropped a bomb near a squadron of cavalry commanded by Constantine's brother, Prince Andrew. The General's reasoning, sentimental for a republican, was that such near aggression to a prince of the royal house was bound to provoke the Greeks to fight the Germans. Temporarily disappointed on this point, the General soon received other encouragement. The Bulgarians began to advance into Greek Macedonia. A Committee of Public Safety sprang up in Salonika, and from it there developed the League for National Defence. There were demonstrations, more or less spontaneous, in favour of France and Veniselos.

Meanwhile in Athens the Allies had opened up a diplomatic offensive. A large number of minor diplomats, intelligence officers, military and naval attachés and vaguely Secret Service persons invaded the city and endeavoured to encourage the Veniselist cause. One among them, Compton Mackenzie, then a young temporary captain in the Royal Marines, invalided from the Dardanelles, gives in his *Athenian Memories* a witty, bitter-sweet impression of those days. But there was a less humorous side and there were many who were less scrupulous than the genuinely philhellene, pro-Veniselist Captain Mackenzie. Captain de Roquefeuil, the French naval attaché, for instance, whose activities later provoked a French parliamentary inquiry. The French with enthusiasm, and the British without, were dragged into the seamier side of Greek internal politics. A propaganda war was waged in the Greek press, free, uncensored, outspoken and easily bought. Greeks, perhaps some were genuine patriots, were bribed by secret service funds to spy, to demonstrate, and to create trouble.

Constantine endeavoured still to tread the narrow path of neutrality, and in order to balance the Allied occupation of the Aegean islands and Fort Dovatepe, north of Salonika, allowed the Central Powers to occupy Fort Roupel in Eastern Macedonia. He also permitted the secret supply of 20,000 artillery shells to the Serbians from the Greek reserve at Salonika.

Unfortunately as between Constantine and Veniselos the Allies had made up their minds: the King could do no right and the Prime Minister no wrong. Enthusiasm for the Allied cause was equated with patriotism for Greece; those who supported the King were dubbed traitors and in some cases driven into the arms of the Germans. However, propaganda was not enough, so by the autumn of 1916 a large part of the French Mediterranean Fleet, including ten battleships, assembled itself off Salamis. 'It is time that we finished with these diplomats,' remarked de Roquefeuil to Compton Mackenzie.

The French seized Austrian and German merchant ships interned at the Piraeus, demanded the expulsion of German agents and the right to supervise postal and telegraph services. Also present, though somewhat reluctantly, as part of the naval demonstration, were units of the Royal Navy.

In London the high-handedness of the French was beginning to cause concern. Sir Edward Grey's conscience troubled him. King George V wrote to his Prime Minister, Mr. Asquith: 'I cannot help feeling that in this Greek question we have allowed France too much to dictate a policy and that as a Republic she may be somewhat intolerant of, if not anxious to abolish, the monarchy in Greece. But this I am sure is not the policy of my Government.' Apparently the Tsar too thought that France and Britain

48

were immersing themselves too much in Greece's internal affairs. The King went on: 'I cannot refrain from expressing my astonishment and regret at General Sarrail's arbitrary conduct towards those troops who, loyal to their King and Government, refused to join the Revolutionary movement at Salonika. Could not a protest of some kind be sent to the French government against General Sarrail's proceedings, which are so strongly deprecated by M. Zaimis?' The King concluded: 'Public opinion in Greece, as well as the opinion of the King, is evidently changing and if the Allies would treat her kindly and not, if I may say so, in a bullying spirit, she will in all probability join them.'

That Constantine might have been persuaded to join the Allies was also the opinion of Lord Kitchener, who had paid the King a lightning visit when he came to pronounce his final verdict on the failure in the Dardanelles. It was also the view of Sir Francis Elliott, the Minister in Athens. Events were soon taken out of their hands. On September 25th Veniselos, with French assistance, fled to Crete, where he received, naturally enough, an enthusiastic reception. Joined by Admiral Kondouriotis and General Danglis, both heroes of the Balkan Wars, he toured the islands of Chios, Samos, Lesbos, and the Sporades, asking for recruits to fight the Bulgars and the Turks.

On October 9th, the crews of Greek naval vessels having declared for him, he met Sarrail at Salonika and declared himself the head of a provisional government. By November three battalions of a new Greek national army were serving under British command and volunteers were still flowing in. The British, having had to use the Nottinghamshire Yeomanry to put down disturbances among these enthusiasts, were understandably not quite so delighted as Sarrail, who tended to interpret all Greek events in terms of his own country's Revolution.

Still, by the end of the year nearly 23,000 Greeks were prepared to fight in some way or another on the Allied side. In Phaleron Bay, off Athens, another Frenchman who did not share Sarrail's passion for parallels with 1789 was less happy. Vice-Admiral Dartiges du Fournet, commanding the Allied fleets, had an aristocrat's sympathy with the King of Greece but unfortunately also his orders from Paris. At the beginning of October he was ordered to demand from the Greeks control of their navy. The British admiral protested, but 300 French marines were landed and the Greek ships in the Piraeus were handed over to the French, as well as control over the shore batteries.

The incident, said du Fournet, 'afforded him neither pleasure nor pride'. The marines were sent into Athens, naval patrols took over the Piraeus and soon the French also controlled the railways round the capital. Again the British protested, their protests were ignored, and in the interests of Allied solidarity the cruisers *Exmouth* and *Duncan* and a number of smaller craft remained under French command, joined on the same principle by the occasional Italian and Russian vessel. Among the Greeks old memories of British and French naval interference began to be revived and a large number of naval officers turned away from the Veniselist cause. Queen Sophie, naturally enough but fruitlessly, complained to her brother the Kaiser.

Paris increased its demands through the Admiral; the army in Thessaly, loyal to Constantine, must be withdrawn from its position on the flank of the new Macedonian army and artillery batteries were also to be surrendered. With this latter demand the King somewhat surprisingly was prepared to comply, but not his government, nor some of his officers. The idea of handing over their own guns to the French was too much. The Admiral sent an ultimatum threatening to send 3,000 men into Athens.

What followed was confusion piled on confusion. On December 1st, 1916, French and British marines and sailors were landed and fired upon, or were fired upon by, Greek troops. The losses on the Allied side were slightly over 200 killed and wounded. Accusations of treachery were rife on both sides. The Allies withdrew to their ships, leaving the Athenians to their own devices. In the resultant explosive atmosphere a minor civil war broke out. Veniselists and Royalists fought in the streets. Dartiges du Fournet contemplated shelling the city to quell the riots, but happily was dissuaded, because of the risk to the Parthenon.

But the Allies were beyond the point of no return. The riots continued. The King blamed the Veniselists and the British and the French who had conspired with them. The Allied Ministers were withdrawn on December 19th and the Salonika government recognised officially. As the year ended there were two Greek governments, one in Athens and the other in Salonika, and Greece itself was divided into Veniselist and Royalist territory. In Paris, Briand had fallen, to be replaced by Ribot, and in London the energetic Lloyd George had ousted the leisurely Asquith. Greece, it was decided, had to be settled and settled quickly.

Charles Jonnart, the overbearing former Governor-General of Algeria, became the 'High Commissioner' in Athens to a nation both independent and neutral. Harking back nearly a hundred years, and doubtless congratulating themselves on the non-availability of the Tsar, who had troubles of his own, the British and the French resumed their mantle as protecting powers under the Treaty of London, which had made Greece independent, and informed Constantine, with colossal arrogance, that they could no longer tolerate the exercise of his authority.

Veniselos became impatient. Field Marshal Sir Henry Wilson, the new C.I.G.S., remarked 'doubtless we have played fast and loose with Tino' (King Constantine), and French troops landed in force near the Corinth Canal, encountered and overcame resistance and moved on into Thessaly. Greece was to be occupied.

On June 1st the King announced his intention of vacating the throne in favour of his younger son Alexander as the Allies would not accept the Crown Prince. 'How are things today, Papa?' asked Prince Alexander one morning. 'They are as bad as they can be,' replied Constantine, 'you are King.' By the 14th the French had taken over Athens completely, the King left, and three days later his son, now the new King of Greece, received his new Prime Minister, Eleftherios Veniselos.

Three years after its beginning Greece had officially entered the war. What the Germans had achieved with the

Turks in 1914 the Allies achieved with the Greeks in 1917 and by methods equally questionable. Somewhat curiously perhaps, the three Greek divisions under the overall control of British or French generals fought not Turks but Bulgarians for the remainder of the war.

It was doubtless excusable if Allied statesmen almost lost sight of a promise made to Veniselos way back in January 1915.

4

'These ignorant and irresponsible men'
Harold Nicolson

On the afternoon of November 11th, 1918, Kaiser Wilhelm II, having crossed the Dutch frontier into exile, met Count Bentinck, who had been given the duty by the Dutch government of being his temporary host. Having ascertained to his relief that the rather unwilling and apprehensive Bentinck was not a Freemason, the former Supreme War Lord then asked for 'a cup of tea, hot, English tea'.

The war was over.

That night all along the Western Front, their first attempts at fraternisation having been forbidden, the British, French and German troops fired off Very lights, rockets and signal flares from their trenches, no longer needing them to illuminate an enemy.

All the Kaiser's allies had preceded him in defeat. The soldiers of the last Habsburg Emperor, Karl, had found that they were fighting for an empire that no longer existed, and on the last front in Italy the subject nationalities had just faded away. The Bulgarians had signed their armistice

T.G.A.—E

at Salonika on September 30th. On October 1st Damascus, the last important city of the Ottoman Empire, had fallen to the British and their Arab allies. In London the War Cabinet expected daily that the Turks, shorn of their empire and with their army in dissolution, would soon indicate their inability to carry on the struggle. Reports came of Turkish emissaries attempting to open peace negotiations through British diplomats in Switzerland and Greece.

Already the terms of an armistice had been drafted in London, and they were approved on October 7th by the Prime Ministers of Britain, France and Italy at Versailles. On October 8th the pro-German Turkish Cabinet, in which Talaat was Grand Vizier and Enver Minister of War, resigned. On the 13th the Turkish chargé d'affaires in Madrid asked the Spanish government to invite the U.S. President to take upon himself the task of re-establishing peace. Before, however, Woodrow Wilson could consult his allies, the Turks had surrendered to the nation which had formerly been their ally but had become their most formidable adversary.

On October 20th at Mitylene the worn and weary figure of Major-General Sir Charles Townshend was helped aboard H.M.S. *Agamemnon*, the flagship of Vice-Admiral Sir Somerset Gough-Calthorpe, the naval Commander-in-Chief in the Mediterranean. The General, who had the unenviable distinction acquired at Kut el Amara in Mesopotamia of being the only British senior commander during the war to have surrendered to the enemy, had been released by his captors to ask for terms.

Whatever the Turks might have hoped to gain from this rather unofficial approach, the Admiral had to communicate with London. Still the negotiations preserved an air of informality; Britain communicated with her allies but Gough-Calthorpe was authorised to receive representatives. They arrived on the island of Lemnos on October 26th. They were rather a scratch team: Rauf Bey, the bearded Minister of Marine, himself an ex-sailor, Reshid Bey, the Under-Secretary for Foreign Affairs, and a Lieutenant-Colonel Sadullah Bey of the General Staff. For five days, in their morning coats and fezzes, with the Admiral and his staff and General Townshend, they sat round some tables improvised by the captain's coxswain in the Admiral's day cabin. Sometimes cheerfully resigned, more often in tears, they agreed to the signing away of the Ottoman Empire.

Finally, on October 30th, 'on board His Brittanic Majesty's ship *Agamemnon* at Port Mudros, Lemnos', the Armistice was signed, 'to take effect from noon local time on Thursday 31st October 1918'. Drinks were served by the white-coated stewards, Rauf Bey gave the captain's coxswain his largest Turkish treasury note as a souvenir, and it was all over. So informal had the proceedings been that Admiral Gough-Calthorpe forgot to ask the senior French Admiral to be present to attach his signature to the convention. This omission was subsequently officially regretted.

By the terms of the document signed on the *Agamemnon* the Allies were to occupy the Dardanelles and Bosphorus forts, and the Dardanelles were to be cleared of mines and secure access given to the Black Sea. All Turkish war vessels were to be surrendered and the Turkish army demobilised, except for a few troops required for the maintenance of internal order. All ammunition and equipment was to be handed over. Allied prisoners of war and Armenian interned persons were to be collected in Constantinople. At the same time all German and Austrian soldiers and civilians were to be evacuated from Turkish territory.

Finally the Ottoman Empire outside Turkey was to disappear. Much of it was in Allied hands already; the holy cities of Mecca, Baghdad and Jerusalem were all occupied. What students of the Eastern Question from Tsar Nicholas I onwards had been predicting for more than half a century had come to pass. Turkish garrisons in the Hejaz, Hazir, the Yemen, Syria and Mesopotamia were to surrender to the nearest Allied commander. The Turks were to withdraw from north-west Persia, Transcaucasia and Cilicia. In Tripolitania and Cyrenaica they were to surrender to the Italians and the British were to occupy Batum and Baku. The possessions of the sick man of Europe were to be divided up at last.

The Mudros Agreement, however, was merely an armistice, the military terms on which hostilities should cease, and so for a time decisions continued to be made by the military and naval commanders on the spot. General Sir Edmund Allenby in Palestine and Syria, General Sir Francis Wingate in the Hejaz, and General Sir William Marshall in Mesopotamia, each administered the areas which their armies had conquered. The Allied army on the Salonika Front, now under General Franchet d'Esperey, divided itself into two. The mainly French half, not without reflections upon the campaigns of Napoleon, moved towards the Danube. The other half, under General Sir George Milne, consisting of three British, three Greek and one French division, with some Serbian and Italian detachments, swung eastwards to Constantinople.

Admiral Gough-Calthorpe was appointed British High Commissioner at Constantinople; the French appointed Admiral Amet and the Italians, Count Sforza. The Bosphorus and Dardanelles defences were occupied, and British, French and Italian troops were distributed throughout the Gallipoli peninsula and on both sides of the shores of the Sea of Marmora. One British battalion, the 3rd Middlesex Regiment, the 'Die-Hards' since Albuera in the Peninsula, made the ceremonial entry into Constantinople in the traditional manner, King's and Regimental Colours flying, band playing and bayonets fixed, watched by the curious, and seemingly not unfriendly, Turks. The only function of the battalion was to provide guards for the various headquarters being set up in the city, for complete calm reigned. Among the population of one and a half million only a few Turkish soldiers were to be seen. Nine thousand Germans and 1,000 Austrians under Liman von Sanders obeyed their orders and took themselves off quietly to Haider Pasha, a suburb on the Asiatic shore, there to await repatriation.

The atmosphere was hardly that of a conquered army capital. The population went about its daily tasks. The Sultan himself was still in his villa on the Bosphorus; his officers of state and his ministers remained in their Offices.

The French 148th Regiment placed itself in reserve at San Stefano and other Allied regiments made their camps on the sites of old conflicts of the Balkan and Russo-Turkish wars. The Greeks, though there was now no Tsar to object to their presence, merely provided guards for their Embassy and Consulate.

On November 13th Lieutenant-General Sir Henry Maitland-Wilson took over as G.O.C. of all the Allied forces, establishing his headquarters in the English Girls' School in the Grande Rue de Pera, in the European quarter of the city. The British soldiers under his command, many of whom had served all through the war, began to prepare themselves for demobilisation and as they returned home were replaced by young men straight out from England and a number of Indian battalions. These latter, the Moslems among them going to worship in the many mosques, were the final addition which made Constantinople even more cosmopolitan than it had ever been before in its chequered history.

Apart from the native population, which was itself mixed enough, there were now British, Greeks, Italians and Frenchmen. There were Romanians and Serbians. There were Poles who had been Austrians, there were Poles who had been Germans, and Poles who had been Russians. All these various nationalities had gained by the victory the status of allies and it was the High Commissioners' and the G.O.C.'s task to administer this vast population, which the war had introduced into the city.

The Turks, with their own authorities and police force, were left to administer themselves. Lord Curzon, Lord President of the Council, observed that 'the Turkish government, if not cowed, was subservient.' He might just as well have said the Turkish people, for there was no distinction. As Winston Churchill put it: 'Turkey, prostrate, looked up and saw with relief that her conquerors were British.' The picturesque phrase was hardly an exaggeration. All over the Ottoman Empire Turkish soldiers surrendered themselves and their arms to small bodies of British troops, in many cases to individual officers and N.C.O.s. The process of disarmament went on smoothly; weapons and warlike stores flowed in and were collected in enormous dumps guarded by handfuls of British or Indian soldiers. The hero of Gallipoli, Mustapha Kemal, now a general without a job, sent a large consignment of machine-guns.

So co-operative and compliant were the defeated Turks, with their many expressions of regret for being pushed into the war against their old ally by the Germans and the now exiled Enver and Talaat, that authority became a little worried. General Maitland-Wilson issued an order to his subordinate commanders: 'In view of the special mentality of the Turkish ruling classes the British government consider it probable that Turkish propaganda may take the form of attempting to secure the sympathies of senior British officers. You will therefore issue strict orders that all offers of Turkish hospitality are to be refused pending the conclusion of peace. . . .'

For although British troops wandered round Constantinople, as did their allies, enjoying the favourable exchange rate and the cheap drink, trying suspiciously the strange and exotic foods and disregarding the advice of their superiors about the sleazier night spots, peace had not yet been signed. For that they had to wait for the decisions being made in far off Versailles.

On November 18th, 1918, in the House of Lords, it had fallen to Lord Curzon to move the 'humble address congratulating His Majesty on the conclusion of an Armistice and on the prospects of a victorious peace'. Speaking of those prospects Curzon said: 'peace is in no danger whatsoever. The armies have already won peace: it will remain for the statesmen to see that it is honourable and lasting.' Such was the mood of confidence and hope not only of the noble lord but of nearly all the Allied statesmen.

The representatives of twenty-seven nations had gathered together in Paris. In attendance were 500 journalists who had taken literally President Wilson's declaration about 'covenants openly arrived at', waiting for every word, hint or suggestion that fell from the lips of the great men who were re-drawing the map of Europe, if not of the world.

Waiting, too, were the millions of people whose lives were to be lived out within lines drawn on that map. Like the journalists they had to wait a long time. For the first, elementary, criticism of the Peace Conference was that it had no form, no pattern, hardly an agenda. As Winston Churchill testified, weeks and months were wasted on pointless committee talk. Thus the principal victors, Britain, France, the United States, Italy and Japan, frittered away their immediate advantage of supreme military power and the moral effect of their victory.

By the time that the Council of Ten, two representatives from each nation, had reduced itself to a Council of Four, the U.S. President Woodrow Wilson, Lloyd George, Clemenceau, and Orlando, the Prime Ministers of Britain, France and Italy, it was too late. Originally the French had proposed logically and harshly that the victors should simply impose their terms. This, however, was just the sort of peace that President Wilson had sailed across the Atlantic to prevent. The only Head of State at the Conference, he had taken the unprecedented step of attending on behalf of the nation which had suffered least from the war in order to put Europe to rights on the principles of his Fourteen Points. A less determined, less self-righteous, man would have been deterred sooner by the immediate results.

What had seemed reasonable and just in Washington, the principle of self-determination for the subject peoples of the two defeated empires, Habsburg and Ottoman, when applied at Versailles created chaos. The Conference became a sounding board for all the problems of Europe and the Near East. A score of new nations and a number of older ones argued among themselves about their frontiers and sought by fair means or foul to persuade the Big Four to their own point of view.

Further to disillusion the President there was the matter of the Secret Treaties: the agreements entered into by the British and the French before the date of the U.S.A.'s entry into the war. Their nature was such as to confirm his worst suspicions of the old secret diplomacy.

On May 18th, 1915, Britain, by the Constantinople

Agreement, had promised Constantinople and the Straits outright to Russia in return for concessions in Persia. On April 26th, 1915, in an excessively badly drafted document known as the Treaty of London, Italy had been given her first price for entering the war: vague concessions in Asia Minor with the right of occupying Adalia. On May 16th, 1916, the Sykes-Picot Agreement had been entered into on behalf of Britain and France, its object, among others, to reassure the French as to their future share of the Arab lands of Syria, the Lebanon and Adana. This agreement was intended to allay French suspicions that Britain, who had sponsored and encouraged the Arab revolt, intended to use it as a means to increase excessively her own sphere of control and influence. The agreement satisfied the French but enraged the Italians, so that by the Treaty of St. Jean-de-Maurienne of April 17th, 1917, Lloyd George was forced to give them a second and better price: 70,000 square miles of Asia Minor including Smyrna.

Now the Constantinople Agreement had been made with the government of the Tsar, and was simultaneously published and denounced by the Soviet government in 1917. The Treaty of St. Jean-de-Maurienne contained the proviso 'subject to the consent of Russia', and that was no longer obtainable or valid. Still, despite the absence of one former ally the Secret Treaties remained, revealing the desperation of wartime, shocking the high-minded President with their immorality, and bedevilling his well-laid schemes with what remained of their obligations.

There were two other points worth observing: the promises made to the Italians contradicted Edward Grey's original promise to the Greeks, and, while all the agreements were made at the expense of the Ottoman Empire, in the case of those two contradictory bargains the territorial promises were to be carved out of Turkey proper.

Not that any of the delegates at Versailles or their advisers gave much thought to Turkey. The memoirs and biographies of the period testify to the feelings of exasperation and frustration which slowly crept over the overworked participants, as they wrestled with the countless, contradictory

60

issues of peace. The American President's failure to understand the Europe which he was determined to reform; his preoccupation with the League of Nations. The French determination to neutralise Germany militarily and economically for ever. The 'sacred egoism' (the phrase was that of an Italian Prime Minister, an expert in the field), of those nations, Italy and Japan in particular, determined to claim the bribes for their past services. The Congress of Vienna in 1815 had, so it was said, danced. The Conference of Versailles had little time for dancing while it worked, plotted, argued and intrigued to reconcile the claims, religious, racial, geographical and economic, of the new Europe. Each elected representative was spurred on by the knowledge that at home there was an electorate ready to hurl him from power if his demands in the sacred cause of nationalism were not as rapacious and intolerant as its own.

Against this background must be judged the actions of the two Prime Ministers, David Lloyd George and Eleftherios Veniselos. Lloyd George was the only Allied premier to submit himself to a general election between the ending of the war and the opening of the peace negotiations. On December 14th Britain had voted, and the results were out a fortnight later: a sweeping victory for Lloyd George, with 474 of his supporters returned as against a mixed opposition of 222, of whom seventy-three were Sinn Feiners who refused to take their seats at Westminster.

Yet it was a curious victory. Lloyd George had been Prime Minister of a Coalition government since he had replaced Asquith in December 1916. The Asquithian Liberals, including Sir Edward Grey, had gone into opposition and Lloyd George had reigned supreme, relying on Conservative and Coalition Liberal votes. In 1918, in agreement with Andrew Bonar Law, the unassuming, colourless Conservative leader who during the last two years of the war had been Chancellor of the Exchequer, Lloyd George had taken his Coalition to the polls. Each candidate loyal to the Coalition had been provided with a letter signed by Lloyd George and Bonar Law: 'a coupon', Asquith had contemptuously called it.

Ostensibly his motive was to preserve unity in the difficult post-war period and to gain a mandate for the Peace Conference, but the Prime Minister's critics, and there were many, maintained that 'the Coupon Election' was a piece of sharp practice whereby he capitalised, and quickly, on his wartime reputation. In the short term, sharp practice or no, Lloyd George's tactics seemed justified, but in the long term there were dangers. Only twenty-six opposition Liberals had been returned, Asquith himself had lost his seat, the old Liberal Party was vitually destroyed, but Lloyd George was himself a Liberal. Henceforth he relied on Conservative votes, and Conservatives, although they acknowledged the reputation and abilities of 'the Welsh wizard', owed their ultimate party loyalty not to the Prime Minister but to Bonar Law, now Lord Privy Seal, Leader of the House of Commons, and in all save name, Deputy Prime Minister.

At the moment there was no sign of rift or dissension between Lloyd George and his loyal Conservative lieutenant. There were a few clouds on the horizon, it is true, but they were but the size of men's hands. *The Times* and the *Daily Mail* disapproved of the Government, but that was to be expected of papers owned by the megalomaniacal Lord Northcliffe, notoriously anti-Lloyd George since the Prime Minister had curtly refused his demand for a seat at the Peace Conference and a place in the Cabinet for his son.

The House of Commons, like *The Times*, had changed. Asquith described it as the worst he had ever seen, but then doubtless the defeated Asquith was a trifle biased. The comment, attributed to Stanley Baldwin, a future Conservative Prime Minister, that it was 'full of hard-faced men who looked as if they had done well out of the war', summed it up. The leaders of the Conservative Party with business backgrounds, such as Baldwin himself and Bonar Law, were men of undoubted integrity, but over many of their supporters on the back benches there hung an aura of quick money made while better men died.

The Government, after the election, had, perhaps unfortunately, changed very little. The wartime pattern of an inner caucus of powerful men lingered on, exacerbated by the Prime Minister's habit of taking advice from whomsoever he chose rather than conforming to any regular method of consultation. These powerful men formed an ill-matched team.

F. E. Smith, now ennobled as Viscount Birkenhead, the Lord Chancellor, was a brilliant lawyer, with a tongue like a razor whether drunk or sober. Consumed by personal ambition he also fancied himself as a philosopher and a politician and was neither. A. J. Balfour, soon to relinquish the Foreign Office to his second-in-command Lord Curzon, was an ex-Prime Minister and an elder statesman retaining the manner and the habits of thought of a previous generation, with no aptitude for the new, harsh world of post-war politics.

His successor, Lord Curzon, had been Viceroy of India at the age of thirty-nine, and hoped to be Prime Minister before he died. Undoubtedly the best-informed Foreign Secretary, especially upon the East, that Britain had ever had, there was something not quite right about Curzon. With his Roman face, his back and shoulders rigidly encased in a surgical steel corset to correct a curvature of the spine, he seemed determined to live up to the couplet of his undergraduate days:

'I am George Nathaniel Curzon,
I am a very important person,
To lesser men I do not speak,
I dine at Blenheim once a week.'

This, however, was the exterior he presented to the world. Beneath there was an over-sensitive, intelligent man with vast industry, application and knowledge, but lacking in that last ounce of resolution necessary in a statesman. Pontifical, verbose, opinionated, prone to see slights where none existed, the Foreign Secretary was not an easy colleague. Nor was George Nathaniel Curzon, Baron Curzon of Kedleston, Baron Ravensdale, Viscount Scarsdale, 1st Earl Curzon of Kedleston, Knight of the Garter, Knight Grand Commander of the Star of India, Knight Grand Commander of the Order of the Indian Empire, politically a person with whom to go tiger-shooting.

At the other end of the spectrum was Lloyd George's Secretary of State for the Colonies and also the Air Department, Winston Churchill. Himself a Liberal, an admirer and pre-war colleague of the Prime Minister, he possessed in abundance that loyalty and resolution which Curzon lacked. Unfortunately the Gallipoli failure still hung round his neck like an albatross, and his re-introduction to office in the last year of the war was described as 'an insult to the Army and Navy'. He was unpopular with the public and many of his colleagues, who regarded him, with some justice, as impulsive, bellicose and unduly obsessed by the new Bolshevik menace. Perhaps the only true friend Lloyd George had in the government, it was unfortunate that his friendship was a very mixed blessing indeed.

It was not, however, the quality of the men he had chosen that was the Prime Minister's immediate concern but the mood of the electorate. The release at last from four years of war had left the British public in a mood for revenge. The recent election campaign had produced phrases such as 'Hang the Kaiser' and 'Germany must pay'. Fantastic sums were bandied about which it was hoped would be forced out of the defeated enemy by way of reparations. Both Lloyd George and Bonar Law had been very careful themselves to give little actual encouragement to such possibilities, but they had exercised no restraint over their supporters and fellow candidates. So the grossly inflated estimates of self-styled economic experts had, in fact, been promised from the election platforms, and had no doubt contributed to the Coalition victory. Now the lack of vigilance and the passive acquiescence of the two party leaders had come home to roost. Lloyd George was Prime Minister and at Versailles to produce results, and results which he knew he could not produce.

So too was Veniselos, but his objects were clear cut and in the event easier to attain. For three years he had fought and argued to take Greece into the war. Finally he had succeeded, but in the process the King had been deposed, foreign soldiers had invaded Greece and Veniselos had entered Athens escorted by Cretan soldiers in French steel helmets, while the Allied fleet lay off the city. Many of his fellow countrymen had been alienated in consequence. Greece, it is true, was now a victor, but the Prime Minister had to return home with the fruits of victory.

Using all his sagacity and charm Veniselos set about the task of persuading the Council of Four to accept the Greek case for territorial compensation. Apart from his own abilities, which were considerable, he had many advantages on his side and many arguments which he could deploy. The right of self-determination was an obvious one; did not this include all those of Greek race still ruled by the Turks? After all, one of the many half-formed plans which floated about in the air of the Peace Conference was one for the creation of British, French and Italian spheres of influence in Turkey. Originally the Russians, too, had been included. The U.S.A., it was thought, might become the protector of the Armenians. Only Lord Curzon objected to this, and offered three lengthy, erudite memoranda to his government on the subject which were ignored, but even he was in favour of the internationalisation of Constantinople.

Unlike Lord Curzon, the other Allied statesmen had no knowledge of Turkey, or Asia Minor for that matter, and Veniselos' request to take up Edward Grey's offer had the advantage of simplicity and directness, plus the fact that it imposed no extra tasks on anyone except the Greeks. Reparations, the Rhine, the Ruhr, Silesia, Poland—these were the big questions. Why should not the so persuasive M. Veniselos have a bit of the Aegean coast? Only the Italians objected to an extension of Greek influence in the Eastern Mediterranean, but this was simply jealousy, and perhaps that could be assuaged by giving them some other convenient bit of Turkish territory.

So Veniselos, in his curious square black silk skull cap, argued before the Council of Four, and charmed Lloyd George with a reference to the Welsh language and flattered Woodrow Wilson with a compliment on the efficiency of American schools in Albania and a nicely assumed interest

65

in the League of Nations. In the evenings he entertained in his over-heated hotel suite with the two evzone sentries at the door, and delighted his guests by reciting Homer and, more up to date, by relating stories of his struggles in the Cretan hills. The atmosphere distilled was, as Harold Nicolson,[1] at the time one of Lloyd George's advisers, described it, 'a strange medley of charm, brigandage, welt-politik, patriotism and courage'. So taken was Nicolson that in writing to his father on February 25th, 1919, he said: 'I can't tell you the position Veniselos has here. He and Lenin are the only two really great men in Europe.'

An observer from a smaller nation, envious of Veniselos' facility, grudgingly admitted that 'every time Veniselos sees Wilson the map of Europe is changed'. Yet it was not Wilson but Lloyd George who finally tipped the balance in Veniselos' favour. There were so many reasons why the two men should warm to each other. Both were in origin lawyers with humble backgrounds; both were members of proud minority races in their own country; both were impatient of generals and somewhat contemptuous of kings; both, though unfortunately neither realised it, were prone to self-delusion.

There had been many philhellenic English statesmen before in Greece's history, aristocrats reared on the classics and consequently often disillusioned by contact with the living Greek. Men who could dissert with warmth on the Peloponnesian War, but who were very cool with regard to the political rivalries of the present Hellenic kingdom. Lord Curzon was one such, and could have thrown in a history of the Byzantine Empire for good measure, but Lloyd

[1] Harold Nicolson followed his father, Lord Carnock, into the Foreign Office in 1906. Delegation to the Peace Conference in 1919. He resigned from the Foreign Office in 1929, and there followed an uneasy period in politics. In 1931 he was a candidate for Mosley's New Party. From 1935 to 1945 he was a National Labour M.P. In 1947 he joined the Labour Party.

Happier in literature than diplomacy or politics, he wrote, among many works, studies of Byron (dedicated to Veniselos), of his father, of Curzon and the official biography of George V. Knighted in 1953, he died in 1968.

George's enthusiasm was not based on Thucydides. The old Liberal Nonconformist feeling for a small Christian nation oppressed by the unbeliever was strong in him, and the mantle of Gladstone had fallen on his very un-Gladstonian shoulders. It was not the sea battle of Aegospotami in 405 B.C. which intrigued him, but the future of the Greeks, as he told Churchill, as a seafaring nation, friendly to Britain, dominating the Eastern Mediterranean and protecting the route to India.

The Prime Minister of Great Britain had to his own satisfaction rediscovered the Greeks and had fallen under the spell of Veniselos. Marshal Foch might advise the French against the project and Field Marshal Sir Henry Wilson might also be very doubtful from the military point of view, but soldiers had never been his favourite counsellors. Lloyd George himself was a little hazy about the details in his enthusiasm; for instance, when negotiating with the Italian delegation he had taken a contour map to be an ethnographic one and had pointed out green valleys as Greeks and brown hills as Turks to further his argument. Finally there was the virtually unvoiced argument, but one which was understood and appreciated very well by the British delegation and particularly the Prime Minister: if the Greeks returned from the Peace Conference empty handed the chances of Veniselos, the friend of Britain, staying in power were very slim indeed.

So, while the Conference moved in its ponderous way towards its main concern, the peace treaty with Germany, Veniselos, with the blessing of Lloyd George, was given his reward in Turkey.

On May 14th, 1919, Harold Nicolson wrote to his wife, Vita Sackville-West, describing how as a member of the 'Greek Committee' he had been called in by Lloyd George to the final consultation the day before. 'So I went in. There were Wilson and Clemenceau with their armchairs drawn close over my map on the hearth rug. I was there about half an hour—talking and objecting . . . The President was extremely nice and so was Ll. G. Clemenceau was cantankerous. The "*mais voyons, jeune homme*" style. It is appalling that these ignorant and irresponsible men should be cutting Asia Minor to bits as if they were dividing a cake. And with no one there except me, who incidentally have nothing to do with Asia Minor.'

Nicolson, full of foreboding, went off to draft the appropriate resolutions. Wilson, Lloyd George and Clemenceau had taken advantage of the absence of the Italian Prime Minister, Orlando, who had withdrawn his delegation in a huff over Fiume and was the only objector, to give Veniselos his head. Unofficially their permission had been conveyed to him beforehand, so that he could forestall any possible action in the same area by the Italians, who might rely on the St.-Jean-de-Maurienne Treaty.

So on May 15th, under the protection of the guns of their own and the Allied fleets, the Greeks landed three divisions at Smyrna.

Lloyd George was not familiar with Thucydides, but Veniselos was to occupy one of his periods of exile with the translation of that particular author. Doubtless, therefore, he could have recalled the passage in Book VI where Alcibiades, encouraging the Athenians on their way to their disastrous invasion of Sicily, says:

'In the assurance therefore that in going abroad we shall increase our power at home, let us set out on this voyage . . . Our security is guaranteed by our navy, so that we can either stay there, if things go well, or come back again. . . .'

5

'*The Turk was still alive*'
Winston Churchill

The entry of Greek troops into Smyrna provoked no head-lines in the world press.

Turkey, like Germany and Austria-Hungary, was a defeated nation. Germany had been forced to accept Allied armies of occupation. The empire of the Habsburgs had obligingly split itself into its component parts. Austria and Hungary were now merely two penniless ill-fed republics. The Allies seemed all-powerful. Doubtless in time at Versailles they would get round to a formal peace treaty with the Ottoman Empire as well, but at the moment it seemed a useful territorial pool from which to reward old friends.

M. Veniselos, noted Harold Nicolson, was perturbed to hear that the Greek troops had behaved badly on entering Smyrna, but no one else was particularly concerned. No one, that is, save the British sailors on board their warships in the harbour who watched the scene.

The remnants of the Turkish army still in Smyrna were in no condition to offer any resistance and the Greeks entered the city like conquerors. Monsignor Chrystosomos, the returned Archbishop of Smyrna, stood on the quay in full canonicals and blessed the troops as they disembarked. Any Turkish soldiers who could be found were disarmed and led off as prisoners of war. Then suddenly the centuries-old hatred of Greek for Turk became too much for a nation never renowned for its calm in either victory or defeat. The Greek inhabitants of Smyrna, inflamed by the sight of defeated Turks, began to join in. The hated fezzes, symbols of foreign rule, were knocked from the heads of prisoners and the Turks were forced to tread on them. Any Turk who showed signs of resistance was manhandled or humiliated. Tempers frayed and shots were fired. Within hours over thirty Turkish officers had been killed, and numbers of dead and wounded soldiers, shot or bayoneted, lay along the quay.

More Greek soldiers were disembarked from the troop-ships and under their protection the Smyrna Greeks began to avenge their years of subservience. Soon the whole port area was in complete disorder, any Turk was in danger. Indeed a few old-fashioned Greeks, or persons of mixed race with which any port abounds, who on this side of the Aegean wore the fez as their normal headgear, were taken for Turks by the troops and suffered accordingly.

At Versailles the statesmen and their staffs, Greeks and Turks forgotten, returned to their maps and their resolutions, and their triple task of drawing up peace treaties, redistributing Europe and giving form and substance to Woodrow Wilson's concept of a League of Nations. From his ship in Smyrna harbour a British naval officer saw a Greek woman crouch over a wounded Turkish soldier who had cried out for water and urinate into his mouth. Other officers were astounded and horrified to see that neither Greek officers nor soldiers showed any inclination to prevent such abominations, but were content to let their compatriots run riot. Soon British sailors were watching the bodies of dead Turks floating past in the water of the harbour.

Eventually Admiral Gough-Calthorpe, in his capacity as High Commissioner, demanded of the Greek admiral that order be restored, and also complained officially to M.

Stergiades, also a 'High Commissioner' and in effect the new Civil Governor of Smyrna. Unfortunately, matters were out of the hands of Stergiades. He, a reasonable man, a Veniselist who wanted to see the Prime Minister's policy succeed and who consequently wished to reconcile all the inhabitants of Smyrna to Greek rule, was powerless and in despair. For far more typical of the attitude of the new Greek colonists was that of the reinstated Archbishop Chrysostomos, who saw the invasion in simple terms of cross against crescent. The Governor soon had cause to disagree with the Archbishop's public utterances which were more suited in tone to the times of the Greek War of Independence than to the twentieth century. Nevertheless Chrysostomos, a not uncommon type of Greek political priest, persisted and used inflammatory language whenever the opportunity occurred.

One such occasion was when the Archbishop was confronted with Nourredin Pasha, the outgoing Turkish governor, who was being allowed to return to Constantinople. The Archbishop objected, saying that he would have preferred to see Nourredin shot. Archbishop and Governor were to meet again. At present, however, despite the efforts of Stergiades on the spot, and the concern of Veniselos who was still in Paris, the Greek occupation seemed to have started in the worst possible way. On the insistence of Veniselos an inquiry was later held into the violence of those first days, but it did nothing to eradicate the impression that the new rule in Smyrna and the vilayet of Aidin was to mean oppression for the Turks. The British and U.S. consuls telegraphed their home governments pointing out that their worst fears had been confirmed. The American missionaries in Anatolia, who had been opposed to the settlement from the start, again sent their views to President Woodrow Wilson. What notice was taken of these communications by the busy men in Paris is not known, but it was too late now: the Greeks were committed and in any event showed no signs of being in the mood to listen to advice.

Anyhow, what had they to fear? The Turks were defeated

and the now 'redeemed' Greek population of Smyrna danced in the streets, treading underfoot any Turkish flags or symbols they could find and shouting 'Zito Veniselos'. After all, were there not as many Greeks as Turks in Smyrna, and were not the British and French, the allies of Greece, all powerful?

Actually, in fairness, nothing said or done at this time by the British and French or even the Italian governments gave the Greeks any cause to think otherwise. The co-operation of wartime looked as if it would continue. Indeed, only three weeks before the Smyrna landing, Greek troops had actually been fighting alongside French in the only sphere of operations where Allied troops were still on active service in any numbers: in the chaos of post-Revolution Russia. For some time two of their divisions, provided by the ever-helpful Veniselos, had been engaged with two French divisions, plus a Polish and a Romanian contingent, in trying to stem the Bolshevik advance around Odessa and in the Crimea. However, to the disgust of Clemenceau, who like Churchill had hopes of the venture, the French troops became disheartened and disaffected. They began to sport red rosettes, circulate subversive pamphlets and news sheets, and were soon on the verge of mutiny.

On April 6th, 1919, the last French troopship sailed from Odessa, on hurried orders from Paris, leaving the Crimea, except for Kertch at the eastern extremity, to the Soviets. The Greek troops, still staunch, left with them, and it was thought advisable in these last stages that each French warship on which the crews had refused to obey their officers should be 'marked' by a vessel of the Greek navy. Many Greek soldiers and sailors were transferred, no doubt to their own relief, to the less onerous task of swelling the occupying forces in Anatolia. For that operation, at this time and for a considerable time to come, was regarded as being, militarily speaking, a walk-over. In fact, hardly a military operation at all.

The Turks, with their army disintegrated and their capital occupied, were not thought capable of resistance.

The Sultan, it was said, had burst into tears of impotent rage at the news of the Smyrna landing, but what could the Sultan, looking at the guns of an Allied battle fleet from his palace window, do? Somehow the distinction was never made between the Sultan, a prisoner in Constantinople, and his subjects. The Allies observed the effete cosmopolitan society of the capital and dealt with a government of polite puppets, but saw no difference between such as these and the tough, simple peasantry of the Anatolian uplands.

Yet there were warning signs for those who had eyes to see them.

Even the British, who had slipped easily into the role of benevolent rulers to yet another Asiatic nation, were beginning to notice a change in the attitude of the Turks in Anatolia after Smyrna. The arms stopped rolling in, isolated sentries and outposts were sniped at, and the orders of British officers were no longer obeyed. The mixed British and Indian force occupying the Ismid peninsula opposite Constantinople might even have been excused for thinking that the war had broken out again. In July, 1919, they suddenly found that a body of over 400 Turkish soldiers had infiltrated into the peninsula and blown up the bridge at Gebze and occupied the village. The communications of all the British forces ran along the coast and the bridge was a vital link in the chain. So, on the 12th of July a combined force of cavalry, Indian infantry and an artillery battery set out from the base at Touzla to recapture the village and repair the bridge. On the 13th the first object was achieved and the bridge was rebuilt by sappers within three days, but not before a minor battle had been fought. It was distinguished by a charge by the 20th Hussars which, as it turned out, was to be the last ever executed by a complete British cavalry regiment.

The Hussars, wielding their swords in the thin morning sun, and killing twenty-five Turks in the process, went down the path of military history, but there was another perhaps more significant aspect of the action round the village of Gebze. The conduct of the Turks. Although described as a mere 'band of Turkish Nationalists' they 'behaved most admirably'. They did not panic, although surprised by the 20th Hussars who charged right through them, then wheeled and charged again. Even after the second charge they stood their ground, firing back and hitting several horses and wounding an officer and a trooper. Finally, threatened by a battalion of advancing Garhwalis they retired, but 'deliberately and quite coolly', dispersing into the rough surrounding countryside. The British, with their imperial background, could class the incident with one of a thousand such others on the North-West Frontier of India, but there were obviously still soldiers in Turkey who, if given a cause and a leader, would have to be taken into account.

The cause was in fact there already, the one form of nationalism not considered at the Peace Conference, that of the Turks themselves. Now it had been fanned into flame in the hearts of the dour Anatolian peasants by the invasion of their homeland by the despised and hated Greeks. The news of the Smyrna landing had spread like wildfire and needless to say the details of the atrocities lost nothing by repetition. In the Turkish view these atrocities were the final humiliation suffered at the hands of a former subject race, which had only achieved its own independence with the aid of foreign arms, and had now been set by those same powerful friends to rule over Turks.

All that was needed was a leader and he was provided largely through the negligence and short-sightedness of the British.

On April 30th, 1919, Mustapha Kemal had been appointed Inspector-General of the 9th Turkish army in Anatolia and on May 19th had landed at Samsun on the southern shore of the Black Sea, over 300 miles from Constantinople.

The appointment of the thirty-eight-year-old General, the hero of Gallipoli, was by order of the Sultan's puppet government and neither his appointment nor his transfer to Anatolia were objected to by the British authorities. Indeed Kemal, with his past record of disagreement with both the Germans and the Young Turks, was regarded quite favourably. Anatolia was known to be in a state of turmoil, with disbanded soldiers forming themselves into brigand bands. Perhaps this general, apparently still loyal to the Sultan, to whom he had been appointed an A.D.C., would use the remaining regular forces to restore some discipline and order. So it was hoped that on one hand the Greeks could be allowed to invade Anatolia, while at the same time the Turkish army could be employed to restrain the indignation provoked by that same invasion. What was not realised until too late was that Kemal had hidden his own feelings of resentment at the Greek invasion under a stern professional exterior and that he had virtually engineered his own appointment in order to rouse up his fellow countrymen in Anatolia.

He moved with incredible speed. In little over a month, using a mixture of cajolery and threats, now posing as a loyal officer of the Sultan, now appearing as a revolutionary, he gathered round him the nucleus of a resistance movement. Certainly he was not alone, there were many willing helpers, but without him it would not have been done. A loosely constituted but grandly named National Congress met at Sivas and hammered out a Declaration of Intent. At a two-week-long meeting which began on July 23rd at Erzerum, the capital of Eastern Turkey, the Declaration was expanded. There, far from possible interference by the occupying forces, the National Pact was produced. It was a simple document of short paragraphs and set out in general terms a nationalist constitution and limited boundaries for a new Turkey, independent of the old Ottoman Empire. If it had been produced by one of the new European nations, Poland, Czechoslovakia or Yugoslavia, its terms would have been regarded as unexceptionable, even welcome. Yet for Turkey, occupied in part by the British, French, Italians and Greeks, it was a declaration of war.

A few weeks before, when the nature of his activities had become known, the Sultan's government had demanded Kemal's return to Constantinople, and when he had not obeyed he had been dismissed from the Turkish army. In fact Kemal had already anticipated his own dismissal by resigning voluntarily; he realised that from now on he was in truth a revolutionary.

75

In October the government in Constantinople under Damad Ferid, finding itself in an impossible position, resigned. The Allies were now hoist with their own professed doctrines of nationalism and self-determination. As a possible way out they determined to use the machinery granted on paper in 1878 by the Sultan Abdul Hamid and never used. The Turks were to have a general election and it was hoped that the result would show Kemal's movement up as but a temporary enthusiasm. The composition of the newly elected parliament was announced on November 9th; it had a large Nationalist majority. As Winston Churchill put it, 'The Allies were loyal to the principal of representative government: accordingly the Turks had voted. Unhappily, they had almost all of them voted the wrong way.'

In Anatolia, Mustapha Kemal's status increased, and even in Constantinople processions began to march through the streets carrying Star and Crescent banners proclaiming the new Turkey for the Turks. By the beginning of 1920 it was becoming plain that Allied control of Turkey went just as far and no farther than their naval guns could fire and their soldiers march. The Allies were naturally confused, unjustifiably surprised, and quaintly indignant. Again in Churchill's words, written after the event and with the consequent advantage of hindsight: 'Loaded with follies, stained with crimes, rotted by misgovernment, shattered by battle, worn down by long disastrous wars, his empire falling to pieces around him, the Turk was still alive.' Unfortunately the lesson being painfully learnt week by week, almost day by day, by the Allied representatives in Constantinople and by their soldiers in the rest of Turkey did not seem to be absorbed by their political masters at home.

In February of the new year the House of Commons was getting restive. In January the Cabinet had virtually overruled the Prime Minister by deciding that the Peace Treaty with Turkey must allow the Turks to remain in Constantinople. In accord with good constitutional practice it therefore became Lloyd George's unhappy lot to defend this decision in the Commons. A number of backbenchers were considerably annoyed by the fact that

Above The Allies. The Kaiser, the Sultan and Enver Pasha in Constantinople, 1917
Below The Victors. Lieutenant-General Sir Henry Maitland-Wilson welcomes General Franchet d'Espérey to Constantinople, February 1919

Above Harington (in light uniform) watching reinforcements arrive in Constantinople
Below The first refugees from Wrangel's White Russian Army arrive in Constantinople, November 1920

King Constantine

King Alexander

Lloyd George with Poincaré after lunch at 10 Downing Street, 19 June 1922 (*left to right*, seated, Balfour, Poincaré, Lloyd George, Pétain; standing, between Balfour and Poincaré, Worthington-Evans—with cigar)

the decision had been first telegraphed to Admiral de Robeck, the new High Commissioner in Constantinople, and at a later date to the Viceroy of India, Lord Chelmsford, for public announcement without Parliament being given an opportunity to first debate the matter. The move had been an obvious one to placate local feeling in the Turkish capital and Moslem sentiments in India as quickly as possible. Though when the question was finally debated on February 20th, Lloyd George was given no cause to regret the timing whereby, according to Sir Donald Maclean (the temporary leader of the Liberal party until Asquith could be found a safe seat), 'the House and the country had not been fairly treated by the government'.

It was an acrimonious debate and the opinions expressed were various and largely irreconcilable. The Commons was worse than the Cabinet. Sir Donald went on to quote from some of the Prime Minister's previous speeches. In November 1914, for instance, when he had described the Turks as 'a human cancer, a creeping agony in the flesh of the lands which they misgoverned', and in December 1919 when, referring to the Straits, he had said: 'Can we leave those gates which were slammed in our face under the same gate-keeper? They were shut treacherously in our face. We cannot trust the same porter.' Sir Donald wondered why we were now going to trust the same porter and at the same time do nothing to help the Armenians and other Christian minorities still 'under the heel of the Turk'.

Lieutenant-Colonel Guinness was equally concerned about the Christian minorities but felt that driving the Turks out of Constantinople would not help. In his opinion 'We should go in and help Turkey to govern herself.' Many members talked of 'the British pledge' to India and seemed to think that in some strange way Indian Moslem troops had fought Turks only on the understanding that Constantinople should remain Turkish. On the other hand Mr. Adamson wanted the League of Nations to take over and make the city its headquarters—'The Caliph could remain there like the Pope in Rome, with no temporal power.' Lord Robert Cecil also felt that international government by the

League would be the best solution, for 'to leave the Turks there would be to fail in the purpose for which we went to war'. Mr. T. P. O'Connor had the courage to say that he thought that Indian concern was largely artificial. The holy cities of Mecca, Medina, Baghdad and Jerusalem had all been taken from the Turks and 'the history of Constantinople was no source of pleasure or pride to thinking Moslems'. Lieutenant-Commander Kenworthy endeavoured to keep the temperature down by suggesting that the Dardanelles would soon be obsolete strategically because of the increasing use of air routes.

Lloyd George in his speech pointed out that previous arrangements on the future of Constantinople had depended in turn on Russian co-operation and then on American help. Neither was now forthcoming. He then endeavoured to placate the 'Indian lobby' by talking of India's war effort, her influence at the Peace Conference and by a complimentary reference to the Aga Khan. It was not his best speech. He did however re-define for the benefit of the House Britain's present 'peace aims'. They were the freedom of the Straits, the freeing of non-Turkish communities, but the preservation of Turkish self-government in communities mainly Turkish. There must be adequate safeguards for minorities and 'the Turk must be deprived of the power to veto the development of the rich lands under his rule'. To ensure these aims, apparently the Allies would continue to garrison the Straits with the help of the Navy.

Bonar Law, who summed up for the government at the end of the day, followed his chief's line and said little about means but something about ends, the ends that at the moment satisfied the House of Commons, 'that Constantinople shall cease to be a focus for war', and 'that the power of the Turks over subject races shall be prevented'.

When the language of apparent power was used by Ministers of the House of Commons it was not surprising that many honourable members seemed to think that the return of Constantinople to the Turks was too large a concession to a beaten foe. That view was, needless to say, not shared by the Turks. The announcement did nothing to reconcile Nationalist opinion which was more outraged by the Greek invasion than by the Allied occupation, which it had never regarded as being permanent. On January 28th the newly elected Chamber of Deputies in Constantinople had adopted Kemal's 'National Pact'. There was now the distinct possibility that the Allies as well as being faced with a revolt in Anatolia might have one on their hands in Constantinople at the same time. Accordingly on March 16th to prevent such a possibility the city was occupied militarily by British, French and Italian troops. Henceforth the only government there was to be that of the military commanders.

On both sides open antagonism was growing. On April 11th the Allies dissolved the unsatisfactory Chamber, the first properly elected one the Turks had ever had, and arrested a number of Deputies. By way of retaliation and object lesson combined, twelve days later, invulnerable in his new headquarters in Ankara, Mustapha Kemal opened the first meeting of the Turkish Grand National Assembly.

These events might never have been, however, so far as their effect was apparent on the statesmen of Britain, France, Italy and Greece, for on May 13th, at last, the terms of the peace treaty with Turkey, the Treaty of Sèvres, were made public. It was nearly a year and a half from the conclusion of hostilities with Turkey. The treaty was the product of many conferences and discussions and by the time its terms were announced, as many wits remarked, they were about as durable as the famous porcelain from the same town. Even the manner of the treaty's announcement did little to make its acceptance by the Turks more likely. The first they heard of the terms came, not from the Supreme Council at Paris, but from M. Veniselos in Athens. He had been given advance information and decided to use it to boost his own prestige.

Moderate Turkish opinion had been offended by the cavalier treatment meted out to the Ministers and Deputies of their first Parliament and by the high-handed manner of the military occupation of Constantinople. The terms of the Treaty of Sèvres were the last straw; the occupation

79

was temporary, these were to be the permanent conditions of peace. Constantinople, as they knew already, was to remain Turkish. The Arab lands were to be lost, that was inevitable. The French were to have Syria and the British to administer mandates in Palestine and Mesopotamia. The Bosphorus, the Sea of Marmora and the Dardanelles were in some ill-defined way to be converted into an open waterway under international control. That again might have been reasonably expected from a study of past history.

It was the remaining terms which provoked the headlines in the Constantinople newspapers and created sympathisers overnight for the resistance movement in Anatolia. Greece was confirmed in her possession of Smyrna and its hinterland, with some paper talk of a plebiscite which deceived no one. In addition she was to have a majority of the Aegean islands and the Gallipoli peninsula. Western and Eastern Thrace were also to be hers, so that all that remained to Turkey on the European shore was an indefensible strip of land to the west of Constantinople. The Dodecanese islands were confirmed as an Italian possession. A separate independent state of Armenia was to be created on the Russian border with Erzerum as its centre. Kurdistan was to be autonomous. Overall, the hated Capitulations, whereby foreigners enjoyed special rights under the law, were to be reintroduced. The Turkish armed forces were placed under Allied supervision, a gendarmerie was to be established under Allied officers. Turkey's finances were to be effectively in Allied hands. Finally, coincident with the treaty and dependent upon its ratification, Britain, France and Italy agreed upon their future spheres of influence in Turkey on the lines of their old wartime agreements. Turkey, independent Turkey, was to be reduced to Constantinople and the north-western quarter of Anatolia.

In the face of the warnings of Lord Curzon, backed up by the reports of Admiral de Robeck, contrary to the advice of Churchill and the War Office and despite clear indications of lukewarm support by the French and Italians, somehow Lloyd George's enthusiasm and personality had carried the day and at the Villa Nirvana at San Remo the final draft had been agreed. As if Turkey had been in a vacuum for the last seventeen months a treaty had been produced to be ratified by the Turks and enforced if necessary by the Allies.

At the time of the military occupation of Constantinople Field Marshal Sir Henry Wilson, the C.I.G.S., had confided to his diary: 'The Frocks are completely out of touch with realities. They seem to think that their writ runs in Turkey in Asia'. They were to be brought face to face with realities in a very short time indeed. On the same day as the announcement of the terms of the Treaty of Sèvres was made in Athens the French commander in the ancient Cilicia of the Crusaders, the area north of the Syrian border round the Iskenderon Gulf, was forced to sign an armistice with the Turkish Nationalist forces. This in part of an area confirmed by the Sèvres Treaty as a French sphere of influence. The French after ejecting the Emir Feisal from his throne in Damascus had found themselves faced with guerrilla attacks by not only the Syrians but the Turks as well. With weak forces on the spot and with little enthusiasm for what looked like developing into a full-scale war the French, under their one-armed, bearded and normally fire-eating commander, General Gourand, had decided to come to terms. The first of the Allies had broken under the strain. Before the end of the year the French were to evacuate their troops from Marash and retire back to the confines of Syria.

It was an ill omen for the future and a lesson not lost on Mustapha Kemal. In June, under his inspiration but not his control, a small army of irregulars advanced into the Ismid peninsula to try conclusions with the British. They, more resolute than the French, replied with an infantry attack by the Gordon Highlanders—supported by a noisy if relatively harmless barrage provided by the big guns of the Royal Navy. The Turks retreated out of range but the Allied commanders were worried. In Constantinople General Sir George Milne, the G.O.C., had rapidly made his dispositions to defend the city from attack and also to put down sympathetic uprisings from within. As Churchill wrote, 'At last peace with Turkey: and to ratify it, war with Turkey!' The wartime allies were in an impossible position. True, Britain, France and Italy had considerable forces both naval and military deployed in the Near East. Their position however was far from being 'all powerful', as it has so often been described. Nor were they united in their degree of resolution. The illness of President Wilson, following his failure to persuade an isolationist Congress to support his grandiose aims, meant that the U.S.A. was no longer actively concerned in Near Eastern affairs. One ally had disappeared and France and Italy were becoming anxious lest they lose the friendship of Turkey. Only Britain's Prime Minister still retained his enthusiasm for putting the world to rights. Though even he shrank from the prospect of asking the electorate to sanction the all-out use of military and naval force less than two years after the end of the most costly war Britain had ever waged in her history. The means to coerce Turkey did exist but the will to use them was lacking.

Only one army remained, apparently willing, apparently able, to enforce the demands of the Allies, the Greek. The army of a small, poor nation which had been mobilised almost continuously for the last nine years. A nation whose King had been sent into exile by Britain and France. A nation which then had been dragged into the Great War. This was the army, and the nation, which the Allies chose, because they had no choice, to do their dirty work for them.

It was a military decision but it was taken by two politicians, Lloyd George and Veniselos.

Years later Lloyd George was asked by Frank Owen, his biographer, his opinion of Haig. The then ex-Prime Minister went to a portrait of the Field Marshal and placed his hand horizontally across the top of the highly polished cavalry boots. 'He was brilliant,' he said, 'up to there.' Admittedly Douglas Haig was a dull dog and there had been many disagreements and clashes of temperament between the two men. Unfortunately Lloyd George had a similarly poor opinion of all British generals above their boots. It was a prejudice compounded of many elements. Dislike of the social class from which they came, contempt for their frequent lack of intellectual qualities and impatience with their insistence upon details and precision. Consequently when Veniselos 'appeared in the guise of the good fairy', Churchill's phrase, to solve the Allies' problems for them, it was fatally easy for Lloyd George to ignore the professional caution of his military advisers. He knew they failed to share his own enthusiasm for the Greek cause in Asia Minor. He knew they had a low opinion of the military qualities of the Greek army, especially its officers. The current mess joke was that in battle each Greek officer knew that he himself would run away but hoped that his comrades would not. The British generals, like the Conservatives in government and in parliament, were all hopelessly pro-Turk, partly because they respected them as soldiers, partly out of deference to Moslem opinion in India. Any sentiment that the generals had for Greece they reserved, in their snobbish way, for the despised Royal House. The Chief of the Imperial General Staff had expressed the opinion of them all when he complained of the unfair treatment meted out to King Constantine in 1917.

So, when the generals doubted the Greeks, Lloyd George, prejudiced, doubted the generals, and dismissed their views as prejudice. The generals' caution was not, however, unjustified.

When Veniselos had been in London prior to the publication of the Treaty of Sèvres he had been submitted to some searching cross-examination by Winston Churchill, the Secretary of State for War, and Field Marshal Wilson. Their questions on the army in Anatolia were precise and detailed. Cost, morale, leave, strategy and tactics, eventual aims and prospects of success. These were some of the questions put to the Greek Prime Minister, to which his overall answer, while admitting the difficulties, was that the Greeks were where they were in response to the requests of Lloyd George, Clemenceau and Woodrow Wilson. With the support of such powerful allies how could he fail? This was not really the sort of answer his interrogators had been seeking, and so on March 24th Churchill had written to the

Prime Minister as follows: 'With military resources which the Cabinet have cut to the most weak and slender proportions, we are leading the Allies in an attempt to enforce a peace on Turkey which would require great and powerful armies and long, costly operations and occupations. On this world so torn with strife I dread to see you let loose the Greek armies—for all sakes and certainly their sakes.'

To this appeal Lloyd George remained unresponsive. Like the later advice of his generals it conflicted with his inclination and his inclination was to support and use the Greeks. Veniselos was delighted to be so used and the Greek army began its task as a maid of all work almost immediately. With speed and comparative ease Eastern Thrace was cleared of Turkish soldiers and Adrianople occupied. At the same time two Greek divisions were moved northwards from Smyrna and quickly neutralised the army of irregulars which pestered the British and French in the Ismid peninsula. Lloyd George was elated; for the second time in his life he had shown his superiority to the conventional military mind.

There were mutterings in the War Office of overstrained resources, overlong lines of supply and communication and warnings about the increasing danger of organised Turkish resistance. Lloyd George shrugged his shoulders. Veniselos was certain that he could give the Allies further assistance. The Greek generals, perhaps they weren't so concerned about the brilliance of their boots, seemed to be equally sure of themselves. So on June 22nd the Greek army began a general advance eastwards into Anatolia. Once again the confidence of the Greeks and their champion Lloyd George seemed justified. Brusa was captured and the Turks appeared disorganised and more inclined to retreat than stand and fight. The British and French observers and advisers attached to the Greek army were impressed, despite themselves, and wondered sometimes what Mustapha Kemal was doing.

They were soon to learn. Despite the presence of a large Greek army on Turkish soil his activities at about that time were more diplomatic than military. His representatives were in Moscow. In the Russian capital there was a regime somewhat similar if more secure than his own. Uncertain, still in danger, without allies and with no feelings of friendship towards the British, French and Greeks who had attempted to reverse the course of the Revolution. More important perhaps, with no more desire than Kemal to see the Armenian state of the Sèvres Treaty established on its borders. The agreement initialled in Moscow was not over particularised but it was enough. For the moment the interest of the two parties coincided, Turkey's age-old enemy was neutralised, the long Russo-Turkish border was in no danger. Kemal the soldier had secured his flank. On September 28th Turkish forces moved into Armenia and captured Kars. Henceforth Kemal could concentrate on the Greeks.

In Athens, however, in that autumn of 1920 spirits were still high. A Te Deum had been celebrated in the Cathedral for the capture of Brusa. Veniselos, recently returned from Paris where he had narrowly escaped assassination at the hands of two Greek ex-naval officers, was still the man of the hour.

It was then that fate dealt the Greeks and their leader its unkindest and strangest blow.

Alexander, King of the Hellenes, was now twenty-seven years old and, despite the circumstances of his father's exile, his relationship with his masterful Prime Minister was improving. There had been difficulties at first. For a time the young King had been virtually a prisoner in the Tatoi Palace outside Athens. He had seen his parents' portraits removed from official buildings, and from the Palace itself. Even his father's military exploits in the Balkan Wars had been expunged from the school history books. Although he had been forced to drink of the cup of bitterness that seems inseparable from Greek politics, at last, in 1920, King and chief Minister were drawing together.

The reason was a curious one. A year before Alexander had married Aspasia, the attractive daughter of Colonel Manos, his father's Master of the Horse, in Greece a minor salaried position, not as in Britain a state post for a great nobleman. Paradoxically the only marriage ever to be contracted between a Greek king and a woman of native birth and blood was not popular. An allegedly egalitarian nation was jealous of the raising up of Aspasia Manos and would have preferred a foreign princess as the wife of the King. So the love match could only be recognised by a morganatic marriage. Alexander's children would not be in the line of succession to the Greek throne. Veniselos, however, disagreed with his countrymen. He was never a petty-minded man and had developed an affection for the young couple, and in 1920 was working hopefully towards the recognition of the King's wife as Queen. In London, in conversation with Veniselos, King George V had also favoured such a course.

It was not to be.

On October 2nd Alexander was walking his spaniel in the palace gardens and stopped to watch the play of two monkeys, pets of the vineyard keeper. The spaniel joined in and was bitten by the female monkey. Alexander intervened and was himself bitten in the leg by the male. The bite was very painful but not considered serious. Then blood poisoning set in. There were eleven emergency operations. Finally the King was too weak for his leg to be amputated. Two eminent French surgeons *en route* from Marseilles on a Greek destroyer provided by Veniselos were delayed by fierce storms in the Mediterranean. They arrived too late. Within three weeks of the bite the King had died in agony in the arms of his young wife who was expecting their first child.

With a title, 'The Monkey's Bite', more appropriate to Conan Doyle than the annals of a nation, the Greeks now entered the most disastrous period of their history.

6

'I do not know what is happening in Greece'
David Lloyd George

The immediate question was who would be King of Greece?

The demise of the sovereign in an ordinary constitutional monarchy normally brings about few public changes save those of interest to the numismatist and the philatelist. Greece, however, was no ordinary constitutional monarchy, and in addition in 1920 there were special circumstances.

King Constantine, who had never abdicated, was in exile, but an exile which had been imposed upon him by the British and French wartime governments. Prince George, the former Crown Prince, to whom the British and French had also objected, was with his father, as was his younger brother Prince Paul. Aspasia, the morganatic wife of the late King Alexander, was, it was true, expecting a child, but even if it were a boy and proclaimed King on birth there would have had to be a regency in Greece at least until 1938[1]. Veniselos certainly considered the possibility but

[1] The child was a girl, Alexandra, who married King Peter of Yugoslavia, in exile in Britain during the 1939–45 war. Aspasia was created

rejected it, partly because of the permanently precarious state of the Greek monarchy and partly because the establishment of a regency would only have posed another equally difficult question. Who would be Regent? The Prime Minister, although he had been in violent disagreement with one monarch, was not on general principles a republican. So, finally, an invitation was sent to Prince Paul to return to Greece and accept the crown. He replied, whether on his own initiative or on paternal advice can only be conjectured, that he could only become King if the Greek people first rejected his father and his elder brother, both of whom had claims superior to his own. The Greek constitution did not specify that a general election had to be held on the death of the monarch, but now there seemed to be no other method of ascertaining public opinion and resolving the deadlock. Accordingly, Veniselos called the first general election the Greeks had experienced since Constantine had gone into exile.

Properly speaking, the election issue was Veniselos plus Prince Paul versus Constantine. With a mixture of tremendous self-confidence and a sense of fair play the Prime Minister allowed back into Greece his old exiled opponents of the Royalist party to campaign against him. So, as the election got under way, the campaign simplified itself into a two-party fight, with Veniselos at the head of one party and Constantine at the head of the other. The Greeks were now being invited not only to choose a king, but to give their judgment on the last five years. Nowhere was there any doubt of the result, whether in the Veniselist north or the Royalist south. In London, Paris and Rome the inevitable Veniselist victory was anticipated complacently. After all, so it was thought, the name of Veniselos was practically synonymous with Greece. On the evening of November 14th the results were announced. They were unbelievable. Two hundred and fifty seats to the Royalist party, for Veniselos a mere 114. As an added humiliation

a Princess by a relieved Constantine. If her child had been a son, King Alexander had wanted him to be called Philip. Prince Andrew as a sign of affection 'reserved' the name, and gave it to his son, born in 1921.

the Prime Minister and his chief supporters all lost their own seats. Despite the view of his many admirers in Britain, France and Italy, at home, apparently, Veniselos was not Greece.

In the election campaign, fought bitterly on both sides, the Royalists had successfully raked up the past. The blockade of Athens by the Allied fleets, the landing of troops and marines, the return of Veniselos in 1917 backed by foreign bayonets. The half-forgotten humiliations were remembered. Not all the propaganda had to be directed against the foreigner, however. Veniselos had been in Paris too long; in his absence the rule of his lieutenants had been neither light nor impartial. There were many grievances, many allegations of corruption. On November 14th, 1920, Veniselos learned the lesson already learned by Woodrow Wilson, that statesmanlike prestige abroad does not guarantee political success at home. Surprised, hurt, and angry, he immediately resigned both as Prime Minister and party leader and three days later left Greece by sea for Italy, despite the entreaties of his supporters whom he left to fend for themselves as best they might.

In London, when he received the news, Lloyd George, conquering his dismay, merely shrugged his shoulders and turning to Churchill said with a grin, 'Now I am the only one left.' It was true. Of the great men of the war and the Peace Conference Wilson was an invalid with little time to live, Clemenceau, the old 'Tiger', had been pushed aside, and Orlando had also been defeated in a general election. Their decisions, however, had placed a Greek army in Asia Minor and at the same time roused the Turks to a dangerous mood of hatred not only against Greeks but any foreigner still on Turkish soil. Now Lloyd George, as the sole legatee of those policies, had to face the fact that Veniselos, his hero and trusted agent, had been ousted and the despised Constantine was to return. Not by some military coup, that would have been almost tolerable, but by popular acclaim. It was a poor time for a man who had been brought up in the nineteenth century Liberal belief that universal suffrage cured all political ills.

The Turks had been allowed to vote and had opted for Mustapha Kemal. The Greeks had gone to the polls and chosen Constantine. 'It almost makes one despair of democracy', wrote Lloyd George to Veniselos, now in Paris. Still, democracy had to be served, and at home the Cabinet, at least, had no doubts as to Britain's proper attitude to the newly elected government in Greece.

On December 2nd Sir Donald Maclean, the Member for Midlothian and Peebles, asked a Private Notice Question of the Leader of the House of Commons with regard to the Greek situation. Bonar Law produced the prepared answer in reply to the arranged question and announced the text of the Note which had been sent that day to Athens. 'The British, French and Italian governments have constantly in the past given proof of their good will towards the Greek people and have favoured the attainment of their secular aspirations. They have therefore been all the more keenly surprised by the events which have just occurred in Greece. They have no wish to interfere in the internal affairs of Greece, but they feel bound to declare publicly that the restoration to the Throne of Greece of a King whose disloyal attitude and conduct towards the Allies during the war caused them great embarrassment and loss could only be regarded by them as a ratification by Greece of his hostile acts. This step would create a new and unfavourable situation in the relations between Greece and the Allies, and in that case the three governments reserve to themselves complete liberty in dealing with the situation thus created.'

On December 6th Cecil Harmsworth, the Under Secretary of State for Foreign Affairs, he was Lord Northcliffe's son, gave some indication of the 'new and unfavourable situation'. In February 1918 the British government had offered credit of over £10 million to the Greek government. Veniselos had so far drawn £6½ million. 'The new Greek government have now been informed,' said Mr. Harmsworth, 'that in the event of the return of the ex-King Constantine to the throne of Greece no further financial assistance will be afforded. . . .'

The Note and this piece of polite blackmail arrived in

Athens just before the Greeks embarked on a plebiscite which was held on the straight issue: should Constantine return or not? Neither was published by the Greeks, but perhaps it would have made little difference. The plebiscite reiterated more forcefully the verdict of the general election. On December 19th Constantine, with his Queen and the Crown Prince, disembarked from the cruiser *Averoff* which had brought them from Venice and entered Athens to acknowledge the welcome of the cheering crowds. In 1917 he had said, 'Alex is King only in my place. I shall return.'

When to their surprise he did, the first reaction of the Allied statesmen had been conditioned entirely by their memories of his attitude during the war. Their pride was hurt by the fact that the tiny Greek nation, for which they felt they had done so much, should presume to reinstate a king who had failed to throw his subjects happily into a world war on their side. The Kaiser was now peacefully sawing logs in exile at Doorn; that his brother-in-law should return to his kingdom was thought to be intolerable. Only Lloyd George and Curzon, who agreed about little else, from their very different points of view felt that Constantine or no, Greece could not be deserted entirely. The majority opinion was summed up by Churchill: 'For the sake of Veniselos much had to be endured, but for Constantine less than nothing.'

The first quick reaction was anger; the second, and more lasting, was relief. The return of King Constantine, it was realised, provided the Allies with an excellent excuse for quietly ditching the Greeks, for the affairs of Greece and Turkey were becoming very troublesome indeed. Looking back on the old year of 1920, the Allies could find little cause for self-congratulation. True, the Treaty of Sèvres had been ratified by the Turks. It had been presented to the Sultan's government on June 10th and had been signed on August 10th. The interval had been taken up in finding a government spineless or cynical enough to sign it. Finally Damad Ferid, who had married one of the Sultan's sisters, had been appointed Grand Vizier, and had formed just such a government. He was an acknowledged expert in these matters, but this time he had to concoct a complete administration of nonentities. For the signature was a farce, and actually more of a farce than the Allies realised, for even the despised, compliant Ferid, 'a very good imitation of an English gentleman', thought Count Sforza, was secretly in communication with the Nationalists.

It was becoming painfully obvious that the Turks were not going to submit tamely to the Treaty of Sèvres. The noble concept of an Armenian state had disappeared under the hooves of the occupying Russian and Turkish cavalry in December. The peacemakers had achieved a minor miracle and had driven Russians and Turks to co-operate for the first time since the days of Peter the Great. Armenia was now divided between the new Russia and the new Turkey, and there was nothing its creators in London, Paris and Washington could do to save it or its unhappy, persecuted population. Other provisions of the shortest-lived treaty in modern history were being not so much torn up as quietly consigned to the wastepaper basket. The spheres of influence, British, French and Italian, it was becoming plain, would be denied those nations by force of arms if necessary. At the change of the year all that remained were the zones of occupation: the Greek spreading out from Smyrna, and the international zone on both sides of the Straits. As a guarantee of the latter the Allies had their soldiers on the spot, their warships in the Sea of Marmora and, for the moment, their possession of Constantinople.

The Treaty itself, although founded on a number of false premises, such as the continued active interest of the U.S.A. and the passivity of the Turks, had possessed a certain Draconian logic. Now the Allies were left with a few rags and tatters of that document, and little of either political or military logic remained.

Greek action in Anatolia had originally been tolerable and possible within the framework of a grand design, however ill conceived. Now the grand design was fading away. The Allies began to recall the cost of assisting Greece. The British taxpayer alone had lent nearly £16 million since 1914. The Italians, jealous of the Greeks from the start, and the French, with financial interests in the old Empire, began to think of the advantages, political and economic, which might be gained by friendship with the new Turkey. The British had troubles enough in the ex-Turkish domains of Palestine, Egypt and Mesopotamia. The French were still trying to subdue Syria. The Greeks, of course, had helped out in the past, but it looked as if it was going to be difficult to give them any help in return. None of the three involved nations, Britain, France and Italy, in declining order of enthusiasm, were prepared to go to war with Turkey to enforce the peace terms of a war which had ended only two years before. For the sake of Veniselos much that could not be performed had been half-promised, but had not the return of Constantine conveniently wiped the slate clean?

Three days after King Constantine entered Athens and just before it adjourned for the Christmas recess, the House of Commons debated the situation in the Near East. Like most debates on foreign affairs it was often imprecise and rambling. Members, as is their wont on these occasions, rode their own hobby horses into the ground. Yet there was one significant common factor discernible: the change in attitude of Britain's elected representatives in less than a year, especially among the Conservatives who formed the majority of the Government party. Gone were the old arrogant assumptions about Turkey, to be replaced by a desire, as Members frequently put it, to be 'realistic' and 'practical'. Members had experienced some disappointments in the last year and there was no dearth of criticism of the government from the government side of the House.

Lieutenant-Colonel Guinness, the Member for Bury St. Edmunds, was typical. He began by saying that he hoped that the Allies had at last realised the true position in Asia Minor and were now 'prepared to base a new policy not on dreams but on hard facts'. Those who had made the Treaty of Sèvres had been 'misled owing to the influence of the Greek argument', and had made the mistake of judging the strength of a whole people 'by the power and genius of one exceptional man who has since been very emphatically repudiated by Greece'. The Greeks had now, he believed, 'chosen a King and a Prime Minister who stand for a policy of peace'. Therefore, went his argument, the prop of the whole Near Eastern policy had disappeared. 'The two other Powers concerned, France and Italy, show every wish to reconsider the Turkish position in a manner favourable towards Turkey'. The unfortunate impression was that Britain still held out; therefore, he concluded, in our own interests 'the first step would seem to be for the Allies to get into touch with the Ankara government either through Constantinople or better still direct'. One speaker who had had direct experience of negotiating with the Turks was Major-General Sir Charles Townshend, the emissary at Mudros in 1918 and before that a Turkish prisoner of war. Now an M.P., he agreed with Guinness, but was even more direct and soldierly, and considerably briefer. 'I only wish to say we ought to approach Kemal.'

One did not need to be as Celtic and responsive as Lloyd George to sense the new feeling. Consequently, when the Prime Minister came to reply, with his back to the wall, he relied, as so often before in that situation, upon his powers of oratory. Yes, he was prepared to negotiate, but with whom? The Constantinople government was still the legal government. 'I do not say it is the *de facto* government but it is the government we have set up.' Therefore the British could not negotiate with a general who was in revolt. It had been suggested that this general with his army could drive the Greeks into the sea and the Allies into the Bosphorus. But, said the Prime Minister, look what had happened. 'In ten days it was scattered, by Greek forces, without the slightest difficulty and the Greeks assured me that they could march right through to the Dardanelles, and that if the Powers asked them, they would march right through to Ankara. I have not the slightest doubt about that.' Honourable gentlemen had suggested that Smyrna should be returned and that Britain should negotiate for peace. 'Peace with whom? Peace with Mustapha Kemal, who is here today and will vanish tomorrow?'

The Welsh wizard was warming to his work, and having disposed of Kemal he turned to the Greeks. 'Because there is a little trouble in Erzerum, because there is a general election in Greece, the result of which we abhor, do not let us change the whole of our policy in the East. The Mediterranean is vital to Britain. We want the friendship of the Greek people, a people whose friendship is vital to us in that part of the world, whatever we do. They will multiply and wax strong; they will make their political blunders, just like any other people, but they will grow, they will become stronger. They are a people of vital intelligence, of energy and they have shown they have courage.'

Then a note of humility and togetherness. 'Do not let us rush into this matter. I do not know what is happening in Greece. I do not quite know what is happening in Asia Minor. Who does?' It was a measure of the Prime Minister's oratorial power that there were no interjections at this stage.

The final appeal was to caution, which the House of Commons generally finds irresistible. The House and the British public were begged not 'to rush into tearing up treaties which took a great deal of reflection' and so 'restore conditions which very nearly proved fatal to us in the Great War'. The Prime Minister was triumphant, the House was quietened and doubtless the Greek Ambassador reported to Athens what he had seen and heard from the Diplomatic Gallery.

Much now depended on what Constantine and his Prime Minister M. Rhallis would do. Their first action did much to reinforce the view that he should be abandoned to his own devices, especially in Britain. There, since the Great Reform Bill ninety years ago, it had been a sort of national joke that, in countries less well regulated than their own, parties victorious at elections promptly replaced not only Ministers but state officials and employees as well. It didn't happen in Britain, thank God, where democracy worked properly, but the poor misguided foreigner, so it was understood, changed everyone 'down to the village post-master'. This was precisely what Constantine did do.

Churchill found himself echoing the classic phrase: 'The new government busied themselves in expelling from every form of public employment all Veniselist officials from bishops, judges, university professors and schoolmasters, down even to the charwoman in the public offices.' Doubtless the fact that all of them had first been given their posts because they were Veniselists was Constantine's excuse, but his wholesale purge of public offices further blackened the King's name in the West and did real harm to one institution on which he would have soon to rely—the Greek army. There the reorganisation took on fantastic proportions. General Paraskeropoulos, the Commander-in-Chief in Smyrna, resigned and left for France on the day the King entered Athens. A purge was expected, of course, but it is doubtful if even the General estimated its character correctly. Over 1,500 officers, from generals to lieutenants, previously dismissed under Veniselos, were reinstated and promoted to the rank they would have held if their service had been unbroken. Conversely, a smaller number of senior Veniselist officers were demoted or dismissed. Their juniors who remained automatically became trouble-makers.

The army in Asia Minor was turned completely upside down. It was political tit-for-tat, but it was military madness. Experienced officers, known and trusted by their men, were whisked away to be replaced by unknowns who had been out of the army for four years, and in many cases had seen no active service since the Balkan Wars. At the same time, attempts to inculcate a new spirit of subservience and devotion to the Sovereign merely irritated and antagonised soldiers who in some years of fighting on the Salonika Front, in Russia, and in Anatolia, had developed their own *esprit de corps* independent of politicians or kings in Athens. Only in his appointment of a new commander-in-chief did Constantine show any wisdom. General Papoulas had risen from the ranks, and in 1911 and 1912 had proved himself an excellent infantry commander. Promoted to general, in December 1916 he had stood by the King, and had been tried later by a Veniselist court martial in consequence. Significantly, he was acquitted. He was, as even his enemies had recognised, a simple, loyal, non-political soldier, something of a rarity in Greece. From the day of his appointment in Smyrna he devoted himself to the task of re-establishing unity; he at least was completely impartial and concerned only with military efficiency. He became in time a popular if not brilliant commander, but the task he had set himself, of healing the rifts in the Anatolian army, was well beyond the capabilities of any one man.

Meanwhile the Royal Hellenic Navy suffered in a similar, if less sensational, way than the army, so that there too the first fruits of the new regime were distrust, jealousy and dissension. Visiting British officers found that Greek naval officers on the same ship would not speak to each other. A poor preparation for Constantine's next move, which took the most experienced diplomats and foreign observers completely by surprise.

As the Royalist 'ticket' at the recent election had been basically the reversal of all that Veniselos had stood for and done in the last five years, they, like the Member of Parliament for Bury St. Edmunds, had reasonably assumed that the war in Anatolia would soon be brought to an end. That course would have had a great deal to recommend it. Greece was a poor country, now deprived of foreign aid, and the army in Anatolia was costing a million pounds a month. It would also have had the virtue of consistency. Constantine had been pushed off his throne because he refused to be dragged into what he regarded as a dangerous and possibly unsuccessful war. In 1917 he had refused because 'he was answerable before God'. In 1921, the terms and responsibilities of his kingship presumably unchanged, in 'a mad outbreak of regal vanity' as Lloyd George saw it, the King decided to out-Veniselos Veniselos. Egged on by his military advisers, Constantine decided not only to follow the policy of his rival but, though deprived of all semblance of Allied support, to step up the war against the Turks. Colonel Exadactylos of the General Staff said that Anatolia could be pacified in three months.

Foreign statesmen who had thought, wrongly, that Veniselos had been rejected because of the unpopularity of the war were thunderstruck. The charm of the great Cretan statesman still dazzled their eyes, and the fact that even he had used the old device of a grandiose foreign policy to allay discontent at home had escaped them. The war, or at least the idea of territorial gain, was still popular. Constantine could only have abandoned it at his peril. His fault was not, as Lloyd George suggested, megalomania, but merely a desire to please.

So in the early days of January, 1921, the Greek army in Anatolia moved over to the offensive and began a series of reconnaissances in force eastwards. For the moment at least, military logic was on the side of its new commanders. In the previous year, while Veniselos had still been in power, the Greek army had followed no particular strategic pattern in its movements. It had fanned out from Smyrna; it had taken Brusa; but overall it tended simply to conform to the tactical demands made upon it by the irregular warfare waged by the Turks. The army had taken its opponents where it had found them, or else where the Allies had indicated. Indeed, one of the last acts of the Veniselists had been to discontinue penetration eastwards at the request of their allies, when the General Staffs in London and Paris had become concerned as to just how far the Greeks intended to go. Consequently the line was an haphazard one, neither offensive nor defensive, extending from Smyrna on three virtually disconnected fronts.

Now, with the severance of relations between the Supreme Allied Council and Constantine's government, all foreign military advice had been withdrawn. The Ambassadors remained in Athens, but were instructed to have no dealings with the King and his court, although they could continue to communicate with the government if necessary. Nothing more, however, was to be allowed. Rear-Admiral Kelly, the Chief of the British Naval Mission, who had in December accepted the Grand Cross of the Redeemer from the King for his services to the Greek Navy, was curtly ordered by Lord Curzon to return it. In a proclamation to his troops the King still referred to 'the Allied Army in Anatolia', but that was a mere puff for home consumption to boost morale.

A few British, French and Italian officers remained with the army but only as observers; there was no more advice, no more restrictions. The Greek army, then, under General Papoulas, was free to proceed to tidy up its front preparatory to the spring offensive, for it was no secret that there was to be an offensive. The war was to be ended not by a negotiated peace, nor by some territorial formula devised by the Great Powers, but by a straight Greek victory over the Turks. The quick successes of the Balkan Wars were to be repeated, and this time by the Greeks alone. Certainly there was a new spirit of ambition abroad among the officers of the General Staff in those early days. Gaining something in panache from their new royal master and taking their cue from him, they began to talk confidently of two rather disparate objectives, Ankara and Constantinople. Whether either was attainable would remain to be seen, for in both cities, simultaneously with the Greek advance, events were taking place which were significantly to affect the future.

A state of civil war now existed between the two. In Constantinople a combination of the Sultan, the Allies' minion, Damad Ferid, and the Sheikh of Islam, the supreme religious authority, had denounced Kemal and his associates as rebels, sentenced them to death and technically imposed a duty on all Moslems to kill them as a religious duty. Kemal had retaliated by arranging for a tame ulema (religious council) in Ankara to return the compliment, making an exception, of course, for the person of the Sultan and Caliph, whom it was convenient and politic still to represent as an unwilling prisoner of the Allied Powers. On behalf of the Sultan men were now being recruited into an army to oppose Kemal; an army which, legally at least, was still the Turkish Regular Army, but in composition was more akin to the Irish 'Black and Tans' and considerably less effective. This force was pushed into the Ismid peninsula and occupied a sector of north-western Anatolia.

So now, in Constantinople on the one hand, the Sultan and Caliph, with the Grand Vizier and the empty panoply of the old Ottoman Empire; on the other, in Ankara, Mustapha Kemal and the Grand National Assembly. It suited the Allies to boost the status of the legal government, as Lloyd George had done in the House of Commons, and conversely to minimise the influence of Mustapha Kemal. It was not, however, a confrontation between equals, and the Allies knew it. Throughout 1920 the divergence between the two cities had become more clearly defined, as if iron filings had been scattered over the two opposed poles of a magnet. In size, appearance, population and atmosphere alone they could not have presented a more striking contrast.

Constantinople, the capital of an empire, with its fascinating mixture of architectural styles, races, languages and manners. A city, too, poised between Europe and Asia, which had managed to absorb the vices of both and thus acquire an indefinable atmosphere of Ottoman decadence overlaid with something akin to the tawdry gaiety of Napoleon III's Paris.

Ankara, on the other hand, was still no more than an overgrown country town, with a few large buildings and fewer still hotels and restaurants, its primitive streets filled with archaic horse or bullock-drawn transport. Situated on an arid plain in the middle of nowhere, it had no pretensions to be anything more than what it was: a simple, backward, provincial Turkish town, with little apart from a railway station and a telegraph office to show for its contact with the twentieth century. Its population, a mere 20,000, consisted of dour, insular Anatolian peasants, seemingly almost indifferent to the events taking place under their noses. Yet Ankara was Turkey, and Constantinople just a city.

At all levels Turkish opinion was turning towards Kemal and recruits were flowing into Anatolia. Statesmen, soldiers and private individuals would just slip away from Constantinople and make their secret ways past Allied guards and cordons to emerge as members of the Nationalist movement in Anatolia. One such was an able career soldier, Ismet Pasha, lately at the Ministry of War in Constantinople, soon to become Kemal's trusted Chief of Staff and destined one day to be the second President of Turkey. That eventuality, though, could not have been even remotely contemplated in 1920, for the access of men and enthusiasm had its considerable embarrassments and dangers. At times Mustapha Kemal's position was as precarious and difficult as his worst enemies could have desired. As in any resistance movement at the beginning there were rival groups, and many of the leaders of irregular bands were jealous of Kemal's position, which they were convinced they could fill better themselves. Some were mere power-seekers, others genuinely disagreed with Kemal's conduct of affairs or were impatient with his apparent delay in getting to grips with the Greeks. Often the Grand National Assembly with its 369 members was less than helpful. Privately, Kemal had scant respect for such a body; Carlyle's description of the British House of Commons as 'a talking shop' would have summed up his view. Nevertheless, the Assembly, however irritating, impractical and disorderly, was his claim and justification for power, so it had to be soothed, flattered and persuaded.

Typically, the loss of Brusa to the Greeks had much affected the Assembly; not so much as a military objective, but for sentimental and religious reasons, for Brusa had been the original Ottoman capital in the fourteenth century. There was situated the famous Green Mosque, and there lay, under magnificent tombs, Osman, the founder of the dynasty, the Sultan Murad I, killed in the hour of his victory over the Serbs at Kossovo, and Murad II, conqueror of Salonika and Corinth. When the loss of this holy city was discussed some of the Deputies literally wept. Kemal, who cared no more for the mouldering heroes of the dynasty than for the living incumbent in Constantinople, hid his feelings of contempt, mollified the Deputies, and made his practical military plans for the future with his small band of intimates in his headquarters at the Agricultural School.

The Deputies, who were well meaning if weak and silly, received soft words, but to those among the rebel leaders who coveted his place Kemal offered nothing save force. An army had to be formed in Anatolia and an army with only one leader. Quite ruthlessly, therefore, Kemal broke or destroyed his rivals, and their followers were converted from rifle-carrying brigands into disciplined soldiers. Ruthlessness was part of his nature, but Mustapha Kemal had in any event ample excuse in the difficulties and dangers of his position.

There were perils from without as well as within. The U.S.S.R. had not given its friendship to him entirely platonically. Financial assistance (he had now received a million roubles) and military co-operation in Armenia were neither without strings. The propagandists in Moscow wrote enthusiastically of the Nationalist movement in Turkey as yet another manifestation of the coming world revolution, and in the autumn of 1920 a large Soviet embassy arrived in Ankara. Kemal's brief pleasure at this first sign of official recognition was severely tempered by the fact that at the same time Communist agents descended on Turkey and commenced their undercover activities. Some Turks had already become converted to Marxism, and many were intrigued, at a time of change and revolution in their own country, by its success in Russia. Kemal, totally opposed to its doctrine, was realistic enough to appear friendly to Soviet diplomats and the Soviet government while at the same time systematically extirpating any signs of nascent Communism in his own ranks. He had no illusions about the long-term intentions of his Russian neighbour and quickly saw the danger of the Communists 'taking over' his own revolution. In extreme cases his methods were swift and violent. Mustapha Subhi, one of the Soviet's foremost agitators and agents, when he became dangerous, simply disappeared from the deck of his ship in the Black Sea.

It was not always so simple, however, to deal with a threat which had the twin advantages of apparent internationalism and social revolution. Furthermore, the two former leaders of the old Committee of Union and Progress, Enver and Talaat[1], were now in Moscow advising and

[1] Both met violent ends: Enver in Turkestan leading a minor revolt, Talaat in Berlin at the hands of an Armenian. Djavid, the third member of the trio, was executed in 1926, allegedly for complicity in an attempt upon Kemal's life.

helping their new masters, and it was some time before Kemal would really be convinced that Turkey had freed herself from the embraces of the Russian bear.

Both Admiral de Robeck, the High Commissioner at Constantinople, and the British War Office, in an appreciation, had predicted the likelihood of 'Kemal being driven into the hands of the Bolsheviks', and in 1920 their pessimistic forecast was only prevented from becoming true by the resolute actions of Mustapha Kemal himself. For in this, as in other matters, 1920 was really Kemal's year of crisis. The energy, patience, guile and courage expended by this one man in overcoming the troubles that beset him were truly prodigious. It was in this period, now wheedling acquiescence from the Assembly, now paying lip service to fanatical Moslems, now facing over-mighty irregular leaders with rifles, and at the same time warding off Moscow and putting necessary heart into his closest associates, that Kemal developed what his most perceptive biographer, Lord Kinross, has called his 'third dimension'. The indefinable quality of leadership.

He was not a particularly pleasant man. His humour, such as it was, was brusque and coarse. His manners and habits were still of the camp rather than the drawing-room. It is almost impossible to find a gentle anecdote about him; his manner recalls that curious mixture of directness and gaucherie which characterised the young Napoleon. Napoleon later acquired a thin veneer of civility. Kemal never did. He shocked those of his followers who were strict Moslems by his heavy drinking habits and offended others by his entirely emotionless but energetic pursuit of women. He seemed to possess few humanising qualities; he relaxed only with his drinking cronies and soldiers in the field. Despite his curiously Western appearance and his determination to drag or push his fellow countrymen into the twentieth century, he still retained much of the arrogance and insensitivity of the old Turk. He was admired and feared but not much loved. Nevertheless, by the early weeks of 1921 when the army he had fashioned, and behind it the people he had inspired, prepared to face a renewed assault by the Greeks, he was undoubtedly the leader of the Turkish nation.

*   *   *

In Constantinople the question posed by Admiral de Robeck to Lord Curzon in June 1920 was still unanswered. 'We are already fighting Turkey,' telegraphed the Admiral, 'are we to continue a new war observing that the Peace Treaty has united practically all Turks?' If the Allies were contemplating such a war they were ill prepared to wage it.

In the early part of the year General Sir George Milne, who commanded the British Army of the Black Sea, had cause to complain, not for the first time, of the high-handed actions and attitude of General Franchet d'Esperey, the Supreme Commander of the Allied Armies in Constantinople. Eventually the French Ambassador in London confessed to Lord Curzon that the General 'had shown a complete lack of tact and judgment'. Soon Franchet d'Esperey was granted long and indefinite leave. 'The French government realised that it would be agreeable news to His Majesty's Government,' remarked Sir George Grahame, the Minister in Paris, when he confided the decision to London.

The removal of one tempestuous general, 'desperate Frankie' as he was known to the British, did not, however, solve the basic problem of co-operation. By a personal appeal to the French President which included many pointed references to French supreme military command in the war, Lloyd George managed to establish that in future the armies in Turkey would be commanded by a British general, but still the Allies continued to drift apart. Reports flowed in to London testifying to speeches and actions by senior French and Italian officers and officials in occupied Turkey which showed clearly that both nations were undoubtedly trying to curry favour with the Nationalists while placing all the blame for Turkey's plight upon the British. It was still just possible to place some trust in the French but the Italians plainly had gone over to the enemy. 'They are already on bad terms with the Greeks in the Aidin vilayet', reported the War Office, 'and the whole trend of their policy has been rather less than loyal to the Allies.' On occasions Italian and Greek soldiers fired on each other. So bad did the situation become that Lord Curzon raised the matter with the Italian Foreign Minister when the Allied Council met at Spa, but with no success. As he informed the Ambassador in Rome: 'Count Sforza appeared throughout our conversations to be animated personally by most friendly intentions but he made no great effort to disguise that his countrymen were not always similarly inclined.' Even this was a favourable estimate, and Count Sforza, who had been the Italian High Commissioner in Constantinople in 1919, was, if not anti-British, certainly anti-Greek.

It was rapidly becoming, it seemed, a military problem, and one that was being left to be solved by the British and the Greeks, who were, after Constantine's return, no longer allies. The War Office appreciation of the situation which was presented to the Cabinet put the matter bluntly. Of the Turks it said, 'political power had passed to the Nationalists', and therefore, so far as the position of the British forces was concerned, 'the occupation of the War Office at Constantinople may therefore not have much effect from the point of view of military control'. Of the Greek army in Anatolia: 'The Greek position is not tactically or strategically good. It is divided into sectors by ridges running east and west with very little transverse communication. The Greek morale is rather uncertain.'

Finally, as seemed possible, if it came to the British alone, 'the military assets of England are barely sufficient, if even they are sufficient, for the needs of the British Empire and beyond our present efforts in Batum, Constantinople and the Straits, Palestine, Egypt and Mesopotamia nothing more can be done with the forces at our disposal'.

The forces at the disposal of the government in Britain were forty-nine infantry battalions in England, of which some were earmarked for use in case of industrial unrest and others were largely made up of newly joined recruits. In Ireland, pinned down by what was still a civil war, there were twenty-eight infantry battalions, an irreducible minimum. Towards the end of the year the approximate numbers of

Allied troops in Turkey, including Constantinople, were 10,000 British, 8,000 Indians, 8,000 French and 2,000 Italians. The Indian troops were, however, soon to return home, and the British and French garrisons be drastically reduced. The Greek army then numbered approximately 100,000 soldiers on active service. There were no reliable estimates for the size of the Turkish Nationalist Army, but it was thought to be a few thousands less than the Greek.

This was the situation in late 1920, when the personalities at Constantinople changed. Damad Ferid, having served his purpose, had retired to Carlsbad for, it was said, a cure. His place as Grand Vizier was taken by Tewfik Pasha, who included at least two Ministers of known Nationalist sympathies in his new Cabinet. Admiral de Robeck, who had doubled the posts of High Commissioner in Constantinople and Commander-in-Chief of the Mediterranean Fleet, reverted to purely naval employment and was replaced by Sir Horace Rumbold, a professional diplomat, whose last post had been as Minister in tranquil Berne. The third change of face, and it was to be far the most significant, was that of military commander. In November General Sir George Milne handed over to Lieutenant-General Sir Charles Harington.

On December 31st, 1920, Sir Horace Rumbold, from his new post, telegraphed a New Year message to Lord Curzon at the Foreign Office. 'The general outlook is very obscure and unsatisfactory,' he said.

7

'The whole thing is a ramp'
Field Marshal Sir Henry Wilson

In 1918, even before the 'Coupon Election', Bonar Law, the faithful Tory lieutenant, had said of Lloyd George: 'He can be Prime Minister for life, if he likes.' The result of that general election had seemed to confirm the view held by many politicians, Liberal as well as Conservative, that Lloyd George was unbeatable, and his own view that he was indispensable. The public at large was perfectly content that the architect of victory should also shape the peace. Accordingly the Prime Minister was almost entirely absent from Britain and the House of Commons until the end of 1919, occupied at Versailles and elsewhere with the making of peace.

Now, by the end of 1920, Balfour's half-condescending, half-admiring 'Little Man' of the Peace Conferences had deteriorated, in Parliamentary conversation, to 'the Goat'. The expression was not meant kindly and alluded to more than the Prime Minister's Welsh ancestry. Lord Vansittart,[1]

[1] Robert Vansittart. Secretary to Curzon, 1920–24. Assistant Under Secretary of State for Foreign Affairs, Permanent Private Secretary to

then at the Foreign Office, has observed: 'He had qualities. His wife had virtues, she needed them.' The point was not Lloyd George's private life. Other Ministers of the Crown, before and since, have had faults, amorous or alcoholic, winked at by their colleagues and, when in the know, the public as well. The point was that the sly jokes and innuendoes were merely symptoms; in little more than a year Lloyd George's political reputation had declined and his status had diminished. Some part of the process was not his fault and was as near inevitable as history can be.

The high hopes raised among the victors by the conclusion of the war and their dashing by its aftermath is now a platitude. At the time, however, the contrast was seen as the great disillusionment. Especially was this so in Britain, where a pacific and prosperous nation which had entered the war reluctantly and with no territorial ambitions, found that after an enormous expenditure of men and money it was in debt, with a mounting toll of unemployment and as many, if not more, unsolved problems as in 1914.

This disappointment both among politicians and the public may have been naive but it was felt none the less, and in such times, irrespective of responsibility, the public blames those it has elected. One of the problems which had soured pre-war politics was still unsolved after the war. In Ireland, sparked off by the Easter Rebellion in 1916, civil war still raged; fought out with a Balkan intensity between rival groupings of Irishmen, while the British attempted the thankless task of maintaining law and order and endeavoured to protect the pro-British Ulstermen at the same time. Lloyd George was no more destined than any of his predecessors at Westminster to produce a magical solution to the Irish problem, but his failure in a sphere where success was impossible was held against him just the same.

Baldwin and Ramsay MacDonald. Permanent Under Secretary of State, 1930–38. Chief Diplomatic Adviser to the Foreign Secretary, 1938–41. The latter post had more prestige than power, for though successively M.V.O., C.M.G., C.B., K.C.B., G.C.M.G., G.C.B., P.C. and a peer, he was unpopular with cautious governments for his outspoken views, especially on Nazi Germany. He died in 1957.

In another part of the British dominions, equally emotive in effect but vastly more important, the war and its aftermath had produced unrest. During the war India had raised the largest volunteer army in the Empire and had been promised 'responsible government within the framework of the British Empire' as its reward. The India Act of 1919, based on the joint recommendations of Edwin Montagu, the Secretary of State for India, and Lord Chelmsford, the Viceroy, went part of the way. Montagu himself believed that India should have had immediate Dominion status, but the Act only allowed self-government by progressive but slow and complicated stages.

Political disappointment thrived on current economic depression and an ex-lawyer called Gandhi became active among the mill hands of Ahmadabad and Amritsar. The government armed itself by the Rowlatt Act with wide powers of coercion. In April 1919 martial law was declared in the Punjab and on the 13th of that month, in Amritsar, Major-General Dyer ordered his troops to open fire on an unarmed crowd of demonstrators, killing 379 of them. The massacre in the Jallianwala Bagh cast a shadow over India and precluded for years to come any chances of co-operation between moderate Indian opinion and the British.

So far, in Ireland and India, it can be argued that Lloyd George's government had been dogged by ill-luck. Unfortunately, however, it was a government which had at the same time quite cheerfully taken on further Imperial responsibilities. Egypt was now in effect ruled by Britain, and mandates had been accepted for Iraq (formerly Mesopotamia) and Palestine. All three territories became almost immediately, for differing reasons, trouble spots, necessitating the presence of considerable garrisons of troops. In fact in the early 20's it became increasingly difficult to find among the spheres of administration or influence abroad any place on the map where trouble of one sort or another was not brewing for the British. Soon Persia and Afghanistan were to be added to the crisis list. The British commitment was enormous, particularly in the Middle East and Asia, particularly in countries which had large or predominant

Moslem populations. In this context it was beginning to seem as if further involvement with Turkey and Constantinople and the sensitive problem of the Caliphate could only increase Britain's unpopularity.

To his critics Lloyd George seemed to be living in a dream world, a hangover from the palmy days of the wartime alliances. Conferences, meetings and discussions abroad still occupied a great deal of his time and energy. The British, the French, the Italians, and the Japanese continued to meet as the Supreme Allied Council in an atmosphere of great importance and solemnity, as if they still controlled their ex-enemies and many others besides. The conferences were now known, however, as Lloyd George's Circuses, for to judge by results the Allies were neither co-operating very well nor very effectively. In Germany extreme Right and extreme Left were at each other's throats. Further east the Poles under Pilsudski had, after years of oppression, become expansionist themselves, and were simultaneously fighting Germans and Russians. Hungary, it appeared, was well on the way to becoming a second Russia. The Italians were prepared to fight the Yugoslavs over disputed frontiers on the Adriatic, but washed their hands of larger problems. The French and Belgians wished to occupy the Ruhr in the hope of extracting reparations from the near bankrupt Germans. The British through compassion or realism hung back, and were accused of disloyalty in consequence.

In November 1920, General Baron Wrangel, sometime commander of the Tsarevich's own Guard Cossacks, the last and most efficient White commander fighting the Red army, followed in the wake of General Yudenitch, Admiral Kolchak and General Denikin, and admitted defeat.

In seventy-five overcrowded ships he, with what remained of his army and their dependents, left the Crimea and arrived in Constantinople. Many were wounded, many suffering from cholera, all pitiful, starving and penniless. The last active attempt by the Allies to stem the course of the Russian Revolution had failed. Something like £3 millions' worth of armaments and aid recently supplied to Wrangel had been thrown away, and in a dramatic manner the problems of

British foreign policy had overlapped. For the clothing, feeding and lodging of this vast influx of refugees was the first problem that faced General Harington within days of his arrival as the new Commander-in-Chief.

So, while Lady Harington organised a system of coloured tickets, coloured tubs and helpers with coloured aprons whereby 90,000 refugees, who spoke no English, could be fed swiftly from soup kitchens, the victorious General Tuchachevsky was able to turn round his Red Army and concentrate it against the Poles. In the Turkish capital useless Russian currency notes of enormous face value were collected by British soldiers as curios and the bazaars were deluged with the personal valuables of the refugees: jewellery, fur coats, Cossack hats and daggers, officers' swords, medals and decorations. The soldiers of the garrison gave up their rations so willingly to the refugees that in the case of the Hampshire Regiment they had to be forbidden by order of the G.O.C. Today in Britain there are a number of old soldiers who still tell the time by exquisite, blue-enamelled watches, decorated with the two-headed eagle of Nicholas II, the last Tsar of all the Russias, sold by their original recipients for food.

Wrangel's ex-soldiers took any job they could find with the British or the French, cleaning barrack rooms or tending horses. The more skilled attached themselves to units as interpreters and signals linesmen. A descendant of one of Tsar Alexander's marshals who had fought Napoleon earned a pittance by driving a fatigue wagon. Sir Horace Rumbold reflected gloomily on the fate of the many Russian women who drifted into the night life of a city not renowned for its high moral tone, even without the complication of an invasion of destitute Europeans. 'I don't think I've behaved worse in my life,' said one British officer later, confirming Sir Horace's fears; 'they all said they were countesses in their own country, of course, but I doubt it.'

So the Russians, who had coveted the city for a century, came to Constantinople, and the thundering choruses and reponses of the Orthodox Church were at last heard in the city: drifting up from the refugee camps where the inmates lived on British and French charity. The irony was certainly not lost on General Harington, who had been appointed by an ebullient Churchill three months before. The Secretary of State for War had just received a telegram which said that Wrangel was advancing. 'Only ninety-eight more miles to Moscow and Winston Churchill comes into his own,' he had said on that occasion. Churchill, perhaps because he feared Bolshevism most, had always entertained high hopes of the policy of intervention. Lloyd George had not, and now that the cause was irretrievably lost could congratulate himself on his prescience and concentrate on more important issues.

As 1921 began there were many, but the most important was his own position. It was unique. A Liberal all his life, he was in office as Prime Minister by courtesy of the Tory majority in the House of Commons. He was that very curious thing, in Lord Beaverbrook's phrase, 'a Prime Minister without a party'. In the sphere of home policy this didn't matter a great deal. The problems of unemployment, industrial unrest and strikes, and even Ireland, were such that out of desperation government and majority party hung together. At best it could be regarded as unity in the face of common danger; at worst as mere desire to cling to power and office. Whichever it was, and it was frequently something in between, for the moment it worked, if not very well.

In the sphere of foreign policy, however, there were already real and alarming disagreements. Within the Cabinet the Prime Minister was passionately pro-Greek. The Foreign Secretary, Lord Curzon, in his magisterial way, favoured some equitable settlement between Greeks and Turks and still hankered after the internationalisation of Constantinople. Edwin Montagu, the Secretary of State for India, was hyper-sensitively concerned about the millions of Moslems ruled by his department and was anxious for a settlement, any settlement, with the Turks. He was soon in receipt of powerful support from New Delhi. The newly appointed Viceroy, Rufus Isaacs, Marquis of Reading, who had already in a fantastic career been Lord

Chief Justice and Britain's wartime Ambassador in the United States, was, like Montagu, a Jew and a Liberal, and the two men formed a powerful partnership. Because of their own race and religion, they felt that they were peculiarly fitted, certainly more so than their Gentile colleagues, to appreciate and interpret the desires and aspirations of the numerous races and religions of India. Winston Churchill, who had first seen action as a cavalry subaltern in India and never forgot the Imperial heritage, was equally concerned about Moslem sentiment and was unimpressed by the Prime Minister's vision of a new Greek Empire. The Lord Chancellor, Birkenhead, who tended to accept his political opinions second-hand, as usual sided with Churchill.

On March 17th, 1921, Lloyd George suffered a serious loss. Bonar Law, his trusted Tory second, whose duller, more prosaic qualities so complemented his own erratic brilliance, was forced to resign through ill health. He went to France for a long convalescence. The Tory party elected in his place Austen Chamberlain, a boring, correct man who had inherited few if any of the qualities of 'Joe', his famous father. Chamberlain, who had been Chancellor of the Exchequer, took Bonar Law's place as Lord Privy Seal, and was succeeded as Chancellor by Sir Robert Horne, whom Lord Curzon thought 'a vulgar fellow'.

These were the 'strong men' of the government. Few of them supported Lloyd George's foreign policy; most of them had deepening doubts about his home policy; nearly all of them disliked each other. With the rest of the curious collection of Ministers who visited the luxurious house at Lympne of Sir Philip Sassoon, the Prime Minister's rich but otherwise undistinguished Parliamentary Private Secretary, they sang comic songs of an evening (a favourite diversion), and hoped that Lloyd George would find a way out. The Prime Minister, when persuaded to participate, would sing a Welsh hymn.

Their trust, such as it was, was not reflected in the House of Commons. Among other things the Tories were worried about the Near East; they placed little reliance on the Greeks and were beginning to revert to the traditional 'grand old Turk' mentality of Disraeli's day. Miss Frances Stevenson, Lloyd George's secretary and his intimate companion, recorded in her diary that the Tories were beginning to use the phrase 'the Turk is a gentleman'. For a party which has always cloaked its realism with sentiment that phrase was enough. The Turk looked as if he was going to be a successful gentleman.

On the Opposition side of the House of Commons, in the diminished ranks of the old Liberal Party and the new Labour party, there were a number of M.P.s who wished the Greeks well, but none treasured the same sentiment towards Lloyd George. Lord Beaverbrook, himself an arch intriguer and privy to many secrets, dates the beginning of 'the Plots' against the Prime Minister by his Cabinet colleagues from this period. Beaverbrook himself, of course, had his own axe to grind; he was seeking a new Prime Minister who would advocate a less adventurous foreign policy and put into practice his own pet scheme of Empire Free Trade. Nevertheless his general diagnosis was correct.

Hitherto Lloyd George had stayed in the saddle with the ease of a man adept at cycling with no hands. From now on he was forced more and more often to make convulsive grabs at the handlebars.

*   *   *

On January 6th, 1921, the Greek army began a general advance into Anatolia. Their ultimate aim was the capture of Ankara, but the short-term objectives were the taking of Eskishehir and Afyon Karahisar, key junction towns on the main Smyrna–Ankara railway line.

The Greek army was divided into two groups, the northern concentrated at Brusa and the southern at Ushak. The northern group consisted of four infantry divisions (18,000 men) and the southern was made up of seven infantry divisions and a cavalry brigade (33,000 men). The front of about forty miles between these two concentrations was lightly held, as was the rest of the Greek line which stretched from the Sea of Marmora in the north down to the south of Smyrna.

There was little subtlety about the battle which followed. Against the Greek northern group the Turks assembled nine divisions, six infantry and three mounted infantry (23,000 men) to the west of Eskishehir. To protect Afyon Karahisar to the south they concentrated a force of ten infantry and two cavalry divisions (25,000 men). Overall, at the two concentrations and along the connecting front, the Greeks had a slight superiority in numbers, something like 3,000 more men than the Turks. In addition they were superior in field artillery and had more than twice the number of machine-guns per battalion than their opponents. In fact, where technical and mechanical equipment, transport, aircraft and weapons were concerned, the advantage was decidedly with the Greeks. The only apparent factor in the Turks' favour was that they would be fighting a defensive battle in difficult terrain over which the Greeks would have to advance, in most cases with the gradient against them. Nevertheless there were no doubts in the minds of the officers on the Greek General Staff that the operation would be successful.

On January 10th the main thrust was made on the northern sector from Brusa towards Eskishehir. Later the Turks were to talk of the first battle of Inönü. The battle, compared with those of the Great War, was a small affair. For a day, fighting in snow and slush, the Turks commanded by Ismet Pasha resolutely held their ground in their prepared position in the valley of Inönü. On the second day they counter-attacked with great persistence and courage. Greek confidence turned to surprise and consternation, and the new Royalist commanders were compelled to admit defeat and order a retreat back to Brusa. It was a small victory, but there were mammoth celebrations in Ankara. For the first time a disciplined and trained Turkish army had met the Greeks on anything like equal terms and it had repulsed them. The disappointed Greeks retired to lick their wounds and prepare for their next offensive in the better weather that would come with the spring. Before that could happen, however, and no doubt influenced by the surprise result at Inönü, the Allies decided to take a hand. There was to be another conference.

In February an invitation was sent to the Greek government, the Sultan's government in Constantinople, and to the Ankara government, to attend a conference in London to discuss the terms of the Treaty of Sèvres. The chair at the conference was, needless to say, to be taken by the British Prime Minister. Lloyd George undoubtedly believed, as another Prime Minister, Harold Macmillan, was to put it forty years later: 'jaw, jaw is better than war, war'; but the conference was from the beginning to end a solemn farce. The invitation to the three governments, at first sight reasonable, was in fact ridiculous. The Constantinople government would obviously not recognise what it regarded as a rebel regime in Ankara. Kemal and his Grand National Assembly, with the facts on their side, refused to accept that Constantinople had any jurisdiction over Anatolia. The Greeks saw that if they accepted that Kemal's government was the lawful government of Turkey they destroyed the basis of their own case, and with it the reasons for their presence in Turkey. The only party who derived any satisfaction from the triple invitation was Kemal, who had thereby received his first recognition from the Allies as the *de facto* ruler of Turkey.

Still, perhaps because Lloyd George's name possessed some residual magic, more likely because each thought that they could lose nothing by appearing to be reasonable, the three delegations came to London. Tewfik Pasha, the Grand Vizier, headed the representatives of the crumbling power of the Ottomans; Kemal sent Bekir Sami Bey, his Foreign Secretary. The Chief of the Greek delegation was M. Kalogeropoulos, a former Prime Minister[1] and now Foreign Minister. He was accompanied by a trio of colonels, Exadactylos, Sariyannis and Lacon.

[1] The category was substantial. The Prime Ministers of Greece were: in 1914, Veniselos; 1915, Veniselos, Gounaris, Veniselos, Zaimis, Skouloudis; 1916, Zaimis, Kalogeropoulos, Lambros; 1917, Zaimis, Veniselos; 1918, Veniselos; 1919, Veniselos; 1920, Veniselos, Rhallis, Kalogeropoulos; 1921, Gounaris; 1922, Gounaris, Kalogeropoulos.

By some piece of superb Foreign Office administrative bungling, or perhaps it was subtle policy, the two Turkish delegations were accommodated in the same hotel, the Savoy. They occupied separate floors and at first refused to speak to each other. Unfortunately neither delegation gave Lloyd George any reason to change his poor opinion of the Turks.

Tewfik Pasha appeared to be ill and spent a great deal of time confined to his bed. His subordinates took their cue from him and hardly attended the conference proceedings at all, leaving the field clear to the Nationalists.

Bekir Sami Bey, nattily dressed in European morning dress, both irritated and offended Lloyd George. On his way to London he had stopped off at Rome to visit the Italian Foreign Minister, Count Sforza, who was also to attend the conference as the head of his own country's delegation. The Italians were rightly suspected by the British of being the least reliable of the Allies. Sforza, the inheritor of a famous Renaissance name not exactly associated with straight dealing, was doubly unpopular, being regarded as outrageously vain (Vansittart calls him 'the Peacock Man') and equally dishonest.

Once at the conference table Bekir Sami displayed, to Lloyd George's mind, the typical Oriental habits of negotiation. He first claimed the Straits, Smyrna and Constantinople, the maximum Turkish demand, and then relapsed into language which made it increasingly difficult for the Allies to know what he really did expect. No doubt the British Prime Minister's patience was strained to breaking point when Bekir Sami was absent from the conference for a whole day, and, as Lloyd George reported indignantly to King George V later, 'finally was traced to a sodomy house in the East End'.

It was not a very successful conference. The negotiations lasted from February 23rd to March 12th. Tewfik remained at the Savoy Hotel and the Greeks predictably refused to sit down in the same room as the delegates from Ankara. The Greek demands under Constantine were substantially the same as under Veniselos: eastern Thrace up to Constantinople and the Smyrna province. The French and British suggested, true to the old and previously ignored Wilson principles, the holding of plebiscites. The Turks accepted, the Greeks refused. Forced to climb down, Briand for France and Lloyd George for Britain relented on the Straits and Constantinople, conceded Kurdistan, and suggested that the newly created League of Nations might look into the question of Armenia. As Armenia, and a large number of Armenians, were no more, this last suggestion was an empty and pointless gesture which only served to make the other terms less acceptable to the Turks.

The real question though was Smyrna. Should the Greeks be allowed to remain there? The Allies' suggestion was that the province should become autonomous, independent of Turkey and technically independent of Greece as well. It was a transparent fiction and doubtless Bekir Sami saw it as such. Without expressing agreement the three delegations returned to Constantinople, Ankara and Athens. All that Lloyd George had succeeded in doing, despite the warnings of Churchill, Curzon, Field Marshal Wilson and General Gourand, who accompanied Briand, was to convince the Turks that he was opposed to their aspirations and to leave an impression with the Greeks that he would help them to achieve theirs. This atmosphere of partiality was heightened by the arrival in London, during the conference, of M. Gounaris, the Greek Prime Minister, apparently for private talks with Lloyd George.

So far as the Turks were concerned perhaps this didn't matter; Lloyd George, though not his government, was anti-Turk, and Bekir Sami would have been blind and foolish not to recognise it. So far as the Greeks were concerned, however, the impression remaining after the London Conference was positively dangerous. Founded on nothing more substantial than their own hopes, buoyed up by encouraging and sympathetic expressions, they left London with the conviction that the most famous statesman of the day would give them help.

On the principle, therefore, that the British Prime Minister, like the gods, would help those who helped themselves, on March 23rd the Greeks renewed their offensive in Anatolia. By a word here and a smile there Lloyd George had started the guns firing again. The Greek official excuse was that they were acting in self-defence. Field Marshal Wilson was unconvinced. During the London Conference he had attended several Cabinet meetings and tendered advice which had not been accepted. The comments in his diary are revealing:

March 2nd. During the duration of the Conference.

'The Greeks have refused Lloyd George's proposal for a Commission to sit at Smyrna to decide who the place belongs to! They very wisely stand pat on the fact that the Frocks gave it to them.'

March 11th. The day before the Allies formulated their proposals.

'Amazing *volte-face* on the part of the Frocks at 10.30 last night in regard to Turkey. They have agreed to withdraw the Allied troops from Constantinople, to withdraw the Greek troops from everywhere in Asia Minor except Smyrna town, to allow the Turks to have troops in Constantinople etc. All this at last in the right direction, but why it was done I cannot imagine. An amazing performance. I suppose the Frocks think it quite natural. Perhaps they hope that by keeping Greeks in Smyrna the Turks will refuse the whole thing and so they will throw the whole blame on Turkey.'

March 14th. Two days after the conclusion of the Conference.

'. . . several indications that the Greeks are going to attack the Turks at Afyon Karahisar and Eskishehir. If this is done at Lloyd George's instigation it will be pretty hot stuff. The Turks meanwhile have occupied Batum. What a rotten peace the Frocks made.'

March 22nd. After the Cabinet meeting of that day. The Cabinet had discussed the Greek offensive.

'. . . Fisher [H. A. L. Fisher, President of the Board of Education] put up a feeble protest. But Lloyd George said there was a great concentration of Turkish troops in front of the Greeks and that it was impossible to prevent the Greeks attacking in self-defence. So far as our (and Greek) information goes, there is no concentration of Turks on that railway, and therefore the coming attack is entirely uncalled for and wholly unprovoked. And Lloyd George knows this. The whole thing is a ramp and a disgusting ramp.' The Field Marshal in the same entry goes on to say that the Greek chargé d'affaires had been to see him in the hope that the Manissa Division (of the Greek army) could remain under General Harington's command. '. . . this of course to embroil us', wrote Wilson, and concluded: 'The whole thing is disgusting. In my opinion the end of this will be the total ruin of the Greeks—the friends of Lloyd George.'

The day after the Chief of the Imperial General Staff put down his pen the Greeks began their week-long battle. The objectives were the same as in the January fighting. In the south they captured Afyon Karahisar comparatively easily and advanced along the road to Konya, nearly due south of and less than 200 miles from Ankara. Once again in the north the fighting was heavy before Eskishehir. The Greeks again reached Inönü and once again were held by Ismet Pasha. The difference though between the second and the first battle of Inönü lay in the duration of the battle and the intensity of the fighting. The Greeks committed all their available forces and threw them at the Turks' defensive positions and artillery. It was the familiar situation of the Great War: the advantage lay with the defence. Greek losses were very heavy indeed and after their troops were exhausted the Turks counter-attacked. After the first battle of Inönü the Greeks retired; after the second they retreated, beaten and in confusion.

Two foreign correspondents with the Greek army have left their impressions. Both were to become known to posterity. The *Toronto Daily Star* had sent out an American called Ernest Hemingway, and the *Manchester Guardian* had commissioned an academically inclined young man named Arnold Toynbee. As might be expected, Hemingway was taken by the drama and violence of it all. The steady, slow persistence of the Turks; the evzones of the Greek Royal Guard lying dead in their ballet-length kilts, stocking caps and pom-pommed shoes. Like many Americans he was hopelessly biased against the Royalist regime, and attributed the defeat of the Greek army entirely to the absence of its Veniselist officers. Toynbee was more sober, serious and analytical. Like so many Englishmen of his education and inclinations he had begun by being pro-Greek, but gradually, acting on the evidence of his eyes, he had come to doubt the justice and the wisdom of their cause. As he accompanied the Greeks on their chaotic retreat by lorry, ox-cart and mule, he noticed the emergence of a myth. The myth of foreign intervention.

Previously the Greeks had been superior militarily to the Turks. If not in courage then technically: in expertise, in organisation, in the use of equipment and weapons. Now the despised, simple, illiterate Turk had won. The explanation must lie in the help of the Russians, the French and the Italians. Officers and advisers of these nationalities were sworn to by eye witnesses as being present, in their own uniforms, assisting the Turks. In time many philhellenes were to believe this, but it was nonsense. What Toynbee heard was the Greeks beginning subconsciously to formulate their excuses for defeat.

*   *   *

For Lloyd George, the friend of the Greeks, the news of the second battle of Inönü came at a period of depression.

The post-war economic boom, aided by the reopening of export markets closed during the war, began to peter out in the winter of 1920, and had disappeared entirely by the spring of 1921. Unemployment more than doubled between December 1920 and March 1921. In June 1921 it was to reach the record figure of over two millions. In the coal mines there was a lock out and the three most powerful trades unions, the National Union of Mineworkers, the National Union of Railwaymen and the Transport and General Workers' Union, 'the Triple Alliance', seemed to be on the verge of calling a general strike. In the delicate sphere of local authority housing Christopher Addison, the Minister of Health whose responsibility it was, having spent vast sums of public money in an inflated market, was forced from office in March 1921. Lloyd George made him Lord Privy Seal for the moment, but 'the Housing Scandal' threatened to engulf not only Addison but also the Prime Minister who had appointed him.

Across the Irish Channel there was, as always, 'John Bull's other island', which engaged so much of England's attention and generated so much Irish and Anglo-Irish passion. The Republic, with de Valera as President, existed side by side with the old British government at Dublin Castle. The situation would have been ludicrous if it had not also been tragic. There were nearly 50,000 troops there; 10,000 men of the armed Royal Irish Constabulary plus the Black and Tans and the even tougher and less scrupulous Auxiliary Division, and it was not enough. Assassination, terrorism and savage reprisals were the order of the day. Field Marshal Wilson, like so many professional soldiers an Ulsterman, told Lloyd George that only a full-scale war could restore law and order.

Feeding on the atmosphere of crisis and failure 'the Plots', as Beaverbrook called them, to replace Lloyd George, increased. Now the plotters, and they consisted of practically all the members of the government, were presented with two failures in an area of foreign policy which was peculiarly Lloyd George's own. The London Conference had failed ignominiously and, as was suspected but not known at the time, both the French and the Italians had tried to do economic deals with Kemal behind Britain's back. The British government had officially declared its neutrality in the Graeco-Turkish war, but it was impossible to ignore the fact that British influence and prestige were still linked to the fate of the Greek army. By his behind-the-scenes encouragement and his public utterances Lloyd George had bound up his own destiny with that of the Greeks. He had created in the public mind, in both Britain and Greece, a relationship which didn't exist.

The British were no longer the allies of Greece; they supplied no arms, no money or assistance. They had no control over the decisions of the Greek King, his politicians or his generals. Yet the Turks could not believe this and were convinced that all Greek actions were somehow inspired by the machinations of Lloyd George. Worse still, in their turn the Greeks, from the King downwards, were equally convinced that in an emergency the British, or at least their leader, would come to their aid. In Churchill's words, the Greeks still believed 'the great man is with us, and in his own way and in his own time and by his own wizardry he will bring us the vital aid we need.' The Greeks were, of course, deluded, but in fairness to them it must be said that Lloyd George never could bring himself to disillusion them. It was a dangerous situation for the Greeks, and it was to prove equally dangerous for Lloyd George.

It was at this time that he confided to Miss Stevenson that he had no friends. Politically at home that was true. Foreign statesmen remarked on the fact that he no longer controlled his Cabinet colleagues. If there had been such a thing in 1921 as a National Opinion Poll it would have shown that his popularity rating had slumped. By the strong line that he was forced to take over strikes he had forfeited the support of the working class. The propertied classes were in favour of his measures, but both disliked and distrusted him personally. The two press barons, Lords Northcliffe and Beaverbrook, opposed him; the former pathologically, the latter on grounds of policy. Their respective newspapers, *The Times* and *Daily Mail* and the *Daily Express*, dutifully reflected the views of their proprietors. The rest of the press was at best lukewarm, with the exception of the *Daily Telegraph*, which pursued a 'patriotic' coalition line.

He toyed with the idea of forming a new party and, more practically, with the possibility of going to the country 'so that men should stand up and be counted'. The rumour of a pending general election got about and his colleagues prepared themselves to knife their leader and each other. Lloyd George had to deny the possibility of a general election and disavow his own responsibility for the rumour. Distrust consequently increased.

Paradoxically the Prime Minister, who though bellicose

and militant was not a militarist, had in the Near East to rely on military men. Lloyd George, who had said 'the difference between Winston Churchill and me is that he likes war and I don't', was now forced to depend upon soldiers, the Greek and his own. The man who had an aversion to the military caste, who had at times both despised and disliked them in the Great War, had now again to give them his orders and rely on their abilities and discretion because there was no one else upon whom he could rely. Lloyd George's opinion of soldiers could be summed up in the words of his friend H. G. Wells, who in his *Outline of History* had written, 'the professional military mind is by necessity an inferior and unimaginative mind: no man of high intellectual quality would willingly imprison his mind in such a calling'. Yet Lloyd George's fate, and so much else besides, now depended upon a war being fought out between Greeks and Turks and on the advice of one British soldier in London and the actions of another in Constantinople: in London Field Marshal Sir Henry Wilson, the Chief of the Imperial General Staff; in Constantinople Lieutenant-General Sir Charles Harington, the Commander-in-Chief of the Allied armies.

There was nothing about either to recommend them to Lloyd George as agents of his policy. Wilson was an incredibly tall Anglo-Irishman who happened, owing to French governessess when a boy, to be able to speak perfect French. He was energetic, impulsive and stupendously outspoken. When Commandant of the Staff College before the Great War he had met General Foch, his French opposite number, and they had immediately struck up a firm friendship. Together after the war they had been resolutely opposed to the introduction of the Greeks into Anatolia. Few British generals admired politicians; Wilson positively loathed them. 'The Frocks' to him were both ignorant and contemptible and none more so than the present incumbent of the position of His Majesty's First Minister. The Field Marshal, not surprisingly, had a sort of genius for rubbing politicians up the wrong way. During the Curragh 'mutiny' in 1914, when officers in Ireland had appeared to prefer resignation rather than be employed to coerce Ulster, he had made enemies in the Asquith government. In 1921 he was still passionately convinced that it was the politicians alone who were responsible for the chaos that was his native country. He regarded Lloyd George's fatalistic attitude over the Armenians as contemptible and his ambitions for Greece as insane. Veniselos was a schemer; President Wilson ('my Cousin' in his diary) was totally divorced from reality. Perhaps Winston Churchill was the only politician for whom he had any regard at all, but only on the occasions when he agreed with the Chief of the Imperial General Staff. Imbued with a tremendous down-to-earth common sense, reinforced by his professional training and experience, the hazy, meandering generalisations of politicians in committee were agony to him, and their often-revealed self-interest despicable. At the time of the Peace Conference he had written: 'The poor Frocks still seem to think that someone is listening to them. It is pathetic.'

Charles Harington was another Irish professional soldier; less of a character than Wilson, whom he greatly admired, but just as much a type that was basically antipathetic to Lloyd George. Forty-eight years old in 1920, he was the son of an Indian indigo planter. Educated at Cheltenham and Sandhurst, passing in 20th and passing out 120th, he had entered the King's Regiment in 1892. He had served in the war in South Africa, but his main interest at this period was games, at which he excelled, especially cricket. At this time, too, he was almost entirely lacking in ambition. While an instructor at Sandhurst he had applied for the permanent post of messing officer because that position, although it would have necessitated his retirement from the active list, offered unrivalled opportunities for cricket, rackets and hockey. He was not accepted, and later gained entrance to the Staff College, much to his own surprise. The Commandant at the time was Brigadier-General Henry Wilson.

At Staff College something happened to Harington which changed his image of a conventional Anglo-Irish games-loving soldier, married to a soldier's daughter and with little apparent interest in the higher reaches of his profession. He left Staff College in 1908 and from then on his career was that of the model, rising, able staff officer.

At the War Office from 1908 to 1911, he was then appointed Brigade Major to the 6th Brigade stationed at Aldershot. Its commander was Brigadier-General Douglas Haig. After a year with his regiment, in the crisis-laden months of June and July 1914 Harington was in the vital Mobilisation Branch of the War Office. When war came he was promoted and became a colonel on the staff of III Corps; then Brigadier-General, General Staff, to the Canadian Corps, and on June 13th, 1916, Major-General, and Chief of Staff to General Sir Herbert Plumer, the commander of the 2nd Army. By general consensus of opinion Plumer, despite his old-fashioned, white-moustached, pot-bellied appearance was the ablest British commander in France. 'Plum', as he was universally called, was also the only general who had the slightest claim to be known by and be popular with the troops under his command. At a time of distant incompetence and indifference to casualties, 'Plum' and his Chief of Staff stood out as exceptious to both rules.

Sir Philip Gibbs[1] described Harington at this period: 'A thin, nervous, highly strung man, with extreme simplicity of manner and clarity of intelligence, he impressed me as a brain of the highest temper and quality in Staff work. His memory for detail was like a card-index system, yet his mind was not clogged with detail. For the first time, in his presence and over his maps, I saw that after all there was such a thing as the science of war and that it was not always a fetish of elementary ideas raised to the nth degree of pomposity as I had been led to believe by contact with other generals and staff officers.' Later Harington served in Italy, and after the war as Deputy Chief of the Imperial General Staff under his old mentor, Sir Henry Wilson, before being appointed to Constantinople.

[1] Philip Gibbs, literary editor of *Daily Mail*, *Daily Chronicle* and *Tribune*. 1915–18, war correspondent for *Telegraph* and *Chronicle*. Novelist. Knighted 1920.

What Lloyd George knew of Harington's character and abilities can only be surmised, but it is interesting to observe one difference of degree between Wilson's and Harington's attitude to their political masters. Wilson, perhaps because, as his detractors alleged, he wanted to play the politician himself, disliked politicians; Harington was simply indifferent. Only once, he recalled, did he ever bother to ensure that he was on a register of electors. During the general election he went and listened to all the parliamentary candidates. None of them mentioned the defence of the Empire, so he went home and voted for none. To 'Tim' Harington it was as simple as that. Needless to say, to David Lloyd George this attitude would have been genuinely incomprehensible.

Poles apart, then, though they were in character and attitude, almost archetypes of their respective professions, these two totally different men were to be brought by the events in the Near East very close to each other indeed.

8

'*As unpleasant towards Kemal
as possible*'
David Lloyd George

In Anatolia, in the spring of 1921, two armies, Greek and
Turkish, counted their casualties and prepared to face
each other again. Both sides were beginning to realise that
the next battle would decide the fate of Turkey. Those
British soldiers, however, who came to Constantinople at
that time, could well have been excused for not thinking
of it as a city at the centre of a crisis.

The soldiers of 'the Army of the Black Sea', as it was still
called, could be divided into types, whether officers or other
ranks. The distinguishing mark was the medal ribbons, or
lack of them, on their tunics. The little oblongs of coloured
ribbon stitched tightly over their left breast pockets effectively divided up those who had served in the Great War,
whether as Regulars, volunteers, or conscripts, from the
newly joined Regulars of the peacetime army. Many of the
wartime soldiers had held higher ranks than their present
ones. It was common to find captains with brevets and
D.S.O.s or M.C.s who had commanded battalions, and

sergeants with D.C.M.s or M.M.s who had been regimental sergeant-majors.

The young subalterns and recruits were intrigued by their first spell of overseas service, but the older men who had survived Flanders or Palestine hardly took the present situation seriously. There was a slight spice of danger in that no one quite knew what the Turkish population of Constantinople might do, and outside the city limits arms and ammunition were carried as a matter of course. On the other side of the Bosphorus, in the Ismid Peninsula and at Chanak, positions were manned on an emergency basis, armed patrols were sent out, and there was always the possibility of being sniped at by Nationalists or brigands, often indistinguishable. Still it was nothing like active service as many had known it. Perhaps the closest parallel was the North-West Frontier of India, with one important difference. There the warlike Afridis and Mahsuds meant business; in Turkey there was no enemy, just a state of chaos created by the politicians.

The soldiers' view of the local population was a simple one. The Turks as shopkeepers and traders were relatively honest and straightforward. Greeks, Armenians and all the other mixtures of races loosely classified as Levantines, were not. For them there was none of the respect which the British entertained for the fighting qualities of their former enemy. Soldiers, as always, simply took the locals as they found them, and 'the old Turk was all right'. There was also something in this attitude of the automatic British Imperial preference for simple Asiatic races as opposed to complicated Latins. The average British soldier had no more regard for the Greeks, their erstwhile allies, than they had for the French or the Italians, their present ones.

The French and Italian private soldiers they regarded as dirty and slovenly, and their officers as overdressed, strutting turkey-cocks. At the highest levels of diplomacy and military command there were attempts at co-operation which were more or less successful. At lower levels, however, the highly trained and disciplined British soldier simply did not take his country's allies seriously. A dapper little

Italian major who rebuked a brawny Scots private for not saluting him had his hat knocked off, his fly buttons ripped open, and was then pushed contemptuously into the gutter.

The man in the ranks in those days was neither as well informed nor as sophisticated as his equivalent today. Emphatically not Wellington's soldier enlisted for drink, nor Kipling's, he was still a man who wanted a bit of adventure, a bit of travel, and whose life was therefore bounded by his regiment, his comrades, the sergeant and 'the officer', as he called him, meaning his platoon or troop lieutenant. The unemployment situation helped to fill the ranks: 'I wasn't too keen on guns or horses, but I lived near the depot at Woolwich and there were five of us in the family', was how one gunner summarised his reasons for taking the King's shilling in 1920. Promotion was slow in peacetime. From private to R.S.M. could take twenty years; from the ranks to a commission was a rarity save as a quartermaster. Socially a vast gap still yawned between private soldier and commissioned officer.

If not the aristocracy or the gentry, certainly the upper middle class officered the British army. The majority of officers came from the public schools. In the 'smart' regiments the Guards, the cavalry and horse artillery, the Rifle Brigade and the King's Royal Rifle Corps, a few hundred pounds a year was still a necessity. In the line infantry and the artillery it helped. Only in the 'technical' and less socially ambitious corps such as the Engineers and Signals, or the Service and Ordnance Corps, could a junior officer hope to live on his pay. In passing, and in part explanation, it may be observed that such considerations were not only relevant in the armed services. Nevile Henderson, the deputy High Commissioner in Constantinople at the time, said that without £400 per annum of private income as a young man he could not have remained in the Diplomatic Service.

Not only socially but in a sense militarily as well, it was an old-fashioned army. The Battle of Cambrai is popularly supposed to have ushered in the era of mechanised warfare. For the Army of the Black Sea, at least so far as equipment was concerned, that battle might never have been fought.

There were no tanks, few armoured cars; cavalry was still cavalry—on horses, still carrying swords. Field guns were pulled by teams of six horses; medium artillery by eight heavy Clydesdales. The R.A.S.C. moved their supplies by horse-drawn wagons and each infantry battalion had its allocation of horses to pull its unit transport. Pack artillery, with guns in sections on the backs of mules, was still much in evidence. The only concession to modernity was a few heavy gun tractors and some rickety lorries, plus the presence of a squadron of R.A.F. biplanes and some seaplanes supplied by the navy.

Weapons were the same as they had been in 1914: the Lee-Enfield rifle and long bayonet, the officers' ·45 revolver; the only automatic weapons were the Lewis gun and the Vickers machine-gun, belt-fed and mounted on a tripod. Uniform, too, had not changed: the tight-buttoned khaki tunic, trousers, puttees and boots for the infantry, breeches and puttees for mounted soldiers. Highland regiments still retained the kilt on active service. Officers of the rank of major and above, in all arms, still wore breeches, boots and spurs. In one respect the Black Sea Army presented an even more old-fashioned aspect: in summer they wore the large cumbrous and useless 'Wolseley' sun helmet. The Turkish climate was something of a problem, hot in summer, freezingly cold in winter, and a few brave or nonconformist spirits took advantage of it to wear the far more comfortable peaked cap all the year round. For the majority, however, Regimental Orders and the eye of the adjutant and the R.S.M. preserved them in summer in headgear which would not have been unfamiliar to Queen Victoria.

Perhaps because of the headdress with its overtones of Imperial wars, the contemporary photographs of the period look older than their forty-six years. Two points have to be remembered. First, this was essentially an army coming back to peacetime habits, dress and attitudes of mind. Hence there was a quite definite drive, as always after any war, to return to the pre-war style of military behaviour. Secondly, although the British army was beginning once again to insist on punctilious ceremonial and general 'spit and polish', which had received a nasty knock in the mud and lice of the Western Front, comparatively this was the most efficient army in the Middle East. Better trained, better disciplined, well fed and well cared for medically, it was superior to both the French and Italian forces and, needless to say, to the ill-equipped Greek and Turkish armies. Its morale was high. Partly because of its efficiency, partly because of the automatic advances in welfare which had been brought about by the war, but also because of the personality of its commander, General Harington.

All those who knew him testify to what they call, simply, 'his kindness', not always an outstanding characteristic of generals. Nevile Henderson, who as Deputy High Commissioner saw him daily, regarded it as almost a fault. The army, he admitted, was 'super efficient', but its commander, he thought, was 'too gentle and nice'.

Harington's subordinate officers and the men under his command would not have agreed. The General spared no effort to make their lot as pleasant as possible. It would have been very easy in a city such as Constantinople to allow a situation to develop whereby the officers enjoyed all its many facilities for expensive sports, hunting, polo, shooting, fishing and yachting, and amused themselves in the evening in the night clubs, while their men languished in barracks, or spent all their money in cheap drinking dens cum brothels. Harington spared no effort to encourage team games and other recreations in which the men could take part.

Some idea of the problems he encountered can be gained from the *Y.M.C.A. Guide to Constantinople*, a pocket book issued to all soldiers. As well as giving information on money exchange, shops, curios, restaurants and cafés, trains, trams, steamers and sports grounds, it included a warning about counterfeit paper money which was palmed off on the unsuspecting, and advised soldiers how to avoid offending Moslem religious susceptibilities. The most illuminating section was at the end, under the heading 'Health Hints'. 'Take at least seven hours' sleep if you can get it. Take a sponge bath every morning if you can get nothing better. Eat only those foods which you know to be good and properly cooked, drink water only when you know the source to be pure or after it has been boiled, do not drink or eat too much of anything. Take some form of vigorous exercise if you wish to preserve your health. Get into the game, form high ideas of sex relations, sexual intercourse is not a physical necessity for the preservation of virility. Remember the folks at home, think clean thoughts, eat clean foods, drink clean drinks.' A trifle paternalistic and naive by modern standards maybe, but Harington himself, who contributed a foreword, never hesitated to make a simple approach to simple men and was repaid by their loyalty.

His relations were also excellent with his two opposite numbers: General Charpy, who commanded the French forces, and General Mombelli, who commanded the Italian. The three generals were, if fact, in better accord than the three High Commissioners, Sir Horace Rumbold, General Pellé and the Marquis Garroni. Henderson described Pellé as 'a gentleman', but did not use that expression, his highest compliment, when referring to the Italian marquis. All three High Commissioners were, however, in complete agreement in one respect: their dislike of Admiral Bristol of the United States Navy, who arrived in 1921 and behaved as if he too were a High Commissioner.

The United States had not been at war with Turkey and the Admiral's presence with a few warships was a hangover from the Wilson period and his duties were consequently ill defined. He was a difficult, pugnacious man and did nothing to lessen the resentment of the High Commissioners by his habit of trying to interfere in what they regarded as their exclusive sphere of action. The High Commissioners did not admit him to their consultations. The Admiral retaliated by ordering the crews of his ships to refrain from paying the usual compliment of manning ship and saluting when the High Commissioners' yachts passed them in the Bosphorus.

Meanwhile, despite these diverting squabbles in high places, life in Constantinople continued almost as if the

Allied fleets and armies were not there at all, and the city itself was still the capital of Turkey. Wrangel's Russians, although at times, as Henderson observed, they made the Grand Rue de Pera 'more like the Nevsky Prospect of St. Petersburg', were slowly being absorbed into the population. The more enterprising opened up stalls and little shops, or got work in the restaurants and night clubs; the unlucky ones came to be accepted as part of the scene, selling flowers mournfully on street corners. The wife of an officer in the Essex regiment used to notice one in particular: a Cossack, still bristling with weapons, trying to sell bunches of Madonna lilies.

The Russians were not the only refugees. In addition some thousands of Turks, fearful of Kemal, or simply displaced in one way or another from Thrace or Anatolia, flooded into the safety of the city. Among them, as the Allies suspected, were a fair number of Kemalist agents who, as well as sending back information, occupied themselves with the ever-increasing traffic of arms and volunteers into Anatolia. The majority, though, were genuine refugees; part of the flotsam of any war and delighted to enjoy the comparative security of Allied protection. To them too Constantinople must have appeared a peaceful city. Apart from the Allied soldiers to be seen in the streets, it must have seemed as if the events of the last eight years had never been. The Sultan, Mehmed Vahid-ed-Din, Mehmed VI, Caliph of all the Mussulmans, still resided in the Dolma Bagtche Palace. On Fridays he could be seen taking his part in the solemn procession to prayer, the Selamlik, in the Great Mosque. Surrounded by troops, courtiers and functionaries and travelling in an open landau, the elderly, moustached gentleman in a blue uniform and crimson fez gave no indication to the spectators that he was no longer, like his predecessors, 'the shadow of God on earth', absolute and omnipotent. His fleet lay rusting in the Bosphorus; one of its few seaworthy vessels, the *Makouk*, was now Sir Horace Rumbold's official yacht. His once powerful army owed allegiance to another, and the men he could rely on had dwindled to a handful of retainers and household troops.

Though paid every outward sign of respect, he was no longer even a pawn in the diplomatic and military game being played out around him. His fate, and that of so many others, would be decided in Anatolia.

One of the players in the game, Lloyd George, received in the late spring and early summer a measure of domestic encouragement which quickly restored his mercurial spirits. Duly reported in the *British Wireless Press*, a two-page newsheet compiled by the Royal Corps of Signals, the British troops in Constantinople learned that there would not now be a General Strike in Britain and that a truce had been declared in Ireland.

On the 15th of April, the 'Black Day' of the British Labour movement, as many socialists called it, the Triple Alliance of the big unions broke apart. Two union leaders, Ernest Bevin of the dockers' wing of the T. & G.W.U., and J. H. Thomas of the N.U.R., both destined in their time to become Cabinet Ministers,[1] decided that they could not support by joint strike action the demand of the miners for higher wages and better conditions. The T. & G.W.U. and the N.U.R. were prepared to negotiate; the N.U.M., under its president Herbert Smith, wanted to fight. The miners, on their own, lost, and were forced to return to work for their old wages and with no improvement in the harsh conditions of their employment. The middle classes, and others who had never been down a coal mine in their lives, purred with relief. Wages soon fell in other industries as well, and Lloyd George thought that he had gained another lease of political life.

The Irish truce, which was signed on July 8th by De Valera, the President of the Irish Republic, brought fighting

---

[1] Thomas, between 1924 and 1936, was Colonial Secretary, Lord Privy Seal and Dominions Secretary, but had to leave public life after revealing Budget secrets. Bevin was a member of the War Cabinet 1940–5 and Foreign Secretary 1945–50. Both retained their working-class accents, Thomas for conscious effect. When he remarked publicly that he had 'an 'ell of an 'eadache', Birkenhead said, 'What you need is a couple of aspirates.' Thomas did not speak to Birkenhead again. Bevin once mystified the Foreign Office by reference to 'addock arrangements' (*ad hoc*).

to an end three days later. The agreement, and the secret negotiations which had preceded it, had arisen out of the lengthy and fantastically complicated Government of Ireland Act, which Lloyd George had devised in an effort to satisfy everyone. The Act was unworkable but, because the Irish Republican Army was nearly beaten, as one of its leaders admitted, and because the British were tired of repression, it provided a basis for peaceful discussion. The Irish were not to be reconciled, that was too much to be hoped, but the truce of July paved the way for the Treaty of December, 1921. Henceforth the Irish might fight among themselves in the Republic, and Ulster would be separate, but Britain would no longer be directly involved, and the last British troops were to leave almost exactly a year later.

It was not a victory but it was a relief to all save the ultra-Conservative, often of Irish ancestry, who persisted in regarding it as a surrender. Their attitude was bigoted and unreasonable, but those who had influence stored up their resentment and added to their growing list of criticisms of the Prime Minister. Lloyd George himself could reasonably think that some of his troubles were over, bask a little in the glow of the Dominion Prime Ministers' Conference, which assembled in London in June, and return again to what Count Sforza called his obsession—the Greeks and the Turks in the Near East.

Like a juggler he had caught two balls but another was still in the air.

*　　　*　　　*

Events in Anatolia had not stood still. The reverse in the spring had exacerbated the differences within the Greek army. The easy explanation of these differences lay in the return of the Royalist officers and the removal of the Veniselists. Actually, the situation was far more complicated than that.

Originally, in 1917, Veniselos had dismissed nearly 3,000 officers who had not supported his revolutionary government. As the Greek army had expanded, their places,

136

and more, had been filled by quickly promoted men regarded as reliable by the new regime. Foolish measures had been resorted to in order to provide the necessary numbers. Many N.C.O.s had been commissioned as junior officers and then literally had to be taught to read and write like many of the new recruits. British officers working with the Greeks were considerably surprised, then and later, to find company and platoon officers who were for all practical purposes illiterate.

With the return of Constantine as many as possible of the dismissed officers, including Prince Andrew, the King's brother, were reinstated. Senior Veniselist officers, especially those who had actively campaigned against the King's return, were, not surprisingly, in their turn dismissed. Others, fearing dismissal or demotion, tried to foment mutiny, resigned, or just deserted. General Papoulas had endeavoured to forget the past and had retained as many former Veniselists as possible. At the same time he had to try to satisfy the demands of the Royalist officers, who felt that their loyalty to the King should guarantee preferment. In consequence the army had what Prince Andrew called 'a plethora of generals and colonels', both in Anatolia and Greece, under-employed and of divergent political loyalties.

In June, 1921, King Constantine, hoping to recreate some sort of unity, reverted to his first profession and love, and was proclaimed Supreme Commander of the Greek forces in Asia. With a fanfare from the Athens press he sailed for Smyrna, there to set up his headquarters. For the loyal journalist there appeared to be many happy and encouraging portents. A second Constantine had landed in Asia Minor; the first Christian king to do so since Richard I of England, Cœur de Lion, during the Crusades.

Landing at Smyrna in the uniform of a field marshal, he received a rapturous reception from saluting officers and cheering crowds of Greek civilians. Not content with the blue and white Hellenic flags exhibited from every building, one enthusiastic well-wisher produced a Turkish flag for the King to walk over. Constantine acknowledged the cheers and declared himself confident of defeating the

Turkish army and thus destroying the power of Mustapha Kemal. A few days later he embarked on a large-scale inspection of his armies, encouraging all those he met with talk of the coming offensive.

Prince Andrew also went to Anatolia at this time to take command of the recently formed 12th Division, and has left his impressions of the morale of the army. Undoubtedly Constantine's presence acted as a fillip; he had a way with soldiers and talked to them as a fellow soldier and not a king. Nevertheless there were still serious dissensions, especially among the officers, many of whom were still declared Veniselists. The army itself had been increased in strength from 110,000 in January to nearly 200,000 men, the largest army the Greeks had ever been able to put into the field. The new units were a valuable addition, of course, but they were formed, like Prince Andrew's own command, for the most part of untried, young recruits. Their officers also were in many cases over-confident and inexperienced. Yet the most serious fault of the Greek army was not the training and certainly not the courage of its private soldiers, but lay in the higher reaches of command.

It is not clear precisely what authority the King himself wielded. He was an experienced soldier and not an unskilled one; nevertheless he wore a field marshal's uniform because he was King, and a king who had to accept the advice of his military advisers. Advice was often conflicting; intrigue and self interest were rife. No one in the Greek army, despite its crowned commander, had the clear monolithic authority of its enemy, Mustapha Kemal. Despite these disadvantages, on July 9th the Greek army, in Churchill's words, began 'marching steadily forward through harsh and difficult country to engage in the greatest campaign undertaken by Greece since Classic times'.

In London, a few weeks previously, on the 1st, 2nd and 9th of June, a special Cabinet committee had been meeting. It was called the Committee on the Future of Constantinople, but it also considered other matters. On June 1st the committee: Lloyd George, Curzon, Edwin Montagu, Churchill, now Secretary for the Colonies, his successor at the War Office, Sir Laming Worthington-Evans, and Sir Alfred Mond, the Minister of Health, had the benefit of the advice of Sir Henry Wilson and General Harington.

Lord Curzon spoke first, and what he had to report spoke volumes for the attitude of the British government. Constantine might rule in Greece but the Cabinet was still more interested in the views of Greece's exiled ex-Prime Minister. Curzon had had a conversation with Sir John Stavridi, formerly Consul-General in London. Stavridi had undertaken to see Veniselos on Saturday next in Paris and return with his views on the Sunday. The Prime Minister was in a pessimistic frame of mind. Kemal had now become 'a formidable menace', and France, because of her extensive financial interests, and Italy also, had surreptitiously ranged themselves on his side. Lloyd George suggested that Britain should 'make herself as unpleasant towards Kemal as possible', and 'support the Greeks on condition that they accepted our advice as to military command organisation and strategy and our guidance as to policy'.

At the same time it was suggested that Greek ambitions should not be furthered, and new terms of peace be devised to put before the Turks. Perhaps the Aga Khan, 'who could speak as Mohammedan to Mohammedan', might be sent to explain the alternatives of opposition or peace to Kemal? Apparently the Aga Khan, whilst undergoing a cure in Switzerland, had been approached by 'moderates from Ankara'. Unfortunately moderates such as Bekir Sami Bey, of the London Conference, had now been replaced by extremists.

The Prime Minister hoped that active co-operation could be obtained in India for a policy of 'arming to make peace'. Concessions to the Turks, as to the Irish, were wasted; both nations would merely ask for more. Regrettable though the French and Italian attitudes had been, they did not seem to have profited either, as their overtures appeared to have been rejected. On the other hand 'there was no reason to believe that the Turks had lost their fundamental confidence in British good faith'. The Committee discussed the probability of early offensive actions by both Greeks and Turks. General Harington did not regard the Greek prospects as favourable, mainly because of 'the disastrous policy' of superseding tried officers on account of their Veniselist sympathies.

Nevertheless, it was wondered if Lord Curzon might ascertain the views not only of Veniselos but of King Constantine as well. The Prime Minister thought that perhaps the King too might have misgivings about the prospects of success. In those circumstances would not the Greeks welcome British mediation? Constantinople would have to be held as a bargaining counter for use against Kemal. The Greeks might, of course, withdraw their troops from the Ismid peninsula, in which case 'it would be a great responsibility to order the small number of British troops to remain in Constantinople against the expressed views of the Chief of the Imperial General Staff and General Harington'.

Edwin Montagu pointed out that he had informed Indian Moslem representatives of the concessions offered at the London Conference. He had assured them that their religious sentiments had been, and would be, fully respected. Rather surprisingly he then went on to say that if Ankara would not accept the London terms, he was in favour of assisting the Greeks. Sir Henry Wilson said that it was as impossible to deal with Kemal merely by holding a position at Constantinople as it was to deal with Sinn Fein by sitting at Dublin. He, like Harington, doubted the ability of the Greeks to hold their position. Bluntly, either the British made a sufficient effort to inflict a decisive defeat on the enemy or they withdrew.

The Committee concluded its deliberations with a general discussion. The difficulties of dealing a serious blow at Kemal. What pressure could be put on the Greeks if they refused to accept our offers? Could Thrace be guaranteed? Was any arrangement possible with Bulgaria? No one knew what the French would do in Constantinople.

On the next day General Harington was no longer present, although Sir Henry Wilson was, being joined by Mr. H. A. L. Fisher, the President of the Board of Education, an historian, a Liberal, pro-Greek and anti-Turk. Wilson began by saying that he had consulted the War Office, the Admiralty and the Air Staff as to the practicability of holding the Gallipoli peninsula. The Admiralty had obviously not lost its fears provoked by the Gallipoli campaign. Both sides of the Straits would have to be held by land forces if ships were to be passed through. There were fears that the Turks would obtain mines, perhaps even submarines, 'from the Bolsheviks'.

Once again the Committee wondered what offer would secure the friendship of Mustapha Kemal. Smyrna? Constantinople and the Straits? Batum and Baku? No one knew whether the Greeks would place themselves in the hands of the British, and if so 'whether they were worth supporting'. It was emphasised that the Greeks must have no justification for thinking that Britain had betrayed them. 'It was King Constantine who had ruined their prospects and we must not allow the odium to be transferred to our shoulders.'

The basic difficulty was still to ascertain the true position of the Greeks. Lord Curzon undertook to invite Veniselos to London. Lloyd George asked Sir Henry Wilson to send an officer to make a special report on the Greek army, but not, however, until Veniselos had been sounded 'as to how such a proposal was likely to be received by the present Greek government'. Lord Curzon expressed his willingness to go to Paris to discuss the whole question with the French government. It was decided, as Wilson had informed the Committee, that 'there was no day-to-day danger' at Constantinople, that the forces there should not be reinforced at present. Finally, reference was made to the situation in Afghanistan, where it was thought that now that 'Kemal had thrown in his lot with the extremists and Bolsheviks' the rulers in Kabul would be more disposed to favour the British.

The most interesting point about this Cabinet Committee meeting was the consideration of a letter from Winston Churchill to the Prime Minister which contained a number of proposals. The letter was dated June 2nd, 1921, and read as follows:

My dear Prime Minister,

I am trying to sum up in a short space what I think we ought now to do about the Middle Eastern situation. I do not go into the past, but we are now very nearly at the end of our means of dealing with it. I do not feel sure that it is not too late, whatever we do, to retrieve the position. We are drifting steadily and rapidly towards what will in fact be a defeat of England by Turkey. That is a terrible thing to happen, undoing all the fruits of the victories we have gained and exposing us to disastrous consequences through all the large Middle Eastern provinces where we are so vulnerable. The only hope I see lies in the following course of action, which I put forward on the assumption that the situation is not altered decisively one way or the other by the battle believed to be impending between the Greeks and the Turks.

(1) Go to the Greeks at once and demand from them—

    (a) Their acceptance of the terms which we prescribe. (What these terms should be will be mentioned later.)

    (b) The reorganisation of their army in accordance with British advice.

    (c) Accept British military guidance in their dispositions, which should comprise without delay a backward concentration much nearer the Smyrna coast.

    (d) A division of troops for Ismid and another for the Dardanelles under General Harington.

Offer the Greeks, subject to the above, the support of Britain—

    (e) Moral.

    (f) Naval.

    (g) Munitions.

    (h) Credit.

Tell them that unless they accept these conditions we shall—

    (i) Disinterest ourselves absolutely in their future.

    (j) Hold ourselves perfectly free to make any arrangements with the Bulgarians or Turks calculated to safeguard our position in regard to Constantinople and to keep the Straits open.

(2) If the Greeks accept—and they must do so within about the next ten days—send someone like the Aga Khan to Mustapha Kemal to say 'We are willing to make peace with you, and between you and the Greeks on the terms set out below, and, in addition, to extend British friendship and commercial assistance to Turkey. If you do not within a brief period of time accept these terms, we shall make operative the arrangements set out in paragraph (1) with the Greeks.'

(3) Reinforce Constantinople with every available man and ship.

(4) Tell the whole story quite plainly to the French, inviting their co-operation in the plan both by joining us in the diplomacy and by reinforcing Constantinople. Make it perfectly clear to them that if they fail to help us in this matter it will be another disastrous episode in the Alliance and force us more and more to reconsider our general position. (I think you will find the French are genuinely disturbed at the undue growth of Kemal's power and demands, and that there has been a great change of attitude in the last few weeks.)

(5) Now for the terms. I think they should be the recent London terms, as modified in detail by your later understandings, plus the evacuation of Smyrna by the Greek troops, with special guarantees to Christians. I do not think there is any chance of getting peace without the evacuation of Smyrna. The fact that we are ready to countenance it will prove to the French the sincerity of our desire for peace with Mustapha Kemal and make them more ready to co-operate with us.

(6) Before you reject this unpalatable view, I hope you will realise what the alternative is in the absence of some great Greek victory:

    (i)   The Greeks will either be driven out of Smyrna or else kept defending it at great expense so long that they will be ruined.

    (ii) We shall have to leave Constantinople very quickly and in circumstances of humiliation.

(iii) The French will invite Mustapha Kemal to come into Constantinople and try to curry favour with him there. The Italians will support the French.

(iv) Mustapha Kemal will return to Constantinople or send his agents there. He will raise a considerable army out of the discontented and desperate men who throng the city. In his own time he will attack and re-conquer Thrace.

(v) We shall not be able to hold our position on the Gallipoli Peninsula. It is much too large to be held except for a very short time by the forces which we can afford to supply.

(vi) We shall be disturbed in Mosul, the reduction of troops will be arrested, and I shall have to come to Parliament for a very heavy Supplementary Estimate. We may even have a general rising there. The same applies to Palestine, where Arabs and Turks will easily make common cause against us in consequence of the Arab hatred of Zionism. Egypt you have got on your hands already. Then there is the Afghan position.

(7) I now learn that the League of Nations wish to postpone the Mandates for Palestine and Mesopotamia until the Americans are satisfied, i.e., indefinite postponement. I ought to warn you that if this course is followed, and if at the same time the Turkish situation degenerates in a disastrous manner, it will be impossible for us to maintain our position either in Palestine or in Mesopotamia, and that the only wise and safe course would be to take advantage of the postponement of the Mandates and resign them both and quit the two countries at the earliest possible moment, as the expense to which we shall be put will be wholly unwarrantable.

Yours, etc.,
WINSTON S. CHURCHILL

The Cabinet Committee 'felt, however, that it would be useless to approach the Greeks with an offer of this kind'.

The third meeting took place not in the Prime Minister's

room at the House of Commons, as had its two predecessors, but at Chequers, the Prime Minister's official residence in Buckinghamshire, as Lloyd George was unwell and had been ordered by his doctors not to travel to London. Curzon, Churchill, Montagu, Worthington-Evans and Mond attended, with Sir Henry Wilson. The meeting commenced at 12 noon, and with a short break for lunch continued through until 3.30 p.m. There was a lot to consider. Veniselos had visited London earlier in the week and had been seen by Lord Curzon, the Prime Minister, and Sir Henry Wilson. Curzon having, at some length, rehearsed the present situation, had then asked Veniselos if he had been in power in Athens would he have regarded an Allied attempt at mediation, which involved some sacrifice of Greek claims, as an act of treachery?

M. Veniselos, although naturally disclaiming any knowledge of the views of the actual Greek government (Curzon himself had said 'they were difficult to ascertain'), went on to say that he could see 'nothing incompatible with the dignity of Greece' in such an approach. If he had been in the place of the existing Greek government he would not have resented such an overture. 'The Allies,' he said, 'would of course have to safeguard themselves against the possibility of an accusation that they had given away the Greek people.' At the present time, however, he was doubtful of the likelihood of success; if they intended to act the Allies should act promptly. He thought the Allies should approach both Ankara and Constantinople. If the proposed negotiations were unsuccessful, said Veniselos, 'the Greek government could not maintain their position in Asia Minor for more than six months without Allied support'. Curzon could only counter by stressing the extreme unpopularity in Britain and France of any new war with Turkey.

Lloyd George told the Committee that when he had seen Veniselos, the ex-Prime Minister had insisted that if Kemal refused to negotiate the only alternative for the Allies to active support for Greece was a humiliating surrender, involving not only being driven out of Constantinople but eventually also from Mesopotamia, Syria and Palestine. The more, Lloyd George said, he had dwelt on the impossibility of another war with Turkey, the more Veniselos had insisted that the Greek army was the only barrier between the Allies and a humiliating succession of withdrawals. Veniselos had also impressed upon him that any attempt by the Allies to get rid of King Constantine would 'only rally the Greeks to him and establish him more firmly on the throne'.

Sir Henry Wilson had confined his discussion with Veniselos to purely military matters. Veniselos had said that he wished to make it clear that he had no part in a proposed *coup d'état* said to be contemplated against the present Royalist officers. Nevertheless 'if the Greek army continued to be conducted as at present, within six months it would cease to exist'. In order to re-establish the Greek army General Paraskeropoulos would have to be reinstated, and most of the officers changed, 'down to battalion commanders'. 'In return for these concessions King Constantine would demand good terms.'

When the Committee had digested the views of their old ally they considered the result of the labours of the Foreign Office and the War Office. A great deal of information had been gathered and none of it made pleasant reading. From the French Military Attaché in Athens it was learned that: '*la moral de l'armée grecque en Asie-Mineure aurait baissée. Les soldats seraient mécontents de leur logement et aussi de la nourriture qu'ils reçoivent. On constaterait d'assez nombreuses désertions et même les déserteurs formeraient des bandes qui parcourent le pays. Enfin beaucoup de soldats se plaignent des chefs nouveaux qui leur ont été donnés.*'

General Harington reported that: 'The return to the Army of Royalist officers as exemplified in the III Corps at Brusa, has resulted in a general loss of efficiency. It appears to be the practice either to employ Royalists in sinecures at the base or give them commands, while retaining at hand under their orders a senior National Defence Officer capable of giving advice. It is urged against the Royalist officers that not only have they had no practical experience but that they lack the offensive spirit, and in many cases have no desire to run into any personal danger. The troops realise this and, on their return from the reconnaissance in force, were openly calling for their old officers and deriding the Royalists.' Lord Granville, the Ambassador in Athens, reported that General Nider, who had been replaced by a Royalist, had told the head of the French Military Mission that morale at the front was excellent because the troops had been told that this was to be the last offensive, but 'that it will go to pieces if this is shown to be false'.

G.H.Q. in Constantinople listed a whole host of defects. There was no intercommunication between columns on the march. By day it was restricted to liaison by officers and by night to field W/T sets. 'Visual and telegraphic communications did not exist.' Barbed-wire entanglement posts had to be pulled out by hand under machine-gun fire because there were no wire cutters available and artillery had failed to cut a path beforehand. Transport was badly organised and cavalry ill-used. 'Greek intelligence as usual was very bad.' The only bright spot was the soldiers' boots which 'were reported to be good', although all other equipment made of leather had broken. Sir Harry Lamb, the Consul-General, reported from Smyrna that over 10,000 new troops had landed during April and were moving towards Ishak. 'Discipline of troops arriving appears defective and much bad feeling is being excited by their behaviour towards Mussulman population, firing at minarets and molesting men, women and children in the streets. Authorities fully alive to possible danger but unable to restrain men.'

The Italian military representative with the Greek army reported 'rebellion among the troops and other minor difficulties'. Both sides in the conflict 'were afraid to appeal to the Powers as they feel it would be an acknowledgment of weakness'. The British military representative in Smyrna reported as follows: 'M. Stergiades, the Greek High Commissioner, informed me that he was far from satisfied with the state of affairs in the Greek occupied zone. Till a few months ago the population of the area under Greek control had been quiet and contented and the administration of the country had begun to show good results. With the arrival, however, of new officers and soldiers from Greece who were ignorant as to how to behave in Asia Minor (I imagine M. Stergiades meant those officers and men who arrived after the elections but it is difficult to fire a question when the Greek High Commissioner has commenced his conversational barrage), trouble started and the Turkish population became incensed at various undesirable incidents which took place.'

The Greeks too were convinced that the Bolsheviks were supplying arms and equipment to the Turks. They had over 200 guns on the front and apparently unlimited ammunition, and this could not all have come from the Italians or from Constantinople. The supplies must be coming by way of the Black Sea ports. The British representative had cross-examined a staff officer, Colonel Sarryanis, and asked him how this had been discovered, for before that there had been 'Italian and Constantinople help', and then latterly 'French help'. The Colonel replied that it had long been known, 'but only since the last operations had the Greeks begun to realise to what extent the Bolsheviks must have helped Kemal'. Finally Gounaris, the Prime Minister, accompanied by Theotokis, the War Minister, had visited the Greek army, being alarmed by reports received in Athens of low morale. 'Their reception everywhere by the soldiers was moderately enthusiastic but not wildly so.'

On top of all this melancholy information the Committee had also for its consideration two long telegrams. The first was from G.H.Q. in Constantinople and informed them in great detail of a plot to take over the Greek army in Anatolia. The moving spirits were Stergiades, Argyropoulos and Admiral Kondouriotis. The Admiral, despite the denial given to Sir Henry Wilson, was without doubt in touch with Veniselos, who was prepared to be 'High Commissioner' in London. It was hoped that the government in Athens would flee, but if not, there were plans for a repeat of the 1917 revolution. The Greeks were told by Sir Horace Rumbold and General Harington that British assistance could not be expected, as it was 'an entirely Greek affair'.

The second telegram was from the Viceroy of India, who was much disturbed by Moslem agitation, and even more by the likely effect of actions by the British govern-

148

ment which could be represented as 'another proof of the desire of the Christian to destroy the Moslem'. These views had also been communicated to the Secretary of State for India. Deteriorating relations with Ankara were prejudicing the conclusion of a satisfactory treaty with Afghanistan. The propaganda and intrigues of the ubiquitous Bolshevik were also much feared.

In the face of this glut of information the Cabinet Committee decided to ask for more. The British Military Attaché in Athens would make a special report on the command, staff and officers of the Greek army. In addition a General Officer was to be sent to Asia Minor qualified 'to give authoritative advice to the British government on the important military aspects of the problem confronting them'. Meanwhile, in the sphere of action, the War Office was to prepare plans for assisting the Greeks with munitions, war material and money but not men. The Admiralty was to examine the possibility of blockading Turkish ports to prevent munitions arriving across the Black Sea from Russia.

The Greeks could have all this and perhaps permission to engage British ex-service men who 'might be willing to volunteer'. The London Conference terms modified would be offered. Smyrna might be autonomous but the Greek army would have to leave Asia Minor. The Turks would have the prospect of extensions of territory to the east, though unspecified, and 'friendly assistance' after the peace. The terms would be presented to the French government and Lord Curzon undertook to visit Paris and talk to Aristide Briand, the new Prime Minister, and the only French politician that the English could bear.

It might have worked. The pliable Briand was persuaded. The Greeks, however, refused. All issues would be put to the wager of battle. On the 10th of July their army resumed the offensive and to everyone's surprise captured Eskishehir and continued to advance towards Ankara. Doubtless Lloyd George was confirmed in his belief, shared with another British Prime Minister, that 'no lesson seems to be so deeply inculcated by the experience of life as that you should never trust experts'.

9

'Anything short of decisive victory was defeat'
Winston Churchill

The Greeks had elected to put the fate of their country
to the final test of battle. They had lost in the region of
8,000 men killed and wounded to gain Eskishehir and
Afyon Karahisar. On the 20th of July, the day they entered
Eskishehir, King Constantine returned from Athens to
resume command in person. He was in time to witness a
general Turkish counter-attack on the next day. It was
repulsed, and the Turkish army began to retire beyond the
Sakarya river. They retreated thirty miles and were now
only fifty miles from Ankara. They began to prepare to
defend their new capital. Ismet Pasha, who commanded, was
in despair; as a general and a man he was prone, in any
event, to fits of despondency, but he had reason. Turkish
losses were at least the equal of the Greek, and in addition he
had lost 4,000 prisoners. His only consolation was that, despite
the Greek victory and their occupation of Turkish territory,
the Turkish army, though defeated, was still intact.

King Constantine and his military advisers were correspondingly elated. The capture of Ankara now seemed a distinct possibility. It was not, however, a purely military objective, and Constantine had no intention of permanently occupying the city or of ruling the Turks. Ankara was to be captured to drive out and humiliate Kemal's Nationalist government. Once that was done it was assumed that a new Turkish government, either in Anatolia or Constantinople, would be forced to accept the Greek occupation of Smyrna and its hinterland, perhaps even cede Constantinople itself, still the ultimate goal in the minds of many ambitious Greeks.

It seems that General Papoulas, the Commander-in-Chief, was more cautious, and would have preferred to dig in west of the Sakarya with the intention of defeating the inevitable Turkish counter-attack. He still hoped to destroy the Turkish army, but his advice was overborne by the rest of the General Staff in favour of the chances of a more spectacular political victory. None of the Greek general officers appeared to realise that they were now fighting a whole nation, and that even if the Turkish army were forced to retreat, even if Ankara were captured, fighting would still continue, whether by regular soldiers or by guerrillas. Many of the Greek senior officers, like Constantine himself, had been trained or influenced by German military methods, but even the great von Moltke had condescended to study the campaigns of Napoleon. It was a pity that no officer of influence in the Greek army in Anatolia had absorbed the lessons to be learnt from his invasion of Russia. The parallels were very close. The great distance involved, the difficult terrain, the inhospitable climate: freezing cold in winter, blisteringly hot in summer. The danger to lines of communication from guerrillas, the virtual impossibility of subduing a whole population. Even the Turkish strategy of retreating before an invading army into the interior was similar to that adopted by the Russians under Kutusov in 1812. Most important of all, Ankara as an ultimate objective was likely to prove as illusory as Moscow. In 1812 Napoleon, in Danzig, had asked his staff, 'How many miles to Moscow?' His marshals had stayed silent. Finally Colonel Rapp, a blunt man from

Alsace, had replied, 'Too many, sire.' The distance from Smyrna to Ankara, even as the crow flies, is over 320 miles, but presumably Constantine never asked the question.

On August 10th, 1921, the Greek army began its general advance across the most difficult country it had yet encountered: the arid steppe land of Anatolia. It did not meet its enemy in force until August 23rd, but by then its effectiveness had been considerably reduced. Almost everything that could go wrong with an army did go wrong. Owing to bad maps and faulty reconnaissance, the line of route planned for some of the formations led across near-desert, with no water supplies to be found. Cavalry and artillery horses, being Greek-bred and therefore unadaptable to a regime of little water and scarce food, died first. Motor transport, in which the Greeks had a decided advantage over the Turks, was simply knocked to pieces by the ground it had to cover. Ox-carts, camels and mules had to be used, but this meant that much heavy equipment had to be jettisoned and the rate of the advance was reduced to the speed of the slowest ox. The army was not prepared for what was in fact a desert campaign; there were nothing like enough water trucks and food was short as well. Further west the Greeks had been able to live off the country; on the dusty sun-baked plateau there was nothing. Many soldiers fell ill with stomach complaints, sunstroke, heat exhaustion and malaria. Medicines and other necessities ran short; luxuries such as coffee and cigarettes did not exist. On the 23rd of August, weary and dispirited, the Greeks met the enemy which had been waiting for them.

Mustapha Kemal had now assumed full command in the field, but for weeks previously he had been functioning as dictator of the Turkish people to prepare them for this battle. Almost literally, as Lord Kinross remarks, ploughshares had been turned into swords. War equipment had been turned out by every little factory in Ankara, in some cases virtually by hand. Every household had been asked to provide one sheet to serve as material for bandages. For the first time in their history Turkish women had taken an active part in warfare. Their Moslem seclusion put aside, they served in any capacity from nurses to beasts of burden carrying shells, ammunition and supplies. Every man and boy was used in an attempt to redress the balance of the Greek's numerical superiority, for they had 50,000 men committed to the battle as against the Turkish 44,000, although 8,000 more Turks were on their way from Cilicia.

Kemal's advantage lay in his position: to the east of the Sakarya river, hemmed in on both flanks by its tributaries. Behind him the Ankara railway, vital for supplies and reserves. He, at least, had learnt some of the lessons of the Great War: the advantage which lay with the defence, the importance of speed of reinforcement. There was one other advantage he possessed. The Russians at Plevna and at the Chataldja lines in the nineteenth century, the British at Gallipoli in the twentieth century, had both been forced to recognise the superb qualities of the Turk as a defensive soldier. Dour, dogged, stubborn and unimaginative, the hardy Anatolian peasant was the ideal infantryman. Not in attack, where he lacked the élan of other contenders for the palm such as the Scottish Highlander, the Gurkha, or the Greek evzone, but in defence, in the situation where he had to stand, fight and die; and that was precisely what Kemal required of him at the Sakarya river.

This was the wall against which General Papoulas threw his men for the next twenty-two days and nights. It was one of the longest pitched battles in history. The fighting was bloody and savage. The Greeks suffered at the outset from a last-minute change of plan. Originally Papoulas had intended to approach the Turkish position by a flanking movement from the south, but the overstretching of his line and a rumour of Turkish troop movements, false as it turned out, dissuaded him. He therefore decided to bridge the main Sakarya river and the two armies met virtually head on. Bearing in mind the circumstances of their approach march the Greeks fought with incredible gallantry and there were moments when the battle seemed theirs. Kemal, however, hung on. Still recovering from a broken rib caused by a fall from his horse, dressed, as other military dictators mock humble before and after him, in the uniform of a private soldier, the Turkish commander suffered torments as companies, regiments and divisions were halved. Forced by his injury to be static, drinking coffee instead of his customary heavy intake of alcohol, he nevertheless preserved his clarity of mind and purpose. The two armies fought themselves to a standstill. Both were short of ammunition and had suffered enormous casualties. The Greeks had lost 18,000 men, the Turks nearly as many.

By the 9th of September their earlier privations were telling on the Greeks; the first request of prisoners was for food. The Turks were just capable of one more counterattack; the Greeks were not. They made a brief attempt to dig themselves in but it was beaten down. On the evening of September 11th, on the orders of its king, the Greek army retreated westwards across the Sakarya river, protected to the last by its artillery, which sacrificed itself in the process.

Apparently it was stalemate, but in reality it was defeat. Churchill put his finger on it when he wrote: 'the Greeks had involved themselves in a politico-strategic situation where anything short of decisive victory was defeat; and the Turks were in a position where anything short of overwhelming defeat was victory'. Henceforth, although there was to be a large Greek army in Anatolia, it was to be an army on the defensive. The tables had been turned. The Grand National Assembly in Ankara, which had not been slow to express its doubts, fears and jealousies in the past, gave Mustapha Kemal the rank of Marshal and the ancient title of Ghazi, politely rendered as 'conqueror', but literally and historically, 'destroyer of the Christians'.

*   *   *

After the battle of the Sakarya river, again in Churchill's words: 'There was a pause in the march of events; an interlude in discussion; a gap in policy.' In one respect he was wrong, discussion continued. Most of it was to no purpose, but it took time and occupied men's minds, and allowed them to persuade themselves that they were doing something while in reality they were merely waiting.

Certainly this was so in Britain. Three very different observers have left their assessments of the character of Lord Curzon. Harold Nicolson, who had an affection for him, Sforza, the Italian Foreign Minister, who disliked and despised him, and Winston Churchill, who poached on his foreign policy preserves and was irritated when rebuked. All three agreed that he somehow lacked moral courage, but, more important, that in his conduct of foreign affairs he had one fatal defect. Sforza wrote: 'Lord Curzon's greatest pleasure in life, at any rate when I knew him and we were colleagues in a great many Inter-Allied conferences, was to state a case in a long and flowery speech, or in a dozen pages of beautiful English, and then—then to lose almost all interest in the further development of the idea. For all his English pride it never occurred to him that he might use the immense power of the British Empire to enforce certain recommendations or wishes of his . . . .' So Lord Curzon in his capacity as Foreign Secretary and also in his dealings with his Cabinet colleagues. Lloyd George knew perfectly well that although Curzon disagreed with him and actively disliked him, he would never push his disagreement and dislike to the point of resignation.

The diplomatic vice of stating a case, however well, and then leaving lesser mortals to profit from it or act upon it if they chose, seemed to be catching in late 1921 and early 1922. It had affected Curzon's colleagues as well. Only Winston Churchill was prepared to take action to stop the Anatolian war, if not against the Turks, then against the Greeks. Could not the Mediterranean fleet blockade their ports and thus force them to see reason? He put the suggestion in an official memorandum to Lloyd George and Curzon. Neither replied. So for almost a year after the Sakarya battle the British government, officially neutral, seemed to do nothing. The Greek army, in the winter of 1921–2, suffered incredible hardships. In the Anatolian winter, short of all supplies, frequently unpaid, its morale sank even further, but somehow it remained in position, watching and waiting for the Turks to move. There was no longer any question of the Greeks themselves taking the initiative. They had suffered 30,000 battle casualties since the beginning of their advance, and their numbers were being reduced daily by sickness.

Prince Andrew, who now commanded the Second Army Corps on the right of the line, completely disillusioned with the conduct of the war and after several disagreements with the General Staff, resigned his command in disgust and returned to Greece. Many, no doubt, would have liked to follow his example. The miracle was that the Greek army did remain. The tragedy was that they still cherished hopes of assistance, assistance from the man who had so often praised their fighting qualities and encouraged their imperial ambitions: David Lloyd George, known to the Greeks, who knew no other foreign statesman, by the only bit of his name they could pronounce, simply 'George'.

Of course, and it has been the excuse of statesmen since time immemorial, there were many other matters to claim his attention, domestic, foreign and Imperial. Europe was still a problem, more especially Germany, and as usual there was no dearth of conferences. One, pregnant with troubles for the future, did not necessitate the presence of the Prime Minister. Arthur Balfour, still Lord Privy Seal, 'the hack negotiator', as he called himself, was despatched to the Washington Naval Conference at the end of the year. It was genuine disarmament. Britain, the U.S.A. and Japan all agreed to limit their building of naval vessels. Unfortunately the Japanese felt aggrieved at not being treated as a first-class Power and being cold-shouldered out of the 'parity' which was to exist between the U.S. and Britain. Unknowingly the seeds of a future war were sown; Britain failed to maintain her strength in the Far East and lost her ally. Singapore was not thought to need fortification or reinforcement, and Balfour returned to his countrymen to be invested with the Order of the Garter, soon to be followed by an Earldom.

In October, 1921, another envoy had left Britain with rather more ceremony than the self-effacing Mr. Balfour. On the 26th H.M.S. *Renown* had steamed out of Portsmouth harbour to the boom of a twenty-one-gun salute, bearing the

Prince of Wales on the first part of his tour of India and the Far East. In Canada, Australia and New Zealand he had been a huge, literally a riotous, success. It was now thought that he should visit the other Imperial possessions to which he would succeed in the fullness of time.

The Prince arrived in India in November and was at once involved in a highly organised tour of both British India and the Princely States. In fact the visit itself had been a cause of some concern to the Viceroy, Lord Reading, and Edwin Montagu, the Secretary of State. Gandhi was increasing his activities and his following and was beginning to be worshipped almost as a saint. His 'non-co-operation' movement was taking hold, and the business of keeping law and order was becoming increasingly difficult. It was feared that the presence of the Heir to the Throne would inevitably provoke demonstrations, perhaps even violence. As it turned out, the form of protest chosen by Gandhi and his rising lieutenant Jawaharlal Nehru, who was jailed as a precaution for the duration of the visit, took the form of the boycott, the 'hartal'. British officialdom's counter measure, the traditional distribution of free food and refreshments to the poor on the visit of a great personage, was itself countered by a rumour spread by Gandhi's agents that the food was poisoned. Appalled by evidence of poverty the Prince had commanded that something be done about it, so the Indian Government had decided to remove the poor! The Prince of Wales, welcomed by 'official' India and the native princes, had also to drive through some deserted streets and attend functions where Indian civilians were noticeably absent. Characteristically, at the end of his tour, he wrote in a mood of self-criticism to Lord Reading, Montagu and his father, George V, complaining of a feeling of inadequacy and also of the excessive measures taken for his protection, which prevented him from meeting Indians. George V's reassuring reply to his son is not without interest. Speaking of the general deterioration of British-Indian relations he wrote: 'The war and the situation in Turkey and Montagu's reforms have no doubt produced the unrest which now exists.'

The 'situation in Turkey' was one which the Viceroy and the Secretary of State were perpetually urging the government to remedy. Politicians, such as Lloyd George, with no experience of India, forgot the basic facts of the Indian Empire. 'The brightest jewel' in the Imperial crown was a conquered state. Since the Great Mutiny of 1857 its British administrators had always hidden away in the inner recesses of their minds the fear that it could happen again. India was an armed camp. The Princes, from the Nizam of Hyderabad, reputedly the richest man in the world, who ruled an area as large as a Balkan state, down to petty Nawabs who had a few villages, all maintained their own state forces. In Hyderabad, Gwalior and Kashmir these were each equivalent to a division; in the smallest states the army diminished to a platoon. Eighteen thousand of these soldiers, paid for and sometimes led by their rulers, had served overseas in the Great War, in France, Egypt, Gallipoli, Mesopotamia and Palestine. 'The Princes', as George V pointed out to his son in the same letter, 'are all loyal and if there was real trouble they would at once come to the assistance of the Government with all their troops. . . .' For in addition to the ever-turbulent North-West Frontier, there was always the prospect of 'trouble' in India. 'A certain amount of discontent', as it was put officially, was to be expected. To deal with it in British India (i.e. those territories not ruled by the princes) an Indian army officered by the British was maintained at something like 200,000 men. (In the Great War it had risen to 573,000.) In addition there was a vast garrison of the British army which, a lesson of the Mutiny, until 1935 controlled all the artillery save a few light mountain guns.

Now in the Indian army, the permanent residents, so to speak, the larger part of the recruits came from the so-called 'martial races' of the Punjab and were Moslems. There were also, of course, Sikhs, Rajputs and Dogras, as well as the mercenary Gurkhas, who were all differing castes of Hindu, but since the Mutiny the British had tended to rely more and more upon Moslems from the north as soldiers and as policemen. Moslems too, as a minority fearful of being engulfed in an independent Hindu-dominated India, tended to support the British Raj. They were, in the King Emperor's phrase, more 'loyal'.

Therefore when Moslem leaders and communities showed signs of disaffection, the administration, from district officer to Viceroy, became concerned. Gandhi's following was largely Hindu. If at the same time large sections of the Moslem population were becoming anti-British because of the British attitude to Turkey, then the principle of 'divide and rule', never voiced but often practised, was in danger of collapse. Consequently Lord Reading, by telegram from New Delhi, and Edwin Montagu, in Cabinet, constantly tried to impress upon Lloyd George the harm that was being done in India by Britain's continued occupation of Constantinople and her apparent intention to hand over a large part of Turkey to the Greeks.

It is easy to see why their arguments fell on deaf ears. The counter-arguments were simple. The alleged strength of Moslem religious feeling was not difficult to decry. During the war, Arabs led by the Sherif of Mecca had fought the Sultan and Caliph. Moslem soldiers of the Indian army had cheerfully fought the Turks. Even at the moment there were eight Indian battalions under Sir Charles Harington's command. In 1920 the War Office, in an appreciation of the Turkish situation under the heading 'Psychological and sentimental', had said on the subject of the occupation of Constantinople: 'In Anatolia and Kurdistan where it might be expected to be of supreme importance, it seems doubtful if it is really vital.' Of the Moslem religion: 'It is useful as a rallying cry, as propaganda and as a stalking horse in foreign politics.'

The War Office was in fact right. Mustapha Kemal was indifferent to religion and impatient to jerk his countrymen into the twentieth century. The observances and the prohibitions of Islam were anathema to him. Nevertheless he was prepared to use any means that came to hand to embarrass the Allied Powers. If pan-Islamic sentiment could gain sympathy for Turkey then it should be utilised. The British rule over millions of Moslems in India was an obvious target. From January 1921 until November, Sir Henry Dobbs was engaged in Kabul in the task of hammering out some sort of treaty between the government of India and Afghanistan to conclude the Amir's abortive and unsuccessful war. The mountain kingdom, almost perpetually at odds with India, provided a happy hunting ground for Kemalist agents spreading doubt and dissension.

In India proper the Khalifat movement of active Moslems, with a little encouragement, practically did Kemal's work for him. There was a genuine sentiment not so much for the Caliph or the 'holy place' aspect of Constantinople as for the fact that Turkey, the only truly independent Moslem country in the world, seemed to be oppressed by Greece, France, Italy and Britain. Especially by Britain, from whom many Indian Moslems wanted their freedom. At the same time as petitions were presented to the Viceroy and deputations organised to argue that a just peace should be made with Turkey, in Indian towns and villages collections were made to aid Kemal in his fight to throw off foreign oppression. The Aga Khan, whose name had been mentioned in the Cabinet as a possible emissary to Kemal, now found himself, as spiritual head of the Ismaili sect of the Shia Moslems, using all his considerable influence to persuade Lloyd George, a personal friend, to drop his pro-Greek policies. To no avail. As Curzon reported: 'The Prime Minister is as philhellene as ever.'

On March 1st, 1922, still under constant bombardment from leaders of Moslem opinion, Reading sent to Montagu a telegram which again stressed the intensity of Moslem feeling in India. The Government of India regarded as essential three conditions: 'The evacuation of Constantinople, the Sultan's suzerainty over the Holy Places, and thirdly restoration of Ottoman Thrace including the sacred Moslem city of Adrianople and the unreserved restoration of Smyrna.' They were a curious set of contradictory demands, ignoring as they did the division which existed between Kemal and the Sultan. Nevertheless they represented the Indian view and Reading asked that they might be published. Montagu, without consulting the Cabinet, authorised publication.

Reading, assuming he had Cabinet authority, published the whole telegram in India. Curzon, when told by Montagu what he had done, was speechless, but did manage to write a letter. It contained some good Curzon broadsides. 'That I should be asked to go into Conference at Paris while a subordinate branch of the British government 6,000 miles away dictates to the British government what line it thinks I ought to pursue in Thrace seems to me quite intolerable.

. . . If the Government of India, because it rules over a large body of Moslems, is entitled to express and publish its views about what we do in Smyrna or Thrace, why not equally Egypt, the Sudan, Palestine, Arabia, the Malay Peninsula, or any other part of the Moslem world? Is Indian opinion always to be a final Court of Moslem appeal? I hope this may be the last of these unfortunate pronouncements.' It was. On March 9th, two days later, Lloyd George summoned Montagu and sacked him.

Montagu had acted stupidly, and his excuse, that he didn't think there was going to be Cabinet meeting early enough to consider what he regarded as an urgent matter, was feeble in the extreme. On March 11th, overwhelmed by his dismissal, he made an excessively bitter speech to his Cambridge constituents. He had been sacrificed to the Die-Hard Tories who did not like Lloyd George's Irish policy. All the Liberals were being sacrificed. (The ill-fated Addison had recently resigned.) The Coalition was breaking up. The Tories, he said truthfully, disliked him. So 'the great genius who presides over our destinies had done for them what they could not do for themselves and presented them with what they so long desired, my head on a charger'. With such a man in charge the official reason for his dismissal, Cabinet responsibility, said Montagu, was a joke. Lloyd George was variously referred to as 'genius', 'wizard' and 'dictator'. 'I have never,' said Montagu, 'been able to understand from what motive his pro-Greek policy was dictated. . . . I do not know in whose interest it is. I am certain that it is calamitous to the British Empire.' In the 1922 general election Montagu lost his seat. Two years later he was dead, a disappointed man of forty-five.

*   *   *

Elsewhere political heads were rolling and for less serious reasons.

In January 1922 there had been yet another Allied Conference, this time at Cannes. Turkey was on the agenda, but the most important event turned out to be a golf match. Lloyd George persuaded Briand, whose only sport was the traditional one of the French bourgeois, coarse fishing, to join him. Indeed he offered to instruct him. Briand's performance, even under tuition, was ludicrous and humiliating. There were photographs. The Paris press went beserk. The French displayed their characteristic lack of an English sense of humour. The Chamber of Deputies had at the time as many shades of political opinion as a prism. Briand was replaced by Poincaré, of whom Curzon said: 'The eternal and to me most repugnant Poincaré; when firmly handled he is amenable.'

The Marquess Curzon of Kedleston was quite wrong. Months previously the French government had determined to get something out of the Turkish affair. The French had made up their minds that the cause of the Greeks, certainly without Veniselos, was lost, and that Kemal was the coming man in the Near East. Both the French and Italians had made tentative advances to the Nationalists behind the back of the British at the time of the London Conference. Their offer then had been the complete withdrawal of French troops from the Syrian frontier area, and the withdrawal of Italians from Adalia, both nations to be compensated by economic concessions. This, to Kemal, smacked far too much of the old European financial and economic domination of the Ottoman Empire, and he rejected both offers.

In June 1921 the French tried again. 'The French were playing up to Kemal all this time in the most deplorable manner and trying to win his good graces behind our backs,' said Nevile Henderson. As their emissary to carry out this task they sent to Constantinople M. Franklin Bouillon, a former deputy and president of the Chamber's Committee for Foreign Affairs. Although he arrived on a warship, Franklin Bouillon's status was sufficiently ambiguous to allow his government to recognise any achievement and disavow any failure. If the French government had deliberately set out to pick a man who would antagonise their British allies they could not have chosen his superior. Fat, luxuriantly moustached, loquacious, interfering and virtually unsnubbable, 'Boiling Frankie' was almost a cartoon Frenchman. When Nevile Henderson first saw him he was wearing 'a dark suit with a pair of very vivid yellow boots'.

Franklin Bouillon first saw Kemal in June, 1921, and again in October, after the battle of the Sakarya river. On October 20th he achieved his object. On that day an agreement was signed in Ankara which meant in fact that France had withdrawn from the cold war with Turkey. The Syrian frontier would be adjusted to Turkey's advantage; the only remaining French troops in Turkey would be in Constantinople. In return the French received concessions with regard to the Baghdad Railway. From now on, though not stated specifically in any written agreement, their considerable financial and economic interests in Turkey would be secure.

The Royal Signals wireless operators on the eastern shore of the Bosphorus, who had recently been in communication with Ankara regarding the exchange of a number of prisoners taken by both sides, used their knowledge of the wavelength to intercept a long coded message. The text of the French agreement was taken by despatch rider to Pavlo; from there by drazine, a motor truck with rail wheels, along the Anatolian railway to Haidar Pasha, and thence by motor launch to Constantinople. The code was broken and the message was recoded and transmitted to London. In Nevile Henderson's words, 'The French had ratted.' Sir Horace Rumbold and Lord Curzon, in their turn, were suitably horrified. Where the French had gone the Italians were sure to follow.

The Cannes Conference, as has been related, proved a fiasco. Briand had fallen and Poincaré, his successor, despite Lord Curzon's opinion, with an agreement in being with Mustapha Kemal was likely to be an unco-operative ally. It was beginning to look uncomfortably as if the British were to be left on their own, their only friends the Greeks, whose army still hung on grimly in Anatolia.

Nevile Henderson has described this period as 'just drifting along' in Constantinople, but in fact the soldiers were more alive to the dangers than the diplomats and their masters the politicians. Lloyd George's attitude at this time was Mr. Micawber's, and while he waited for something to turn up he still hoped vaguely that the Greeks would be able to help him out. Harington, less confident than Lloyd George of the Greeks' ability to pull British chestnuts out of the fire, decided to take the initiative himself. From his intelligence reports he knew that the Nationalists were daily gaining in strength; that financial aid was being supplied, if only in small quantities, by the Russians, and that both the French and the Italians were handing over large quantities of arms to Kemal—arms for which they had no further use as they evacuated their spheres of influence, and which came in particularly handy as sweeteners for their future relations with the coming men in Turkey.

Harington, 'a resolute man', as Sforza, who had no reason to like him, called him, saw his opportunity in the fact that there were a number of British soldiers held prisoner in Nationalist hands. Prominent among them was Major Rawlinson, brother to the Great War general now Commander-in-Chief in India. Rawlinson, like the others, had been captured when the Turks in Anatolia, at the time of the Smyrna landing, had turned against the occupying powers, broken into the dumps of surrendered arms and taken prisoner British supervising officers. While negotiating for the return of these officers Harington tried to establish direct relations with Kemal. Contact was made, but unfortunately Harington's hands were tied by Sir Horace Rumbold, more under the control of Whitehall than his military commander. In the circumstances there was little enough that Harington could offer Kemal and the informal negotiations were broken off.

Perforce the General had to return to his military duties,

training and caring for the troops in Constantinople and the garrisons on both sides of the Straits. He managed at the same time, though fifty years old, to be the best cricketer among many enthusiasts in his army and to emulate Leander and Byron by swimming the Bosphorus.

Militarily it was stalemate again. In June, 1922, Harington was given an additional reason for feeling downcast, apart from the failure of his attempt at diplomacy, by a personal loss. On the 22nd, just after unveiling a war memorial plaque at Liverpool Street Station, Sir Henry Wilson was shot dead on the steps of his house in Eaton Place by two Irish gunmen. Earlier in the year he had been eased out as Chief of the Imperial General Staff and had been elected M.P. for an Ulster constituency, and that, for his murderers, had seemingly been enough. By his death the British army lost its only field marshal by violence, and Lloyd George lost a critic. Marshal Foch, who had with 'Henri' opposed the Greek adventure from the start, spoke of 'my old and trusted comrade and best friend', and crossed from France to be a pall-bearer and give Lady Wilson his arm at the funeral in St. Paul's.

The same afternoon Winston Churchill had to address an angry House of Commons on the Irish question, and promised among other things to cordon off North from South with troops. The subsequent debate was marked by an intervention by Bonar Law, now apparently restored to health and political activity. The next day, in Dublin, Rory O'Connor, the leader of the I.R.A., and his men, in occupation of the Four Courts, were being shelled by the troops of Michael Collins, the Free State leader, with field guns obligingly lent by the British Commander-in-Chief. O'Connor was later to be shot without trial and Collins to be murdered in an ambush, but the affairs of Ireland were increasingly becoming Ireland's own. A legacy of bitterness nevertheless remained in British politics, especially in the hearts of many die-hard Tories, which expressed itself, however unjustly and illogically, in dissatisfaction with Lloyd George and all his policies. Others besides Lord Beaverbrook were beginning to look to the returned Bonar

Law for salvation. Bonar Law himself, although naturally he had strong feelings about Ulster, the home of his ancestors, at this stage showed no signs of disloyalty to his old chief. Anyhow foreign affairs were not his forte, and it was once again in the field of foreign affairs, and once again in the Near East, that the next crisis for the Coalition government occurred.

On July 29th the British Ambassador in Athens was invited to the Greek Foreign Office, there to receive an official note from the hands of the Minister informing him that the Greek government had decided that the only way to restore peace was to occupy Constantinople with Greek forces. The Greeks showed every intention of putting their decision into effect. Two days previously the Greek warships at Constantinople had slipped away, ostensibly to carry out exercises in the Sea of Marmora. On orders from King Constantine, the new Commander-in-Chief in Anatolia, General Hajianestis, had secretly and swiftly moved two of his divisions by sea to reinforce the Greek troops already in Thrace, and was preparing to advance the whole force to the Chataldja lines, the last defence for Constantinople. Ever since, the Greek threat to the Turkish capital has been described as a gambler's final throw, but there was, at the time, a great deal of military logic to support it.

The Greek army in Anatolia was in desperate straits. It had failed to reach Ankara and the chance would never come again. General Papoulas, following continued disagreements with the Ministry of War in Athens over strategy and supplies, had, with his whole staff, resigned in May. Constantinople was, of course, Turkish, but it had a large Greek population, plus thousands of inhabitants whose race, like their allegiance, was at least problematical. The Allied garrison was small, and in any event British, French and Italians were still technically at war with Turkey and in occupation, like the Greeks, of enemy territory. With Constantinople in Greek hands, would not the Greeks, and the Allies as well, have the strongest card in their hands to play against Kemal in Ankara?

Naturally enough Constantine and his advisers were

a⁺tracted by the idea of taking the ancient capital of the Byzantine Empire, with all the consequent prestige that they would gain thereby. A triumphant entry into Constantinople would easily outweigh the reverse on the Sakarya river. These considerations aside, however, and accepting that they were probably the emotional springs of action, the straight politico-military argument had force, and a chance of success. The British, French and Italians, especially the British with their pro-Greek Prime Minister, might not be prepared to assist in Anatolia, but would they be prepared to fight the Greek army to keep it out of Constantinople? Would the Allies, who had encouraged the Greeks to go into Anatolia in the first place, now wage war against them to prevent them from minimising some of their losses?

The decision had to be made in Constantinople. Sir Horace Rumbold was on leave and Nevile Henderson deputised in his place, so the decision was arrived at jointly by Henderson and Harington. The General had no doubts. He could visualise the two populations, Greek and Turkish, fighting in the streets of the city. 'I simply could not believe the report which I was getting on this mad prospect,' he said. Swiftly he inspected the Chataldja lines, running across the peninsula from the Sea of Marmora to the Black Sea, thirty miles west of the Bosphorus. 'The finest natural position in the world,' was how the dead Wilson had described them. The lines were reinforced with British and French troops and the command given to the French general, Charpy. The newly appointed Mediterranean C.-in-C., Admiral Sir Osmond Brock, put to sea from Constantinople in his flagship, the *Iron Duke*, taking with him five other capital ships, *Benbow*, *King George V*, *Marlborough*, *Ajax* and *Centurion*, with a seaplane carrier and nine destroyers. The 3rd Light Cruiser Squadron took on fuel and ammunition at Malta and steamed full speed eastwards across the Mediterranean.

Henderson drafted, and Harington altered and then issued, a proclamation stating that any attack on Constantinople from whatever direction, that is from either Greeks or Turks, would be unhesitatingly opposed by the Allied forces. The

167

Allied High Commissioners, General Pellé and Garroni, approved. The government in London, when formally approached by the Greek government for permission to invade Constantinople, backed up the actions of its men on the spot. The Greeks, with a powerful British fleet in the Sea of Marmora and the Chataldja lines held against them, could do nothing save bow to superior force and order their troops to halt their advance. Harington, who had been offered by the Turks 20,000 men to help him if necessary, described the situation as Gilbertian. Henderson wrote later: 'I have always personally hated my action on that occasion. . . .'

The last move but one was Lloyd George's. Doubtless from the kindest of motives and as a sop to wounded Greek pride, in a speech in the House of Commons he praised the courage and endurance of the Greek troops, and ended with a series of ambiguous phrases which seemed to indicate that there were limits to his patience with Kemal and that perhaps next time Britain would help the Greeks.

Extracts from this extraordinary speech were published by command of King Constantine as an Order of the Day to his soldiers. Greek morale rose again, but not for long, for the last move was Mustapha Kemal's. Undeterred by Lloyd George's eloquence and judging it against his actions, on August 26th he launched his long-prepared major offensive against the Greek army in Anatolia. Weakened by the two divisions transferred to Thrace the Greek army began to retreat. Kemal had told his troops that their goal was the Mediterranean. On September 9th the Turks entered Smyrna. 'Here's a bloody mess,' was Lloyd George's comment when told the news.

10

'There is nothing to fight about any more'
Mustapha Kemal

When the news of the wholesale retreat of the Greek army had first reached G.H.Q. in Constantinople, General Harington had immediately signalled one of his liaison officers: 'Can't someone get on a tub and stop them?'

Apparently no one could, least of all the recently appointed Greek Commander-in-Chief, General Hajianestis, referred to by Lloyd George in Cabinet as 'some kind of mental defective'. The description was not an abusive comment on the general's military abilities, but literally true. In his younger days Hajianestis had been both a gallant and efficient soldier, but upon his elevation to the rank of general he had degenerated into a mere courtier wearing military uniform. Like Lord Cardigan in the Crimean War his command post was his yacht, this time moored in Smyrna harbour. Cardigan, however, did leave his yacht to lead the charge of the Light Brigade. Hajianestis led no charges but stayed on board, occasionally visiting the odd waterside restaurant. The reason for his actions was the justification for the Prime Minister's remark, for by the time the general reached Anatolia he was mentally sick. On some days he was convinced that his legs were made of some brittle material, sugar or glass, and would break if he walked on them. On others he would lie on his bed, firmly of the opinion that he was dead. In the field of mental illness these are common enough delusions, but they are rarely encountered among army commanders on active service. Emphatically the fifty-eight-year-old General Hajianestis was not the man to stand on a tub and endeavour to stop his troops running away. At the last moment he was relieved of his command, but by then it was too late. General Tricoupis, his successor, only learned of his appointment after he himself had been captured by the Turks.

The morale of the Greek army had snapped completely. For too long it had been kept in position in Anatolia, badly supplied, apparently neglected by Athens, constantly harried by the enemy. When the Turks advanced the Greek army disintegrated as a fighting force. Soldiers refused to obey their officers, officers refused to obey their generals. The retreat became a rout. Reinforcements hastily sent to Smyrna refused to disembark. Discipline gone, the Greek army became a vengeful, frightened mob. On its way to the coast it vented its fury on Turkish civilians, killing and plundering, burning villages, and defiling mosques by slaughtering pigs, abhorrent to Moslems, within their precincts. Some units still preserved their discipline and managed therefore to put up some resistance to the Turks, but in the majority of cases panic supplanted reason, and the path to the sea was marked by a trail of abandoned artillery and ammunition and piles of discarded rifles and equipment. In the final stages even the hardy Turkish cavalry, on their tough little ponies, found it impossible to keep up with the retreating enemy.

So the wheel had turned full circle. Once again the Allied fleets lay in Smyrna harbour. On September 3rd the Greeks, realising that their position was hopeless, had called upon their former allies to use their influence to bring about an armistice. To no avail. It would have been a hopeless task in any event. The Turks could not have been held back at this stage, and the Greeks were divided as to whether to stay and fight round Smyrna or evacuate. General Poly-menakos, Commander-in-Chief in succession to Tricoupis, backed up by Theotokis, the War Minister, was in favour of making a last stand. General Hajianestis, though no longer in command, still exercised a baleful and indecisive influence. Stergiades, the High Commissioner in Smyrna, had given up all hope and pressed for immediate evacuation.

Because of conflicting rumours and announcements, both soldiers and civilians in Smyrna were in a state of chronic indecision, verging on panic, for a week before the Turks appeared. Consequently the arrival of British, French, Italian, American and Greek warships boosted morale enormously, until it was realised that they were there only to rescue their own nationals, whereupon spirits plunged again and the Smyrniots awaited the coming of their conquerors with something like apathy.

In the short week before the Turks were sighted the harbour at Smyrna looked like an international naval regatta. Only the Greek ships *Kilkis*, *Lemnos*, *Helle* and the cruiser *Averoff*, which had brought King Constantine back from exile, were active. The *Averoff* and *Lemnos* had been present when the jubilant Greeks had entered Smyrna in 1919. On the other ships there was little for the companies to do but watch and wait. The catalogue was almost Homeric: H.M.S. *Iron Duke*, the flagship of Admiral Brock, the Commander-in-Chief in the Mediterranean, and the *King George V;* then *Ajax*, her replacement, and the cruiser *Cardiff* with a number of attendant destroyers. The French *Waldeck-Rousseau*, soon to be joined by three armoured cruisers, *Jean Bart*, *Edgar Quinet* and *Ernest Renan*. The Italian flagship, the slim elegant cruiser *Venezia*, escorted by destroyers. A day later four U.S. destroyers, *Simpson*, *Litchfield*, *Edsel* and *Lawrence*, under Captain Hepburn, arrived and dropped anchor alongside the British.

The officers and crews of these ships watched the tragedy of Smyrna unfold itself across the long seafront as if on a cinema screen. There were daily instalments.

On September 4th a Greek hospital ship filled up with wounded and left the harbour. The next day the British put ashore marines and seamen to act as guards for the steamers which had been requisitioned to transport refugees. Orders were issued for the inspection of passports and consular documents, the Royal Navy having taken over the task of evacuating Dutch as well as British nationals. In fact neither the British nor the Dutch colony seemed anxious to leave, as the Greek High Command was still issuing statements which suggested that Smyrna would be held against the Turks. Rumours still abounded that the Allied fleets would help to keep the enemy at bay. More wounded Greek soldiers were evacuated and trainloads of field guns, limbers and stores were seen to arrive at the railway pier. Thousands of weary, footsore Greek civilians, with their belongings and their children, began to swarm into the town. The weather was swelteringly hot. 'Words fail to convey even a small part of the misery seen that day,' said a naval officer.

On September 6th the first of the British refugees, mostly Maltese and Cypriots, began to leave on the S.S. *Magira* and *Antioch*. Then the sailors started to get their first glimpse of the retreating Greek army. On horses, donkey and foot, some armed, others without equipment, unshaven and dirty, many of them with rags wrapped round their feet in place of boots. 'A demoralised army without discipline, order, life or interest,' was how one eyewitness described them.

A transport arrived from Thrace with fresh troops, rumoured to be intended as reinforcements to cover the town. To the disciplined eyes of the Royal Navy they looked no better than the men straggling along the harbour road. The whole of the seafront was now filled with Greeks, mainly women and children, who just sat on their small piles of belongings without food or shelter. It became apparent that the Greek transports would evacuate soldiers and no one else. The civilians were to be left to their fate. Monsignor Chrysostomos, the Archbishop of Smyrna, in conversation with a naval officer, was furious to hear that the British did not intend to use their 'big guns' on the Turks when they arrived.

172

Above Mustapha Kemal inspects his troops in Anatolia,
March 1922
Below General Papoulas and his staff in Anatolia, March 1922.
General Papoulas (white moustache) has on his right
Crown Prince George of Greece

British and French warships at Constantinople, 1922

Above Turkish infantry advancing on Smyrna, August 1922
Below Greek artillery prepare for attack, Anatolia, July 1922

On September 7th martial law was proclaimed by the Greeks. Looting of the warehouses on the sea front could be seen to be in full swing. Another transport arrived with Greek troops, who shouted and jeered at their comrades who were embarking. A number of generals arrived from Athens but at the same time squadron after squadron of Greek cavalry began to move through the town. These, it was learnt, were the rearguard, the last disciplined troops the Greeks possessed, and were to be evacuated from Chesme, opposite the island of Chios, forty miles west along the coast. They were soon followed by General Polymenakos, the Commander-in-Chief, and his staff. The same evening M. Stergiades, the Greek High Commissioner, followed by shouts and jeers from those he left behind, took refuge on the *Iron Duke*. On September 8th more and more refugees crowded into the town by rail, some hanging on outside the carriages, and on foot. The warships prepared armed parties to go ashore if necessary. The last of the British refugees embarked. The Greek warships left the harbour. A Turkish aeroplane was seen to circle over the town. The British and French landed strong, armed patrols to guard property and consulates from the crowds of looters, many of whom were themselves by now armed with rifles and revolvers abandoned by the soldiers.

Mr. Horton, the U.S. Consul-General at Smyrna, telegraphed to the Acting Secretary of State: 'Turkish forces expected to arrive tomorrow night or morning after. Please telegraph urgently what will be my relations if any with the Kemalist military or civil authorities.' The reply he received from Washington was not particularly helpful in that he was reminded that 'your government recognises the existing regime neither in Greece nor in Asia Minor, and that diplomatic relations with the Sublime Porte [i.e. the Constantinople government] have not been resumed.' Mr. Horton was therefore 'to remain unofficially at his post', and do his best. On September 9th Admiral Bristol in Constantinople also communicated with Washington. 'Smyrna situation most alarming. Greek troops in panic and pouring into city. Repeated threats by Greek officers to burn town. Aidin and Nazilli already burned. On September 6th American, English and French and Italian consuls telegraphed Greek Minister of War, Theotokis, asking for assurances Smyrna would not be burned or pillaged. Theotokis replied he could give no such assurances.'

Also on September 9th, a Saturday, a little after nine o'clock in the morning, Captain Thesiger, having just inspected the naval guard mounted at the gasworks (the company was British owned), found himself facing long lines of Turkish cavalry riding into the town. The Turks had arrived. Captain Thesiger and the Turkish cavalry colonel spoke amicably enough together in bad French. The Allies were trying to maintain order until the Turks arrived. Thesiger advised the colonel to avoid the back streets to prevent bloodshed. The cavalry accordingly resumed their advance along the sea front.

The impression they made on the British was favourable. They had a few days' growth of beard on their faces; they looked tough, tired and hard bitten and they were neither smart nor particularly clean. On their saddles they carried all manner of equipment and plunder from guitars to brass jugs and carpets, but nevertheless they had an appearance of discipline about them. As they continued through the town there were rifle and revolver shots from the houses. Some of the Turks were wounded. They drew their swords, but 'under provocation the discipline of the Turks still held'. Panic-stricken, hundreds of Greeks fled before them and took refuge on the lighters and barges in the harbour. The British, seeing that many of these refugees were armed, confiscated their weapons and threw arms and ammunition into the sea. The Navy then supplied this 'panicked mass of humanity' with cooked potatoes and drinking water.

More and more Turkish troops moved into the town, and soon French, Italian, Spanish, Belgian and American flags began to appear on the houses along the waterfront. Some genuinely indicated foreign property; others were flown in the hope that they would warn off the Turks or the rabble of refugees and looters which swarmed in the streets. Beyond the harbour area sporadic rifle fire could be heard.

Sir Harry Lamb, the British Consul-General, and Commodore Barry Domville, Admiral Brock's Chief of Staff, met the Turkish advance-guard commander, Ferik Salahaddin Bey, and agreed to continue to police the town until Turkish gendarmerie arrived. There were a few scenes of violence as Armenians and Greeks attacked the incoming Turks. Turkish civilians were now beginning to arm themselves to carry out reprisals.

Sunday, September 10th, was comparatively quiet, but a number of long-range shells landed in or around the town, presumably fired by the Greek warships protecting the road to Chesme. The Royal Marine guard at the gasworks reported over 300 dead during the night and numerous incidents of murder, rape and looting. A number of refugees attempted to swim to the British battleships. Mustapha Kemal was observed entering the town in a motor car surrounded by his staff and a large escort of lancers. On September 11th a number of corpses were seen floating in the harbour including 'apparently a soldier crucified on a box lid'. Boats put out from the naval vessels and sank a large number of these bodies by attaching iron fire bars to them. At night fires could be seen burning inland.

Sir Harry Lamb, having been ordered to have no official dealings with Mustapha Kemal, in fact met him by chance in the street and was told curtly by the Turkish leader that he still considered himself at war with the British. Admiral Brock sent Commodore Domville to call upon Kemal officially and Kemal admitted that he had spoken on the spur of the moment and there the matter ended, although it was noticeable that with the French and Italian representatives the Marshal was far more friendly.

In Smyrna itself there were now a number of distinguishable groups. The Turkish army itself, still reasonably disciplined and kept in hand, Turkish irregulars, later arrivals, over whom less control was exercised, and the Turkish civilian population, wild with joy at their deliverance. Then came the Greeks and Armenians, locals and refugees, existing as best they could and collecting in great crowds within sight of the Allied warships, from which they still

175

expected some form of protection. Seemingly imperturbable, the great ships lay at anchor, and at sunrise and sunset the Marine bugles rang out over the harbour as the ensigns were hoisted and lowered ceremonially.

On shore a number of wheels continued to turn full circle. Mustapha Kemal visited the municipal buildings still decorated with portraits of King Constantine. Remembering the Greek King's entry into Smyrna, one of his crowd of admirers spread a Greek flag on the floor. The Marshal refused to do as was expected and tread on it. 'That is a sign of a country's independence,' he said, and walked round it. Monsignor Chrysostomos had another meeting with Nourredin Pasha, whom once he had said ought to be shot. Nourredin, now military governor, had not forgotten, and reminding the Archbishop of their last meeting, told him that he was to be hanged forthwith. Willing hands started to take Chrysostomos to the nearest tree, but a Turkish mob joined in and gouged out his eyes, and he was dead before a rope could be put round his neck.

The scene presented by the Smyrna waterfront was now indescribable. Thousands of refugees, discarded belongings and transport. In the water corpses still floated, and in the shallows stood numbers of horses and mules, hamstrung or blinded by the retreating Greeks so that they would be useless to the Turks. There was, however, one more ordeal for Smyrna to suffer. On the afternoon of September 13th columns of smoke were seen rising over the Armenian quarter. On the 14th Admiral Bristol again telegraphed the Acting Secretary of State: 'Wireless just received from my chief of staff at Smyrna states city is burning . . .' During the night of the 13th the fire had spread throughout the northern part of the town. All the buildings facing the harbour went up in one mammoth conflagration.

On board the British flagship Ward Price, the indefatigable foreign correspondent of the *Daily Mail*, who, said Nevile Henderson, 'dropped like a vulture from the sky' on a news story, typed his dispatch. 'What I see as I stand on the deck of the *Iron Duke* is an unbroken wall of fire, two miles long, in which twenty distinct volcanoes of raging flames are throwing up jagged, writhing tongues to a height of a hundred feet. Picture a constant projection into a red hot sky of gigantic incandescent balloons, burning oil spots in the Aegean, the air filled with nauseous smells, while parching clouds, cinders and sparks drift across us—and you can have but a glimmering of the scene of appalling and majestic destruction which we are watching.' A naval officer's description was shorter. He said, 'it would hold its own with Dante'.

Refugees threw themselves and their children into the sea. The foreign admirals, originally with strict orders to take on board only their own nationals, put out boats. Captain Hepburn reported to Admiral Bristol: 'All men of war in harbour loaded with refugees.' In the next few days the foreign warships and commandeered merchantmen evacuated from Smyrna 213,480 men, women and children, who were taken to Greece or distributed about the islands of the Aegean. Three-quarters of Smyrna was a smouldering ruin.

To this day Turks argue that the fire was started by Greeks or Armenians as a continuation of the 'scorched earth' policy they had carried out in the interior. The Greeks maintain that the fire, however it started, was spread by the Turks as a deliberate act of vandalism and revenge. They point out that only the Turkish quarter survived. The Turks stress that in Smyrna the Moslem quarter is to the south, and every afternoon the prevailing wind, the 'imbat', blows south-west to north-east and would naturally carry flames from the Armenian quarter towards the Greek and away from the Turkish quarter. Certain it is that Mustapha Kemal had no hand in the matter. He was not, however, much perturbed by the fire and its effect. He merely regarded it as a fitting end to the Greek empire in Asia Minor, as did his officers and soldiers, who did nothing to control the blaze and little to save human life. For them 'Giaur Izmir', infidel Smyrna, was no more.

*   *   *

In Britain in September the House of Commons was in recess. It was the political close season when Ministers and Members of Parliament rested from their labours. The more conscientious, or those with small majorities, visited their constituencies. The others took their holidays. For the Cabinet and the government this autumn was not to be a period of relaxation. As the Turkish army advanced towards Smyrna, there was a Cabinet meeting on September 7th at 10 Downing Street, presided over by the Prime Minister. As usual on these occasions the proceedings began with a résumé of the situation by the Foreign Secretary. The Prime Minister might despise and dislike him, his Cabinet colleagues might be irritated by him, but it was generally accepted that in stating a case elegantly and accurately Lord Curzon had no equal.

Curzon referred briefly to the agreement which had existed between the Allies in March, when all the Powers had appeared to be of the opinion that an armistice should be imposed on Greeks and Turks. Since then the situation had deteriorated 'due to the consistent treachery of the French'. Delays and obstacles had been invented in Paris. Behind the backs of their allies the French had been in constant communication with Mustapha Kemal, encouraging him to ignore Allied pronouncements. 'It now appeared that there was no possibility of resistance by the Greek Army. The Turks had had enormous advantages through receiving military equipment and arms in large quantities from France and Italy.'

The Greek request to Britain to impose an armistice had been passed on to the French and the Italians. The French had said that the Greeks must evacuate Asia Minor first; the Italians had not even replied. Now 'it was possible that the Turkish army would be in Smyrna within a few days'. Lord Curzon had received reports of the Greeks killing and ill-treating the Turkish population as they retreated. He had warned the Greek government, which had done nothing, and now there would be a serious refugee problem. The American Relief Organisation and the League of Nations had been informed.

178

It looked as if the real question now was the Straits. If Britain yielded to the Turks, then 'the whole of the fruits of the war as to the Balkan situation would be thrown away'. Kemal might well advance and threaten the Ismid peninsula and Constantinople. The Foreign Secretary felt that the French, suspicious as always, would not leave the British alone in Constantinople; therefore danger was not to be apprehended there. General Harington was confident that with the aid of the French and Italians he could suppress any rising in the Turkish capital. There were also, Curzon reminded the Cabinet, 400,000 Greeks in Constantinople, and now that they were leaving Asia Minor they would of course be stronger in Europe. The Cabinet apparently accepted that having only recently kept the Greeks out of Constantinople they could now use them to defend it.

Winston Churchill was not in favour of a bargain with the Turks 'to ensure the safety of the Greek army', but 'the line of deep water separating Asia from Europe was a line of great significance and we must make that line secure by every means within our power'. He wondered if the Bulgarians, 'the best fighting people in the Balkans', although an ex-enemy nation, might be persuaded to play some part.

The Prime Minister, unlike Curzon and Churchill, was still not reconciled to the defeat of the Greeks. He 'suspected that defeat had been engineered by Constantine'. He was doubtful 'if the Greek army had suffered a complete débâcle. The Turks had claimed to have captured only 10,000 prisoners.' That was true at that date, but there were soon to be 40,000 Greek prisoners taken in the Smyrna area and 30,000 counted dead. Like Churchill, Lloyd George was concerned, if not obsessed, by the Straits. 'In no circumstances,' he said, 'could we allow the Gallipoli peninsula to be held by the Turks. It was the most important strategic position in the world and the closing of the Straits had prolonged the war by two years.'

Lloyd George was, of course, referring to the 1914–18 War, and what he said in that context was undeniably true. He did not, however, advance any reasons as to why the Straits were particularly important to Britain in 1922.

During the war the British had unsuccessfully stormed Gallipoli in order to defeat the Turks and relieve Russia. Now the Prime Minister seemed to see the imminent possibility of that operation being carried out in reverse. 'It was inconceivable,' he said, 'that [the British] should allow the Turks to gain possession of the Gallipoli peninsula and we should fight to prevent their doing so. The Peninsula was easily defended against a great sea power like ourselves and if it were in the occupation of a great sea power it would be impregnable.' Churchill's suggestion with regard to Bulgaria he considered to be valuable save for 'an insuperable difficulty': the Romanians and the Yugoslavs were bitterly opposed to the Bulgarians. Whether Lloyd George was being sarcastic or not it is impossible to tell. He ended by saying that he considered 'it was possible that the Greeks under their new commander-in-chief may fight and improve the situation'.

Lord Lee, the First Lord of the Admiralty, who had just returned from Constantinople, contributed the reassuring news that he had formed the view that in that city British prestige was far higher than that of the French or the Italians. Thus inspired, the Cabinet decided that Lord Curzon should continue his diplomatic efforts with the Allies. That the naval forces should be increased in the area to prevent Kemalists gaining access to the Gallipoli peninsula. That in the peninsula itself, which was at present occupied by French troops, there should now be British troops as well. That if the Turks attacked in the Ismid peninsula General Harington could be at liberty to withdraw to Constantinople, but that any attempt to cross the Bosphorus to Constantinople 'should be resisted by the full strength of the British forces by sea and land'. Finally, despite the hopes of the Prime Minister with regard to a last stand by the Greek army, British civil ships should be diverted to Smyrna to take away foreign refugees if necessary.

On September 11th the Prime Minister held a conference at lunchtime at his country home at Churt. It was a small gathering: Sir Laming Worthington-Evans, the Secretary of State for War, Lord Lee, the First Lord, and Lieutenant-

General Chetwode, the Adjutant-General, with Colonel Bartholomew from the War Office. It had become plain that General Harington did not fully understand, or possibly would not understand, what the Cabinet was telling him to do. It was probable that Mustapha Kemal would soon threaten Chanak or demand that the British troops there should be withdrawn. Therefore the troops should be withdrawn before the demand was made.

General Chetwode interposed to say that in the view of the War Office and the Admiralty if Chanak were evacuated and Kemal brought up guns, it would be difficult, if not impossible, for destroyers, cruisers or supply ships to pass up the Straits. The Prime Minister did not comment on this point directly, but replied with the rather curious statement that 'in the eventuality of a war in the future in which the Turks were on the side of our enemies it was vital that we should retain the control of the Straits and be able to cover Constantinople to plant guns on Gallipoli which could destroy Turkish batteries on the Asiatic side. This was the permanent policy to be borne in mind.'

General Chetwode wisely did not intervene again, and accordingly Lord Curzon sent a telegram to Sir Horace Rumbold and the War Office sent one to General Harington, the intention presumably being that this time the recipients would each be able to understand the language of their respective professions. The contents were virtually the same and the shorter instructions to General Harington will suffice. 'As Cabinet do not intend to hold Chanak we do not propose to reinforce there; you can evacuate at your discretion, after informing Allied generals.' 'As we do not intend to defend the Ismid peninsula you may, at your discretion, also withdraw those troops.' The only discretion allowed to the General was that if French or Italian troops were sent to Chanak the evacuation there might be postponed. It was hoped that a declaration could be secured from the Allies that the Kemalists would not be allowed to move from Asia into Europe. If the Allies did not co-operate then Britain would 'act alone', and the navy would prevent any transports from crossing. It was suggested that the troops from Chanak should be transferred to Gallipoli.

By the time of the next Cabinet meeting there were no Greek troops left in Asia Minor save as unburied corpses or prisoners of war. The Greeks' entry into Smyrna three years ago had made no headlines. Their evacuation, the total defeat of their army, the burning of Smyrna, and criticism of Lloyd George, was now splashed across the top of every newspaper. By far the most sensational and critical, though nonetheless accurate for its anti-Lloyd George tone, was the *Daily Mail*.

Ward Price was still in Smyrna, moving about in his own special way. Having cadged a lift on the *Iron Duke*, he now managed a spectacular scoop by gaining an interview with Mustapha Kemal. It was published on September 15th. 'There is nothing to fight about any more,' Kemal told Ward Price. 'The frontiers we claim for Turkey exclude Syria and Mesopotamia but compose all the areas principally populated by the Turkish race. Our demands remain the same after our recent victory as they were before. We ask for Asia Minor, Thrace up to the River Maritza and Constantinople. We are prepared to give every security for the free passage of the Dardanelles, which we will undertake not to fortify. It is only right that the Powers should agree to our creating such defensive works on the Sea of Marmora as will protect Constantinople against a surprise attack.'

Ward Price asked Kemal what he would do if the Allies refused to hand over Constantinople. 'We must have our capital,' said the Ghazi, 'and I should in that case be obliged to march on Constantinople with my army, which would be an affair of only a few days. I much prefer to obtain possession by negotiation though, naturally, I cannot wait indefinitely.' Elsewhere in the *Daily Mail* it was reported that Stamboul, the Turkish quarter of Constantinople, occupied by the French, was scarlet with Turkish flags celebrating the great victory, and that in Athens the Cabinet had resigned. Rumours that King Constantine had left his capital were officially denied.

If Lloyd George did not accept some of the statements in the *Daily Mail* because of its well-known bias against his own government, any doubts he might have had about the total collapse of the Greeks must have been dispelled by a report in the *Sunday Express* two days later. It was written by Lord Beaverbrook, the newspaper's proprietor, who, as well as writing copy, was on Lloyd George's own instructions unofficially looking at the situation in the Near East and reporting back to the Prime Minister. Beaverbrook cabled his despatch from Athens, where he watched troops, and old men, women and children being disembarked. There were no civilian men between seventeen and forty-five years of age because they had been rounded up by the Turks and detained in Anatolia as Turkish subjects. 'The disembarkation was a painful sight. As each haggard infantry man limped on shore he was deprived of his rifle, but every second man had no rifle left.' Beaverbrook expected that the men would be formed up and marched off to barracks, but there were no officers and few N.C.O.s. 'The men drifted off into the town with two months' leave (in the middle of a war!) in a hopeless disorderly stream, with nothing to distinguish them but a dirty uniform and a transportation pass to some distant home.'

Athens was full of talk of revolution, but by whom and against whom was not clear. Beaverbrook continued: 'If there is a strong demand for the return of Veniselos I did not discover it, and the general opinion appeared to be that Athens would be a good place for the ex-Premier to avoid.' Constantine was blamed, Veniselos was blamed, though in whispers and behind hands. 'One liberty of speech the Athenians still retain—the right to damn all the Allies, collectively and separately. They blame the English and they curse the French. They consider that England persuaded them to enter into this adventure, which has turned out such a ghastly failure, and that Mr. Lloyd George has been either unable or unwilling to come to the rescue of his own.' Perhaps Lord Beaverbrook was being tactful. Others had heard the Greeks on both sides of the Aegean cursing and chanting 'Misfortune to George'. In Greece Beaverbrook also heard from the returning soldiers what Toynbee had first heard months ago in Anatolia, the excuse of foreign

183

help: 'that the Kemalist armies, even down to companies, are commanded by distinguished French officers, that the Turkish plan of campaign was prepared by French generals, and that nothing could stand against the technical skill learned on the Western Front against the Germans.'

Dispirited, disillusioned and resentful, the thousands of refugees crowded into Athens. Those who were lucky were accommodated in private houses, the theatres and the National Opera House, where each box was filled with a family while others slept in rows in the auditorium or on the stairways. The Queen of the Hellenes gave up a villa. The Old Palace in Constitution Square was turned into a relief headquarters, where bread was distributed daily and lists of arriving refugees posted so that families and relations could find each other. Food was short, and shops, open for only half the day, had to be guarded by police and troops. Thousands of refugees camped in home-made tents or shelters made out of oil-drums. The beach at the Piraeus, the port of Athens, was covered by an entire encampment of refugees living in the open air, dressed in clothes made of old sacks and wearing on their feet sandals cut out of car tyres. What remained of the Army of Anatolia was disbanded and allowed to drift home, spreading tales of death, incompetence and treachery throughout Greece.

All the grandiose plans hatched by the Allied statesmen in Paris less than three years ago had reduced themselves to this: thousands of bereaved, penniless refugees cast up in Greece and the Aegean islands, and thousands of dead, Greek and Turkish, left in Anatolia. The glittering concept of a new Greek Empire which Veniselos had foisted on a gullible Lloyd George and a naive Woodrow Wilson had resulted in the biggest disaster suffered by the Greeks in modern times.

The twin project of an Armenian state under American mandate and an international zone on both sides of the Straits, again under the control of the U.S.A., had faded almost as soon as Woodrow Wilson sailed home in July 1919. Perhaps if he had consulted the Republicans, perhaps if he had made a conciliatory gesture towards them, then

184

the Treaty of Versailles might have been ratified by the Senate. As it was, the mood of the United States, 'which had burnt its fingers with the Philippines', was firmly opposed to any agreement which smacked of external commitments. The President's direct appeal to the electorate with his tour of the Middle and Far West might have brought about a change of heart, but his collapse on September 25th and subsequent partial paralysis brought such schemes to an end. On March 4th, 1921, Woodrow Wilson, unnominated by the Democrats at the election, had just managed to drive in an open car to the Capitol with the Republican President-elect, Harding. He lingered on until February 3rd, 1924, curiously enough outliving Harding, who died of apoplexy in August 1923; but his dreams of U.S. participation in the League of Nations and the affairs of the Near East had all died in 1919.

In France, Clemenceau, who had backed Wilson and Lloyd George, had fallen from power soon after the Peace Conference, to be succeeded by men progressively more determined to avoid embroilment with Turkey. Poincaré, now in power as Prime Minister, had been President in 1914, and had, in addition to his predecessors' regard for French economic interests in Turkey, an innate distrust of the British, perhaps formed in those August days in 1914 when Britain had appeared reluctant to support France. Franklin-Bouillon for France had been followed to Ankara by Tuozzi on behalf of Italy. Orlando and his foreign minister, Sonnino, had been rejected by the electorate soon after the war, and with them had gone any possibility that Italy would pursue Imperial policies in Asia Minor or support those who did, especially if they were Greeks.

So the U.S. mandates had been a dead letter almost from the start. The areas of control and influence assigned to France and Italy by the Treaty of Sèvres had been abandoned virtually before that treaty was signed, and the Treaty itself had remained unratified by both French and Italian governments. All that had remained of the grand design for the partition of Turkey had been the Greek enclave round Smyrna and the Allied occupation of Constantinople and the Straits. Veniselos had followed Wilson, Clemenceau and Orlando. Now the Greek army, the last vestige of Lloyd George's dream of an Asia Minor populated by industrious, Christian, Latin peasants, reviving again the colonies of Greek and Roman civilisation, had been driven into the sea. All the calculations and assessments of race, origin, language, religion and birth-rate, which had persuaded him that Italians, Greeks and Armenians could and should establish themselves in Turkey, had been blown away by Kemal's guns, many of which had been made in French and Italian factories.

Now, in the autumn of 1922, there was a new victorious Turkish army and nation, led by a resolute skilful commander, who demanded not only the lands he had reconquered but Constantinople and Eastern Thrace as well. Standing in the line of his advance were small French and Italian garrisons, whose orders emanated from governments which, so far as the British were concerned, were worse than broken reeds. Alongside them were a few thousand British troops— the Indian battalions had been withdrawn earlier in the year—and in the Sea of Marmora the British fleet. In Britain there was an indifferent population, a hostile press, a critical Parliament, a divided Cabinet—and Lloyd George.

I I

'Work on the defences continued all day'
Colonel D. I. Shuttleworth

In the space of four years, from the surrender of the Turks on board the *Agamemnon* to the burning of Smyrna, a revolution had occurred in the military and political situation in the Near East. Perhaps the speed with which events had taken place, perhaps their dramatic nature, had left British statesmen gasping and bewildered.

In 1922 they seemed quite incapable of comprehending what had happened. Admittedly each change of fortune had been sudden and more catastrophic than the last. The Turkish revival, the death of King Alexander, the defeat of Veniselos, the return of Constantine and the Greek defeat had followed each other remorselessly and with a kind of insane logic. Still the final result, if not its magnitude, had been predicted by Henry Wilson and Churchill, among others. Lloyd George had not been without contrary advice and prophecies of disaster. He had, however, chosen to ignore any opinion but his own, and to interpret optimistically any event which seemed to run contrary to his own preconceived notions.

As late as 1938, when his *Truth about the Peace Treaties* was published, he resolutely refused to shoulder any of the blame for himself. If the Greeks had been slaughtered it was the fault of King Constantine and his incompetent generals. If the Armenians had had their hopes raised only to be dashed to the ground the fault was Lord Curzon's. If the government had failed to appreciate the new vigour of the Turks it was the fault of British Military Intelligence, 'never more unintelligent', which had not kept it properly informed. If Britain was left alone it was not the fault of the British Prime Minister but of the self-seeking French and Italians, who had shortsightedly deserted their ally. If the Turks were now triumphant some part of the blame attached to the pro-Turkish proclivities of British generals and Conservative Members of Parliament.

The arguments, punctuated as they are by Gladstonian diatribes against the Turks, only sound tolerable if declaimed aloud so as to take on some of the author's eloquence. Read silently they merely indicate disappointment and an almost hysterical desire for self-justification. When Lloyd George does descend to the precise he advances the causes which, in his view, had to be defended in 1922: the internationalisation of Constantinople, the Bosphorus and the Dardanelles, the expulsion of the Turks from Europe and the protection of the Christian minorities under Turkish rule.

In 1938 these were very old-fashioned concepts indeed; they were, in fact, almost equally old-fashioned in 1922. These were the problems which had pre-occupied British statesmen in the nineteenth century. Together they had constituted the Eastern Question at a time when the Ottoman Empire, for good or ill, had still been a reality. In 1922 there was no Ottoman Empire left; there was but a shadow of a Sultan and Caliph. All that remained was Turkey, as much a national state as the new Austria, Poland or Yugoslavia.

Still, four years after the war, Lloyd George's arguments had a certain force, the force of sentiment and eloquence if not of logic. During the war the Turks had massacred Armenians and ill treated Greeks, both of whom they had regarded as disloyal and potentially rebellious subjects.

Should they be allowed to resume their rule over those that had survived? Again during the war Turkish control of the Straits had imposed a stranglehold on Russia, Britain's ally. Might not a hostile Turkey, during another war, similarly impose its will on the countries bordering the Black Sea? In order to try and break that stranglehold the British, with the Australians, the New Zealanders, the Indians and the French, had died in their thousands on the beaches and rocky heights of Gallipoli. Now that Gallipoli was occupied should it be tamely handed back to the Turks and so, it was thought, those sacrifices be made vain and pointless?

These were the main arguments. There were other minor ones intended to back them up, ranging from a repetition of King Constantine's pro-German sentiments to the harsh treatment meted out by the Turks to British prisoners of war captured when General Townshend surrendered Kut. There were, however, pertinent questions which, if asked, destroyed most, if not all, of these arguments.

Was Britain likely to want to penetrate into the Black Sea? Why assume that Turkey would be hostile to Russia? Was international control workable or even possible? What specific British interest was threatened by Turkish control of the Straits? What could be done in practice for the Armenians or the Greeks in Turkey? Because their predecessors had fought and died there, were British troops to remain on the Gallipoli peninsula in perpetuity? Were the prejudices and hates of the wartime period to last for ever?

All Lloyd George's views in 1922 were hangovers from the Great War, as were his regrets over French and Italian 'desertion'. It was as if he could not realise that he was no longer the great wartime leader, controlling vast armies and fleets, surrounded by powerful allies, fawned upon by lesser powers anxious for some of the spoils of victory. The moment when, at 4 p.m. on June 29th, 1919, he had sat down in the Hall of Mirrors at Versailles and had begun his letter to George V: 'Mr. Lloyd George with his humble duty to Your Majesty has the honour to announce . . .' and had gone on to inform the King of the signing of the peace

189

treaty, that moment had been his greatest, and three years later he could not realise that the power and the glory of that day could not be recalled.

Nor could he realise that the Treaty of Versailles and the other treaties, including Sèvres, were not, in his own words, 'the greatest measure of national liberation of subject nations ever achieved by any war settlement on record' and therefore by implication perfect and inviolable. Now the incompetent Greeks, the brutal Turks and the cowardly French and Italians had spoilt it all. Undoubtedly in 1922 Lloyd George's pride was hurt. He was like an old man looking back with regret on the prowess and skill of his youth. He was still, however, Prime Minister of Great Britain.

It would be unfair to suggest that some at least of Lloyd George's sentiments were not shared by his colleagues. Lord Curzon also talked of 'the objects for which we had fought the war'. Other members of the Coalition government, itself a survival of the piping days of war, still hankered after the lost sense of national unity and purpose and were offended that a former enemy, and the most despised at that, should so soon snap his fingers in the face of his conqueror. There was, too, a curious atmosphere about the whole matter as if the days of 1914 had returned again. The same Turkish enemy; once again strategic consideration of the Gallipoli peninsula; again an assessment of morale in Constantinople. The Commander-in-Chief in the Mediterranean telegraphed to ask if the *Goeben*, now the *Sultan Yavuz Selim*, should be torpedoed, although that particular warship had been at anchor for years and 'had a hole in its side that you could drive a tramcar through'.

On one man particularly this revival of the war against Turkey, the talk of military and naval movements, the possibility of violent action exercised an irresistible fascination: Winston Churchill. The Secretary of State for the Colonies had been hitherto the Prime Minister's sternest and most perceptive critic in the Cabinet. He had warned him of the possible resurgence of the Turks; he had advised against too much reliance upon the Greeks; he had pointed

190

out the dangers of indecisive policies. Now when Mustapha Kemal presumed to dictate his peace terms to the British Empire Churchill's pride was aroused. 'Defeat is a nauseating draught; and that the victors in the greatest of all wars should gulp it down was not readily to be accepted', he wrote. 'So having done my utmost for three years to procure a friendly peace with Mustapha Kemal and the withdrawal of the Greeks from Asia Minor, and having consistently opposed my friend the Prime Minister upon this issue, I now found myself wholeheartedly upon his side in resisting the consequences of the policy which I had condemned.'

Friendship? Loyalty? Duty? Something of all three, plus a zest, of which Lloyd George had once complained, for military conflict, which made Churchill like the biblical war-horse which 'saith among the trumpets Ha Ha', and 'smelleth the battle afar off'.

The possibility of a fight had roused again the cavalry subaltern never far below the surface of the statesman. 'The government might break up and we might be relieved of our burden. The nation might not support us; they could find others to advise them. The press might howl, the Allies might bolt.' The truculence and pugnaciousness that a later generation was to know well were at once displayed. Lloyd George had found an ally.

In Churchill's wake there followed, as was to be expected, Lord Birkenhead, and with less enthusiasm Lord Balfour, Austen Chamberlain and Laming Worthington-Evans. The latter, who was Secretary of State for War, was soon to find himself a very busy man, for the military preparations had begun. The evacuation of the Greek Southern Army through Smyrna and Chesme, and the Northern Army by way of Brusa, had left the Allied forces occupying the so-called Neutral Zone on the Asiatic shore of the Straits, directly exposed to the Turkish armies.

The purpose of the Neutral Zone was to protect both shores of the Dardanelles, the Sea of Marmora and the Bosphorus. The drawing of the boundaries had been carried out in a sweeping way with little regard to possible defensive strategy or even the configuration of the terrain. It was as if a ruler had been placed on the map, its centre line running diagonally through the two exits of the Sea of Marmora, and the zones created where the ruler overlapped the European and Asiatic shores. Consequently in Anatolia there were two zones linked by a narrow strip of coastline: opposite the Gallipoli peninsula the southern zone, comprising the villayet of Chanak and the town of the same name, and opposite Constantinople the area of the Ismid peninsula.

The strategic considerations in respect of these areas were an interesting variation on those which had been in the minds of statesmen, generals and admirals in 1917, when the Allies had tried to wrest control from the occupying Turks. Now the situation was reversed. The British fleet was in the Sea of Marmora, and as there was no likelihood that it would be required to sail through the Bosphorus to the Black Sea, the important exit to the Sea of Marmora was the Dardanelles. Constantinople could in any event be dominated from the Sea of Marmora. The Turkish army was on the Asiatic shore and would have to be transported by water if it was to take either Gallipoli or Constantinople, and of the two the Gallipoli peninsula was held to be the more important. This for two reasons: the peninsula controlled the Dardanelles, and Constantinople was already promised at some future date to the Turks. Therefore in London the priorities for defence were judged to be Gallipoli, Constantinople, Chanak and the Ismid peninsula; that is, the Ismid peninsula could be evacuated first, then Chanak, and so on in reverse order. In fact a strict domino theory of withdrawal was almost impossible in practice, and it was this divergence between practice and theory which occasioned Harington's and Rumbold's disagreement with the Cabinet.

Both the Dardanelles and the Bosphorus could be spanned by gunfire from either shore, so that no position could be considered in isolation from its fellow. If the Gallipoli peninsula were to be defended *and* the Dardanelles dominated then Chanak had to be defended as well. The lesson of the Gallipoli campaign was that there had to be both military and naval predominance to be effective, and that a fleet entering, or of course leaving, the Sea of Marmora was very much at the mercy of whomsoever held either shore. The Allied fleet in position was very powerful indeed, but naval guns were limited in their effect when used against shore targets, and the ships that carried them were very vulnerable either to mines or shore batteries. In a sense, therefore, the naval possession of the Sea of Marmora was less of an advantage than it appeared at first sight. The Turks, then, in 1922, if they were allowed by Allied evacuation to occupy the whole of the Asiatic shore, would be in a considerably stronger position than the Allies in 1917, when they had tried to breach the Dardanelles while an enemy held both Asiatic and European shores.

It was, therefore, for these reasons that within days of the Greek evacuation Harington, backed up by Admiral Brock, determined that Chanak should be held against the Turks if necessary. Of course, Harington's view, though agreed to by Rumbold, the High Commissioner, was in no sense a political decision. The General, perhaps less than anyone else concerned, wished to see war break out between Britain and the Turks. If, however, his political masters decided that a course was to be followed other than that of complete evacuation, then militarily it was his duty to ensure that that course, if possible, should be successful. The evacuation of the Asiatic shore and then defiance from the European shore, even with the help of the Navy, was in his view if not an impossibility, certainly a very dangerous course indeed, and one which might well end in disaster or humiliation. Better therefore to stick to what remained of the letter of the law and hold as much of the neutral zone as was feasible, to which technically both the French and Italians were also committed, and at the same time retain in one's own hands some advantage and flexibility, useful whether the outcome was war or negotiation.

In the days after September 9th, as the Turkish army flowed eastwards in the wake of the departing Greeks, the risk of war between British and Turks suddenly became a possibility.

From the return of Constantine to the Greek throne and

the consequent suspension of official relations between the British government and the King of the Hellenes, the position of the British army in Anatolia vis-à-vis the Greeks had been a curious one. Originally when General Harington had arrived in Constantinople he had commanded not only British, French and Italian troops but Greek as well. A division commanded by General Gargalides stationed in the Ismid peninsula and a detached regiment at Beicos obeyed his orders. When the Greeks ceased to be allies these troops were taken from Harington's control, and at almost the same time the French and Italian governments indicated that their troops were not to be employed in Asia under the British Commander-in-Chief. Henceforth the British became merely distant observers of the battles to the eastwards between Greeks and Turks for dominance in Anatolia.

Relations between the armies of the two ex-allies remained cordial, for in a sense they still opposed the same enemy, although the Greek role was active and that of the British passive. British forces, though small, still held Constantinople and on the Asiatic shore occupied positions in the rear of the Greek front line. Greek warships were still allowed in the Sea of Marmora and the Bosphorus, and British warships, in turn, used Smyrna as a friendly port. From their vantage point in Anatolia, while they occupied themselves with punitive expeditions against the bands of Turkish irregulars which roamed between the Greek back areas and their own positions, the British could observe the Greek army closely as it prepared to advance on Ankara.

General Harington had already submitted an official report to the Prime Minister on the state of the Greek army, but it had been too pessimistic for Lloyd George's taste. Another general officer must therefore be sent out to have a closer look and report over Harington's head. The War Office, no more enamoured of this proposal than was Harington, effected a compromise. Major-General T. O. Marden, the commander of the British troops under the Commander-in-Chief, was ordered in June 1921 to provide this second opinion. On the 19th he left for Smyrna by destroyer with Major T. G. G. Heywood, who had been

Chief Intelligence Officer with the Salonika army, and Major M. A. B. Johnston, the British Military Attaché. The Greeks offered no objection to this rather curious mission on behalf of a nation with which they were no longer in diplomatic communication.

General Papoulas, the then Commander-in-Chief, welcomed General Marden and gave him every facility, including a motor car and, as interpreter, a Greek corporal who had left Eton the year before. Marden worked hard at his mission and inspected virtually the whole of the Greek army. The General Staff talked frankly to him of their plans for an offensive, plans which were not yet known to their battalion commanders. At one stage an official invitation was extended to Marden and Harington to have dinner with the Greek army in Ankara. At every unit he visited there were playings of the British national anthem, cheers for Great Britain and often for Lloyd George as well. Every infantry company had its large photograph of King Constantine placed in a prominent position encircled with laurel leaves, and 'all seemed happy and extremely confident'.

It was Marden's job, however, to look below the surface at essentials, and by these he was less impressed. The Greek private soldier was hardy and could march all day on the simplest and most meagre rations, but his uniform and equipment were filthy, such as 'to make a British non-commissioned officer weep'. Much, of course, has to be allowed for Marden's British prejudice in favour of shininess for all things military from boots to mess cans, but there were other more disturbing features about the Greek army than its lack of 'bull'. So far as temperament went the Greeks were in complete contrast to the Turks; in a heady advance they would fight gallantly but they had a dislike of slogging defensive actions. Curiously this was a view with which Lloyd George, much later, was to agree, comparing the Greeks in this respect to the French. Again, allowances have to be made for the temperament of the observer. General Marden found the Greeks excitable and liable to let off ammunition at any target, good or bad. But then, perhaps, some of

Kemal's irregulars, if he had had an opportunity of inspecting them, would not have possessed the fire discipline of, say, the Grenadier Guards.

The most serious defect of the Greeks lay in the quality of their officers. Regimental officers seemed to take little interest in their men. No Greek officer would, like his British equivalent, inspect his men's feet after a long march before he removed one single article of his own equipment. Marden's impression was that the relationship between officers and men, and indeed officers with each other, 'was not sufficiently strong to repair a disaster'. Furthermore, above the regimental level the junior staff officers were of poor quality, and 'the technical services for carrying out a complicated plan [were] distinctly weak'. Of the commanders who had been trained properly some had been to the French, some to the German Staff Colleges, so that their techniques were not the same and their tactical methods were not dovetailed as in a nationally trained officer corps. Finally, and most damning of all, however trained, 'the senior officers were all politicians'.

So General Marden submitted his report, which did not differ in essentials from that of Harington; in 1921 it appeared 'with luck the Greeks would succeed'. Lloyd George, the recipient of the report, of course hoped so and convinced himself that the Greeks would have that luck, but it was not to be. A little more than a year later Marden found himself commanding the British outposts against which the backwash of the defeated Greek army had surged and which were now menaced by the Turks, following in hot pursuit of their beaten and totally demoralised foe.

It was not, of course, the first crisis to face the General. Since the date of Marden's report there had been a number of strictly military problems, each one of which had provoked action by the Allies. The crises themselves had been of differing degrees of seriousness. Frequently there had been concern about the Turkish population in Constantinople. As the fluctuations in the fortunes of Mustapha Kemal had affected his compatriots, or as they had been affected by the political actions of the Allies, the military commanders had

196

thought it necessary to take active steps to be ready to put down an internal revolution. Fortunately they never had to go beyond posting guards at strategic points and staging demonstration marches through the city. The latter, disconcertingly, the Turks had seemed to find thoroughly enjoyable, frequently clapping the regimental bands.

Then, at one time, Wrangel's refugee Russians had provoked a crisis. Of the total number of nearly 120,000, 30,000 had been soldiers possessing arms and ammunition. Many of these armed men who did not succeed in gaining employment from the Allies were herded off, still under some form of military discipline, to a vast camp on the Gallipoli peninsula. There they had been supervised by the French, who eventually had to provide guards and sentries to keep them in order. Inevitably this situation had led to all kinds of friction, and more than once both British and French commanders had been prepared to prevent by force a Russian attack on Constantinople. Finally, in this one respect, the emergence of Kemal and the nationalist movement in Turkey had done the Allies a good turn. Kemalist propaganda sheets appeared on walls in Constantinople threatening death or expulsion for the 'Whites', and as the Turkish army advanced westwards the Russians began to think in terms of defending themselves and Constantinople against Turkish invaders.

On May 13th, 1921, when Kemal's army was fully occupied in Anatolia, the Allies had established their neutral zones to protect the Straits, and the lines of demarcation had been drawn along the Asiatic shore of the Dardanelles. Paradoxically the first testing of these quite arbitrary and wrongly named areas of occupation, which had been agreed with the Greeks and the Sultan's government, had come a little more than a year later and from the west, when the Greeks, in their final desperate gesture, had threatened the Chataldja lines and Constantinople. On that occasion, perhaps because there was no time for reflection, the news had been announced at an inter-Allied horse show. There had been a conference of senior officers on the spot and the British, French and Italians had managed to preserve a united front. Now, in the autumn of 1922, co-operation seemed far less likely. The situation was much more serious and it would have to be solved one way or the other by the British.

At the beginning of September Lloyd George was still optimistic about the powers of resistance of the Greek army. At least in the presence of his Cabinet colleagues he appeared to believe the Greeks when they said they would make a last stand at Smyrna. The town and its surrounding area, the original Allied concession to the Greeks, had recently been declared an autonomous province by Stergiades, the High Commissioner. This action, presumably with the connivance of the government in Athens, was intended to show that at this late hour the Greeks demanded no more of Asia Minor than was their right under the peace treaties. Perhaps it was also intended to provoke the Allies into defence of their given word. If such was the intention, as a diplomatic manœuvre it was a dismal failure; the French and the Italians were almost as indifferent as the Turks, and the British Cabinet took the declaration to mean that the Greeks would and could defend Smyrna.

The soldiers on the spot were far less sanguine than the politicians at home and, as they heard of the speed and manner of the Greek retreat, were certainly not able to share the Prime Minister's well-preserved optimism. Accordingly, on September 9th, the day that the first elements of the Turkish advance-guard entered Smyrna, Colonel D. I. Shuttleworth received his orders from General Harington to take command at Chanak and to put it into a state to repel attack. He left Constantinople on the 10th with his staff captain and arrived at Chanak on the morning of the 11th.

His orders were to prevent the Turks from crossing the neutral boundary. Chanak was to be defended against all attack until further orders were given. At the same time, as background to his written orders, Colonel Shuttleworth was informed orally that a prolonged defence of Chanak was not contemplated at the moment and that he might have to consider eventually a withdrawal under fire to

198

Gallipoli. As an extra task he was also to look into another question, that of the Sanjak of Chanak, the area round the town which extended outside the military boundary. It was now denuded of Greek troops but still occupied by a battalion of Turkish gendarmerie, officered by the British but owing allegiance to the Sultan.

The forces Shuttleworth found at his disposal at Chanak to accomplish these objects were hardly excessive for the purpose. To oppose a Turkish army which, it was presumed, would soon drive northwards from Smyrna, Colonel Shuttleworth had under his command one squadron of the 3rd Hussars, 92nd Battery, Royal Field Artillery, armed with eighteen-pounders, a section of Royal Engineers, and one infantry battalion, the 1st Loyal Regiment, plus the Turkish gendarmerie battalion which he was told beforehand he was in no circumstances to employ against their compatriots in Kemal's army. On arrival Shuttleworth found that outside the neutral area in the Sanjak of Chanak there was considerable disorder. Turkish irregulars, often a polite term to describe mere brigands, were already pillaging the dwellings of Greeks and Armenians and ill treating the civilian refugees left behind by the Greek army. The Mutessarif of Chanak (a combination of English mayor and French prefect) had taken over the Sanjak in the name of the Sultan, relying on the Turkish gendarmes, but with little effect. It was soon obvious that many of the Turks were now pro-Kemal and it was extremely doubtful if they would obey their British supervising officers. Shuttleworth therefore decided that he could not control the whole neutral zone, but must concentrate on the purely military problem, for which he could only rely on his handful of British troops.

On September 11th Shuttleworth carried out a reconnaissance of the ground he had to defend with the company commanders of the Loyal Regiment, the commanding officer being down with fever. The position was very far from ideal. The boundary of the actual neutral zone ran from Karabiga on the southern coast of the Sea of Marmora southwards through Biga and Bayramic down to the Aegean coast, opposite the island of Lesbos. To defend this line would have meant manning a front of something like eighty miles and was an obvious impossibility. Shuttleworth decided to defend the coast of the Dardanelles from Chanak to Nagara Point. Both places were vital. Nagara Point was the cable end to Europe and it was also important that this section of the Dardanelles, where it took a sharp right-hand, almost right-angled, bend opposite Kilia, should be held from both shores. Chanak itself, a small town of some 8,000 Turkish inhabitants, controlled the Narrows, as its name implied the narrowest section of the Dardanelles, the distance from Chanak to Kilid Bahr on the opposite shore being less than a mile, at one point not more than 1,500 yards. This vital neck of waterway had been heavily fortified by the Turks in the late war. As Shuttleworth doubtless recalled, it was here, on March 18th, 1915, when the Allied fleet had made the first move in the Gallipoli campaign, that the Turks had placed their heaviest concentration of shore batteries.

The distance, however, from Chanak to Nagara Point was six miles, and at the moment even that as a defended front was impossible with the forces on the spot. Shuttleworth therefore decided to prepare a defensive ring around Chanak itself, with Nagara Point, where there was an old Turkish fort, as a detached position. As Nagara and Chanak were connected by a metalled road running along the coast and protected and concealed by overhanging cliffs; the two positions, unless completely overrun, were not cut off from each other. This arrangement was not without its dangers, but it did mean that the British would now only have to defend two positions: Chanak, with a frontage of 5,500 yards, and Nagara Point, with a frontage of 1,500 yards. Shuttleworth had been promised reinforcements but had been given no date for their arrival, and because he had no idea of the probable movements of the Turks he had to be ready to fight with his tiny force the next day if necessary. What that next day would bring Shuttleworth had no means of telling.

Outside Chanak the rest of the world was still digesting the news from Smyrna. The greater part of the British

Mediterranean fleet was concentrated there, concerning itself with the saving of as many refugees as possible. What the movements were of Turkish troops beyond Smyrna was not known. There were no aircraft available to carry out reconnaissance, and the Greek spies, who until the defeat of their army had kept the British informed of the movements of irregulars outside the neutral zone, had now all disappeared. At this moment the eyes and ears of the commander at Chanak were, just as for any nineteenth-century commander, his cavalry patrols. So Shuttleworth's information was limited to the powers of observation and the speed of the hundred men and horses of his squadron of 3rd Hussars, which, divided into troops, roamed the rough, hilly country to the east.

Having cut his commitments to the bone Shuttleworth's problems were far from over, for he then had to consider his method of defence for his two positions. Both Chanak and Nagara presented considerable difficulties. Chanak itself was a flat brick-and-mud town scarcely a mile square, situated on the northern bank of the estuary of the small River Koja, which runs with several meanderings almost due east and west. The central part of the town was divided into Turkish, Armenian, Jewish and Greek quarters, the Turkish being to the west of the town and the others stretching in that order to the east. It was a small compact town, the only extension being along the coast to the north for a little over a mile to the old Military Hospital, which, standing on a slight hill, provided an observation post. The town itself was militarily indefensible, therefore a defence line of trenches and wire had to be constructed outside the town limits and to the east. Here lay the essential difficulty, for Chanak is overlooked at a distance of four miles by a ridge of hills, Asmali Tepe, Bairah Tepe and Damyeri Tepe, rising to a maximum height of 1,000 feet. The ridge almost encircles the town with a chain of hills, save to the north and south, where the high ground slopes down to the coast. At the centre, the hills are pierced by the valley of the Koja, at this point a shallow stream with a bed approximately fifty yards wide. Obviously for an attacking enemy the ridge provided excellent means of observation of the whole of the Chanak defence works, and, of course, for bombardment by artillery.

As some compensation, however, the ground was rough, the hills steeply sloped and, apart from a few crude tracks, the ridge offered considerable obstacles to the movement of anything save infantrymen on their feet. All told, Shuttleworth, perhaps a little optimistically, thought that the hills afforded as many disadvantages to potential attackers as problems for the defenders. If the Turks possessed a great deal of artillery and ammunition, then in time, with the advantage of direct observation, they might be able to swamp the defences of Chanak. Shuttleworth therefore made his decision for the siting of his own lines on the basis of a compromise. Any defence of Chanak had to be a defence in depth, and to achieve this he would have to have reinforcements by way of more troops on the ground and, as a second best, gun support from the Navy. At the same time he had to bear in mind his primary purpose: to prevent the Turks reaching the Narrows with artillery. The nearer to the hills the more likely he was to prevent the Turks from closing the Narrows, but the nearer he went, the more he exposed his own troops to machine-gun and possibly artillery fire.

Whichever way the problem was approached risks had to be taken, and the risk he took was of planning a defence line which could only be reasonably secure when he was provided with more troops. Accordingly his men were set to the task of digging trenches about two miles out from Chanak which would afford them and the hoped for reinforcements a good field of fire. The trenches, when protected by barbed wire, would also provide some protection against an infantry attack by the Turks. The work on these trenches began on September 12th, every available man being used for the task. The only exceptions were the squadron of Hussars patrolling to the south (the direction from whence the Turkish advance was expected, Smyrna being 140 miles away) and a platoon of the Loyal Regiment, uneasily mounted on mules, which watched to the north. On the same night a report was received from one of the British officers of gendarmerie at Ezine, about twenty miles from Chanak on the old neutral line, that a division of Turkish cavalry was six hours' march away from him, and that two more Turkish divisions had reached Edremit, a further forty miles distant to the south-east.

At six o'clock on the morning of the 13th, Major Harenc, the senior British officer of the gendarmerie, who knew the area well and spoke Turkish, was sent off in a motor car to Ezine to investigate and report. At the same time Colonel Shuttleworth tried to persuade the Turkish authorities outside his area to allow Greek and Armenian Christians to evacuate their homes. The gendarmerie battalion was now obviously useless and not to be relied upon, as pro-Kemal sympathies were on the increase. The authorities were obstinate or indifferent. Shuttleworth, meeting a blank wall of obstinate non-co-operation, eventually gave up; he did his best to warn the Greeks and Armenians and then withdrew his remaining British officers behind his rudimentary defences.

His next task was to evacuate civilians from the town of Chanak itself. Using his old friend, the Mutessarif, he met here with more success. The elders of each community, Christian and Moslem, were approached and began the task of persuading the population that they must be prepared to leave. Shuttleworth signalled Constantinople for assistance from the Royal Navy to help with the evacuation if necessary, although a large number of civilians, seeing the obvious preparations for war, began to leave the town on foot or by their own primitive transport.

On the evening of September 12th Chanak had at last received some measure of reinforcement in the very tangible shape of the battleship *Ajax*, which had sailed north from Smyrna and now anchored in the Narrows. Captain Trewby of the *Ajax* was immediately in consultation with the artillery officers at Chanak, preparing plans for a naval barrage and the use of the battleship's powerful searchlights. The next morning parties of sailors and marines landed to assist the soldiers in the task of digging trenches and preparing barbed-wire entanglements. The weather was hot, the work tiring and boring, and the company of H.M.S. *Ajax*, which had been met on landing by Colonel Shuttleworth and piles of spades and shovels, was not without its loud comments on the strange habits of 'Pongoes'.

Despite the jaundiced view of the blue-jackets, the work of entrenching was more important than the presence of the *Ajax* as a floating gun platform. The large and impressive ship's armament was capable of flinging high velocity, armour-piercing shells a distance of over twelve miles on a flat trajectory, but the Turks, when they arrived at Chanak, would be but four miles away and protected by the rough and difficult ground. In addition, though the Navy was loath to admit it, bombardment by ships' guns designed to fire over a flat surface, the sea, at other warships, had been curiously ineffective against forces and emplacements on land.

There were other arrivals at Chanak besides the *Ajax*. On the morning of the 13th Colonel Shuttleworth was pleased to welcome another squadron of the 3rd Hussars, another battery of field artillery and, somewhat to his surprise, out of the blue a seventy-man detachment of Italian infantry, which appeared to be quite happy and willing to join in the digging operations. The horses and guns of the British detachment gave considerable difficulty on landing, as the piers at Chanak harbour, through years of neglect, were rotten and unreliable. However, by the morning of September 14th, all British troops were on shore, and the Chanak commander was in some sort of state to receive a more illustrious visitor.

Purely by chance Field Marshal Lord Plumer, the Governor of Malta, was on his way to visit Harington, his old Chief of Staff, and sniffing excitement and action had decided to call at Chanak on the way. Shuttleworth reported the situation to Lord Plumer, who inspected the defences, sent a short signal to Harington at Constantinople 'All well here', and departed, doubtless with food for thought. While the Field Marshal was present the Mutessarif reported that he had been on the telephone to the Turkish commander at Edremit and had told him that the Allies were prepared to use force to defend the principle of neutrality. Major Harenc returned to report Turkish irregulars at Ezine. In the afternoon Commodore Domville arrived by seaplane from Smyrna to announce that the Turks intended to advance on the Straits and Constantinople by winter.

Colonel Shuttleworth wrote his usual note in his report for that day: 'Work on the defences continued all day'.

*'A stand for something which was not of
any great value'*
Austen Chamberlain

By September 14th Chanak was protected by a line of
three trenches and British flags were placed along the
boundaries. The Italian contingent wished to put up their
own flag but found that unfortunately any flags they
possessed had been left in Constantinople. The Italian
commander promised to obtain some without delay.
General Harington informed Colonel Shuttleworth that as
bold a front as possible had to be put up in the face of a sudden advance by the Turks. In the event, however, of a serious
prolonged attack, Shuttleworth was to withdraw his force
to Gallipoli. With typical generosity Harington said, what he
was to repeat often in the next few weeks, that whatever
course his subordinates decided on he would accept full
responsibility.

In Constantinople Harington's own superior and old
friend, Lord Plumer, had taken on responsibilities of his
own. On arrival there, after a few words with the Commander-
in-Chief, the Field Marshal sent two telegrams, one to

Lloyd George, the other to the War Office, saying in both cases that he entirely approved of Harington's actions and dispositions. At the same time he ordered the despatch of the 2nd Royal Sussex Regiment and the 1st Gordon Highlanders from Malta to Chanak. It was a somewhat old-fashoned interpretation of his powers as Governor of Malta, but such was Plumer's reputation that he got away with it. A day later the *Iron Duke*, Admiral Brock's flagship, arrived off Chanak from Smyrna. The Admiral, also on his own responsibility, promised Shuttleworth a minimum of one battleship, two light cruisers and five destroyers to help with the defence of the town. If the politicians wanted a battle neither Plumer nor Brock were prepared to see it lost by half-hearted measures. If Lloyd George was determined to defy Kemal then it would not be done by words alone.

What exactly the Turks were doing still remained something of a mystery. Patrols of the 3rd Hussars reported that along the neutral line telegraph and telephone lines to Chanak had been cut, and that cavalry had been seen in strength at Guenen, east of Biga. On the other hand a new addition to Shuttleworth's forces, five elderly Short seaplanes supplied by the carrier H.M.S. *Pegasus*, reported no movement on the roads leading to Chanak. These seaplanes, slow, vulnerable and wildly inappropriate for reconnaissance work over rough hilly country, took great risks coming down to tree-top height to look at Anatolian roads and villages but could still find no sign of the enemy. Yet the day after the pilots and observers had rendered their reports the 3rd Hussars, on the ground, confirmed Turkish occupation of Ezine and Biga. A report was received from a friendly Turk that at Ezine preparations were being made to bake 17,500 loaves of bread in expectation of the troops to come. A British flag from the neutral line was delivered at Saracheli by a solitary Turkish officer. The Mutessarif was given the unenviable task of replacing it. The 3rd Hussars occupied Sarracheli but found no sign of Turkish troops. To Shuttleworth it was a puzzling situation, but he came to the conclusion that the Turks must be moving by night and hiding by day. He could only hazard guesses as to what these tactics presaged or their eventual attitude when they finally came into contact with Allied troops.

On September 16th there was another addition to the garrison. The band of the Loyal Regiment was paraded with a guard of honour to welcome the arrival of the French contribution to Allied solidarity. It was a curious ceremony, for this little bit of pageantry could scarcely disguise the fact that the regimental band and guard of the British regiment was almost equal in numbers to the whole French contingent, a weak company of the 66th Regiment and twenty-four colourful members of the 1st Moroccan Spahis. Shuttleworth showed the French officers round the defences. There were now three Allied flags flying at Chanak to impress the Turks, the Italians having repaired their previous omission and the French having come prepared, at least, in this respect.

A plan was devised to blow up the road from Ezine if necessary, engineers in Ford vans being ready to drive to two selected points to explode charges. There was still, with regard to this and other preparations, an inevitable air of amateur improvisation at Chanak, imposed by the chronic shortage of both front line and technical troops. The piers on both sides of the Narrows were only put into working order by the efforts of Lieutenant-Colonel Hughes of the Australian army and a party of Australian and New Zealand N.C.O.s, who were present by chance on Gallipoli as part of the Imperial War Graves Commission, concerned with the battles of five years ago. This resourceful officer, looking well ahead, also began to prepare a landing strip for aircraft on Gallipoli and to pipe a fresh water supply to Kilia on the European shore to be used as a reserve for Chanak. These arrangements were vitally necessary, as Chanak depended for everything save milk, eggs and bread upon supplies from Constantinople. To avoid the possibility of being starved out Colonel Shuttleworth had to put in hand the construction of a bakery, and arrangements for a supply of fresh meat. As the numbers of the garrison increased, medical and sanitary services had also to be provided.

Day by day the build up at Chanak increased, but it

was largely a matter of services and facilities; the actual number of fighting troops was still pathetically small. On September 17th another battleship appeared in the Narrows, H.M.S. *Marlborough,* which three years before had rescued from the Crimea the Dowager Empress Maria Fedorovna, widow of Alexander III and mother of Nicholas II, and the Grand Duke Nicholas, the former Commander-in-Chief of the armies of the last Tsar. Demonstrating again the Navy's capability for any task, this time the *Marlborough* landed naval machine-gun and Lewis-gun teams, which were swiftly integrated with the infantry, and also began unloading twelve-pounder guns to supplement the field-artillery battery. Rear-Admiral Kelly, who commanded the 4th Battle Squadron, promised another battleship for Kum Kale and one for Gallipoli to provide some of the artillery support the army so conspicuously lacked. The Admiral also informed Shuttleworth that he had plans to set up naval six-inch guns on shore if necessary. Such aid and assistance was, of course, welcome, but there was a grave danger that the ubiquity and apparent omnipotence of the Navy might blind the eyes of the government to the fact that there was still only one battalion of infantry occupying the trenches outside Chanak. If the Turks did attack the only function of all these splendid battleships might be to facilitate the withdrawal of a few hundred soldiers.

On September 15th, while Smyrna still smouldered and while at Chanak soldiers, sailors and marines dug trenches, filled sandbags and wrestled with reels of barbed wire, the Cabinet met in Downing Street at 4 p.m. Sir Laming Worthington-Evans, the Secretary of State for War, not perhaps before it was time, produced a map showing the strength and disposition of the Allied forces on both sides of the Straits.

Excluding the units at Chanak the total British forces in the area, including Constantinople, were five infantry battalions, the remaining squadron and headquarters of the 3rd Hussars, two companies of engineers, three batteries of field guns, an armoured train and five naval seaplanes, plus a number of scratch gun sections made up by the Royal

Navy. The French had six infantry battalions, some armoured cars and light tanks, three squadrons of cavalry, three batteries of artillery and twelve aeroplanes. The Italians had one infantry battalion in Constantinople and the cadre of a locally raised force of Turks officered by Italians. On the European side of the Straits in Thrace there was now an irregular but armed and equipped force of 6,000 Turks. South of the Ismid peninsula there were calculated to be about 20,000 Turkish regulars. Around Chanak the size of the Turkish forces was estimated to be 5,000 men, with 40,000 more in the Smyrna area. The total Allied forces amounted to 7,600 men, twenty-eight guns, twelve tanks and armoured cars, twelve aeroplanes and five seaplanes.

The Cabinet, not surprisingly, came to the conclusion that this force was inadequate to hold its present positions. General Harington had made it plain that he could not hold Constantinople for long unless he could also hold the opposite shore, on the Asiatic side of the Bosphorus, at Scutari, the site of Florence Nightingale's famous hospital in the Crimean War. The Cabinet digested the fact that the Bosphorus varied in width from 600 to 1,200 yards, and the First Lord of the Admiralty explained the difficulty of stopping small craft carrying troops from crossing, unless both sides were held by the Allies. The Cabinet then gave itself up to Lord Curzon, who embarked upon a description of the general situation. As usual he did not stint himself for words; his explanation was lengthy and detailed. He began with the evacuation of the Greeks and he told his colleagues of the meeting between Sir Harry Lamb and Mustapha Kemal in Smyrna. He then produced some encouraging news: it seemed likely that a conference could be held between the Allies and the Greeks and Turks. The Italians favoured Venice as the venue; Lord Curzon did not. He preferred the idea of Paris, providing that some agreement could be reached beforehand with the French. He was prepared to visit Poincaré to bring this about. Lord Hardinge, the Ambassador in Paris, Curzon conceded, possessed great authority. (Like Curzon he too had been Viceroy of India, and in fact the two men detested each other.) Nevertheless the issue was surely of sufficient importance to justify a personal visit by the Foreign Secretary. The Cabinet agreed.

The idea of yet another international conference also appeared attractive to a majority of the Cabinet, and a conference which would not only include the two belligerents and the Allies but as many other interested parties as could be persuaded to attend. So Lord Curzon was given the task of persuading Poincaré, who had only recently snubbed Lloyd George at Boulogne by taking his lunch at the Prefecture while the British Prime Minister had to fend for himself in the station buffet, to return to the Allied fold. While in Paris Lord Curzon could try to bring in the Serbs,[1] as the King of the Serbs, Croats and Slovenes and his prime minister were there at the moment, and perhaps extend invitations to the Romanians and the Bulgarians as well.

Winston Churchill was the first to indicate any desire to break away from conjecture upon these high diplomatic possibilities and return to the military situation in the Straits. He was 'wholly opposed to any attempt to carry out a bluff without force'. General Harington had indicated that if the positions had to be defended both sides of the Straits should be held. Then, in Churchill's view, so be it, and reinforcements would have to be sent out. As regards the view of the public, Churchill, still a Liberal, thought 'Liberal opinion would be a great deal influenced by the recent atrocities and Conservative opinion would not be willing to see the British flag trampled on'. Lord Curzon had mentioned the League of Nations. Churchill thought that if other interested powers such as Greece, Serbia and Romania were to be invited to a conference, then they should be asked to send a military contingent. 'This would confront the Turkish forces with six flags instead of three flags

[1] After 1918 Serbia, with Montenegro, Croatia, Slovenia, Bosnia-Herzegovina and part of Macedonia, became 'the Kingdom of the Serbs, Croats and Slovenes' and later Yugoslavia. In the early 20's both 'Serbia' and 'Yugoslavia' were, however, used indiscriminately by foreigners to describe the new state.

which was in itself something of a League of Nations.'
Finally the Secretary of State for the Colonies wondered if
the Empire might not be prepared to put up a force to
defend Gallipoli.

Austen Chamberlain, the Lord Privy Seal, was much
more cautious. He was not a brilliant man but steady and
sensible. Reasonably enough he wondered how Turkey was
to be dominated from the Straits and Constantinople. That
had been the argument at the time of the Dardanelles
expedition. Now the British held the positions they had fought
for then, but Turkey was not subdued. Did Churchill
contemplate holding the Straits permanently? Apparently
not. Then, said Chamberlain, he did not want the British
representative at the conference 'to make a stand for
something which was not of any great value'. At this point
the Prime Minister decided to state his views. There was
already something like a division in the Cabinet. Churchill
was for making a stand; Chamberlain was doubtful. The
two service Ministers, Lord Lee at the Admiralty and
Worthington-Evans at the War Office, tended to be more
concerned with departmental details than the rights and
wrongs of policy. Lord Curzon put his trust in a number of
diplomatic moves to be carried out by himself. Lloyd
George was quite simple in his determination not to 'run
away before Mustapha Kemal'. No questions of the British
position at Mosul or in Iraq were going to deflect him from
Britain's 'supreme interest in the freedom of the Straits'.
He was in favour therefore of the despatch of reinforcements.
Whether a division was necessary to defend Constantinople
would have to be discussed, but whatever the details the
point was that the British must be in sufficient strength.
He was, however, 'entirely opposed to approaching the
French government as a suppliant for assistance'. What
about Romania and Serbia? He had read in the *Morning
Post* that the Serbians did not want the Turks back. The
same applied to Romania. Both governments should be
approached immediately and asked not merely for a brigade,
but for whatever force they would be prepared to send.

Lord Curzon was somewhat sceptical about so much

help, but Lloyd George was not to be deflected and wondered also what the Greeks could do. 'They must have several divisions available,' he said. 'Combining the Greek, Romanian, Serbian and British forces a considerable army would be available. If Mustapha Kemal crossed the Straits with 60,000 rifles then he would be met by 60,000 plus the British fleet. The time had come,' thought Lloyd George, 'to do something concrete.'

If the combination he suggested could be formed, then the British representatives at a conference would not have 'to throw themselves at the feet of M. Poincaré'. Lord Curzon was still doubtful and warned against 'building too enthusiastically on these proposals', but Lloyd George was now constructing castles in the air at great speed, from the roof downwards. 'The Czechoslovaks would be bound to stand in with Romania and Yugoslavia and the French were influenced by the Czechs.' The mood became catching; Churchill wanted the Bulgarians in too. Soon in everyone's mind, save Curzon's, there was a picture of a gigantic alliance of nearly the whole of Eastern Europe opposed to the Turks. The idea of Imperial help was again put forward: Sir Hamar Greenwood, the Chief Secretary for Ireland, suggested that Australia and New Zealand ought to be asked to co-operate. Churchill wondered about more aeroplanes. Worthington-Evans thought a division could get to Constantinople in under three weeks and asked if the battalions at Malta and Gibraltar could be used. It was decided reluctantly that there was no point in asking the U.S.A. to participate despite her 'large missionary interests in Turkey'.

Lloyd George then produced another piece of helpful gossip. Mr. A. T. Sylvester, one of his secretaries, had been told by a representative of the *Daily Telegraph* of a conversation with the Serbian chargé d'affaires in London. Apparently the Serbs were opposed to the idea of the Turks returning to Thrace. The Prime Minister had similar information about the attitude of the Romanians. Lord Hardinge in Paris could therefore approach the King of Serbia immediately. Austen Chamberlain suggested that

Winston Churchill should send a telegram to each of the Dominions asking for a battalion. Churchill said that the telegram would be sent by the Prime Minister but that he would be prepared to draft it.

Curzon, still fighting for facts, asked 'what answer he was to give when asked where the forces were to be sent'. Lloyd George said that the governments concerned should be told to send a representative to General Harington 'to make the necessary arrangements'. Curzon then wanted to know if he was to tell the French that the British government would send a division, even if it would not. He was told that it would be premature to decide that point until replies had been received from Serbia and Romania. Churchill and Chamberlain then wanted to know something a little more specific about sending aircraft from Egypt, but the Prime Minister was content to leave such matters to the Air Ministry and Admiralty experts. He was much more concerned about what the Greeks could do. The Minister in Athens, he thought, could find out and report.

Lord Curzon's predicament can well be understood; there seemed to be many ideas but few decisions. In the end the Cabinet decided to try something of everything. The approaches to the Balkan nations should be made for military participation, the reward being their presence at the proposed conference. The Greeks would be asked what they could do to defend the Straits. General Harington would provide, once again, information on the state of the Greek army. Lord Curzon would see M. Poincaré and inform him that if the French would send reinforcements to Constantinople then so would the British. Reserves would not be called out and leave would not be stopped, but a division was to be put in a state of readiness. The battalions at Malta and Gibraltar should move forthwith. Two squadrons of aeroplanes would move from Egypt. The naval Commander-in-Chief in the Mediterranean should be authorised 'to take any action he may deem necessary to secure or destroy' any transports conveying Turkish forces to Europe. Finally, Churchill should draft a telegram for Lloyd George to be sent to the Dominion Prime Ministers, inviting their co-operation 'in the despatch of military reinforcements'.

On that Friday Miss Frances Stevenson, Lloyd George's secretary, was waiting in the Cabinet ante-room. 'My door opened and L.G. and Churchill walked in from the Cabinet Room. L.G. asked me to take down from Churchill the text of what I realised was to be a telegram asking for their support in the event of a war with Turkey. I was horrified at the unwisdom of the message, conveying as it did the prospect of renewed warfare on a grand scale. L.G. and Churchill took the draft back into the Cabinet Room, where the meeting was in progress. Shall I send L.G. in a note warning him against such action? But then again I thought he will never agree to such a telegram being sent. The next thing I knew was that the telegram had gone.'

The next day, a Saturday, Winston Churchill, in a fit of over-zealousness, released the news of the telegram to the British press, too late for the Sunday papers but in time for the Monday ones. He forgot, however, the difference in time between Britain and the Dominions, and he failed to check what time the telegram had been sent from London. In Canada, Australia and New Zealand the telegram from London was not decoded until Monday, but by that time the three Prime Ministers had received their first intimation of the request from their own newspapers on Sunday morning. Mackenzie King, the Canadian Prime Minister, did not in fact see a newspaper that morning until a reporter asked him what action he intended to take. As none of the Dominion governments had been consulted beforehand, it was not perhaps the best manner in which they should first hear of a request which they regarded, in any event, as being peremptory and Imperialistic, reminiscent of the days when their countries had been mere colonies, ruled and controlled from London.

Mackenzie King replied in very clear terms, indicating that his countrymen had no wish to be embroiled in a new war and that even if any military action were contemplated the Canadian Parliament would have to be consulted first. This broad hint was apparently lost on the British Cabinet, which had shown no indication so far of wishing to recall the British Parliament so that its views might be ascertained. The Australian Prime Minister's reply was equally discouraging if less critical, although he also complained about the lack of previous consultation. In South Africa the Prime Minister, Jan Smuts, was on a lengthy tour of the Union and, perhaps tactfully, never sent an official reply at all. The Newfoundland government indicated that it was in agreement with the home Cabinet but made no offer of military assistance. Only from New Zealand came the sort of reply which Churchill had hoped would flow in from all the Dominions: New Zealand would send a battalion, perhaps a brigade if necessary. The British Cabinet decided that the news of this heartening offer of support could be made public, but that the cause of Imperial unity would not be best served by advertising the Canadian or the Australian responses.

Churchill's muddle over the telegrams was not the only one. The Cabinet was contemplating a military operation; it was getting within sight of the outbreak of a war. Yet a very dangerous gap yawned between the actions of military and naval personnel on the spot and the information on which the Cabinet gave its orders. There were a number of reasons why this situation came about. For three years Lloyd George had pursued a twin obsession: an exaggerated admiration for the Greeks and an excessive hatred of the Turks. Neither view was shared by his military and diplomatic advisers and many of his Ministers were but lukewarm. Of course government servants such as Harington or Rumbold did not necessarily have to agree with the policies of their political master. They had a duty merely to obey or resign. Soldiers and civil servants have, before and since, carried out measures with which privately they have disagreed, that being a condition of their service. Unfortunately, however, Lloyd George had not been consistent. He had encouraged the Greeks, had helped to fire their imagination with grandiose notions, and had then left them to fend for themselves. Consequently by 1922 it was not so much that Service Chiefs and Foreign Office officials disagreed with the basic premises of the Prime Minister's policy in the Near East, as that they were irritated and exasperated by the manner in which he had attempted to put it into practice. Their own advice had been ignored and they had seen a policy of half-measures end in failure. Now that a crisis approached which might well demand action, and action which could mean war, they feared that Britain might be pushed into an unnecessary conflict inadvertently. Overall, they did not trust the Prime Minister.

Churchill's 'small group of resolute men' was not trusted either. Churchill himself was regarded as an impetuous fire-eater, Birkenhead as a clever adventurer; the rest were nonentities. Curzon was knowledgeable and able and with all his faults a reasonable man. Unfortunately his chief fault was that, unlike the others, he lacked resolution. With Lloyd George in charge it did not make up an impressive team. The Prime Minister was undoubtedly excited by the possibility of a showdown with Turkey. Those who might have to translate his enthusiasm into action were not.

To make matters worse the Prime Minister's peculiar method of doing business was becoming notorious. Curzon had frequently complained of his habit of not consulting the Cabinet collectively, but of dealing with its individual members separately. There had been a great deal to Edwin Montagu's jibe about Cabinet government having become a joke. Lloyd George was undoubtedly adept at getting his own way by devious means. The obverse of the coin was his manner of obtaining advice. It was as if he had a positive antipathy towards taking official guidance. The view of a newspaper man, a foreign diplomat, even a mere dinner-table companion, although only given in passing, was preferable to the carefully marshalled opinions of the Foreign Office or the War Office. Perhaps one can spare a measure of sympathy for Lloyd George, perpetually burdened with Lord Curzon's balanced and erudite lectures, and therefore understand the reasons for his formation of what came to be called the 'Garden Suburb'. The phrase described the Prime Minister's private corps of advisers and helpers quartered in Whitehall Gardens. Nevertheless the Garden Suburb worked separately and by different methods and

standards from those of the 'regular' Civil Service, whose
functions it appeared to usurp. In short, with Lloyd George
senior Service officers, high-ranking Civil Servants, and a
number of Ministers were never quite sure where they stood.
The Service chiefs, in particular, with the likelihood of a
war on their hands, desperately wanted to know where
they stood. This was especially true in the Near East where
the first shots would be fired. Consequently generals and
admirals tended, far from home, to take matters a little
into their own hands; not because they wanted a war, but
because they wanted to prevent one. To do this, in their
opinion, if the Straits were to be defended then they would
have to be seen to be defended properly, by guns and men
and not just the words of Lloyd George in London. Field
Marshal Lord Plumer had looked at the Chanak defences
and had decided to act. The 2nd Royal Sussex and the 1st
Gordon Highlanders were therefore warned on the 14th
September to embark for Chanak. The Royal Sussex arrived
on the 18th and the Gordons on the 20th September. The
Cabinet, however, only considered the question of moving
one battalion from Malta on September 15th. Similarly
the Cabinet, in late September, found itself wondering about
possible danger from Turkish guns still in place along both
sides of the Straits. They were relics from the Gallipoli
campaign, but were they not still serviceable and therefore
dangerous? Actually the question by the time it was asked
was an academic one. Weeks before the Royal Navy had
landed at each battery and removed the breech mechanisms;
and the army had followed, blowing up all stores of ammunition they could find.

These examples, and there were others, can be regarded
and explained simply as the Navy and the Army pursuing
their own tasks in their own way, but they did also bear
witness to a degree of independence of London not often
encountered in the twentieth century. Doubtless nowadays
a Cabinet Minister would have flown out to Chanak to see
for himself. Admittedly air travel in 1922 was neither so
certain nor as rapid as it is today, as the one man who did
fly out discovered. He was Major-General Anderson,

appointed as Chief of Staff to Harington to 'stiffen him up', in Nevile Henderson's view. Anderson's pilot was the famous aviator Alan Cobham, but the plane broke down in Austria, so that Anderson arrived too late to be of any use. Still, Churchill during the 1939–45 war had a penchant for finding out for himself by looking at battle-fronts. It seems therefore somewhat strange that he didn't at least make an effort to do the same in 1922. Even a visit by the Prime Minister himself would not have been out of the question. The journey from London to Constantinople could be accomplished in three days of comfort and safety on board the Orient Express.

Whatever the reason, no Cabinet Minister from London did make the trip, and so the men who made the ultimate decisions relied upon reports and telegrams and summaries, second-hand opinions and hearsay evidence. Maybe this fact did not affect Lloyd George very much, for the simple and regrettable reason that he did not pay much attention to official opinions anyway, and seemed to come to some of his decisions by a process akin to clairvoyance. Again, the importance of the fact-finding tour by the politician can be exaggerated. It is possible, for instance, for the distinguished visitor to see only what his hosts wish him to see. Nevertheless a visit to Chanak in 1922 would have been of value in one respect: that the government would then have realised precisely what Harington was defending, and consequently why it seemed so frequently to be at cross purposes with him. Throughout the Cabinet minutes there occurs the phrase 'the neutral zone'. Harington is 'defending the neutral zone'; he will take action 'if the neutral zone is violated'; 'the neutral zone must be respected by Turkish troops'; 'Kemal's troops will be liable to attack if they cross the neutral zone', and so on. But Shuttleworth was defending, militarily, only the Chanak area and Nagara Point. The neutral zone presented a front of eighty miles, and although, through Plumer's prompt action, there were now two more infantry battalions at Shuttleworth's disposal, defence of that line had always been out of the question. In the neutral zone there were only mounted patrols of the

3rd Hussars and the Loyals, moving about on the lookout for the advancing Turks.

As has been seen, however, the Cabinet was not much addicted to studying maps, and the impression in London was that the whole area of the neutral zone, roughly eighty miles by twenty-five, would and could be held against Mustapha Kemal's forces. The zone itself, which was a creation of the Allies and the Sultan's government, was not, of course, recognised by the Turkish leader. To Kemal and the National Assembly the line of demarcation was merely a line drawn across the map of their own country by powers which they did not accept as having any authority to do so. Furthermore the British, French and Italian commanders on the spot attached very little importance to the line either. It followed no natural features, so that it had no strategic or tactical significance. It had only been relevant when a Greek army had been in Anatolia as marking very roughly the administrative boundaries between the two sets of occupying forces. The Greek wall of men having gone, as a position to be held against the whole of the Turkish army the neutral zone was referred to by senior British officers as a 'farce' and a 'bluff'.

There was no military reason why Mustapha Kemal should recognise or respect it, and none of the Allied soldiers expected that he would. Perhaps in London the politicians thought that the presence of one British soldier carrying the Union Jack was enough to deter the Turkish army flushed with victory. In Anatolia there were no such illusions. To Shuttleworth and his superiors, Marden and Harington, it was obvious that the only deterrent to Kemal's sweeping on to the Straits and Constantinople was a strong military posture on the Asian shore. The position at Chanak Harington estimated could be held for four to six weeks; perhaps for longer if reinforced by infantry and artillery and backed up by the fleet.

In order to attack it and possibly capture it Mustapha Kemal would have to make a positive decision to wage war. This, as Harington put it, 'taking on the whole of the British Empire', he was convinced Kemal did not want to do. The Turkish army, despite its victories over the Greeks, was not in the best of condition to accept another and far more powerful adversary. The Turks had suffered many casualties and lost many prisoners. Their equipment was not of the best. They were short of artillery and ammunition. They had few aeroplanes. The whole army was in need of reorganisation. To say this was not to denigrate the fighting qualities of the Turks. No man of Harington's generation, with Gallipoli but five years in the past, was likely to underestimate the terrific powers of endurance of 'Mehmedchik', the Turkish private soldier. If there was an incident, if shots were fired, the Turks would fight and fight well. They were less well disciplined than the British; if they were provoked and firing broke out then it was doubtful if their officers would be capable of controlling them. Harington intended, however, that the Turks should not be provoked, either by the soldiers under his command or by dangerous or impossible situations manufactured by politicians in Downing Street. A show of force, or the one soldier with a Union Jack, the reliance upon prestige alone, might well create a provocative situation and produce the very result it was intended to prevent. The danger lay in hasty actions, overbearing attitudes and inadequate means. The safe course, in Harington's view, was to attempt nothing beyond one's capabilities, but at the same time to give no encouragement to those Turks, less level-headed than Kemal, who might think that the Allies could be stampeded into the sea in the wake of the Greeks.

On September 19th Colonel Shuttleworth, on receiving reports of the advance of large formations of Turkish cavalry, began to withdraw his own cavalry and mounted infantry patrols nearer to Chanak. He also prepared plans for the employment of his small French detachment. On September 20th the Gordon Highlanders arrived from Malta but with orders that they were not to disembark but were to remain on board their transport in readiness. The French detachment, some requisitioned Turkish country carts with solid wooden wheels carrying their baggage and supplies, moved off for Okjiler to watch the road from Bayramic.

A few hours after they had departed, Colonel Shuttleworth received a telegram from General Harington informing him that by order of their respective governments the French and Italian troops were to be withdrawn entirely from Anatolia, and were to proceed forthwith to Constantinople. The telegram also contained a warning that in the circumstances Shuttleworth might expect a Turkish advance on his position to follow upon the withdrawal. The French and Italian flags were taken down and by 1 a.m. on the morning of September 21st the Highlanders were disembarked and taking their places in the trenches. The withdrawal of the French and Italians had a simple but discouraging explanation. Generals Charpy and Mombelli, the French and Italian commanders in Constantinople, recalling Allied co-operation to keep out the Greeks a few months previously, had been perfectly willing to assist their British colleague to repel the Turks. The detachments they had ordered to Chanak had been small because they had been sent purely on their own responsibility. However, when news of this measure of participation, minimal though it was, reached Paris and Rome, the two Prime Ministers had immediately reversed the decision of their generals. If there was fighting to be done, it would have to be done by British soldiers alone.

On the same day as the French and Italian troops were withdrawn and the flags were taken down, Lord Curzon in Paris prepared himself for his first meeting with Raymond Poincaré, the French Prime Minister. Curzon had been joined the night before by Admiral of the Fleet Lord Beatty. Originally the Cabinet had intended to send with the Foreign Secretary Lord Birkenhead, the Lord Chancellor, as co-negotiator. Then, perhaps because it was thought that naval matters would inevitably arise, the Lord Chancellor had been replaced by the First Sea Lord.

David Beatty, the holder of that office and therefore the professional head of the Navy, had been a rear-admiral at the unprecedented age of thirty-eight, the youngest since Nelson. He had won the D.S.O. as a lieutenant in command of a gunboat on the Nile during the campaign in the Sudan. It had been his first meeting with Churchill, at the time attached to the 21st Lancers. A brave, dashing sailor, Beatty had owed much to Churchill since that date. An Anglo-Irishman of modest means, his upward path had been made at least more comfortable by his marriage to the beautiful Ethel Tree, the divorced daughter of Marshall Field, the American retail-store millionaire. Her wealth had provided him with many luxuries: hunting in Leicestershire, grouse-shooting in Scotland, and a yacht, and it had given him a certain independence with regard to what he considered to be second-rate naval posts.

Curiously, the possession of a rich American wife was an attribute which Beatty shared with both Lord Curzon and the Admiral's civilian chief, Lord Lee, the First Lord of the Admiralty. Actually Lord Curzon had had two such: his first wife, Miss Leiter, dying in 1906, he had married Mrs. Duggan, a widow, in 1917. In Lord Lee's case his wife's wealth undoubtedly buttressed up his own moderate abilities; his peerage had followed his gift of his house Chequers to the nation as a country residence for the Prime Minister of the day. But marriage to a rich American was the only shared characteristic between the humdrum First Lord of the Admiralty and his First Sea Lord. Lee was modest in attainments and demeanour. Beatty was neither. At Jutland he had commanded the Battle-Cruiser Fleet in a dashing manner which had unfairly eclipsed the more sober conduct of Jellicoe, his superior, who commanded the Grand Fleet. Soon he had replaced Jellicoe, and at the end of the war had received an earldom and been promoted Admiral of the Fleet. Now, in 1922, Beatty to the British public was a hero. With his actor's good looks it was not a role he declined. Neither the length of his hair nor the number of the buttons on his uniform jacket conformed to naval regulations. His gold-braided peaked cap was worn jauntily at an angle. As well as a hero Beatty was a character. So, of course, was Lord Birkenhead, but he was also a tough brilliant advocate of immense skill and experience. Beatty, for all his prestige at home, was merely a sailor. As the Anglo-French negotiations were to turn out Lord Curzon would have been better advised to have taken a good lawyer.

13

'Do you not think it terrible that I should be treated in this manner?'
Lord Curzon

On the same day, September 16th, as Winston Churchill gave the news of the Prime Minister's telegrams to the press, he also handed out an official communiqué to the British people.

As he himself admitted, it was 'censured for being alarmist and provocative in tone and certainly it was ill received in important quarters'. The communiqué was actually drafted by Churchill at Lloyd George's request and was approved by the principal members of the Cabinet, with the exception of Lord Curzon who, although out of London, was, presumably deliberately, not consulted. The language in which the British first heard of their nearness to war was certainly not half-hearted. 'The approach of the Kemalist forces to Constantinople and the Dardanelles and the demands put forward by the Ankara government . . . if assented to, involve nothing less than the loss of the whole results of the victory over Turkey in the last war.'

Nor was there any hint that perhaps other nations

might not be as enthusiastic as the British to defend the peace settlement. 'The British government regard the effective and permanent freedom of the Straits as a vital necessity for the sake of which they are prepared to make exertions. They have learnt with great satisfaction that in this respect their views are shared by France and Italy, the other two Great Powers principally concerned.' Churchill went on to say that both the British and French High Commissioners in Constantinople had been instructed to inform Mustapha Kemal that 'these neutral zones established under the flags of the three Great Powers must be respected'. However, if diplomacy were not enough then force would be necessary to prevent 'a violent and hostile Turkish aggression'.

The reader's blood was then curdled by the thought of the dire results which would follow if Kemal were successful. 'That the Allies should be driven out of Constantinople by the forces of Mustapha Kemal would be an event of the most disastrous character, producing, no doubt, far-reaching reactions throughout all Moslem countries, and not only through all Moslem countries but through all the States defeated in the late war, who would be profoundly encouraged by the spectacle of the undreamed of successes that have attended the efforts of the comparatively weak Turkish forces.'

Precisely how, for example, Germans, Austrians, Hungarians and Bulgarians would be encouraged was not stated, nor did the Secretary of State give any indication of the sort of reaction to be expected from Moslem peoples as divergent in their attitude to the Turks as the Persians, the Arabs and the Indians, or even the Malays. But it was not only the whole Moslem world and Britain's ex-enemies that were likely to be affected: 'The reappearance of the victorious Turk on the European shore would provoke a situation of the gravest character throughout the Balkans, and very likely lead to bloodshed on a large scale in regions already cruelly devastated.' Mustapha Kemal admittedly had asked for Eastern Thrace up to the Maritza, but doubtless this passage was intended to revive the old Liberal memories of massacres in the nineteenth century under the Ottomans. Gladstone also had used the pejorative singular and talked of 'the Turk'.

His Majesty's government was prepared to prevent this 'great danger', however ill-defined, but others were 'deeply and vitally affected'. 'Romania was brought to her ruin in the Great War by the strangulation of the Straits. The union of Turkey and Bulgaria would be productive of deadly consequences to Serbia in particular and to Yugoslavia as a whole. The whole trade of the Danube flowing into the Black Sea is likewise subject to strangulation if the Straits are closed. The engagement of Greek interests in these issues is also self-evident.'

Quite who this was intended to persuade it is difficult to decide. Churchill himself in Cabinet had wondered if the Bulgarians would help. There was no reason at all to think that Kemal wanted to invade Bulgaria. At Smyrna he had stated quite plainly his aims. A 'union' of Turkey and Bulgaria was so much nonsense. Serbia, as part of the new Yugoslavia, was in fact the province furthest from Turkey and not the nearest as might have been imagined. There was no suggestion nor indeed any reason why Kemal should want to close the Straits. As for 'the engagement of Greek interests', it was precisely on this issue that Churchill had criticised Lloyd George's policy, and it was because the Greeks had involved themselves in Turkey that they were now ruined militarily and economically, striving to cope with an invasion of starving, destitute refugees. Nevertheless 'His Majesty's government are therefore addressing themselves to all these Balkan Powers with a view to their taking a part'. The Dominions were also to be invited to send contingents 'in the defence of interests for which they have already made enormous sacrifices and of soil which is hallowed by immortal memories of the Anzacs'.

That Churchill was blamed, however unfairly, for the ghastly failure of the Dardanelles by a number of surviving members of the Australian and New Zealand Army Corps and of the British army, hardly made the last reference the most tactful, but the most serious objection to the passages about foreign and Dominion help was the implication that such help would be granted. If, which is the most charitable explanation, the whole thing was a gigantic bluff meant to dissuade Mustapha Kemal, it failed for the very good reason that he knew that the French, and the Italians, let alone the Balkan countries, would not oppose him. On the other hand, if Churchill's communiqué was meant merely for home consumption in order to rouse up the warlike ardour of his fellow countrymen, it failed equally signally.

Lord Curzon, when he returned from one of his country seats, disapproved of both language and content and talked of 'a flamboyant manifesto'. The British press was even less impressed, and had an 'easy' public. The faith of the man in the street in politicians and their promises had been considerably shaken by the disillusionment of the immediate post-war years. Lloyd George's own glamour as a man sprung from humble origins who had led his country to victory had faded as he appeared more and more in industrial and economic matters to be in the pockets of the bosses. Traditionally indifferent to foreign affairs, the British public had had little reason to pay a great deal of attention to a war between Greeks and Turks. Within the recent memory of every adult one war had arisen out of a squabble in the Balkans. That another should arise again within four years, in 1922, the first year of real peace, seemed intolerable, especially as the causes appeared so unimportant. The British, despite the late war, did not hate the Turks; they had no particular feelings about the Greeks, who were now defeated anyway. That the Turks now wanted Turkey and Constantinople did not seem, on the face of it, unreasonable. Emphatically to the large mass of the people, who had not been consulted, the freedom of the Straits did not appear to be a 'vital necessity'.

Much of this was realised by Lloyd George, who was certainly not insensitive to public opinion. In early September he had given breakfast to Henry Morgenthau at 10 Downing Street. Morgenthau, the former U.S. Ambassador at Constantinople, was violently pro-Greek and had just given an interview to the *Daily Telegraph* and contributed an article to the *Sunday Times*, in both of which he had said that the Allies 'should keep Constantinople out of the hands of the Turks'. The city would be under the protection of the League of Nations and administered by Britain, France and Italy 'and possibly in due time, the United States would join'.

Lloyd George knew that these suggestions were simply not within the realms of possibility, but after he had questioned Morgenthau closely on the Near East question, when Morgenthau appealed for the use of 'the armed might of the British Empire' so that 'the Turk could be hurled back into Asia', the Prime Minister's reply was very significant indeed. 'Mr. Morgenthau,' said Lloyd George, 'I simply can't do it. The Labour crowd and the pacifists right now are trying to make me demobilise the entire army, even trying to make me withdraw the troops in Palestine. They would not stand for a government spending a shilling on anything that involved a military expedition for any purpose.'

Too much should not be made of a conversation to a guest over a breakfast table although, typically, the information he extracted from Morgenthau Lloyd George later related to the Cabinet without acknowledging its source. (Churchill guessed from whom it came and confirmed this with Morgenthau later.) The real point of Lloyd George's answer to Morgenthau lies in his acceptance of the ex-Ambassador's outdated arguments and his view of those who disagreed. Yet it was not just 'the Labour crowd' and 'the pacifists' who were worried by the imminence of war nor was it the sacrifice of shillings that alone concerned them. Liberals and Conservatives, as well as Labour supporters, all resented the thought of the possible sacrifice of men's lives for an object which seemed merely to be a hangover from the peace treaties.

The tone of the British press both moulded and reflected the feelings of its readers. On or about September 20th every paper had a photograph of the waterfront at Chanak, what the *Daily Mail* called a 'little lonely shabby town'.

Leader writers, with little enthusiasm, endeavoured to explain the importance of this hitherto unknown Turkish

228

port in terms of British prestige. For a week or two previously there had been constant stories of the sufferings of the Greek army and the civilian refugees. Undoubtedly at this stage there was considerable public sympathy for their plight, and in consequence a reflected detestation of the Turks who were immediately responsible. With the news that Britain herself might be involved the pendulum began to swing in the opposite direction. The condition of refugees gave place to news of Greek cabinet changes. The new Prime Minister was M. Kalageropoulos, who had led the delegation to the London Conference. There were rumours of impending revolution in Athens. Stories of Turkish massacres and atrocities began to be played down, to be replaced by eye-witness accounts of Greek atrocities perpetrated while their army was in retreat. Hopefully, diplomatic correspondents talked of Allied co-operation, and almost imperceptibly the argument grew that, in terms of moral blame, there was little to choose between Greeks and Turks.

The movement of the Royal Sussex, the Gordon Highlanders and some artillery batteries from Malta to Chanak was announced, and the names of the ships of the Royal Navy which were sailing east were published. The reactions of individual newspapers of course varied. On September 18th the *Daily Mail*, virulently against any possibility of war in the Middle East, carried the broad headline:

'STOP THIS NEW WAR!'

'Cabinet Plan for Great Conflict With the Turks. France and Italy against it. Extraordinary Appeal to the Dominions.' The latter was more true than the leader writer knew, for since the initial rebuff Lloyd George and Churchill had tried again to persuade the Canadian government to make some show of solidarity with Britain.

In his first reply Mackenzie King as well as pointing out the necessity of summoning the Canadian Parliament, had complained about the prior lack of consultation or even information. On the 19th September Lloyd George, seeming not to appreciate these points, again asked for an assurance of support. The reply, signed by Lord Byng, the Governor-

General, was chilling in the extreme. 'We have not thought it necessary to re-assert the loyalty of Canada to the British Empire.'

On the 20th Churchill cabled that a special staff had been organised at the Colonial Office to keep Canada informed, and sent its first report in the hope that now at least all Mackenzie King's resistance would be overcome. These last-minute concessions, however, had no effect. Even if the Canadian Prime Minister's susceptibilities had not been offended by the manner in which he had first been informed of the request, public opinion in Canada, English and French, was firmly opposed to 'European' obligations. The Dominion had internal problems of its own. The aftermath of the Great War and the Allied intervention in Russia, where Canada had been the chief Empire contributor, had produced an isolationist and independent mood, completely unsympathetic to appeals for Imperial unity emanating from Downing Street. After the Cabinet meeting at which the issue was discussed, Mackenzie King entered in his diary, 'all were inclined to feel whole business "an election scheme" of Lloyd George and Co.'

Churchill's final appeal virtually went unanswered. On September 18th the *Daily Express* headline was 'Mobilising the Empire', and in a leader it was predicted that 'if Kemal, besotted with his cheaply won victories, should try to cross the Straits he will rush on complete disaster'. On the same day *The Times* was more diplomatic, although there was considerable sympathy with the French attitude of wanting to avoid war. There was, however, no sympathy wasted on the British government, about which subject two days before, a leader writer had said, 'British Ministers have made mistake after mistake.'

No other newspaper was as outspoken as the *Daily Mail*, which talked of the policy set out in Churchill's communiqué as 'bordering upon insanity', and the next day of Lloyd George and Churchill beginning to 'beat their war-drums'. At the same time readers of that paper were enabled to read a despatch which gave a slightly different impression, for once again Ward Price, despite the fact that he was cordially disliked by every British soldier and official he met, had managed to get himself to 'the sharp end'. According to his despatch he had just ridden round Chanak defences with Colonel Shuttleworth, and 'found nothing but confidence and eager anticipation on the faces of the Lancashire lads' (of the Loyal Regiment, recruited in North Lancashire) 'working in different parts of the line'.

In Ward Price's opinion 'this small force would prove a very unpleasant obstacle for the Turkish army to run up against'. Of course, no British paper, however much it might be opposed to a war, was going to suggest in 1922 that British soldiers were not a match for at least ten times their number of any other nation, and Ward Price at the moment when he wrote his despatch could still speak accurately of 'the united Allies'.

There was general agreement in other newspapers that Lord Curzon, on his way to Paris, was the man. *The Times* backed him and did not rank him as 'one of the Ministers whom they [the British people] distrust'. Lord Curzon, said *The Times*, was *persona grata* in France.

The first news that the Cabinet received of the labours of their colleagues came by telegram telephoned by Lord Hardinge, the Ambassador in Paris, and was received in London at 3.20 p.m. on September 20th.

Apparently the too clever Sforza, now the Italian Ambassador to France, was also present at the Quai d'Orsay at Poincaré's invitation and it was only with difficulty that Curzon had managed to exclude him from the talks for an hour or so in the morning to put the British view in private.

Poincaré had been in communication with General Pellé, the French High Commissioner, who had been to Smyrna to see Kemal. The Turkish leader had talked of being unable to hold back his armies until the territories claimed in the National Pact had been occupied, and said that he would be forced to take action before the winter. The only doubt in Kemal's mind seemed to be over what the Allies would do about Constantinople.

Poincaré dismissed much of this as '*blague*', but said that Kemal would only attend a conference if his claims to

Eastern Thrace and Constantinople were accepted beforehand. In answer to Curzon's request for assistance the French Prime Minister said that 'it was both a moral and physical impossibility for France to resist the Turks if they advanced', and that 'French public opinion would not admit of a shot being fired against a Turk'. In addition, in his opinion, the Turks could not be kept back and 'they could cross to Europe when they pleased'.

Curzon, needless to say, opposed this argument and mentioned the interest of the Balkan states. Poincaré said that the Serbian Prime Minister had told him categorically that he would not move and that the Turks could have Eastern Thrace straight away. Lord Curzon fell back on Romania and the constantly recurring phrase that Britain would not 'sacrifice the entire results of the war'.

The afternoon session was reported by Lord Curzon himself by telephone. He had returned to the attack. Sforza had decided, surprisingly, to be 'helpful rather than otherwise', so he was invited to hear Lord Beatty. When asked if Britain were to bear the sole brunt of a Kemalist attack, Poincaré 'exhibited extreme irritation' and repeated that 'French public opinion would not tolerate the death of a single French soldier at the hands of a Turk or of a single Turk at the hands of a Frenchman'. Curzon asked Poincaré if 'he had measured the full meaning of this extraordinary declaration' and mentioned the Allied defence of the Chataldja lines against the Greeks. This provoked 'a rather lively scene'. Lord Beatty was then brought in to show that the Royal Navy could prevent the Turks from taking Chanak, keep the Straits open and hold the Gallipoli peninsula, as well as preventing an invasion of Thrace across the Sea of Marmora and holding Constantinople. As one of Harington's staff put it, Beatty at that time 'was ready to blow anything and everything sky high'. Poincaré, however, as Curzon ruefully admitted, 'with commendable astuteness had mobilised the French Admiral Grasset to counter all these propositions', which he did, in Curzon's view, 'with great amiability and lack of success'.

The Foreign Secretary turned Grasset's argument about

the impossibility of holding the European shore in favour of holding the Asiatic shore, and then moved on to his proposals for a peace conference to include, as well as the Great Powers, Greece, Turkey, Serbia and Romania, making it clear, though, that there should be no advance agreement with Turkey.

On this latter condition both Poincaré and Sforza appeared doubtful, and were certain that at least the Allies should agree among themselves beforehand. Curzon said he would have to consult his own government, but that Poincaré must use his influence with Kemal, 'which I knew to be supreme', to dissuade him from any act which 'might compel Great Britain to act alone'. The Foreign Secretary ended by informing the Cabinet that 'we may emerge from this very difficult position with success', and urged that Britain should 'desist from any action likely to provoke immediate hostilities'.

This news from Paris was obviously heartening and the Cabinet cabled its congratulations to Lord Curzon. On September 21st Lord Hardinge telephoned from Paris, acknowledging 'the kind words of encouragement' and stating Curzon's proposed terms for the conference, so that they could be approved by the Cabinet. The Foreign Secretary's suggestion was that Constantinople, as promised, should be returned to the Turks, but only after a new Peace Treaty had been signed. So far as Thrace and the shore of the Bosphorus were concerned, he thought that both might be demilitarised under the aegis of the League of Nations and that similar conditions could apply to the Dardanelles. To enforce these conditions upon the French and Italians he intended to use the argument that in the event of disagreement the British would act alone to defend Chanak and Gallipoli, perhaps with the help of the Serbians and Romanians. The Greeks he felt were completely demoralised and could not be relied upon. He placed particular importance upon the concept of League of Nations control as he thought that membership of that body could be held out to the Turks as an inducement to agreement and as a sop to their pride.

His first essential move would be to obtain the agreement

of the French so that they would use their influence with Mustapha Kemal to make him see reason. Curzon was reasonably confident that he could so persuade the French, having, as he felt, shown them the moral weakness of their position in 'deserting the allies from admitted motives of fear'. Needless to say the Cabinet approved of Curzon's actions and proposals and awaited the results of his labours.

On the afternoon of September 22nd Curzon again met Poincaré, and in the evening sent a long telegram to the Cabinet from the British Embassy. It was received in London on the morning of September 23rd. The news was not good. 'Have just returned from meeting of quite unprecedented description,' he began. As soon as the Foreign Secretary had announced his proposals Poincaré had emphasised that the military situation was very dangerous and therefore the only chance of peace was an overture to Kemal promising him Thrace and Adrianople 'without any reserve or qualification'. Curzon demurred, denying Poincaré's pessimistic view of the military balance and saying that if Harington were forced to evacuate Chanak it would only be because the French and Italians had abandoned him. The word infuriated Poincaré for, in Curzon's words, 'he then commenced a second speech by a bitter attack on Harington whom he accused of having deliberately misrepresented to his colleagues the attitude of the French and Italian governments. I instantly and indignantly repudiated this charge; whereupon Poincaré lost all command of his temper and for a quarter of an hour shouted and raved at the top of his voice, putting words into my mouth which I had never uttered, refusing to permit the slightest interruption or correction, saying that he would make public the insult to France, quoting a telegram from Athens to the effect that the British Minister had asked the Greek government to furnish 60,000 men for the defence of Thrace and the Straits, and behaving like a demented schoolmaster screaming at a guilty schoolboy. I have never seen so deplorable or undignified a scene. After enduring this for some time I could stand it no longer and rising, broke up the sitting and left the room.'

Outside the conference room the Marquess Curzon of Kedleston, His Majesty's Principal Secretary of State for Foreign Affairs, burst into tears. It was there that an amazed Count Sforza found him, with tears in his eyes, reviving himself with sips of brandy from a pocket flask. 'Do you not think it terrible that I should be treated in this manner? Never in my life before have I had to endure such speeches,' he said. Sforza said sympathetically that he had in his time suffered similarly, while thinking that Curzon's 'soul was still that of an Oxford student who weeps because he has not won a prize'.

Eventually Poincaré came out and apologised, saying that he had been exasperated by the charge that France had abandoned an ally. Curzon withdrew the expression for the sake of politeness, while knowing 'its incontestable truth'. Half an hour after leaving the conference room Curzon was, with Sforza's help, persuaded back though still indignant with Poincaré. As he bothered to put it in his telegram to his Cabinet colleagues, 'I should not have thought it possible for anyone in such a position, the chairman and host of the proceedings, to make such a display, and it needed more than ordinary self-restraint not to terminate the conference abruptly and announce my intention to return to England.'

So Curzon returned to the conference table and continued his arguments but he had lost the French and with them the Italians. Perhaps a stronger man than the Foreign Secretary, or perhaps merely a different man, by pursuing a 'hard' line could have persuaded the allies to co-operate. Perhaps not. Poincaré was no more enamoured than Mackenzie King of the assumption in Churchill's communiqué that, unconsulted, he would spring to the side of Britain. For anyone, even without Curzon's defects as a negotiator, the cards were stacked against the British. Poincaré had ascertained that the Serbians and the Romanians were prepared to do nothing. He himself was ready to accede to all Mustapha Kemal's demands, tomorrow if necessary, beginning with the grant of Eastern Thrace. 'Absolute surrender', was how Curzon saw it. If the British would not agree, Poincaré suggested, then each nation should send separate Notes to Ankara. Perhaps the British could indicate privately to Kemal that though they were holding back at the moment, they would, of course, agree with him at the conference. Curzon rightly resented this and then proposed a new formula of his own which he had devised while in Paris.

He was prepared to allow General Harington to meet Kemal at some convenient place in Turkey, so as not to involve him in any loss of face, and there the two generals could devise lines behind which the Turkish and Greek armies could retire, pending a final settlement by international conference. Curzon suggested Mudania, on the Sea of Marmora, as a convenient meeting place.

Poincaré was unenthusiastic, seeing no point in further negotiations. Curzon, on the other hand, as he confided to his Cabinet colleagues, saw every point in gaining time. Realising that he could no longer expect any help from the French, Italians, Serbs or Romanians, he was determined that Britain, if alone, should negotiate with the Turks from as strong a position as possible. While the French considered his new proposal and, as he hoped, communicated it to Kemal, the strengthening of the Chanak defences could continue. The ex-Viceroy was much concerned with British prestige, especially in the Moslem world, and though he did not want war was determined that Britain should not be pushed ignominiously out of Asia by the Turks. For although Curzon might break down when shouted at, he did return to the fray, and was prepared to devote all his vast powers of application and industry to a cause he believed in with the intensity of a mystic, the British Empire.

Sforza now decided to intervene, arguing the same case as the French. Would not the British say that Kemal could definitely have Eastern Thrace up to the line of the River Maritza? This, Curzon feared, might well lead to a violent explosion by the Greek army and the Greek population against the Turks already there. Kemal would then insist that he had to go to the aid of his fellow countrymen and the Graeco-Turkish War would break out anew. Curzon felt he could not possibly make any more concessions, and there rested his case. Finally, in his telegram, he asked for the approval of his colleagues for the position he had taken up. There was hardly anything else the Cabinet could do but approve, and hope that Lord Curzon would make the best of a bad job.

Poincaré, in his arguments with Curzon, had made much use of the state of French public opinion, which was opposed to war with the Turks. In fact there was very little to show that on the other side of the Channel the prospect roused any more enthusiasm. The Coalition government had not increased its popularity as the year had worn on. At home the unemployment figures still stood at nearly a million and a half. The sober *Annual Register*, which had described 1921 as the 'most disappointing and depressing period in British commerce and finance for 100 years', could only say of 1922 that it was 'a little less depressing'. The trade unions resented imposed cuts in wages and employers could offer little, or persuaded themselves that they could offer little, in a stagnant economy. In the depressed area of Ebbw Vale, in September, steelworks and collieries employing 10,000 workers simply closed down, owing to constant labour disputes. Although wages were kept down the cost of living was still increasing, being now 80 per cent above the pre-war level. Abroad, the troubles in Ireland continued, with political murders in both North and South. The British were now only marginally responsible, but there were still moments when it was thought that perhaps in the classic cause of 'law and order' Imperial control might have to be reasserted. Unrest continued in India. The Prime Minister's stock had fallen still further. His reputation as a European diplomatist had suffered considerably when the international conference in April at Genoa had been wrecked, to his own obvious disappointment and surprise, by the disturbing Rapallo Agreement between the two outcasts, Soviet Russia and the new German Republic. Personally, too, his image was becoming tarnished. A debate in the Commons on the 'Honours Scandal' had left an impression behind of a Prime Minister who in the recommending of peerages and knighthoods was, to say the least, both

237

generous and indiscriminating.[1] More than dark hints were bandied about concerning the fate of certain party funds.

In this atmosphere the looming crisis over the Straits seemed to many merely the crowning example of incompetence or worse. Warlike measures and utterances looked suspiciously like the efforts of desperate men forced to distract public attention from conditions at home by drumming up enthusiasm for patriotic adventures abroad. Of course policies likely to lead to war are rarely popular. Lloyd George had talked to Morgenthau of 'the Labour crowd' and 'the pacifists'. In this category he could place, for instance, a meeting held at the Kingsway Hall while Curzon was in Paris. The organisers were the Independent Labour Party and the speakers were Ramsay MacDonald, the Labour leader, George Lansbury, and the thirty-four-year-old Fenner Brockway, soon to be an M.P. and then just getting into his stride as a lifelong opponent of violence. Again, the call to prayer by the leaders of the Free Churches and a few days later by the Archbishops of Canterbury and York, could be regarded as a conventional and expected reaction, and not necessarily an adverse comment on the policies of His Majesty's Ministers, who were also prayed for regularly on Sundays—at least in the Church of England.

Of more immediate concern was the mounting tide of press criticism. The *Daily Mail* demanded the recall of Parliament and misquoted the classic phrase, coined during the Crimean War, about 'drifting' towards war. The headline of September 21st said bluntly: 'Get out of Chanak.' The news that the Mayor of Bradford was intending to call a town meeting to protest against war with Turkey inspired the *Mail* to appeal to all other towns to do likewise. *The Times* founded a great deal of its arguments on a letter from Sir Edward Grey, now Lord Grey of Fallodon, the former

[1] Three related matters gave cause for concern. In six years Lloyd George had created ninety-one new peers and in four years distributed forty-nine honours to the press. Titles were also alleged to be purchaseable by donation to political funds; for instance knighthoods at £12,000 and baronetcies at £40,000. There was a Lloyd George Fund in addition to the official fund of the Conservative Party. Conservatives feared that these had become mingled to the disadvantage of the latter.

Foreign Secretary, who said that the government had made 'a terrible mistake' in releasing the Churchill communiqué to the public before there had been any official consultation with the French government. The leader of September 22nd, while wondering if Kemal would accept a conference (General Pellé had found him in 'an uncompromising mood'), also said that even now Downing Street did not seem to have realised its errors and was still contemplating unilateral action.

The only crumb of comfort that Lloyd George could extract from the newspapers came from the *Daily Express* which, on the 20th, although modestly it 'did not pretend to fathom the mysteries which at present obscure inter-Allied politics', did insist on the freedom of the Straits because 'without the freedom of the Straits neither the British Empire nor European civilisation can exist'. So said the leader on September 20th. On the 21st the front page announced that as there were only British troops at Chanak and no Greeks, there was therefore no validity in Kemal's claim to have a right there. This argument was somewhat naive, but the headline read: 'Danger of War Past', and the leader was headed: 'United. The Allies find a way to peace.' Unfortunately, therefore, the one newspaper which gave some grudging support to Lloyd George was wrong in all three particulars.

There were other ordeals for the Prime Minister apart from bombardment by press headlines. At eleven o'clock in the morning of September 21st he received a deputation of thirty members of the General Council of the Trades Union Congress. J. B. Williams, the Chairman of the T.U.C., headed them, but his task was merely to introduce his members. They included four Labour M.P.s, and the three spokesmen were J. H. Thomas, now an M.P., Ben Tillett, and Margaret Bondfield, who seven years later as Minister of Labour was to become the first woman to be a member of the Cabinet and a Privy Counsellor.

None of the speakers was brief. Tillett said that he was, among other things, 'cognisant of the vested interests and the cross purposes of the vested interests', whatever that meant, and that he realised both the gravity of the position and the Prime Minister's responsibility. More precisely, he stated that trade-union opinion, working-class opinion, 'was absolutely antagonistic to the war'. The trades unions had no quarrel with the Turks or the Greeks, and though they were mindful of the connection with Moslem India, 'we should be opposed to war and would organise opposition against any form of war'. Margaret Bondfield thought, as might be expected, that women felt more strongly about the matter than men. Certainly she did not disguise her own feelings. The Cabinet call to the Empire had impressed her with horror, for she had discovered 'the perpetuation of the war mind'. Dealing with a 'holy war' and 'the sanctity of Gallipoli', she said that 'a new war would be the beating of the dead, because they died to prevent any more war'.

J. H. Thomas, in a long rambling speech (he was the only delegate who was interrupted by Lloyd George), referred to the Prime Minister's own professed desire for peace, and in particular to a recent speech at a conference of Nonconformist Churchmen. He said that however united the Cabinet might be, and however determined the Prime Minister, the Labour movement would, in the event of a war, 'use all its influence to persuade our people not to support the war'. Later on he put it directly to Lloyd George: 'We believe that of all the things which have contributed towards this difficulty the chief has been your own attitude. . . .' The Prime Minister refused to be drawn, and when replying seized upon the fact that both Tillett and Thomas had talked of the freedom of the Straits and their belief in the worth of the League of Nations. He himself was solely concerned with the freedom of the Straits, but what if Kemal could not be trusted and the League could not exercise control?

He then treated his audience to a resumé of recent history, not omitting 'the torch of war, pillage, outrage and murder' which might be carried from Asia to Europe. In passing Lloyd George dealt with the Greeks, for one of the delegates had suggested that the British had paid them. Not at all. 'We never paid sixpence to the Greeks; we never gave them support either in money or in arms.' They had tried recently to negotiate a loan in the City but without government aid had failed. 'When the Greeks went to Smyrna we said, "You go there at your own expense; we cannot support you; you take the responsibility," just as the Italians at that moment had gone to Adalia, the French to Cilicia, the Americans were hopeful that they might get a mandate for Armenia—the Greeks went to Smyrna.' Having thus disposed of his old ally Lloyd George returned to all the well-worn arguments about the damage inflicted by Turkish control of the Straits in the Great War. The Labour party had declared at its conference in 1918 for freedom of the Straits under the League. That was precisely his own policy. The Turkish National Pact, however, suggested Turkish control. The Greeks had been prevented at Chatal-dja from occupying Constantinople; now it was the turn of the Turks. It really sounded quite fair and reasonable.

So persuasive was Lloyd George that J. H. Thomas, when the delegates were on the point of leaving, said he 'had clearly indicated what brothers we are in this matter'. Thomas also endeavoured to mention the means for executing what he called 'their joint policy', but at this point Lloyd George thought it politic to disengage, and bidding the delegates farewell, to settle on the terms of a mutually agreed notice to the press. There can be no doubt of Lloyd George's skill; in so far as it was possible with political opponents he had scored a victory.

For the moment the official leaders of the T.U.C. would remain quiet, as would Labour M.P.s in the House of Commons, the Prime Minister having seen their leaders in private and given them the same assurances. Yet in the harsh terms of practical politics Lloyd George had not increased his support in the country; he had only gained acquiescence that was both temporary and conditional. If he thought that those who were opposed to him politically could in some way be brought round to the service of a prime minister above party politics, he was deluding himself.

On September 23rd the note signed by Poincaré, Sforza and Curzon was despatched to Ankara. It was the best that

Curzon had been able to manage after hours of argument. The Turks were invited to send a representative without delay to a meeting to be held at Venice or elsewhere to negotiate a final treaty of peace between Turkey, Greece and the Allies. The other nations invited were Japan, Romania, and Yugoslavia. The Allies 'viewed with favour' the desire of Turkey to recover Thrace as far as the Maritza and Adrianople, but the 'provisional neutrality' of the area was meanwhile proclaimed, i.e. no Turkish troops were to be sent there until the conclusion of the peace treaty. Similarly the Turks could have Constantinople after the peace had been signed. With regard to the Straits the document was somewhat vaguer. The Greeks should retire to a line fixed by the Allied generals in agreement with both Turks and Greeks. In return the Turks must undertake not to send troops into the neutral zone nor to cross the Straits or the Sea of Marmora. It was suggested that Allied generals might meet Mustapha Kemal at Mudania or Ismid. The Allies concluded by saying that they were convinced that 'their appeal will be listened to'. Their grounds for saying that were very flimsy indeed. They offered to support the admission of Turkey into the League of Nations, but they did not state what they would do if Kemal did not agree to their proposals. There was, of course, a very good reason for the omission: France and Italy were not prepared to do anything. Curzon had worked hard to produce a piece of paper, but it was still only a piece of paper and Kemal knew that before it was delivered.

In London, Winston Churchill, presiding over a triumvirate consisting of Beatty, Cavan, and Trenchard, continued with his warlike preparations.

On the same day as the note was sent to Ankara, Turkish cavalry in force crossed the boundary of the neutral zone at Chanak.

14

'We are living on a sort of volcano'
Lieutenant-General Sir Charles Harington

The first Turkish forces to penetrate into the neutral
zone consisted of a cavalry detachment of about 200 men.
At 10 a.m. they were met by a patrol of the 3rd Hussars
under Lieutenant Naylor at Saracheli. The Turks appeared
quite friendly and perhaps as an earnest of their pacific
intentions had their rifles slung over their shoulders, muzzles
downwards. Again, like the cavalry observed by the fleet
at Smyrna, they were not smart as a British cavalry regiment
was smart; but then, as one officer remarked, 'It takes the
British a long time to realise that you can be an efficient
soldier without being clean'. So the Turks' scrubby little
horses were not well groomed, many had staring coats,
their saddles and bridles were not polished to a high gloss
and their stirrup irons were rusty, but the riders were
obviously tough, fighting soldiers.

Lieutenant Naylor, with his own thirty troopers behind
him, asked the Turkish commander to withdraw. The Turk
refused. Naylor then said that he must halt while both

243

of them referred the situation to their superiors. Again the Turkish officer, still in a quite friendly manner, refused. He did not recognise the neutral zone; he had seen no British flags; he could not withdraw without orders although he did not want to fight the British. At this point a much larger body of Turkish horsemen appeared, swelling the total number to over a thousand, so to avoid having his own tiny force completely surrounded Naylor withdrew to Erenkeui, and from there signalled Colonel Shuttleworth at Chanak. The defences were immediately manned and Rear-Admiral Kelly, in command of the 4th Battle Squadron, was informed. That done, Shuttleworth was still in a considerable dilemma. In his own words: 'The situation was quite unanticipated. Peaceful penetration by armed men who did not wish to fight, and yet refused either to withdraw or to halt, had not been foreseen. . . .'

The Admiral was prepared to bombard towns within range of his guns when occupied by an advancing enemy, but these Turkish cavalrymen hardly came into that category. Shuttleworth decided to use again the friendly services of the Mutessarif, who appeared to be 'genuinely distressed' at the situation. At Shuttleworth's request he telephoned his compatriots at Saracheli and informed the Turkish commander that he must leave Erenkeui by 0600 hours the next morning or the British would be compelled to take action, and the responsibility for any bloodshed would therefore rest with him.

Between themselves Admiral Kelly and Colonel Shuttleworth agreed that the bombardment should not in fact commence until 1100 hours, partly so that the Turks should be given ample time to comply, but also so that Harington at Constantinople could be informed. Meanwhile Shuttleworth wrote a personal letter to the Turkish commander to be delivered by one of the gendarmerie, the 3rd Hussars were ordered not to fire unless actually fired upon, and the road and bridge north of Erenkeui were demolished by explosives. The Mutessarif asked to write a letter in Turkish to the Turkish commander impressing upon him the seriousness of the situation, and this was agreed and sent off with Shuttleworth's. Throughout the night the Chanak defence force stood to, expecting a possible attack. On the warships the gun crews prepared to open fire the next morning.

The morning of the 24th brought a rush of telegrams. During the night there had been a rumour through the Mutessarif that the Turks had left Erenkeui at 0430 hours that morning. Whether the rumour was true would have to be confirmed by reconnaissance, but a message from Harington informed Shuttleworth that although the Turks were not to be allowed to approach Chanak in force they were not to be engaged unnecessarily. This message, however, was only in answer to Shuttleworth's first news of a Turkish advance. It was closely followed by Harington's answer to the report on the situation during the night. The General warmly approved of the decision not to open fire and said that as he had now received news of a possible conference to be arranged between the Allies and Kemal, everything must be done to avoid unnecessary engagement. If, however, Shuttleworth was compelled to open fire then his action would be supported by the Commander-in-Chief. During the morning it was discovered that although the Turks had moved out of Erenkeui during the night, they had since returned and were constructing machine-gun emplacements.

Shuttleworth had received no answer to his messages sent to the Turks so that Harington's second orders had only arrived in the nick of time. Harington admitted later that he had gone to bed the previous night fully expecting that by morning hostilities would have broken out. Thus for the first time at Chanak British and Turks had been on the knife edge of war. It was not to be the last.

The situation for Harington was as difficult as can be imagined. He himself was as determined as a man could be in his position that a war should not break out. Nevertheless as a soldier he had a duty to obey orders from London, and also a duty to his own men, whom he could not allow to be overrun by the Turks. At the back of his mind he was convinced that Mustapha Kemal did not want war with Britain, but obviously, from remarks made later in his own autobiography, he must have had some reservations about the attitude of the British government.

The gap in his information was, despite his private belief, the true intention of the Turkish leader. Even with the advantage of hindsight it is difficult to come to a definite conclusion. Undoubtedly around Kemal there were close associates who wanted to go on to Constantinople and the Straits, into Eastern Thrace and perhaps further, possibly to retake Salonika and Macedonia. The defeat of the Greeks, regarded as the tools of Lloyd George, had inspired some of the generals to think in terms of even more sweeping victories. Kemal himself was determined to keep his demands within the bounds of the original National Pact. He had sufficient detachment to see his countrymen through the eyes of others. He knew the feeling of many Europeans about them and could visualise how an armed return to former subject territories would rouse again the only half-dead hatred in the Balkans and among the Great Powers for 'the abominable Turk'. At present the Great Powers were divided, but if his demands became unreasonable, if there was a hint that he intended to revive the Ottoman Empire, then France, Italy and the Balkan nations might well swing round to support the British. In a sense, if he attacked the British, as well as risking defeat he would be proving Lloyd George right. If his troops moved into Europe he would be inviting a crusade against them.

Lord Kinross, Kemal's biographer, portrays him as essentially a man with a clear head, and the ability to assess realities of the great military commander. One cannot argue with the assessment, yet it seems strange that if he was determined not to have war with the British he should have pressed the matter so close at Chanak. Kemal, of course, was a bold man; he may have thought that the British would not back up their threats. He had observed the conduct of Lloyd George towards the Greeks and consequently regarded him as a man of many words and little faith. Nevertheless he must have known that the risks were enormous. A scuffle between two private soldiers outside Chanak; some shots exchanged; a couple of hot-headed or panicky subalterns on either side, or one of each, and the war could have started. Kemal had some estimate of Harington as a man who wanted to avoid a war, but the Commander-in-Chief, although in constant touch, was not at Chanak. Neither for that matter was Kemal. Both had to rely on subordinate officers. British junior officers at Chanak had to remind their men perpetually not to be provoked into firing at the Turks. Perhaps the Turks did likewise, but the Turkish army, which contained many irregular formations, was nothing like so well disciplined as the British. So far as international opinion was concerned, as the Turkish army, flushed with its recent victories, was 'attacking' and the British 'defending', though by means short of gunfire, few people, even in Paris or Rome, would have believed, in the event of an incident, that the British had fired the first shot.

It was therefore a dangerous game, and one in which Kemal had to rely on his own estimate of his opponent's reactions. Some he guessed correctly, but hidden from him was the degree of resolution of the British government. On that it is likely that Kemal, for once in his life, guessed wrongly. He was aware, of course, of the disunity between the Allies. He knew, because it was published in the British press, of the public lack of enthusiasm in Britain for war. It also seemed likely that Harington, as Allied Commander-in-Chief, would try to prevent an outbreak of hostilities. The crux of the matter was whether this was possible, for ultimately Harington, like Rumbold and Brock, took his orders from London.

It was there that the real danger existed. Churchill had said 'the Allies might bolt'. Plainly they had. 'The press might howl.' It did, every day. 'The nation might not support us.' Parliament had not been recalled and neither it nor the electorate had been consulted. Churchill had listed his 'group of resolute men', including Balfour, Austen Chamberlain, Birkenhead and Worthington-Evans, but by the middle of September the group really consisted of himself and the Prime Minister. They 'intended to force the Turk to a negotiated peace before he should set foot in Europe'.

Mustapha Kemal, underestimating his opponents, deliberately delayed replying to the Allied note. The delay in fact gave him no advantage, for warlike preparations went on apace in London during the time-lag. Always impatient of detail of any kind and especially of military detail, Lloyd George, bored by timetables, shipping schedules, gun weights and calibres, equipment and arms, handed over the preparations to Churchill. It was a task that the Secretary of State for the Colonies enjoyed. As First Lord of the Admiralty in 1914 he had delighted, with far more than civilian zest, in controlling the Royal Navy. Now he headed the so-called Committee of Ministers which had charge of a possible war with Turkey. More often than not the only Minister present was Churchill himself. The other members of the Committee were the professional heads of the three Services, Beatty, Cavan and Trenchard.

The function of these three, the Admiral, the General and the Air Chief Marshal, like the Foreign Office and Colonial officials who also attended, was to advise on policy, not to initiate it. Inevitably these functions merged at some points. Senior Service officers have opinions, and their opinions influence their judgment and the advice they offer to their political masters. It is interesting therefore to examine the attitudes taken by the three officers concerned with the central direction of the war planning at this time.

Something of Beatty's career and character has been described already. Arrogant, bold and forceful, he was convinced that the Royal Navy could hold the Straits. Admiral Brock, on the spot, was doubtful, and was not prepared to guarantee that the navy afloat could defeat the Turkish army on land. But for Beatty to have thought that the Navy, a service which had produced Nelson and himself, could in any war be worsted, would have been to question the faith of a lifetime. He was, however, prepared in the Committee to support the viewpoint of another service, the R.A.F., represented by Trenchard. Hugh Trenchard, like Beatty, had owed some part of his preferment to Churchill's help. Beginning life in the Scots Fusiliers, he had been a somewhat unusual soldier. Poor by reason of his father's bankruptcy, he had withdrawn into himself and gained the nickname of 'the Camel' for his aloofness. In the long, hot Indian afternoons, like Churchill before him, he had read seriously while others slept. Severely wounded in the South African War he had gone to Switzerland a hopeless invalid, with one lung shot through and his body paralysed from the hips down. In that condition, in a sort of desperation, he had launched himself down the Cresta Run. Thrown from the toboggan, almost miraculously the violent fall had performed the task of a modern osteopath, and Trenchard had resumed his career.

At the age of thirty-nine he learnt to fly an aeroplane, not in fact very well; but from then onwards his progress was that of the embryo Royal Flying Corps, later to become the Royal Air Force. If one man can be said to have formed and preserved that service as a separate and powerful entity against military and naval prejudice and political indifference, then that one man was Hugh Trenchard. Consequently, but for entirely different reasons, Trenchard was as obsessed with his own service as was Beatty. The Admiral's obsession lay rooted in the past, in 100 years of naval supremacy; the Air Marshal's looked towards the future.

Sandwiched between these two powerful characters, Beatty and Trenchard (the latter had with eminence acquired a new nickname, 'Boom'), was 'Fatty' Cavan, the Chief of the Imperial General Staff. He was not, of course, fat, but lean[1]. Vansittart described him as 'a spare little man who looked as if it would pain him to pain anybody'. He was a very conventional soldier indeed. The son of an Irish peer, from Eton he had gone to Sandhurst and had then been commissioned in the Grenadier Guards. In the late war he had served in France and then in command of a corps in Italy. Finally, in complete command of all British forces there, he had been instrumental in turning the series of

---

[1] It was the age of nicknames. Plumer was 'Plum', Harington was 'Tim', Worthington-Evans was 'Horace', Asquith was 'Squiffy', Birkenhead was 'F.E.', and had been 'Galloper'. Lloyd George had several. Only Curzon escaped. The Foreign Office simply called him 'the Marquess'.

disastrous defeats of the Italians by the Austrians into an Allied victory. With neither the flamboyance of Beatty nor the single-mindedness of Trenchard, Cavan was nevertheless an able soldier, and his task was to persuade the government that the primary need at Chanak was for soldiers.

On the ground there the Turks outnumbered the British to an almost ludicrous extent. In addition in Constantinople, as Harington telegraphed, 'many undesirable elements have drifted into the town and it is known that some 20,000 Turks and probably an equal number of Greeks are armed'. The Commander-in-Chief said that 'we are living on a sort of volcano'. Furthermore, Harington did not share Beatty's confidence that Constantinople could be defended entirely by the Navy. So concerned was he that on September 22nd he arranged for the evacuation of the wives and families of British troops, and laid plans for the embarkation of the British civilian residents at very short notice.

There were still only three battalions of infantry, Loyals, Gordons and Royal Sussex, at Chanak, and in Constantinople three more. One of these, the Irish Guards, had been sent out post-haste to repel the Greeks when they had threatened the city. It was commanded by Harold Alexander, at thirty-one the youngest colonel in the British army. A man who had emerged from the Great War with three wounds, five mentions in despatches, the D.S.O., the M.C., the Legion of Honour and the Russian Order of St. Anne, twenty-two years later he was to be a field marshal and the Commander of the Allied Armies in Italy. Apart from the military distinction of their commanding officer, the Irish Guards had one other advantage. They were up to full strength, an advantage not shared by the other two infantry battalions, which were very weak indeed.

This shortage of men was Cavan's problem. Lloyd George and Churchill, and of course Beatty and Trenchard, all favoured ships and aeroplanes as a substitute. Naturally they were important, and in both respects the British had a decided advantage over the Turks. Nevertheless, naval guns and aeroplanes could not cancel out the Turks' overwhelming superiority in manpower. It was Cavan's task to try to adjust this inbalance. Eventually he had some success but the disparity remained, and his achievement was attended by difficulties and disagreements with his naval and air force colleagues. Some more battalions were moved to Chanak. The 2nd Highland Light Infantry, recruited in the Glasgow slums and known to the rest of the army from their initials H.L.I. as Hell's Last Issue, was in Cairo on the 22nd September. They were preparing for their annual parade, on which they trooped the Assaye Colour, which they carried, in addition to the King's and Regimental Colours, to commemorate the great part they had played under Wellington, then merely General Wellesley, in the Mahratta War. The blanco and the metal polish were put aside, the Colours and the regimental silver deposited in the Ottoman Bank, and the battalion embarked from Alexandria with the 1st King's Own Scottish Borderers from Ismalia within ten hours of receiving their warning order. They arrived at Chanak at 8 a.m. on September 25th. Anchorage for the troopship was difficult to find as the narrows were crowded with the warships of the Mediterranean fleet, their guns trained on the eastern shore.

The H.L.I. took up positions in the line east of Nagara Point and thence northwards to the sea. The Borderers took over a part of the line round Chanak itself, previously sparsely manned by the Loyals. The situation was described to the two battalions by a senior officer as being 'a bit awkward'. As the H.L.I. from their positions could actually see Turkish cavalry on the hills to their front, this was something of an understatement. Colonel Shuttleworth had still received no answer to his letters sent to the Turks. Late at night on September 26th Major-General Marden arrived on the destroyer *Montrose* from Constantinople to take over command from Shuttleworth of the Defence Force which, with the addition of the 2nd Sherwood Foresters hastily moved from Constantinople, had now become two brigades, each of three battalions. The two brigades, the 83rd and the 85th Infantry, were now commanded by Shuttleworth and Colonel A. T. Beckwith respectively. Marden's orders, as he told Shuttleworth and Rear-Admiral

Kelly, were 'not to fight if he could possibly help it'.

Cavan's and Harington's request for more troops was being answered. On their way to Constantinople from England were the 2nd Grenadier Guards, the 3rd Coldstream Guards and the 11th Royal Marine Light Infantry. The 1st Duke of Wellington's Regiment and the 1st South Staffordshire had arrived from Gibralter to take their place with the 1st Buffs and the 2nd Essex Regiment protecting Constantinople on the Asiatic shore. By October 7th Marden would have one more battalion added to each of his brigades, the 2nd Royal Fusiliers and the 2nd Battalion of the Rifle Brigade from Aldershot. The artillery of the Defence Forces now amounted to fourteen 18-pounder guns, six 4-inch howitzers, eight 3·7 howitzers and twelve 6-inch howitzers. In addition there were fifteen naval 12-pounder guns, plus 6-inch guns from H.M.S. *Benbow* which, with incredible effort as each gun weighed $7\frac{1}{2}$ tons, sailors from the fleet had unshipped and manhandled into emplacements improvised out of heavy timbers and concrete blocks. Four battleships, four light cruisers and eight destroyers lay at anchor offshore, but Trenchard had been active as well as Beatty, for simultaneously with Marden's arrival there appeared upon the scene twelve seaplanes, sixteen Snipe aircraft and eight Bristol fighters. A further two squadrons of planes were on their way by sea from Egypt.

So, as Kemal delayed in answering the Allied note of September 23rd, the British forces being ranged against him increased in numbers and firepower. In consequence the odds against successful military action on his part lengthened. It was still open to him, of course, to regard this massing of naval and military might as a gigantic bluff. The circumstances were different, but he had only recently seen the warships of Britain lying massive but impotent off the quay at Smyrna. Apart from the technical difficulties they would not bombard Constantinople. Although during this period he made underground attempts to obtain some of the Sultan's warships, as a soldier who had fought at Gallipoli he knew the limitations imposed upon warships by those narrow waters. So, he must have reasoned, did the British admirals. With regard to the soldiers on land, despite their recent increases he could still comfort himself with a calculation of his own enormous superiority in manpower. Perhaps, therefore, the British were merely putting on a show to save face, the same consideration which impelled him to push his men as close to the Chanak outposts as possible.

From Kemal's point of view the unknown factor in his calculations was still the real intentions of the British government. In this respect external appearances were deceptive. Parliament had not been recalled; some government Ministers were still abroad; King George V was not in his capital but at Balmoral. General Harington was endeavouring to get in touch with Kemalist generals, and Lord Curzon, it was learned, was anxious to have private talks with Kemal's representative, Ali Fethi, who had been in London and was now in Paris or Rome. If, taking all these signs into account, Kemal did think that Lloyd George and his small but powerful body of supporters were not prepared to go to war, a glimpse behind the scenes in London would have been a revelation to him.

Whether they were wise, and whether their decisions, if made public, would have been popular, is not the point. During this period they only received encouragement from two quarters: some qualified support in the columns of the *Daily Telegraph* and a telegram from Lord Jellicoe, the Governor-General of New Zealand, saying that by the night of September 21st 12,000 ex-officers and men and 300 nurses had volunteered for recall. Nevertheless, of their determination there can be no doubt. The King might be at Balmoral, but he was in constant touch with London. His private secretary, Lord Stamfordham, had in his custody the necessary proclamations for the King's signature to declare a state of emergency. The Royal train was waiting at Ballater station ready to whisk the King to London. There a committee of Service officers and senior officials of the Foreign Office and other ministries was considering the putting into force of 'the War Book'. This was the body of regulations and measures which was designed so that the nation could pass from peace to war. It had two stages, 'Precautionary' and 'War'. As the Committee observed, certain measures prescribed in the Precautionary stage had been carried out already. The War Book was designed 'to meet the situation which would arise in the event of a world war in which the whole resources of the Empire would be drawn upon'. The Committee decided 'that is not the situation that now presents itself'. Accordingly, strict censorship, blockade measures and special legislation would, it was thought, be at the moment inappropriate. It would not be that sort of war. Nevertheless those items in the War Book which were designed to alert and prepare the Army, Navy and Air Force and Intelligence departments for the outbreak of hostilities were recommended to the Cabinet for adoption.

A day later the proceedings of Churchill's Committee of Ministers were reported to the Cabinet and approved. Most of the measures proposed concerned the despatch of more troops, including a brigade of artillery and possibly two regiments of cavalry from Egypt. Bombers were offered to Harington should he require them. Harington was also instructed again to warn Kemal that his forces would be liable to attack if they invaded the neutral zone. The Committee, and therefore the Cabinet, was particularly concerned that there should be 'no ambiguity regarding the right of the Allied Commander-in-Chief at Constantinople to take action'.

Only in one likely sphere of activity was there any measure of doubt and that was where naval operations were concerned. Lord Curzon was against 'provocative action', Lloyd George wanted 'no Kemalists on the water'. Admiral Brock continually pointed out that his guns could destroy roads and artillery emplacements but would be of less use against troop concentrations. He also wanted to know if he was expected to clear the Sea of Marmora of every ship afloat. In the event, despite a number of frenzied telegrams, he was never told. On one subject, however, he was given categoric orders. Reports had been received that 'Bolshevist submarines and submarine-chasers and mine layers are to be placed at the disposal of the Turkish Nationalists'. 'Any such craft appearing in the Straits should be attacked.' If they approached the Straits from the Black Sea under the Russian flag they were to be warned off. 'In the event of risk to any Allied ship from the approach of any such craft encountered in the Black Sea or Straits, it should be sunk.' Somewhat strangely 'it was not deemed expedient to warn the Soviet government at present of these intentions'.

While these instructions were pouring out from London the Prime Minister was in the country at Churt, but his own determination and attitude were frighteningly obvious. On September 22nd he telephoned Sir Maurice Hankey, the Secretary to the Cabinet, with advice on the preparations to be passed on to Worthington-Evans, Lord Lee and Winston Churchill. He was concerned because the Kemalists, he understood, had indicated September 30th as the day beyond which they would not wait to have their demands answered. In which case Lloyd George wanted to be ready for them. He was not unduly depressed by the prospect. 'It would be a great triumph if we could defeat a heavy Turkish attack alone, without any assistance from the French and demonstrate to the world that even from a military point of view we are not as helpless as our enemies of every description imagine us to be.' The details of military planning might not concern the Prime Minister, but he was quite prepared to commit the increasing British force in Turkey against Kemal's army. Also, in words made famous in the Suez crisis thirty-four years later, he was prepared, if necessary, that Britain should 'go it alone'.

There were in fact a number of other similarities between 1922 and 1956. Both Prime Ministers had an inner circle of Minister confidants; on both occasions there was considerable popular and press agitation against a war and a failure of Commonwealth nations to come up to Downing Street expectations. There was something of the same atmosphere as well. In 1956 Anthony Eden was determined to teach Nasser a lesson. In 1922 Lloyd George, although unlike Eden he had never met his adversary, undoubtedly treasured a personal feeling against Kemal. Like Nasser, perhaps Kemal could be 'toppled'. The year 1956 produced many rumours of impending internal revolutions to remove Nasser. In just the same way the Cabinet in 1922 was often intrigued and encouraged by stories of Kemal's insecurity and his fear of assassination. In both cases a British Prime Minister misjudged world opinion and the popularity and stability of his opponent. Equally, it appears, both Nasser and Kemal made the initial mistake of thinking that the British would not go to the lengths of war.

Historical parallels should not be strained too far and undoubtedly some factors are common to every crisis, and not all of them can be laid at the door of the politicians. Suez in 1956 produced its crop of military 'nonsenses'. So did Chanak in 1922. The most notable concerned 1,000 men of the Royal Air Force. When the crisis broke in the middle of September they were *en route* by sea on the *Braemar Castle* for Iraq. As Cavan was pressing the question of manpower reinforcements Winston Churchill wondered if these airmen might not be diverted to Turkey. They had no rifles or other arms, he knew, and he realised that they were all technical men, aircraft mechanics and the like. Could they not, however, be utilised to keep order in Constantinople? Trenchard was considerably less than enthusiastic. These men were all needed by the R.A.F. in Iraq, and, he emphasised, were not specially trained for anything other than their technical trades. It was decided, nevertheless, to ask Harington if he wanted them. Harington did not, and said so, but he got them just the same.

The 1,000 airmen arrived in Constantinople. There they performed no useful function and it was decided that as soon as more soldiers came out, the airmen should resume their interrupted journey. At the last moment, however, to assuage their wounded pride, it was decided that they should be allowed to stage a demonstration march through Constantinople, presumably to show the Turks not only the size but the variety of Imperial resources. In their best sky-blue uniforms, still somewhat unfamiliar to those who had known the Royal Flying Corps in khaki and the Royal Naval Air Service in traditional blue, they marched through the city. Their commanding officer was pleased and proud of the bearing of his men, unused to parade-ground drill, until he heard an unmistakably English female voice from the crowd: 'A smart lot, aren't they? But how in God's name did the Portuguese in those adorable blue uniforms get mixed up in this mess?'

It was in fact with reference to reinforcements of aircraft and in no spirit of sarcasm that Harington wrote to Trenchard: 'This is the rummest sort of war I have ever seen. It is mixed up with diplomats of all nations, soldiers and sailors, Greeks and Turks, infidels of every kind and Bolsheviks, and the town is a seething mass of the dirtiest-looking devils you ever saw'; and, in conclusion: 'Thank you so much for all your help. I will do my best to look after the units you are sending me.'

The situation, and not only from the viewpoint of G.H.Q. in Constantinople, now appeared to be a very curious one indeed. Technically the Allies, by their note of September 23rd to Ankara, had served a kind of ultimatum upon Mustapha Kemal. Only one of the Allies, however, Great Britain, was prepared to enforce it. If Kemal returned a truculent answer saying in effect that he did not wish to send a representative to 'Venice or elsewhere' to negotiate with Britons, Frenchmen, Italians, Japanese, Romanians, Yugoslavs and Greeks, what were all those nations, save the British, going to do about it? The answer was nothing. The French and the Italians were half in league with the Turks already, despite the presence of their troops in Constantinople. The Romanians and the Yugoslavs were concerned, of course, but would probably take their lead from France. The Yugoslavs were in fact more suspicious of Bulgaria than Turkey. The Greeks were defeated, and the Japanese were on the other side of the world.

It was up to Britain then, whatever answer Kemal returned, or, as seemed possible, if he returned no answer at all. The British Cabinet had not liked the wording in the note about the neutral zone: 'the provisional neutrality of which has been proclaimed by the Allied governments'. The word 'provisional' stuck in their throats. Lord Curzon explained that it was the strongest phrase the French would accept, as they argued that the status of the territory was merely temporary and that the agreement had been reached not with Kemal but the Sultan. An even simpler explanation was that Poincaré and the French government did not want to fight the Turks. Lloyd George and the British government seemingly did. 'Neutrality', remembering Belgium and the cause of Britain's entry into the 1914–18 War, was a magical word. A nation could go to war to protect 'neutrality', but 'provisional neutrality' was not quite the same thing. Consequently, with the exception of Lord Curzon, the members of the Cabinet in London turned their minds to what was, in their view, another condition in the note, the stipulation in the first sentence that the Turkish government would inform the Allies of their readiness to send a representative to negotiate 'without delay'. As the days passed with no reply from Ankara, Lloyd George began to grow impatient.

The reasons for his impatience were fourfold. First a kind of professional, and perhaps therefore almost subconscious, desire for speed and pace in the negotiations. If there was to be a diplomatic coup or its alternative, military action, then the momentum of the confrontation between Britain and Turkey must be maintained. Troops, aircraft and warships were on their way. If Kemal merely drifted or dallied the urgency would disappear and the steam would go out of the crisis. The second reason lay in Lloyd George's estimate of Kemal's character. To the British Prime Minister Kemal was an Oriental, 'a carpet-seller in a bazaar', who enjoyed haggling for its own sake. Like many devious men of humble Celtic background Lloyd George saw himself as a model of simple peasant rectitude. It was not the way in Llanystumdwy, therefore it would have to be made plain to the Turk that there was only one price.

The third reason for haste on the Prime Minister's part was perhaps the most curious of all. Unlike the previous two it was not subjective, but it depended nevertheless on Lloyd George's state of mind for its acceptance. British Military Intelligence had informed the Cabinet that Kemal himself intended to force the issue by a military advance upon Constantinople and Chanak on September 30th. At a distance of forty-six years it is impossible to trace the source of the information. Certainly it did not emanate from Harington or his headquarters in Constantinople. There had been reports, of course, of Kemal talking of moving before the winter, but Kemalist agents in Paris and London denied that there was any plan for a positive act of war. Whatever the origin of the forecast, the Cabinet believed it to be accurate, and Lloyd George, hitherto sceptical to a degree of military intelligence, accepted what may only have been a rumour or an inspired guess as fact. Therefore September 30th, only seven days from the despatch of the Ankara note, became in his mind the time limit for decision. The last factor which spurred Lloyd George on towards a showdown was complementary to the intelligence report, which it seemed to confirm, but was based on solid fact. It was the deteriorating situation at Chanak.

General Marden had taken over command there on September 26th and on the morning of the next day was able to observe the advance of about 2,000 Turkish cavalry towards Chanak. Standing on the Hospital Hill to the north of the town, through his binoculars he saw a race between a squadron of the 3rd Hussars and a large body of Turkish horsemen for dominance of Asmali Tepe. The Turks won. Accordingly Marden gave the order for all British troops save the Hussars and the company of the Loyal Regiment on their mules to retire behind the barbed-wire defences.

By 3 a.m. on September 28th all the British were inside, manning their defences. Marden telegraphed to Harington for permission to open fire if the Turks attacked, which was granted. Turkish detachments were now appearing on all sides and Marden realised that there must be many tracks through the rough hilly country which were not marked on his own map. It was along these tracks that the Turks were infiltrating round as well as to the front of his position. Immediately he set his men to the task of digging more trenches and putting up more barbed-wire entanglements. The most disturbing factor about this steady advance was

259

the presence, observed for the first time, of Turkish infantry as well as cavalry. Soldiers mounted on horses could not attack good barbed-wire defences; infantry could and would.

On September 25th in London the Cabinet met at twelve noon, with Beatty, Cavan and Trenchard in attendance, and considered General Harington's report on the advance of the Turkish cavalry to Erenkeui and its subsequent retreat. For perhaps the first time there was serious discussion of the basic practicalities of the war which seemed about to break out. Lord Beatty, having consulted with Rear-Admiral Webb who had just returned from the Near East, was now, it appeared, less confident than previously that the navy, unaided, could prevent a Turkish invasion of Constantinople. If Admiral Brock could have been given *carte blanche* earlier then perhaps by now he would have been in a position to deny the city to the Turks. Unfortunately the Admiral had been hampered by political considerations, and, Beatty implied, still was; therefore the best that the navy could do would be to delay the inevitable. Lord Cavan doubted if the French and Italian troops would even co-operate with the British in keeping order in Constantinople. He too thought that a prolonged defence of Constantinople would be impossible. 'In fact,' said Cavan, 'our General was operating from a hostile capital.' Such views were obviously unwelcome to the Prime Minister, who wondered if the 20,000 Greeks in the city could not be enlisted by Harington 'to form a Civil Guard to help in the maintenance of order'.

In the general discussion which followed it fell to Winston Churchill to point out that the Cabinet had only just realised from Harington's report, what they had apparently not realised before, that the Chanak perimeter was only four miles long. Previously it had been understood that it was fifteen miles long. Therefore, said Churchill, the Turks could establish positions on the Dardanelles either to the north or south. Some of the confusion about the neutral zone and Chanak had at last been resolved. The Cabinet for the first time understood that what Marden and his force were defending was not a large area of territory but a small Turkish coastal town protected by trenches and barbed wire, and now hemmed in by considerable numbers of Turks.

Finally, the Prime Minister asked Trenchard hopefully if the R.A.F. could not prevent the Turks from taking Constantinople. If they had possessed the number of machines they had at the end of the war, said Trenchard, in conjunction with the Navy it would have been possible. Now, unfortunately, 'they could delay a Turkish advance along the Ismid Peninsula but they could not guarantee to stop such an advance'. In the light of this information the Cabinet decided to give General Harington new priorities; 'he should hold Chanak and Gallipoli at all costs and, provided his task at Chanak was not endangered, should remain at Constantinople as long as it was possible to do so'. So now the reverse order of importance was the Ismid peninsula, Constantinople and then Chanak and Gallipoli. As Gallipoli was not threatened at the moment and the Turks were in sight, almost within touch, at Chanak, it was there that the conflict, if conflict there was to be, must come. On that day the War Office report on the distribution of Turkish troops was as follows: at Erenkeui over 1,000 men, at Bigha 800 men and 4 guns, north of the gulf of Edremid over 2,000 men and 12 guns. Further east were the 6th and 4th Turkish Corps amounting to 25,000 men and 80 guns, in the Smyrna area there were 24,000 men and 79 guns and, moving on the Ismid peninsula, 11,000 men and 24 guns. 'The situation,' added the War Office, 'appears to be most critical and uncertain.'

On September 27th, at 10 a.m., the Chief of the Imperial General Staff received a telegram from General Harington. It was not very well expressed but its meaning was quite clear. 'Losing a lot of lives in hanging on is what I want to guard against especially if Cabinet then say that they cannot reinforce me. Why not start at once and give Turkey Constantinople and Maritza, having offered them to them, and so end it all. Keep a force and big fleets on Gallipoli with advanced guard Chanak. These small forces trying to stop here and keep order and ordered to fight to last at Chanak, if Mustapha's reply is truculent, are bound to get into difficulties if negotiations are prolonged. There is no time for delay.

Remember Turks are within sight of their goal and are naturally elated. No one is more anxious to avoid a war than I am, but it is the very way to get dragged into one.'

Bearing in mind the Cabinet's instructions, Harington's views were doubtless disturbing enough, but there were other problems on their way for a harassed Lord Cavan and the British Cabinet. On the same day as Harington's telegram arrived, what had begun as a military and naval mutiny on Chios and Mitylene on September 23rd erupted into a full-scale revolution in Athens. On September 27th King Constantine was forced to abdicate in favour of his son, the Crown Prince George, and Greece was in the grip of a conspiracy of colonels. A Colonel Plastiras appeared to be their leader; he had organised an air drop of revolutionary leaflets on Athens. All the conspirators seemed to be military men, but Eleftherios Veneselos, who had been in exile in Paris, was now coming to London as their emissary.

15

'*The moment to avert the disaster has arrived*'
War Office telegram to General Harington

Constantine had never been popular in Britain and his abdication provoked a storm of valedictory abuse in the press. On September 28th the *Daily Express* ran as its headline 'Tino makes his second exit', and talked of 'the traitor king' who 'lays down his sceptre that he may save his life', and later of 'this ludicrous weakling'. *The Times* managed to sound like an Oscar Wilde dowager and called the ex-King of the Hellenes 'a paltry personage'. For the British, Constantine had never seemed able to do the right thing; if in fact he had hung on in Greece and fought out a civil war none of his critics would have become his champions.[1] Now as he prepared to leave Greece for the last time his alleged pro-German sympathies during the 1914–18 War were again revived, and he was represented as either a villain or a fool. All the disasters of Greece, the army's defeat, the destruction of Smyrna, and the pitiful problem of the refugees, were hung round his neck.

[1] Vansittart put the popular view concisely: 'Nobody in my time saw more ups and downs, or deserved the ups less.'

So for a few days he became a crowned scapegoat, a convenient sacrificial victim for policies which had failed. Those newspapers, and they were in the majority, which were opposed to war with Turkey, strengthened their argument by disparaging both the Greeks and, somewhat illogically, the king of whom they had just rid themselves. The pendulum of anti-Greek feeling swung to its limit with a report in all papers on September 27th of a speech by Lord St. Davids which produced the headlined quotation on the Greeks as 'Bad at Fighting but First Class at Murder'. Few people felt quite as strongly as Lord St. Davids, who presumably had his own sources of information as Chairman of the Ottoman Railways. Whether the shareholders he was addressing in London on that occasion agreed with his doubtless entirely objective remarks it is impossible to say; the more general feeling in Britain was simply one of weariness with the affairs of Greece.

In France and the United States, too, politicians and the public alike, although as in Britain they felt a sympathy which was expressed in generous contributions to refugee funds, regarded the new revolution as further confirmation of the 'impossible' nature of Greek politics. Fervent phil-hellenes felt differently of course. Mr. Morgenthau, now in Athens as Chairman of the League of Nations Refugee Settlement Commission, was overjoyed that the man he still referred to as 'the Kaiser's brother-in-law' had again been ejected from his throne. There was still a king in Greece of course, the new George II, which for one of Morgenthau's stark republican prejudices was a pity, but doubtless that would be remedied in time. For sentimental philhellenes like Morgenthau now looked forward confidently to the establishment of a liberal progressive regime, as if the presence of Constantine in Athens had been the only obstacle standing between the Greeks and a life of democratic sweetness and light.

Which just showed how wrong sentimental philhellenes could be about Greece. Actually for nearly a hundred years the burden of expectations placed upon Greece by her admirers had been a heavy one. A poor country, ruled for centuries by the deadening hand of the Turks, with no native dynasty or aristocracy, she had been expected in the nineteenth century, and was now expected in the twentieth, to be able to place herself at one bound beside nations with centuries of civil development. It was not a standard applied to the rest of the Balkan nations, formerly part of the Ottoman Empire. The curse of Greece was her history and her name. Men who called themselves 'Greeks', it was felt, must surely have some aptitude, even if inherited from the fifth century B.C., for democracy; after all, they had invented the word. No one though of Sophia, Bucharest or Belgrade as 'the cradle of democracy'; but Athens, that was different. Hardly a politician or a journalist could resist the phrase. Consequently, often in the teeth of their own experience, the friends of Greece in Western Europe and the U.S.A. hoped that each change of political fortune in Greece might produce a modern Pericles or a race of philosopher-politicians. What in fact the Greeks did produce was the original of a type since become familiar in their native land and elsewhere: the ambitious political colonel on the make.

Traditionally, in Britain professional soldiers tend to be mildly right-wing in their political views and sentimentally royalist in their outlook. In a country, too, where constitutionalism, without a written constitution, has been brought to a fine art, they are divorced from politics. Socially they are, or at least were, drawn from a class which, if not necessarily aristocratic or rich, either thinks, or has been taught to think, that the making of a fortune is not of primary importance. Wide variations exist within the generalisation, of course, and existed in 1922: say from Cavan, rich and aristocratic, to Harington, of very modest means and middle class. Nevertheless in Britain there was a 'type' of army officer, with recognisable and predictable social and political attributes and attitudes, virtues and vices. Even in countries as firmly republican and professionally egalitarian as France and the U.S.A. the 'type' can also still be distinguished.

Nothing further from this accepted pattern can be

imagined than the typical Greek army officer of the 1920's. There was no equivalent of the British 'army family', the French or German squirearchy with one of its sons destined to the profession of arms, or the Southern military family in the States with a grandfather who had fought with Lee and a grandson at West Point. Greek officers were poor for the good reason that no rich Greek wanted his son to be a soldier. They were all politicians, as General Marden had remarked, because they despised practising politicians, not a difficult task. They had few ideals of loyalty to the throne as an institution or personally to the Sovereign. Consequently many were republicans. It cannot however be said that they were democrats. They themselves wished to be politicians, but not politicians exposed to the professional hazard of the ballot box.

The revolution in Greece in 1922 was not a popular rising, despite ample material in a defeated and demobilised army, an invasion of refugees, and a discredited policy, to bring one about. It had started as an organised mutiny and it developed into a military coup. Although for the moment a king was on the throne and Veniselos was prepared to give help and advice, the men who had seized power were republican, authoritarian, and soldiers. A Revolutionary Committee now ruled Greece and its leading spirits were Colonels Plastiras and Gonatas, archetypes of their class and profession.

Plastiras was the prime mover. A republican by conviction, he had supported Veniselos, presumably as the lesser of two evils. In Anatolia he had commanded a brigade of Evzones, the élite corps of the Greek army, with vigour and determination, earning himself two nicknames, 'Black Pepper' from his own men, and the 'Black Devil' from the Turks. On Constantine's return in 1921, hearing a rumour of his own pending dismissal, he had successfully threatened the mutiny of his whole brigade and so stayed in command. Like many future revolutionaries he had not been loved by his military superiors. Prince Andrew had regarded him as a trouble-maker who concentrated more on the prosecution of his own political aims than upon the overall interests of the army. Be that as it may, and with their different backgrounds and opinions it was inevitable that the two soldiers would disagree, the important question was now what use Plastiras would make of the power given him by the army.

It was an interesting question to many outside Greece. Britain was, as always, suspicious of military regimes. Given the condition of Greece at the time it had not been difficult to agree with Lord Beaverbrook and predict some sort of revolution. That it had put into power not a nice, conventional, parliamentary government but a military dictatorship was however a disappointment. When it became known that one of the professed aims of Plastiras was the reorganisation of the Greek army and a fight for eastern Thrace, apprehension changed to alarm. Just as Constantine on his return had been unable to reverse Veniselos' policy in Anatolia, so Plastiras, having ousted Constantine, could not advocate acceptance of Mustapha Kemal's demands. Military dictators do not achieve power on a platform of national humility. Smyrna and the Greek colony in Asia Minor was gone for ever, but there was still eastern Thrace which could be represented as Greek. Plastiras began to prepare the Greek army and people to combat 'a Turkish invasion of the homeland'.

Once more Veniselos, in harness again, was hurrying to London to confer with his old friend Lloyd George. For one British newspaper and its proprietor, Lord Beaverbrook, this was too much like history repeating itself. So the *Daily Express*, which was still prepared to support a government defending British interests, began to differentiate between the holding of the Straits and assistance to the Greeks in eastern Thrace. Beaverbrook had been in Athens and seen one defeated Greek army return. He had not approved of Lloyd George's policies, but if as a result there was to be a show down between the British and the Turks, then, albeit reluctantly, he would take the 'patriotic' line. This did not, however, imply future support for more secret plots hatched out between Veniselos and Lloyd George. Beaverbrook did not trust the Prime Minister and suspected that he had a plan to hold a general election at a time of national crisis, a 'Coupon Election' of a different sort with an appeal to national unity which would once again steamroller his coalition government into power. The *Express* therefore began a campaign designed to undermine such a possibility.

Mustapha Kemal had not only smashed the Greek army but he had also 'smashed the secretly prepared plans of the Coalition for a general election'. 'The fate of political parties in England has been flung into the flames of Smyrna.' The date for the general election, announced the *Express*, had been fixed for October 28th because of 'a subterranean fight for the £2,000,000 in the party war chest'. The Conservative party was to hold its National Conference on November 15th. If there was a general election before then the money could be spent on Coalition candidates, before those Conservatives who were anti-Lloyd George could prevent it. All these plans, argued the *Express*, had now fallen to the ground because the Turks had ruined the Prime Minister's foreign policy. 'The Coalition proposes but Kemal disposes.' This final argument was not, of course, true. Beaverbrook was exposing motives and taking the risk that what he maintained had happened would happen. Under the guise of revealing past policy he hoped to knock away any support for such a policy in the future. As for the other newspapers, the *Daily Mail* was still passionately anti-war, and *The Times* diplomatically concentrated on foreign and not home affairs. The *Manchester Guardian*, Liberal, and in former times pro-Lloyd George, confined itself to pointing out the dangers and futility of war. Only the *Telegraph* stayed rather stodgily in favour of the government, despising rumours, scandals, and back-biting in time of national emergency. Overall it was a disappointing press for Lloyd George and certainly gave no suggestion to the new regime in Greece that it might hope for sympathy or assistance from Britain.

The crisis with its focal point at Chanak was however still in being. The British press and public might be against helping the Greeks or fighting the Turks, but the unknown quantity was still the British Prime Minister. He had encouraged the Greeks before with mere winks and nods;

might he not do it again? Chanak itself had now grown in importance out of all proportion to its strategic significance. Constantinople and the Ismid peninsula could be given up but not Chanak; it was now a matter of prestige. Very few people, and only one newspaper, the *Daily Mail*, actually had the courage to say that it didn't matter either and could be handed over to the Turks tomorrow.

Mustapha Kemal had still not replied to the Allied note when the Greek revolution broke out. Although from his own point of view he must have had reservations about unconditional acceptance of its terms, it seems very likely that events in Greece persuaded him to delay even more. For the advent of Plastiras had re-created the old dangerous, triangular situation between Greece, Turkey and Britain. Britain was opposed to Turkey at Chanak; now Greece was again opposed to Turkey in eastern Thrace. The missing link was the connection between Britain and Greece. The conjunction again of Lloyd George and Veniselos was obviously a dangerous one for Kemal. Officially, of course, there was no alliance or understanding between the two, but an atmosphere of intrigue and behind the scenes plotting clung to any of Lloyd George's dealings with Greece. Kemal was as suspicious as Beaverbrook. From the Turkish point of view it seemed that Britain might fight at Chanak and in Constantinople as well; now it appeared that the Greeks might fight in Thrace where a large proportion of the population was Greek. Not without reason the Turks were very suspicious of British motives and actions; not unnaturally they began to fear that Britain and Greece, with the same enemy, might co-ordinate their efforts. Consequently Kemal took the bold course and stepped up the pressure against the British at Chanak. He hoped that he would settle his differences with them, one way or the other, before the Greeks had time to reorganise themselves in eastern Thrace. His hopes of a peaceful settlement were centred upon two men, Lord Curzon and General Harington. Both on their own initiative were pursuing negotiations with Kemal's representatives. What, however, the Turkish leader could not know was how much power over events the

Foreign Secretary and the Commander-in-Chief actually possessed, for both, in the final analysis, had to take their orders from the Cabinet.

To that extent in the field of diplomacy Kemal committed two mistakes, which as an experienced military commander he should have avoided. First, he underestimated his enemy, and second, he committed himself to a course of action without knowing, as the Duke of Wellington had put it, 'what was on the other side of the hill'.

At Chanak itself, as more and more Turkish infantry appeared and advanced close up to the barbed-wire fences, the Defence Force, now named the 28th Division, could only stand and wait. The total strength of Marden's command was now 3,500 men, made up of two infantry brigades, a cavalry regiment minus one squadron, and in support the artillery batteries. On their way were five more infantry battalions and more artillery, but in the last few days of September these reinforcements, among them the two Guards battalions, the Rifle Brigade and the Royal Fusiliers, were still at sea, scheduled to arrive on October 7th. Even when they arrived some battalions would be earmarked for Constantinople or the Ismid peninsula. Meanwhile Marden and his men had to sweat it out. The men who were there have testified to the curious atmosphere of those days. The scene was like a film set for a battle. Two lines of trenches and emplacements, two fences of barbed wire. There was the likely enemy within sight. Short, stocky men in the main, dressed in dark khaki uniforms with a variety of headgear, from the kalpak, a tall conical fur hat widening towards the crown, to what looked like a sort of peakless military deerstalker. There they were, the Turks, feeding and watering horses, putting up wire and digging, or just standing, smoking cigarettes and watching. At night the searchlights of the battleships played along the valleys and over the rough hills, reflecting on the barbed wire and illuminating the sentries at their posts.

It is difficult to say who bore the greater strain, the gun crews of the fleet waiting night after night for the order from the land to open fire, or the soldiers in their trenches, never knowing when a familiar figure a few hundred yards away might suddenly take cover and convert himself into an enemy. To make the situation more nerve-racking, presumably on orders, the Turks carried out a policy of alternately blowing hot and cold. One day engaging soldiers in conversation in broken English across the wire and begging cigarettes; the next, shouting, jeering and making gestures as if to provoke some hot-tempered sentry to take a pot-shot at them. When new Turkish units appeared or when there were changes in the line it was noticeable that some were as pacific as possible, arriving with their rifles down-pointed, like sportsmen on a shoot, and later walking about without arms; whilst others were edgy and difficult in their manner, looking as if they were spoiling for a fight. It might have been just the different character of the regiments or perhaps of their commanding officers, but it looked suspiciously like orders from Ankara.

On the British side pressure had to be constantly exercised from the top downwards to prevent the rifles going off by themselves. Harington had to restrain Marden and Marden in turn had to restrain Shuttleworth. Lower down the scale, regimental officers constantly reminded their men that they must not open fire without orders. Nearly all the N.C.O.s and most of the older private soldiers had seen service in the 1914–18 War, as had the officers above subaltern rank; it was among the young men with no taste of action that the greatest difficulty was experienced. The 'old sweats' were steady enough; it was the recruits who had never fired a rifle except on the ranges who, as Marden said, 'simply itched to have a fight'. There were differences between the temperament and experience of the regiments to consider as well. The Gordons, who had been in Anatolia before, in 1921, and had lost comrades to Turkish brigands, and the rough, tough H.L.I. were more likely to let off a few rounds in anger than say the less temperamental, more steady going Royal Sussex. Again, both the H.L.I. and the Scottish Borderers had just come from Egypt, not a country at the time which gave the British soldier much reason to be well disposed towards the inhabitants of the Near East.

The most disturbing feeling suffered by the troops was that of being 'hemmed in'. As Marden admitted, the Turks had two complementary advantages. Their British opponents were provided with pre-1914 maps which did not mark roads and tracks constructed by Germans and Turks during the war, and the Turks could make use of their knowledge against the relatively static defence force. In consequence Marden and his subordinate commanders were frequently unpleasantly surprised to observe bodies of Turkish cavalry or infantry suddenly appearing where least expected, especially on the flanks of their position near the coast. It was this very closeness of the enemy, the fact that Turks might turn up round the side of a hill or in front of a barbed-wire fence, that lent the whole business an air of unreality, at times producing incidents which, recollected later, in tranquillity, had their humorous side. Some even at the time caused laughter, and on both sides, for the Turks are not a race without humour, even if of a fairly simple, robust kind. The humour was derived from the nervous tension. It was during this period that one British infantry soldier, while unloading his rifle to clean it, squeezed the trigger on a round still in the breech with the result that a bullet shot off in the direction of a group of Turks. His platoon officer immediately jumped out of the trench and ran towards them shouting that it was an accident. The Turks, presumably fearful that the shouting officer would be followed by his men with bayonets fixed, retired at once to their own trench. The young second lieutenant, with some courage, then stood his ground until, with pantomime gestures and simple English, he persuaded the Turks to come out of their positions and advance towards the British lines again.

At many places those Turks who had picked up some English, generally as prisoners of war, would engage their opposite numbers in conversation and gratefully accept cigarettes, which were apparently in short supply in the Turkish army. This atmosphere of friendliness worried commanding officers on both sides, and frequently chatting groups were broken up by superior authority. One British

officer was positively infuriated by these attempts at fraternisation. Lieutenant-Colonel Craigie-Halkett, the fiery
commanding officer of the Highland Light Infantry, would
scream in Arabic at any Turks he found talking to his
men, not a whit deterred when sometimes they replied in
English. On one such occasion, as he departed on his horse
into the distance, his duty done, a Turk turned to the 'Jocks'
and remarked, 'He has a cruel face, your Colonel. . . .' Other
incidents were less amusing. Turkish officers had obviously
from the start received orders not to recognise the neutral
zone by word or deed. Now that Turkish troops had swarmed
into it right up to the British positions, it had become a
farce. Marden called it simply 'the line that had separated
us from the Greeks'. The next move of the Turks was to
maintain that the British had no right to be at Chanak at
all, and oppose any extension of the defences. There were
numerous arguments about the barbed-wire fences and
frequently Turkish soldiers were seen testing the strength of
the outer perimeters. On a number of occasions the 3rd
Hussars had to draw their swords to ward off Turkish
cavalry who would seize their bridles and try to force them
back inside the main defences. A wiring party of the Loyals
had to form line and advance, in order to drive back Turks
who were encroaching upon their sentries. The Turks
retired slightly, knelt down and loaded their rifles and prepared to open fire. Sensibly, Lieutenant-Colonel Fitzpatrick,
the commanding officer of the Loyals, ordered his own men to
halt and sit down. Eventually the Turks were persuaded to
retire about 300 yards, but the next day they were back,
pushing at the wire and presumably trying to be as provocative as possible.

Nerves were wearing thin, and it was at this time that
Marden formed a mobile column consisting of detachments
of the Loyals and the Royal Sussex, which he intended to use
partly for reconnaissance and partly to push back the Turks
from his own front line. As September 30th got nearer (he
had been given the date as well as Lloyd George), his fear
was that the Turks would be so close to his own men as to
give them a considerable military advantage. The dislike

273

of being shut up in a trap with no room to manœuvre is part of any soldier's mentality, but eventually Marden was persuaded by Harington to abandon this plan as being far too likely to lead to hostilities.

Harington at this time was exercising incredible patience. Through Hamid Bey, the Nationalist spokesman and representative in Constantinople, he was in touch with Mustapha Kemal. In answer to Harington's request for a conference Kemal returned evasive or obstructive replies. He could not consider negotiations until the British stopped helping the Greeks by allowing their fleet into the Sea of Marmora. The British must send no more reinforcements to Chanak and no more guns to Gallipoli. He objected to the demolition of Turkish property that was occurring in and around Chanak; the object of this, as he well knew, was to give the defenders a better field of fire if attacked. These replies, as well as reports on the situation at Chanak, Harington dutifully passed on to the Cabinet in London. There, too, nerves were wearing thin. Harington's news, needless to say, did not help.

Lord Curzon was again in Paris, trying still to preserve some sort of Allied unity. The French could just, but only just, be held to the Allied note, and with them the Italians. All hope could now be given up of assistance from Yugoslavia or Romania. Their representatives in Paris had gone round and round the subject and finally said that they could not contemplate military assistance for fear of Bulgaria and the omnipresent and vaguely defined 'Bolsheviks'. It was extremely doubtful if they had ever seriously intended to be involved. They didn't particularly want to see the Turks returning to Europe; they would of course like a seat at any coming peace conference; but before that peace conference, if there was to be any shooting, they were quite content that it should be left to the British. Acting on a suggestion thrown out by Lloyd George, Lord Curzon, as he probably well knew, had wasted his time.

Curzon however had other causes of complaint. It had obviously puzzled him, as it had not puzzled his colleagues in the Cabinet, why Turkish pressure was being built up against Chanak where there were two British brigades and a lot of artillery, while there was no parallel action in the Ismid peninsula where there was only one brigade. The three battalions of infantry there, commanded by Colonel W. B. Emory, were in an even more precarious position than those at Chanak. They held a line of about five miles in length from the Bosphorus above Scutari, through the Chamlija heights, which overlook Scutari, to Moda, the European suburb on the Sea of Marmora. Behind them was the enemy capital, with its teeming population of Turks and its small garrison of Allied troops. In the Ismid peninsula there were plenty of Turkish troops, and to spare, but they had not advanced steadily and menacingly as at Chanak. The reason behind this apparent inconsistency was suggested in a telegram which Admiral Brock, with Harington's approval, had sent to the Admiralty on September 26th, arriving the next day. 'The Nationalists,' said Brock, 'hesitate to attack Ismid because of the danger of alienating French and Italian sympathy by certain massacres that would take place in the town and other contingencies. The Christian population,' went on the Admiral, 'were in a highly nervous condition. A complete organisation exists in Constantinople for arming large bodies of Turks and the infiltration of undesirable elements by train and ferry from Asia is uninterrupted.' It was obvious that if Kemal moved on Constantinople there would be fighting on a large scale between Turks and Greek and Armenian Christians. Inevitably the garrison would be involved, not only British, but French and Italian as well. The French and the Italians had shown no disposition to leave. Kemal had said on September 27th, in an interview with the *Daily Telegraph* correspondent, 'we must have our capital', but not presumably at the risk of making two more enemies and perhaps creating another Smyrna. The possible damage to foreign property and loss of life among the large international colony was not worth the risk for a city already promised to him in any event.

It was for precisely this reason that Curzon now swung round even more to the view that Constantinople should be held and Chanak abandoned. The British fleet would not bombard the capital; Kemal for all his assumed indifference would not want fighting in the streets. If the British took their stand over the capital of Turkey they could hope for French and Italian support, and thus preserve Allied unity up to and including the peace conference. It is impossible to say if it would have worked. Curzon for all his emotional upsets was a tireless negotiator, and the hackneyed phrase about 'exploring all avenues of approach' might have been coined specially to describe his methods. Sometimes in so doing he lost sight of the ultimate goal. This time he was not given a chance. The rest of the Cabinet had its eyes firmly set on Chanak.

On September 27th Chamberlain, Churchill, Lee, Worthington-Evans and the Service chiefs met together at the Colonial Office at 3 p.m. to prepare for the Cabinet meeting at seven. Curzon was also present but said little, presumably because there was little to say. His colleagues seemed to have made up their minds to have a war.

Chanak could hold out now, it was estimated, for three or four weeks. The difficulties of the situation were known from Harington's telegrams. General mobilisation would provide two divisions which could be sent to Turkey. Lord Cavan, the professional soldier present, wondered if Chanak might not be evacuated as 'a *beau geste*'. The normally pacific Austen Chamberlain would have none of it. 'Proposals for withdrawal,' he said, 'were based on purely military considerations,' and it was his opinion that 'we could not now withdraw from Chanak with credit to ourselves in order to avoid Kemal's irregulars'. He would regard such a withdrawal 'as an humiliation to the British Empire'. Churchill agreed with him. Later Churchill, in dealing with the speed with which reinforcements could be sent on mobilisation, assumed, with no one to contradict him, 'a serious collision on September 30th'. The meeting adjourned preparatory to the Cabinet meeting that evening. No answer had been received from Mustapha Kemal save those passed through Harington. The Cabinet had, four days before, considered putting the whole matter in the hands of the

League of Nations. Churchill and Chamberlain had persuaded Lloyd George that the French might induce the League's Council to insist that the British should leave Chanak before a peace conference was held. This would have been unacceptable so the idea was dropped. Curiously, September 27th was one of the few days on which there was not a rigorous attack upon some aspect of the government's policy in the Near East in any newspaper. The journalists seemed to have assumed that because contact had been made with Kemal and a conference suggested all would be well.

The Cabinet, when it met that evening, with the Prime Minister presiding, dealt with a number of curiously disconnected items. Once again Lloyd George wanted an estimate of the fighting qualities of the Greek army. The Military Attaché in Athens was ordered to find out. Worthington-Evans was instructed to write to the Editor of the *Daily Mail* pointing out that the morale of the troops in the Near East was being affected by 'the tenor of the articles' and that 'the government would have to take steps to secure that the military position was not prejudiced'. The Service chiefs were given another impossible task, this time to report by next morning on the feasibility of holding Constantinople if Chanak were evacuated! The Cabinet then considered, but made no decision regarding, Harington's latest telegram to the War Office.

He was still dealing with Hamid Bey but had also sent a personal telegram to Kemal requesting that Turkish troops move back. Colonel Shuttleworth had issued an ultimatum saying that he would be obliged to use force by 0700 hours on the 28th, but Harington had cancelled it. If Kemal did not reply within forty-eight hours or withdraw his troops he (Harington) would assume that more were moving up. There were seven infantry and four cavalry divisions (23,000) men in the area available to attack Chanak. Dealing with evacuation or defence Harington said, 'I can do whatever you wish. My own personal opinion is that Mustapha will not attack seriously. He is trying to force me into firing the first shot.' Again Harington wished to be assured that if he committed himself to the defence of

Chanak he would swiftly be provided with reinforcements. At the present moment he would, he thought, have to evacuate Constantinople to obtain from there a reserve brigade. The Cabinet decided to tell the General that his telegram was 'being carefully considered'.

From now on, for a few days, the Cabinet or a Conference of Ministers was in almost perpetual session. At 7 p.m. the next day, the 28th, Lloyd George, Churchill, Curzon, Birkenhead, Worthington-Evans, Lee and Robert Horne, the Chancellor of the Exchequer, met together at Downing Street. They had had two previous meetings that day but this, the third, was to enable them to reach certain decisions. One of the matters raised by Kemal was the position of the Greeks. They were at present allowed into the Sea of Marmora with warships, but not troop transports, whereas no Kemalist vessel was allowed there at all. Kemal's argument was that the Sea was not a part of any neutral zone and therefore he should be allowed the same freedom as the Greeks. Harington seems to have been impressed by the argument, but the Cabinet was not. If Kemal did not withdraw from the neutral zone, which the Ministers thought was still possible, then the Greeks would be allowed to move in transports as well. For once there was some logic to the government's decision. Turkey was essentially a land power; Greece still had an advantage at sea. If there was to be a conflict over Thrace then it would be quite unfair for Britain, officially neutral, to allow Kemal to invade Thrace, but not allow the Greeks full freedom to try to prevent him. It was logical, but a sad prospect, meaning, as it would, the failure of diplomacy and a resumption of the Graeco-Turkish War. Presumably, however, even at this stage it was more than a possibility in Lloyd George's mind, as he wanted to know about the state of the Greek army and was prepared to make conditions about Greek vessels referable to Kemal's behaviour towards the British at Chanak.

At 10 p.m. that night a telegram was despatched from the War Office, on Cabinet instructions, to General Harington telling him of this decision and also emphasising that if Mustapha Kemal replied suggesting a meeting it must be with the other Allied generals and a representative of the Greek forces, and not with Harington alone. The second part of the telegram must have considerably surprised the General. It read as follows: 'We are without information whether a clash has occurred at Chanak. We warmly approve forebearance you have shown in face of repeated provocation and the efforts you have made to avert hostilities. You can rely upon our whole-hearted support if, notwithstanding your efforts, fighting breaks out or has broken out in the Chanak zone or hostilities are forced upon you by attempts of the Kemalists to net you in. As soon as it is clear that our troops are seriously engaged we shall mobilise two divisions and call for extra recruits so that reinforcements may be sent to you at the earliest possible moment and meanwhile, in order to reinforce Chanak, you may, if necessary, evacuate Constantinople and Ismid. Our policy is to hold Gallipoli at all costs and to hold on to Chanak so long as this can be done without undue military risk.'

Fifteen minutes later the Foreign Office despatched its telegram to Sir Horace Rumbold, the High Commissioner. It reiterated that a personal meeting confined to Kemal and Harington was to be ruled out as being inconsistent with the Allied note. Further, if there was to be a meeting at Mudania then no concessions should be made beforehand, especially at the expense of the Greeks. The government was obviously a little disappointed that Sir Horace had not communicated his own view on Kemal's proposals, which had come through Harington. Perhaps in those circumstances it was thought fair that Sir Horace should in his turn be kept in the dark about the instructions to the Commander-in-Chief, for no mention was made in the Foreign Office telegram of any of the orders or promises communicated to Harington.

Before the two telegrams were despatched the Cabinet had the opportunity of studying a detailed document which was divided into two parts. The first part was 'an appreciation of the position at Chanak—Constantinople' prepared by the Chiefs of the Naval, General and Air Staffs. The second was an appreciation of the likely situation at Gallipoli and Chanak in October 1922. The first part assumed that Harington, conforming to the Cabinet instructions, would evacuate Constantinople. He could then, it was thought, hold Chanak for three or four weeks. Both the Navy and the R.A.F. would assist him in his task. There was no military reason for evacuating Chanak, but the Turks must be prevented from bringing artillery into the neutral zone. As soon as Chanak was attacked two divisions would have to be mobilised; the troops now on their way would arrive by October 15th, and the two divisions by October 23rd. The General Staff was of the opinion that the first Turkish attack on Chanak would be repulsed, probably with heavy losses to them. However, the force now at Chanak was 'inadequate to stave off a prolonged attack'. Even when the two new divisions arrived the whole force 'could only hold Chanak and Gallipoli and could not clear the neutral zone'. In the second part of the document the General Staff did its best with the task of forecasting events after the first Turkish attack had been repulsed. It was assumed that the Turks would attack 'on or about September 30th', and when repulsed would take up positions within striking distance. Orders would be given in Britain on October 2nd for 'the mobilisation of the Interim Expeditionary Force of two divisions and a cavalry brigade, and their despatch to the Dardanelles for the purpose of driving back the Turks and re-establishing control of the neutral zone'.

Once again, for the politicians, the soldiers did their sums, and compared the strength of the opposing forces. At Constantinople, if he could stay there, Harington had 4 infantry battalions, 2 field-gun batteries and a squadron of cavalry. At Chanak and Gallipoli, 3 squadrons of cavalry, 5 field-gun batteries, 2 pack artillery batteries, 4 medium batteries, 7 infantry battalions and a squadron plus a flight of aircraft. The reinforcements on the way were 5 infantry battalions, 2 pack batteries, a medium artillery brigade and a heavy brigade and 3 more R.A.F. squadrons. All these would have arrived by October 5th. The latest information about the Turks was that the 3rd Army (11,000 men and 24 guns) would probably stay in the Ismid peninsula and watch Constantinople. The 2nd Army (36,000 men and 112 guns) would attack Chanak. The 1st Army (18,000 men and 79 guns) would probably move north from Smyrna and could join the 2nd Army some time after October 2nd.

Shorn of details the General Staff's opinion was that the clearing of the neutral zone would prove to be a 'task of extreme difficulty'. The coming season of the year would be 'most unpropitious for field operations and the hardships to which the troops will be subjected will be much more trying to the British than the Turks who are more or less inured to them'. Reinforcements by the Interim Expeditionary Force would not be enough to ensure success. The message of the appreciation was very clear indeed.

The next morning the Conference of Ministers met at 10 Downing Street at 11.30 a.m. and dealt with a lengthy agenda. King Constantine could have a British warship to take him from Athens to any non-British port. The British Ambassador in Rome was to find out if the Italians had left Constantinople. Lord Balfour at Geneva would be given a free hand on the matter of the Smyrna refugees. The government 'would support the line taken in his speech to the Assembly whatever it was'. The Greeks should be told not to retire from eastern Thrace. The French High Commissioner in Constantinople must be informed that the British would not withdraw from Chanak. The French and Italian admirals at Constantinople should be asked to help prevent Turks crossing to Europe. General Townshend's offer to go as an emissary to Mustapha Kemal should be refused (he went just the same and achieved nothing). All Cabinet and other government Ministers must be recalled to London. Officials of the Board of Trade should be warned to be ready to requisition shipping. It was decided that the Secretary of State for War should not after all write to the Editor of the *Daily Mail*. Finally, it was decided, a telegram should be sent to General Harington to the following effect:

'The Turkish Nationalists are obviously moving up troops and seeking to net your forces in. Cabinet are advised by the General Staff that if we allow continuance of this, the defensive position will be imperilled and that the moment to avert the disaster has arrived. It has therefore been decided by the Cabinet that the Officer Commanding the Turkish forces around Chanak is immediately to be notified that, if his forces are not withdrawn by an hour to be settled by you, at which our combined forces will be in place, all the forces at our disposal—naval, military and aerial—will open fire. In this latter event the air forces should be used so long as the Turkish forces are inside the neutral zone. The time limit should be short and it should not be overlooked that we have received warning regarding the date—September 30th, from our intelligence.'

The soldiers at Chanak had kept their heads, but the statesmen in Downing Street had pulled the trigger.

16

'Like Sir Edward Grey in 1914'
Winston Churchill

The Cabinet had now sent General Harington an order. He was to tell the Turks to remove themselves from the neutral zone within a stated time; if they did not he was to fire on them.

The ultimatum was not to be communicated to Ankara, but simply to the Turkish commander on the spot. The time limit was to be set by Harington and, as Cabinet discussion revealed later, twenty-four hours was regarded as the appropriate period. After twenty-four hours had elapsed, if the Turks had not gone there would be war between Britain and Turkey.

If war came the official reasons were going to be very flimsy indeed. Mustapha Kemal had not replied to the Allied note delivered a week before. In that note, as part of the proposals, the Turkish government had been requested not to send troops into the provisional neutral zone. Yet the troops were there, as Harington said, 'grinning through the wire' at the British. Nevertheless, apart from grabbing the bridles of the 3rd Hussars they had offered no violence to a British soldier. They had been difficult, provocative

283

and at times threatening, but they had not fired a single bullet. The British had not one wounded man to show to prove Turkish 'aggression'. Furthermore, however much the Cabinet closed their eyes to the fact, the Dardanelles Defence Force was on Turkish soil. The boundary of the neutral zone was in no sense a frontier, nor was the perimeter wire fence round Chanak. Constantinople was promised to the Turks and although there was always fear of a pro-Kemal rising in the city, at this moment there were no signs that this was likely to happen. Certainly there had been no aggressive movements by the Turkish troops in the Ismid peninsula, a likely precursor to any attempt to throw out the Allied garrison by force. Of course, the government was prepared to advance other arguments, but they were curiously mixed and in some cases contradictory. The troops at Chanak were now virtually surrounded save for the connection by the sunken road with Nagara Point and behind them the sea. There would be no more British reinforcements arriving until October. If the Turks brought up more artillery, undoubtedly the situation of Marden and his men would be very dangerous indeed. Yet according to the intelligence report the Turks were due to attack on September 30th; therefore they would not have time to bring up more guns. For the British to anticipate a Turkish attack would have no military advantage, not even that of surprise, as the Turks would be warned by the terms of the ultimatum.

The strain on the troops at Chanak was naturally considerable, never knowing when the Turks might attack, being constantly on the alert manning sentry posts and defences. For many of them committal to battle would have been in a sense a relief. Nevertheless, as the War Office had warned the Cabinet, it was a battle in which, although the first attack might be repulsed, thereafter the Defence Force would be in a state of siege waiting for the next attack. Overall, the Cabinet had ordered Harington to demand the evacuation of the whole neutral zone while the War Office had stated quite plainly the military impossibility of clearing it and then holding it with the forces at Harington's disposal. For the British to drive the Turks back permanently it

Above Smyrna in flames, September 1922
Below Refugees on the quay at Smyrna, September 1922

Chanak (view across the Narrows, looking north)

Ismet Pasha at Mudania

Above General Harington and Ismet Pasha at Mudania after the signing of the Armistice.
Below General Harington about to inspect the last Allied parade in Constantinople, 2 October 1923. *From left to right* Nevile Henderson, Lady Harington, General Mombelli, General Harington, Salahaddin Bey, General Charpy.

would be necessary for Marden's force to be backed up by the proposed Expeditionary Force, and quickly, thus embarking upon a minor invasion of Turkey.

In fact, the Cabinet had made history by consulting the three Chiefs of Staff, Army, Navy and Air Force, jointly, for the first time, only to act in a sense clean contrary to their careful and detailed advice. The Cabinet knew that Harington was in touch with Kemal; they knew also that if it came to war they would have no allies. They had the awful warning of the Greek defeat staring them in the face. Yet at this moment they were resolved to embark upon a war with Turkey over a city which they were prepared to give up to the Turks and a neutral zone which was disavowed by nearly all the nations which had created it.

The final argument of the members of the Coalition government was a familiar one: they were acting to defend the rule of law in international affairs and to preserve the sanctity of treaties. It was an argument that had been used on previous occasions and it was to be used in the future. The formula of words had been invoked in 1914 when the Germans entered Belgium; it was to be used when the Germans invaded Poland in 1939; it was to be used again in 1956 at the time of Suez. Unfortunately, despite shelves of books by eminent jurists on the subject, there is no such thing as international law, in the sense of one body of rules observable by all sovereign states and enforceable upon them. International law, so called, when it does function effectively as between states, corporate bodies or individuals, does so only by agreement on both sides. Nearly fifty years after the Chanak crisis there is no international body capable of enforcing its universally accepted decisions upon the states of the world. The strength of the United Nations Organisation is only that of its individual members. Any one nation may take the risk and defy it, and succeed.

In 1922 the League of Nations was new-born, and, as was to be shown later, powerless. In any event, even if there had been an international body capable of judging disputes and enforcing its decisions, the British had not got a particularly good case. There had been a peace treaty with Turkey. The Turkish puppet government had ratified it, but the French and the Italians had not. Plainly the majority of Turks did not accept the peace treaty; equally plainly Mustapha Kemal and his National Assembly was the *de facto* government of Turkey, as Lloyd George had admitted in the House of Commons. By the London Conference the Allies had admitted that the Treaty of Sévres needed revision, and that Kemal's government was entitled to have a say in that process. The neutral zone and the occupation of Constantinople had both been enforced by the Allies upon the Sultan's government. That the new Turkish government should have Constantinople had been conceded. There remained the question of eastern Thrace, in essence a dispute between Turks and Greeks. The Greeks had invaded Turkey and had been repulsed; the two nations were still at war, a war in which Britain, France and Italy were all declared neutrals. Kemal's claim was that eastern Thrace was part of Turkey inhabited by a majority of Turks, that Greeks were molesting the Turkish population, and that he was entitled to follow the war there, fighting the Greek army wherever he could find it. All the counter-arguments of the Allies referred back to the original peace treaty of Sèvres, which had not been signed by the present government of Turkey. All the rights of the Allies were those of conquest. Now, so far as most of Turkey was concerned, Kemal was in turn the conqueror.

So much for the moral and legal content of the justification of a war. There was one further consideration which had nothing to do with morality but had considerable, if not overwhelming, practical importance. The chances of success. There were three possibilities. First, that the Turks would yield, either by submitting to the ultimatum or else withdrawing as soon as Harington's guns began to fire. To think that this was likely to happen was grossly to misread Kemal's character and position. Lloyd George may still have thought of the Turkish leader as some sort of bandit chief whose power would fade away in the smoke from the first discharge of the heavy guns of the British fleet. Others had once held the same view, but by September 1922, after the crushing defeat of the Greeks, the Prime Minister was probably the only person capable of shutting his eyes to the evidence before him. The second and third possibilities depended upon the effect of the first British attack. If it were successful, and the Turks were driven back, there would almost inevitably be an armed uprising in Constantinople. At Chanak the Turks would attack again, and the British would be forced to send more men and guns to the Near East to maintain their position, and might well be dragged into an attempted invasion of Turkey. If on the other hand the first British attack were not successful, there would still in all probability be an uprising in Constantinople and the British might be forced to evacuate there and at Chanak. In which case the government would either have to swallow a mammoth humiliation or else send out a much larger force to exact revenge.

As none of the three alternatives made military or political sense, and as the facts behind them had constantly been presented to the Cabinet by the Service chiefs and argued by politicians and press, the explanation for the telegram of September 29th must be sought in the characters of the senders. Of the four men of weight in the Cabinet, one, Lord Balfour, played no real part in the crisis and none in the decisions. He was strongly anti-Turk and might well on this issue have sided with Lloyd George, but in fact throughout the relevant time he was absent in Geneva as British representative to the League of Nations. His only connection with the crisis was that it became his duty to pass on to the Cabinet the complaints of the Dominion representatives, also at Geneva, as to the paucity of information given them about British intentions and actions.

The three remaining Ministers were Churchill, Birkenhead and Lloyd George. Churchill has given his explanation for his change from an opponent of the whole of British policy in the Near East to being a supporter of war with Turkey. Simply it lay in his pride and pugnacity. Whatever the rights and wrongs, British soldiers were not going to be pushed out by Turks. The whole of the British Empire was not to be humiliated by Mustapha Kemal; therefore as much of the British Empire as could be persuaded was to go to war with Turkey. For outdated reasons and with no regard for the consequences. In the 1939–45 War there were many comparisons made between Churchill and a bulldog. The cartoonists were more accurate than perhaps they knew. A fight produced a blind reaction. Before 1914 he had tolerated, even favoured, votes for women until suffragettes demonstrated at one of his meetings; from then on he had been opposed to them. Once into a fight he dug his teeth in more and more, and closed his eyes. As a war leader in the 40's he frightened two of his own generals, Wavell and Auchinleck, by growling at them. Alexander kept him at bay with soft words and contrary actions. Montgomery growled back, and together they won the battle of El Alamein. In 1922 Churchill was convinced that Mustapha Kemal could be frightened away by growling, and there was no one capable of keeping Churchill on a leash or administering a sharp rap on the muzzle. Least of all his master Lloyd George who, as Prime Minister, and much more than *primus inter pares*, was ultimately responsible. Birkenhead, like Churchill, was naturally pugnacious, his whole life had been a struggle. His grandfather, Thomas Smith, had been a miner and the most renowned bare-fist boxer in the West Riding of Yorkshire. A fight, whether in the ring or the courts, came naturally to a Smith.

It is Lloyd George's motives that are the most interesting. He was not, like Birkenhead, the grandson of a pugilist or Churchill, the grandson of a duke, a simple man. He was wily but he was sensitive; he was pugnacious but he was not a warmonger. In the short term he could be cynical, but in the long term he was often an idealist. Like all Celts he was subject to alternating moods of bursting exuberance and hopeless depression. In September 1922, although he preserved his outward cocky demeanour, he knew that his popularity was fading, that many of his colleagues were itching to desert him. His hopes of Greece had been dashed, the French and the Italians had let him down. He was temporarily disillusioned with politics. At this time he even toyed with the idea of resigning and becoming editor of

The Times. Fleet Street held its breath, and exhaled criticism when he continued as Prime Minister. Many of his critics suggested that he was creating a war atmosphere to keep himself, formerly a war leader, in office. The possibility must have occurred to him. Perhaps he thought the Greeks would help; perhaps he thought that the Turks would run away. Even then there were many risks. It is more likely, though, that Lloyd George's mood was one of personal desperation rather than political calculation. Of Constantine, when he sanctioned his invasion of Turkey, Lloyd George had said that he had acted 'in a mad outbreak of regal vanity'. By his own order to start a war less than two years later the British Prime Minister demonstrated that vanity is not a monopoly of kings.

At this eleventh hour, while the telegram was on its way, three very different men were still working for peace. In Ankara, Franklin Bouillon, with his curious quasi-official position, which undoubtedly gave him a great deal of personal satisfaction, was still in touch with Mustapha Kemal. He argued for acceptance of the Allied note and a conference, needless to say primarily in the interests of France, but in the process he was also striving to avert a war. Harington regarded him as a nuisance, 'a perfect curse' he called him, and in a way it was true, because, carried away by optimism and his own estimate of his skill as a negotiator, he happily misrepresented the willingness of both sides to come to terms. The danger was an obvious one, but for the moment if he could get both sides round a conference table he didn't care. It is difficult to say that he was entirely wrong.

In Constantinople, General Harington, although confined by his own official position to strict accuracy, was also in touch with Kemal through Hamid Bey. Step by step he was trying to persuade Kemal to attend a conference by removing his doubts and fears. Of course the General did not know if Kemal's objections were sincere or not, but with great patience and diplomacy he treated each one as genuine and endeavoured to allay it. The Greeks had not flown aeroplanes over Turkish troops at Ezine. The Greek fleet had been withdrawn from Constantinople on September

27th only 'under the strongest British pressure'. The demo-
litions carried out at Chanak had only been those absolutely
necessary for military purposes. The only shots fired by his
artillery had been to register the guns, and with no aggressive
intent. His representative in eastern Thrace had reported
that there was no foundation in the allegation that Greeks
were burning Turkish villages. Kemal and his representatives gave little away but slowly it seemed as if they might
be being persuaded.

*   *   *

In London, alone among the Cabinet, Lord Curzon had
been active. At 4 p.m. on September 29th he had seen Nihad
Rechad, who was Ali Fethi's deputy and had come at
Curzon's request from France. At 10 p.m. that Friday
evening there was a Cabinet meeting at Curzon's house, 1
Carlton House Terrace. Lloyd George was absent, but
Curzon had persuaded Austen Chamberlain to call the
meeting in view of the importance of what he had to announce. There were at the meeting, besides Chamberlain
and Curzon, Horne, Lord Lee, Churchill and Cavan, the
Chief of the Imperial General Staff. Lord Birkenhead and
Worthington-Evans arrived a little after the proceedings
had commenced and Curzon had begun his report.

Apparently the Foreign Secretary had got on well with
Nihad Rechad, whom he described as 'a gentlemanly
friendly outspoken man, friendly to this country'. Their
conversation however had been full of surprises. Nihad had
begun by saying that he thought that the decision in Paris
(i.e. with regard to the contents of the Allied note) was 'a
work in the interest of peace'. Curzon naturally enough
had replied that 'at the moment it hardly looked like
peace, and that we appeared to be on the brink of hostilities'.
At which Nihad showed considerable surprise and asked
Curzon what on earth he meant. Curzon answered by
stressing Kemal's delay in replying and saying that at Chanak
the Turks were up to the barbed wire, 'and were making
grimaces across it'. He then mentioned the Cabinet's

decision and the orders sent to Harington. Nihad had exclaimed, 'But that means war.' He had not realised the situation was so serious, and could he communicate the conversation to Kemal? Curzon agreed, but suggested that if he did so he should also at the same time seek an explanation of Kemal's 'dilatory and evasive' attitude. Nihad answered by saying that Kemal 'was suffering under two great apprehensions': that the British government was in conspiracy with Athens and was organising Greek military resistance in Thrace and assisting their naval forces in the Straits. Curzon denied any communication with Athens, where in fact there had only been a government for the last two or three days. Nihad then came to Kemal's second fear: that some sort of puppet government would be set up there by the British 'which would prevent the Turks coming into their own'. Curzon denied this too, and stressed that even an interim administration during the peace conference would have to be 'mainly of a Turkish character'. After some more conversation Nihad had promised to report all this to Kemal the next morning. These were the facts, said Curzon, and he then told the Cabinet of his proposals. On the supposition that Nihad was genuine, and remembering 'that a renewal of the war with Turkey would be a most deplorable occurrence and very unpopular', could not the orders to Harington be suspended for twenty-four hours or else the time limit in the ultimatum itself be extended for twenty-four hours?

At first it looked as if Austen Chamberlain would agree. Before Curzon had first seen him he had noticed the headlines in the evening papers which suggested that Kemal had accepted the idea of a conference; one paper had a headline 'Better News'. 'All this,' felt Chamberlain, 'was an ill preparation for the public reception of the decisions taken by the Cabinet.' He had asked Sir Maurice Hankey, the Secretary to the Cabinet, to obtain the Prime Minister's view, and no doubt it would be received later. For himself, however, he felt about Curzon's suggestion 'very doubtful whether military considerations would not render it impracticable'. Curzon said that he personally trusted Nihad, but admitted that if 'the military insisted that an additional twenty-four hours would jeopardise the position it would greatly influence him'. Plainly he hoped that they would not.

Birkenhead, who spoke next, was at his most bellicose. He 'had heard nothing which led him to think it [the ultimatum] ought to be modified in the slightest degree'. After all Kemal had received ultimatums before, which he had ignored. Chamberlain intervened to say that Marden had prepared an ultimatum but Harington had cancelled it. Birkenhead said that 'if that was the case he was shocked to hear it'. He had 'no doubt that Parliament and the public would support the government if they proceeded with their plan'. The Lord Chancellor was much concerned lest 'the spirit of the troops be affected by the insolence of the Turks'. Without doubt it had affected Lord Birkenhead.

Robert Horne, the Chancellor of the Exchequer, was more sober and subtle in his judgment. 'Nihad had been sent to "blind" London.' All the 'secret information received' indicated that Kemal had decided to take no notice of British threats. He 'was inclined to distrust Nihad's suggestions altogether'. Curzon demurred, but Horne thought that even if Nihad himself was honest, 'he might be an unconscious agent'. He (Horne) 'would be very sorry to postpone action'. Curzon then asked Cavan for his professional view, but before the general could reply Birkenhead intervened to say that the C.I.G.S. could only talk of the effect of the twenty-four-hours' delay. Quite obviously he did not want a soldier expressing any wider view upon the situation. Thus confined, Cavan said that the telegram 'was a definite straightforward order'. It should be reaching Harington at just about the present time (11 p.m.). Therefore he estimated that Harington would communicate with Marden and Marden with the Turkish commander by about 4 or 5 a.m., possibly 6 a.m. At this point Curzon was apparently rather surprised that all this should go on throughout the night. Hopefully he had assumed that soldiers kept the same hours as the Foreign Office, say ten in the morning to five at night. 'There was no day or night in carrying out military orders,' said the General, sounding like King's Regulations. A counter order in his opinion could not now affect the situation, save to add confusion.

Curzon pointed out that he merely wanted a delay. Chamberlain said that he thought Cavan's opinion was decisive. Lord Lee agreed. Then Churchill, speaking for the first time, no doubt he meant it kindly, struck a note of historic gloom. He sympathised with Lord Curzon 'who was bound to assure himself, like Sir Edward Grey in 1914, that no stone had been left unturned to preserve peace', and he felt 'he had the full right to clear his conscience in the matter. After all, it was his duty more than anyone else's.' Churchill agreed with the generally expressed view 'that it was not physically possible to defer action without the gravest risk. It would almost certainly make General Harington feel that he did not know where he was. He would probably say to himself that this goverment had cold feet.' After reflecting that 'the Cabinet could not undo what had been done', the Colonial Secretary then cheered up a little with the opinion that there might still be peace, at least eventually. 'The Turks might scurry off with some loss,' he thought, 'and Lord Curzon could then again take up the threads of the peace settlement.' Chamberlain was less convinced, and said that 'it was impossible to let off guns without having in mind that greater events might come out of it'. Again Birkenhead intervened impatiently, rather as if he were still the toughest advocate at the English Bar. Did Lord Curzon disagree with the general view?

The Foreign Secretary 'still had his apprehensions', but accepted the physical difficulties of communication and the military opinion. In the circumstances, he said, 'they could only hope for the best'. Then Chamberlain informed them that through Sir Maurice Hankey he had learned that Lloyd George thought 'that the prospects of securing peace by the proposed delay were not commensurate with the military risks involved'. With that the Cabinet adjourned at 11.30 p.m. and they left Lord Curzon in his house with his rejected plan.

On the next day, September 30th, 'as a matter of urgency', the Cabinet met at 10 Downing Street three times, at

293

4 p.m., at 7.45 p.m. and again at 10.30 p.m., the first two times because, to its surprise, it had received no acknowledgment from General Harington to its telegram of September 29th. It had, however, at the first meeting, received a telegram from Hardinge in Paris. Poincaré, not surprisingly, was protesting about the British decision to serve an ultimatum on the Turks without consulting the French government. It was deemed inadvisable to reply to that particular communication for the moment. Even Lord Curzon seemed to think that in not consulting the French some sort of revenge had been exacted for Poincaré's action in withdrawing his troops from Chanak. It was a curious mentality for a government which was constantly complaining of the bad faith of its allies.

With regard to Harington, the Prime Minister was obviously both worried and annoyed, and expressed his opinion that 'General Harington was so much concerned with the political situation—which was not rightly his—that he did not devote sufficient attention to the military situation'. Lord Cavan made some remarks about the heaviness of telegraphic communication with Constantinople in defence of his brother general and the Cabinet adjourned, having drawn up the draft of a rather rude reply to M. Poincaré.

At the second meeting the Prime Minister was still concerned as to what resistance the Greeks could put up in Thrace, and anxious that if Kemal did not withdraw his troops in conformity with the ultimatum then Greek warships and transports should again be allowed complete freedom on the Sea of Marmora. It was obvious that he had never really approved of Harington's prohibitions in the first place. Still no news had been received from General Harington. The Cabinet Ministers were warned to attend again later that evening, when a reply was confidently expected.

It was at the third meeting at 10.30 p.m. that it was gathered from Admiralty and Foreign Office telegrams that not only had hostilities not broken out, but that fairly obviously General Harington had disobeyed the Cabinet's 'peremptory order', and had not even delivered the ultimatum. The Cabinet expressed 'extreme concern'. Apparently

'General Harington was intensely preoccupied with the political situation which aroused misgivings as to whether he was giving sufficient attention to the military situation'. Though an anonymous Cabinet minute, the words are obviously a repetition of Lloyd George's comment at the previous meeting. It now appeared that Harington had disobeyed orders and had the support of Sir Horace Rumbold, the High Commissioner, in so doing.

The normally impersonal and unemotional Cabinet minutes positively seethe with indignation. The Cabinet expressed concern on, among other points, the following:

1. That Sir Horace Rumbold and General Harington should apparently contemplate a meeting between the General and Mustapha Kemal at Mudania while the Turkish Nationalists, in defiance of several remonstrances and warnings, were still actively violating the essential condition laid down in the Paris note of September 23rd . . .

2. That, notwithstanding the truculent attitude of Mustapha Kemal, and his flagrant disregard of the Paris note, the British High Commissioner and General Harington, besides putting pressure on the Greeks with regard to the movements of their warships and transports through the Straits, were anxious that the Powers should compel the Greek army at once to withdraw behind the Maritza line, before the line had even been fixed . . .

3. As to the danger to peace which this attitude seemed to involve.

4. Generally, as to the apparent progressive deterioration of our political position and prestige, particularly from the point of view of the Dominions, as resulting from the failure up to now of our various attempts to secure compliance with the Paris conditions by an enemy whom we had defeated decisively in the Great War and who possessed only a remnant of his former strength.

The third minute contained the most curious observation of the lot, but overall it can only be assumed that the Cabinet led by Lloyd George, having screwed up its courage for a war, was now furious that due to Harington it had not got one.

In this unpromising mood the Ministers awaited a telegram from the General which was reported to be on its way. The Chiefs of Staff, Beatty, Cavan and Trenchard were ordered to be present at the Admiralty at nine o'clock the next morning to help cope with it.

It was a long telegram, and some of the phrases must have infuriated Lloyd George. Harington, as was his way, had not stuck to officialese and it was apparent that not only had he not obeyed the government, but that he would not obey it in the future if the same demands were repeated. The telegram started fairly mildly:

'I share,' said the General, 'the Cabinet's desire to end procrastinations of Kemal and I note decision of Cabinet but I would earnestly beg that the matter be left to my judgment for moment. There is no question of disaster or danger to British forces until Kemalists bring up serious force of guns and infantry.' Harington then went on to stress that he could defend his positions at Chanak. Therefore, he continued, 'To me it seems very inadvisable just at moment when within reach of distance of meeting between Allied Generals and Kemal which Hamid says will be in two or three days and Ankara government are penning their reply to Allied note that I should launch avalanche of fire which will put a match to mine here and everywhere else and from which there will be no drawing back. I have incessantly been working for peace which I thought was the wish of His Majesty's Government. To suppose my not having fired so far at Chanak has been interpreted as sign of weakness is quite wrong because I have been very careful to warn Hamid that I have [undecipherable] powers of England behind me and that I shall not hesitate to use it if time comes.

'I have very carefully considered whether, as we are so far not at war with Kemal, the Turkish cavalry could be best dealt with by using the minimum force to effect my object or whether I should at once employ full force. In order to avoid England being interpreted as aggressor I decided on the former. You must remember the repercussions on Christian population here [i.e. Constantinople] if any actions at Chanak. If we plunged this city into a panic it would [be] deplorable and they are very frightened after Smyrna. My only reserve of troops is in Constantinople. I may have to withdraw from there and it means the desertion of Christian [? women] and [? children]. Confidence has re-appeared in last few days since reinforcements marched in and I was every day feeling more hopeful that I might see the end with principal [*sic*] of the neutral zones preserved without firing a shot and with British flag flying high here. It all hangs, in my opinion, on what can be affected in Thrace.'

There had been no further Turkish advances at Chanak; in fact some troops seemed to have been drawn back.

'I look,' said Harington, 'upon situation as improving daily. [Marden] has now got elbow room he requires and in a few days will be nearing maximum strength with leading units of 1st Brigade within reach and aeroplanes in air. I am naturally anxious to get Kemalists further back and await reply to my request for a Turkish Commander to settle a provisional line on ground with General Marden. Marden reported the position a few days ago as becoming impossible but since then we have got more troops and guns and it is evident Kemalists have had orders not to attack. It was never dangerous. Will you at once confirm or otherwise whether my judgment is overruled. If Kemal's reply to my last request is unsatisfactory I am all in favour of issuing. He does not intend to attack Chanak seriously in my opinion. Have shown this to Brock and Rumbold who agree.'

Now it is only fair to say that there were inconsistencies in Harington's arguments, especially when compared with his previous messages. He now played down the danger to his own troops at Chanak, and perhaps over-emphasised the amiability of the Turks. At the same time he stressed the dangers in Constantinople if he took troops from there, as he indicated that he would have to do. He might be preserving the 'principal' of the neutral zones but little more. Although he said that he was prepared to issue an ultimatum, the judgment on Kemal's reply would be his own, and it was obvious that he did not intend to use force unless compelled by the Turks. From the point of view of the Cabinet his attitude might be intolerable, and plain disobedience to a military order, nevertheless as Harington had received in the last few days a variety of changing and conflicting orders it is not surprising that he had decided to disobey the last and most dangerous of all. His mixed arguments were obviously intended to forestall any attempts by the Cabinet to change its reasoning and force him into hostilities on other grounds.

What happened next depended upon the decision of the Chiefs of Staff. Perhaps, however, Lloyd George was for once a little naive to leave it to them. Dog does not eat dog. Beatty, Cavan and Trenchard, after some thought and reference to a variety of military considerations, decided that 'General Harington's telegram entirely alters situation'. There were some questions to which they still required answers, about the Turkish dispositions, for instance, but of disobedience to 'peremptory orders' there was not a mention. Doubtless if the Cabinet wished to consider such matters it could, but an Admiral of the Fleet, a General and an Air Marshal had presumably decided that discipline was not a subject with which they were competent to deal. Beatty, Cavan and Trenchard were not going to eat Tim Harington.

Curzon was later to confide to Harington that after the third Cabinet meeting there had been a suggestion of passing a vote of censure on his conduct, a proposal to which he (Curzon) had been opposed. If it had happened the Lloyd George government would have found itself in a very curious position indeed, for on October 1st General Harington was informed that Mustapha Kemal would meet him at Mudania in conference with the other Allied generals. The Cabinet, when it heard the news, sat down and began to draft some very precise instructions for the Commander-in-Chief in Constantinople.

Typically, Harington's first thought was not for his political masters, but for the soldiers under his command. So on October 2nd a signal was sent to the 84th Brigade (1st Irish Guards, 1st Buffs, 2nd Essex Regiment) in Constantinople, and the 83rd and 85th Brigades at Chanak, the men who had borne the day-to-day strain of imminent war. The Commander-in-Chief, accompanied by Generals Charpy and Mombelli, was going to Mudania on October 3rd 'to meet Mustapha Kemal Pasha with a view to arranging an armistice. He wishes all ranks to know how much the world has appreciated their self restraint under most trying circumstances.'

At home in Britain those newspapers most against the war, in particular the *Daily Mail*, which three days before, through Ward Price, had predicted that Kemal would accept, and the *Daily Express*, were loud in their praise of Harington. They did not know of the ultimatum which the Cabinet had prepared, but had sensed that the government's attitude was far more intransigent than that of the Commander-in-Chief, and that if any credit accrued from the affair it was his. *London Opinion* published a cartoon which caught the feeling exactly. It was entitled, 'The Soldier Peacemaker holds back the Dogs of War'. The illustration depicted a lean, military Harington pulling back from a precipice, with some difficulty, two enormous surging hounds with the heads of Churchill and Lloyd George.

In London, on Sunday October 1st at 10 a.m., the two originals of the drawing, plus a Cabinet of sixteen members (Balfour was still in Geneva), including the relatively unknown Stanley Baldwin, President of the Board of Trade, had met to consider the new turn to events in the Near East. The Cabinet was obviously less than pleased with General Harington. Although it was now willing to back-pedal on its ultimatum telegram, it was only prepared to do so very slowly indeed. As the events of the last few days were revealed to those Ministers, the majority, who had not been consulted, the inner quorum, Lloyd George, Birkenhead, Churchill, Chamberlain, Horne, Lee and Worthington-Evans, were at great pains to stress that any orders given had been on the advice of the Chiefs of Staff. This was true in the narrowest military sense, but not in the overall political sense. This fact was also, 'without any implication of censure', to be made clear to General Harington. The transparent fiction was also resorted to that the information on which the Prime Minister and his confidants had acted was 'received exclusively from the Constantinople Command'. In other words, if Harington had been landed with an ultimatum to deliver, it was his own fault. Once again Lloyd George (it seemed to be something of a personal hazard) had been misled by unreliable information from the military.

The Cabinet then concentrated on the instructions to be given to Harington for his guidance at the forthcoming conference. There was still a feeling that perhaps the General had not understood precisely the limits of his authority. He had already disobeyed a clear order, but it was as if the Cabinet could not bring itself to admit that he had done so because he thought it was foolish and dangerous. Therefore instructions were sent from the War Office with regard to Mudania, and repeated by the Foreign Office to Rumbold, who was told to instruct the Commander-in-Chief on the policy of His Majesty's government.

In fact there had been no lack of comprehension on Harington's part. In the last month he had received from London a variety of contrary instructions; his strategic priorities had been changed almost daily. It must have been clear to him that the government did not know whether to defend Constantinople, Chanak or Gallipoli. Lloyd George did not want to submit to Mustapha Kemal, but was not sure how and where to defy him.

Properly speaking, the Cabinet gave orders to Rumbold, the High Commissioner, who then gave orders to Harington and Brock. Yet if those orders meant war then it was Harington's responsibility to wage it, so that at the very moment when the Cabinet exercised its full authority, it abdicated power in Turkey to its general on the spot. The only way that Lloyd George could avoid having to take Harington's military opinion was by getting himself another

300

general in Constantinople. An obvious impossibility on the eve of a peace conference, especially as it appeared that Harington was supported by both Rumbold and Brock. Indeed of the three men it now seemed that the modest, quiet, 'kind' general was the most powerful personality. It was not necessarily a development which was bound to be appreciated by one of Lloyd George's views and temperament. Accordingly a long and detailed telegram was despatched to Harington, informing him of many matters which he must have understood already. In addition he was told that the Cabinet policy on serving an ultimatum on the Turks still held good, but that its implementation was to be held in suspense for the moment. It was repeated a number of times that he must confine himself to the purely military considerations and on political matters subordinate himself to Rumbold. It is perhaps significant that in such a long telegram there was no room for a word of congratulation or encouragement for the General in his efforts to preserve peace.

The Cabinet then noted that M. Poincaré had informed the British Ambassador in Paris, Lord Hardinge, that both the French and Italian governments 'considered it essential in the interests of peace that the Greek evacuation of Thrace should take place as soon as possible, an opinion he [Poincaré] understood which was held by the Allied High Commissioners, in Constantinople'. Thrace was obviously going to be the important issue at Mudania and so it figured large in the 'master copy' telegram sent to Rumbold, but the Cabinet wanted to make sure that it was not given up too easily.

'Under Paris agreement sole object of this meeting is to fix line of retirement of Greek forces in eastern Thrace, in accord with Greek and Turkish military authorities, the Ankara government in return for this intervention to undertake not to send troops either before or during final peace conference into neutral zones and not to cross Straits of Marmora.'

The Cabinet was also now concerned lest Harington should take matters into his own hands:

'These conditions must be borne strictly in mind. In accordance with them General Harington, as allied Commander-in-Chief, was instructed by War Office on September 28th to communicate with Allied generals and the representative of Greek forces, and to arrange for their presence. It is presumed that this has been done.'

Lloyd George was determined that the Greeks should not be left out and was not prepared to 'exercise pressure' until the Turks had 'withdrawn entirely from the neutral zones'. Throughout the last four years in the Near East he had used the Greeks to achieve British objects; he was still prepared to do so. That at the same time he favoured what the Greeks regarded as their rights merely made his policy more dangerous. If the Turks would not leave the British alone at Chanak or in the Ismid peninsula then the Greeks would not be deterred by their champion from resisting the Turks in Thrace. Some part of his motive may have been kindness to the Greek cause, but the Greek army in Thrace was in no condition to resist the Turks, as Harington had frequently stated. A resumption of the Graeco-Turkish War in a province with a mixed Greek and Turkish population would have been disastrous for thousands of innocent civilians, and would inevitably have carried the war into the rest of Greece. It was, although Lloyd George could not see it, a time when kindness, so often a selfish sentiment, was scarcely removed from cruelty.

One other instruction to Rumbold is significant in that it shows that even now the British government, having been saved from a war by Harington's good sense, still thought that it knew, as a Cabinet minute put it, how to make 'a bargain with an Oriental'. 'We cannot contemplate,' stated the Foreign Office telegram, 'Mudania meeting being spun out from day to day, in order to enable Mustapha Kemal to strengthen his position at Ismid with a view to invading Europe.'

With a wealth of similar instructions and advice, on October 2nd General Harington embarked on the *Iron Duke*, Brock's flagship, for Mudania.

17

'*We cannot alone act as the policemen of the world*'
Andrew Bonar Law

The scene chosen for the last peace negotiations of the war which had not ended in 1918 was hardly impressive.

As a town Mudania was very much like Chanak: mosquito-infested, with white washed, thick-walled houses, intersected by badly cobbled streets and narrow alleys, the only tall buildings the onion-shaped mosques and the accompanying thin towers of the minarets from which the muezzin called the faithful to prayer at sun up and sun down. It was a town marked by war. What had once been the Christian quarter was now deserted, and in the waters of the little bay the occasional putrefying Greek corpse could still be seen. The distant view did something to compensate for the general flea-bitten appearance of the port itself: behind the town shining grey aloe trees on the low hills, and, discernible in the blue autumn haze across the water, the disputed land of eastern Thrace.

On October 3rd, however, when Harington arrived, he could not enjoy the view, for a raging seasonal storm in the

303

Sea of Marmora washed the streets clean, scoured the crumbling waterfront and drenched a Turkish guard of honour of nearly 200 men, which, with a military band, was turned out in his honour.

For the first hour or so it must have seemed to the General that this unfortunate initial impression was to set the tone for the whole conference, if indeed there was to be a conference at all. For although the three Allied generals were at Mudania, neither Mustapha Kemal nor the Greek representatives were present.

It was soon learnt that Kemal had no intention of attending, for in his place was his most trusted subordinate, the Commander of the Western Army, General Ismet Pasha, the victor of Inönü. When the British government heard of the substitution there was almost another crisis but by then it was too late. Harington had taken the right view that Kemal regarded himself as Head of State and had sent his senior military commander to confer with his British equivalent. Pride and calculation had no doubt played their part in Kemal's decision but Harington was not the type of man to quibble over protocol; his mind was set on essentials. Consequently he was in no mood to listen to what seemed a transparent diplomatic excuse to explain the absence of the Greeks, that the destroyer that was to have brought them had broken down. To make sure that they did not boycott the conference out of pride a British destroyer was despatched across the Sea of Marmora to fetch them.

The next difficulty was accommodation. Mudania boasted of no buildings suitable for a full-scale conference. The Turks had done their best with what they could find: a modest house on the seafront which had once been the Russian consulate. To give it some sort of appearance Anatolian prayer mats had been hung on the walls and the rickety wooden balcony which looked out over the sea had been decorated with a Turkish flag. In the largest room that overlooked the bay two deal tables been covered with green baize, one for the maps, the other for the delegates. The windows were small and barred and allowed in very little light, so for evening work there were placed ready two kitchen oil lamps. There was hardly space round the main table for all the delegates and their staffs, and once they were seated there was no room for anyone else to move. It was a far remove from Versailles, Sèvres and San Remo.

So disposed, the delegates provided an interesting contrast in national types. Harington, tall and lean with his quick nervous gestures, took the head of the table. He had brought with him Colonels Gribbon and Heywood, a legal expert, Major Simms-Marshall, and a young Gunner officer employed on intelligence duties, J. S. Blunt. Lieutenant Blunt spoke Turkish but was under orders to listen rather than speak. Ismet Pasha, the principal Turkish delegate, was a tiny dapper man, black-moustached, and with the placatory smile often worn by those who become hard of hearing at an early age[1]. With him was Tewfik Bey, his Chief of Staff, whose wolfish smile was not placatory, and, to everyone's surprise, Hamid Bey, the Kemalist representative from Constantinople. Hamid might have been of a different race from Ismet and Tewfik; thick-necked and heavy-jowled, with his spiky hair *en brosse* and fierce upturned moustaches, he looked like an imitation Hindenburg. Opposite Ismet sat General Mombelli, grey-haired and grey-faced. On Ismet's left, General Charpy, a film producer's idea of a handsome portly French general. Interspersed between the principals sat the members of their staffs in almost any order, crowded round the table virtually knee to knee.

There were other factors besides the primitive facilities which emphasised the change in Allied fortunes vis-à-vis the Turks since 1918. Mudania, though it was settling peace or war, was essentially a military meeting between equals. In the bay the *Iron Duke* lay at anchor, providing Harington with his sleeping quarters and wireless communication with Constantinople and demonstrating Britain's naval might. On shore, however, the town swarmed with

[1] Ernest Hemingway, who saw Ismet at Lausanne in 1923, maintained that he pretended to be deaf to disguise his bad French, a social failing in any educated Turk. Apparently Hemingway alone realised this. Mustapha Kemal, who knew Ismet for twenty years, never found out.

Turkish soldiers. Cavalry regiments were constantly trotting through the narrow streets. To the British it sometimes seemed as if it was the same regiment which passed and re-passed the windows of the conference room in order to impress the Allies. Harington redressed the balance to some extent by asking the conference guards, through Blunt, if they had been British prisoners of war, and when a number said they had, asking them if they had all been well fed. The smiles and nods he received in reply seemed to indicate they had never eaten so well before or since.

The big peace conferences after the war had of course taken place in a blaze of publicity. At Mudania by contrast there was very much a sense of isolation. Two visitors, neither entirely welcome, did however appear, and their presence might almost have been predicted. Fresh from his talks with Mustapha Kemal the loquacious Franklin Bouillon burst upon the scene, with an assistant who turned out to be a correspondent of *Le Matin*. Franklin Bouillon was convinced that his was the credit for the whole conference. He offered his services to Harington but was chillingly dismissed. Thereafter he oscillated busily between the Turkish delegation and that of his own countrymen. The other arrival was just as predictable—Ward Price of the *Daily Mail*, who had followed every twist and turn of events in the Near East for the last eighteen months. He quickly demonstrated the enviable facility of possessing better means of communicating his copy to London than those available to Harington for official messages through the Royal Navy and the Foreign Office. Of course Ward Price's task was simple compared with Harington's, for the flow of official telegrams was immense; from Rumbold in Constantinople, from the Cabinet in London and, an added complication, from Curzon, who was now in Paris working furiously to keep the vestige of Allied unity alive while the conference lasted. Inevitably a number of mistakes and undecipherable groups of words and letters occur in the telegrams; there was a confusing number of duplications and often the overlapping of instructions and reports. The problem of accurate and speedy communication only added to the difficulties of the conference and in consequence the strains placed upon Harington.

At home in Britain, now that it was learnt that the Mudania meeting had begun, it was confidently assumed in the newspapers that a peaceful settlement would be reached within days. In a sense this was a reasonable assumption for it was difficult to see what Britain had been preparing to fight about. At the seedy little town on the Sea of Marmora however, Harington was forced to see things differently.

On October 2nd Franklin Bouillon had seen the Allied High Commissioners, Rumbold, Pellé and Garroni, in Constantinople and had given them a glowing picture of the Turks' willingness to come to terms. Now at Mudania it became obvious that his forecast had been hopelessly over-optimistic and that he must have given the impression to the Turks that the Allied generals would be able to take political decisions on their own responsibility or else that somehow he himself would be able to sway the governments to authorise the generals to do so. To Harington it looked like a gigantic bluff; one of his staff described Franklin Bouillon as 'a most amusing fellow, but a thoroughly disreputable politician'. In fairness, however, it was likely that Franklin Bouillon deluded himself. At Mudania he does not seem to have realised that the British regarded him as a dangerous nuisance, that the Italians did not trust him and that his own countrymen had a much lower opinion of his abilities than the one he held himself. He had been a favourite of Briand's and therefore cut very little ice with Poincaré; General Charpy in any event, out of respect and friendship, tended if he could to side with Harington. Only with the Turks did Franklin Bouillon exercise an influence, and it was counter-productive, as his indulgent interpretation of Allied, especially British, intentions, tended to stiffen their own resistance.

For this and other reasons the first sessions round the cramped table were very difficult indeed. Despite the fact that Ismet Pasha was there it was obvious that all his decisions would have to be ratified by Mustapha Kemal and behind him the shadowy National Assembly in Ankara. In

307

fact, although there were many 'authoritative' statements from Paris that Kemal was about to do so, he had not yet replied to the Allied note of September 23rd. Eastern Thrace must be promised before he would agree. This Harington could not do; he had to be assured about the neutral zones first and the Greeks, in occupation of eastern Thrace, had not yet appeared. Needless to say the Turks saw this reluctance on Harington's part as confirmation of their suspicion that the British were somehow still in league with the Greeks.

It was not only Mustapha Kemal and his delegation at Mudania that harboured the suspicion. Lord Beaverbrook's *Daily Express*, which on October 1st had hoped that the government 'will be more than careful in its dealings with Veniselos', carried on the 2nd a headline 'VENISELOS THE WARMONGER'. During the next few days the *Express* informed its readers of the arrival in London of Sir Basil Zaharoff to join Veniselos, and 'the eloquence and the money bags of the Greek mission being then united they will plan a new descent on the Foreign Office'. According to the *Express*, there existed a 'great intrigue to save Greece'; there were secret conferences being held at Sir John Stavridi's house in Surrey and the Highgate home of Sir Arthur Crosfield, whose wife came from a prominent Greek shipping family. It was in fact not just a good newspaper story. Veniselos was undoubtedly trying to gain support in London for the Greek cause. Lloyd George had promised Curzon that he would be very careful and have nothing to do with the Greeks but it is extremely doubtful if he kept his promise. Once more there was an atmosphere of backstairs intrigue about the Prime Minister's concern for Greece.

At the centre again was Sir Basil Zaharoff, whose alleged influence on Lloyd George caused angry questions in the House of Commons. A confidant of Veniselos, his detractors said that he had begun life as a brothel tout in Constantinople; certainly his origins were obscure and made more obscure by his own carefully cultivated air of an international mystery man. By occupation he was a financier and armaments agent and had been knighted by the British after

the 1914–18 War for his services. Professionally and patrioti-
cally, if the word applied, he had been concerned with the
supply of arms to the Greeks in the recent war and had
shared Veniselos' dream of a Greek empire in Asia Minor.
At one stage he was supposed to be financing the Greek army
out of his own pocket. Reasonably enough the *Daily Express*
and Lord Curzon shied away from such contacts, but there
was in reality little to fear. The cause of the Greeks was not
to be revived even by the British Prime Minister, whom Sir
John Stavridi customarily addressed in correspondence as
'My dear Great Man'.

While General Harington was still locked in negotiations
at Mudania with Ismet Pasha, who was proving infuriatingly
obstinate, on October 7th a letter was published in both
The Times and the *Daily Express*. It was the day after the
Greek delegates had at last arrived at Mudania, seasick from
their voyage in a destroyer at high speed in a rough sea.
They were General Mazarakis, and Colonel Sarryanis who
in happier days had been at the London Conference and had
once been confident of a Greek victory in Anatolia. The
letter was written by Andrew Bonar Law, the ex-Conserva-
tive leader. At first it seemed to agree with the stand taken
by the government:

'When the Greek forces were annihilated in Asia Minor
and driven into the sea at Smyrna, it seems to me certain
that unless a decisive warning had been issued the Turkish
forces flushed with victory would have attempted to enter
Constantinople and cross into Thrace.'

In which case Bonar Law thought war in the Balkans
might have resulted.

'It was therefore undoubtedly right that the British
government should endeavour to prevent these misfortunes.'

That said, however, Bonar Law came to the real point of
his letter:

'It is not however right that the burden of taking necessary
action should fall on the British Empire alone. The prevention
of war and massacre in Constantinople and the Balkans is
not specially a British interest, it is the interest of humanity.
The retention also of the freedom of the Straits is not

especially a British interest; it is the interest of the world. We are at the Straits and in Constantinople, not by our own action alone, but by the will of the Allied Powers which won the war, and America is one of these Powers.

'What then in such circumstances ought we to do? Clearly the British Empire, which includes the largest body of Mahomedans in any state, ought not to show any hostility or unfairness to the Turks.

'I see rumours in different newspapers, which I do not credit, that the French representative with the Kemalist forces has encouraged them to make impossible demands. The course of action for our own government seems to me clear. We cannot alone act as the policemen of the world. The financial and social condition of this country makes that impossible.'

The letter concluded by suggesting a tough approach to the French to preserve mutual interests, but it was the phrase 'we cannot alone act as the policemen of the world' which stuck.

Three days before, Veniselos, in an eloquent letter, had challenged the slur of warmonger by much reference to Greek assistance during the war, and had made an appeal on behalf of the Greeks in eastern Thrace who would be annihilated by the Turks, as would their compatriots in Constantinople. The *Daily Mail* unfairly stigmatised his appeal as a call for 'a holy war against Moslems'. It was a long letter and he related much past history from the Greek and his own point of view, but did conclude with what was in effect his minimum suggestion, that the Allies should occupy eastern Thrace and supervise its handover to the Turks. Veniselos' letter had sparked off a heated and detailed correspondence. Nihad Rechad, for instance, put the Turkish case, and Caclamanos, the Greek Minister in London, supported Veniselos, but Bonar Law's letter concentrated his readers' minds on the present British position and not in a sense favourable to the policies of the government. His arguments were immediately praised by both *The Times* and the *Daily Express* and from the evidence of the correspondence columns they struck chords

310

of response in the breasts of many Tory back-bench Members of Parliament. Obviously there was trouble ahead for the Coalition government and its leader Lloyd George.

Meanwhile at Mudania Harington still endeavoured to soften the Turks and at the same time convince them of his sincerity. Kemal had now formally accepted the Allied note of September 23rd and at Chanak General Marden had managed to persuade the local Turkish commander to withdraw his men a thousand yards from the British defences. Lord Curzon was again in Paris, attempting to preserve some measure of Anglo-French understanding and co-operation. This, however, was the moment chosen by the Turks, presumably on Kemal's instructions, as he and Ismet were in constant contact by telegram and telephone, to demonstrate that obtuseness and arrogance in negotiation which had infuriated even pro-Turkish Englishmen for a century. The pressure was relaxed at Chanak but Harington began to receive reports of a build-up of Turkish forces in the Ismid peninsula. Ismet indicated that unless eastern Thrace was handed over immediately and all Allied units departed he would be compelled to put his army into motion.

Harington had worked hard for peace, probably, as he realised, having jeopardised his career in the process, but there were limits to his tolerance and patience. Technically speaking, according to his instructions from the Cabinet, he still had the power originally vested in him to deliver an ultimatum of short duration and on its expiry to give the order to open fire.

He returned to Constantinople to consult with Rumbold, but also in order, as far as it was possible, to prepare the city to resist a Turkish attack. There he had the consolation of seeing more reinforcements arriving, including the 2nd Grenadier Guards, who marched through the city led by the pipes and drums of the Irish Guards and the regimental band of the Buffs. A few days later the 3rd Coldstream Guards were also to disembark along with the Royal Fusiliers and a battalion of the Royal Marine Light Infantry. The arrival of so many crack troops as proud of their ceremonial as their fighting traditions was not entirely appreciated by the population of the city still used to the languors of the Ottoman. One commanding officer received a letter from a Turk saying that 'the residents near the Barracks would be much obliged if you would stop such frequent use of the bugle as it is very disturbing for many who wish to rest in the early part of the morning'.

The telegrams between Constantinople and London flowed thick and fast. The Admiralty telegraphed Admiral Brock, who was warned not to take hostile action until further instructions if the Turks advanced across the Ismid peninsula because 'the French and Italians have in effect gone back on the Paris note. If on the other hand we are attacked at Chanak this will be an act of war against the British Empire.' However, 'in event of Turkish advance on Ismid neutral zone your orders to stop Greek men-of-war and transports entering Sea of Marmora are cancelled'.

Rumbold telegraphed to the Foreign Office: 'Generals hoped that this protocol [giving the Turks most of their demands] would have been signed today but at the last moment Ismet Pasha demanded that eastern Thrace should be handed over to the Turks before the peace treaty and that all the Allied contingents and missions should be withdrawn. The demand is of course entirely at variance with Allies proposal of September 23rd. Ismet Pasha intimated that he would set his troops in motion if Allied generals did not agree to this proposal, which annuls the whole basis of the conference. Turks [have?] just requested permission to transport to eastern Thrace an unlimited force of gendarmerie which might in effect be an army . . .' Rumbold went on to say that the French and Italian High Commissioners were prepared to concede almost anything but that General Harington suggested that the British government should authorise him to tell the Turks that Britain would 'summon' the Greeks to leave eastern Thrace at once but Allied troops would then replace the Greeks. The meeting between the High Commissioners and their generals had been acrimonious to a degree. The ubiquitous Franklin Bouillon had wormed his way in again and was told by Rumbold that his 'impolicy was pernicious'. Even the Marquis Garroni had felt impelled to remind the Frenchman that he did not represent the Italian government. The Turks had now demanded Karagatch, a suburb of Adrianople. Rumbold began to think that they would try to grab western Thrace as well.

Lord Curzon in Paris was still having great difficulties when Harington returned to Mudania. The French and Italian generals, unlike their High Commissioners, were in favour of Allied troops replacing the Greeks in eastern Thrace. To have got this far, Rumbold realised, was an achievement, because the Turks' stratagem had been, with Franklin Bouillon's help, to persuade the generals to sign an agreement allowing the Turks in straight away. Harington at Mudania, where the crew of the *Iron Duke* were fusing shells preparatory to action, was instructed to play for time. He took the opportunity to upbraid Ismet for his breach of faith in ordering the advance of 3,000 cavalry and infantry with artillery into the Ismid peninsula and threatened to oppose him with all available forces unless he withdrew. In fact, as Rumbold informed Lord Curzon, he intended to wait upon events in Paris. At this time Ward Price recorded that the General was looking fine-drawn and had taken to smoking cigarettes on the balcony overlooking the sea in the interludes from the conference table.

Thus the prospects for peace now depended upon Curzon in Paris and Harington at Mudania, with Rumbold in Constantinople acting as intermediary and interpreter. Lloyd George, Churchill and Birkenhead, who dominated the Cabinet, were silent, presumably now content to rely upon the decisions of a general who had disobeyed them and a Foreign Secretary who disagreed with them.

At Mudania, still buffeted by autumn storms, the sessions continued with frequent interruptions and adjournments so that the delegates could send and receive telegrams. Turkish regiments continued to move through the town and occasionally a military band would strike up strident Turkish airs presumably on orders to entertain the delegates. The British, French and Italian officers stretched their legs in the uninspiring little town and were saluted punctiliously by the Turkish soldiery. General Mazarakis seemed to have resigned his country's affairs into the hands of his former allies and took little part in the discussions. Harington, realising that it was his only advantage, worked hard at preserving unity between himself and Charpy and Mombelli. The three generals had, of course, known each other for some time and had worked together amicably in Constantinople. A memory of common effort during the Great War still lingered among the generals, even if it was sadly absent among the statesmen. This residual cameraderie was undoubtedly encouraged by the attitude of the one other principal at the conference, Ismet Pasha.

The part he played is difficult to assess. Small and unimpressive, yet he was reputed to be the most popular general in the Turkish army. Like many deaf men he often appeared stupid; certainly he did not like the task of negotiator which had been thrust upon him. What Harington could not know was the amount of discretion he had been given by Kemal, whether his frequent consultations with the Ghazi were necessary or mere subterfuge. Whatever the instructions he received, the combination of his deafness and suspicion succeeded in irritating the three European generals and thus inadvertently increased their regard for each other. One of Harington's staff talked of the Turks' 'moments of dense and almost childlike obstinacy'. There were rumours that Kemal, although officially in Ankara, was nearer at hand, in Brusa for instance; the temptation upon Harington to demand a decision must have been almost insupportable.

Finally, on October 8th, when almost all hope had been abandoned Rumbold was able to signal to Harington that Curzon had managed to persuade the French, not without difficulty as M. Poincaré was helpfully out of Paris, that there must be a provisional inter-Allied occupation of Thrace before the Turks were allowed to move in. Veniselos had agreed to a period of thirty days. Accordingly Harington could present his terms to Ismet, requesting the withdrawal of Turkish troops from the British positions at Chanak and

314

the Ismid peninsula as a compensation for Greek withdrawal beyond the Maritza. Now Harington could stress that there was no question of a majority decision at Mudania; on paper at least the Allies were united. The General's task was to persuade Ismet and behind him Kemal. He prepared with great care a speech which was full of tactful assurances of mutual trust, which painted in the rosiest colours the offers being made to the Turks and finally gave solemn warning of the dangers of non-acceptance. A professional diplomat could not have done better and would probably have done much worse.

Ismet's first response was not encouraging and Harington broke off the negotiations to return to Constantinople for his final instructions, leaving Charpy and Mombelli at Mudania. On his return the next day on board H.M.S. *Carysfort* he was so convinced that the conference would break down that he prepared his final speech: 'We feel that we have done all that is humanly possible. It is useless for me to repeat what I said yesterday. We have given you all in our power. You were asked by the Powers to give very little in return. You have given nothing. I am forced to repeat—nothing . . . We are now at the parting of the ways. Peace on the one side and a very dark future on the other. Your government refuses the former and prefers to plunge a large portion of mankind into . . .'

Harington never finished the draft, for on landing at Mudania he was met by Charpy and Mombelli who told him that the situation had visibly improved, that Ismet had been talking to Kemal several times during the night and that they thought there were only six minor points outstanding.

Even at this last moment, however, General Harington was again to be placed in a personal dilemma by the government at home. Waiting for him in the conference room was a telegram authorising him to start operations. A second arrived confirming the first. The flicker of Allied unity kept going by Curzon had had its effect on Lloyd George. Harington put both telegrams in his pocket, with another from Marden at Chanak informing him that the position there was again becoming impossible and that he could hold it no longer. Harington authorised him to open fire at a stated hour and then faced Ismet Pasha. In his own words:

'We agreed to transfer the first two points, being purely political, to Lausanne. The next two I won; I don't think they were very important. The next point was the area I had claimed round Chanak. Ismet Pasha said that he could not agree and there was a deadlock. I had been instructed from home that I must get that area. The scene is before me now—that awful room—only an oil lamp. I can see Ismet's Chief of Staff—he never took his eyes off me. I paced up one side of the room saying that I must have that area and would agree to nothing less. Ismet paced up the other side by saying that he would not agree. Then quite suddenly, he said: "*J'accepte.*" I was never so surprised in my life! I have never done any acting, but I think that I must have impressed him as I walked up and down that awful room.'

There only remained the question of the numbers of Turkish gendarmerie to be allowed into Thrace. Major Simms Marshall, the legal adviser, whispered, 'Get a number, it doesn't matter a damn.' Ismet asked 9,000; Harington retired with Charpy and Mombelli and then offered 7,500. Ismet hesitated and Harington stretched across the table, shook his hand and said, 'Here is another 500'—'and we closed on 8,000 well knowing that they would not abide by any number laid down.' Harington realised that it was all over and sent a telegram to Marden cancelling his previous order. The cancellation arrived an hour and a quarter before Marden would have given the order to open fire.

As Harington wrote, 'I did not think of the telegrams in my pocket. I only thought that our nation did not want another war so soon.'

There was still one more thing to do. Charpy and Mombelli were in favour of signing the agreement next day. Harington, who feared that Ismet or Kemal would go back on their word, insisted that the document be drawn up there and then. So the conference sat for another fifteen hours

316

straight through the night. The agreement was rendered into English, French, Italian, Greek and Turkish with some doubtful translation and much slow typing. At 7.15 on the morning of October 11th the agreement was signed by all but Mazarakis, who had retired to a Greek warship. He said he had no authority and anyhow could not contact Athens by wireless. The space for his signature was therefore left blank. The delegates signed the backs of Turkish piastre notes as souvenirs, a Turkish military band struck up again and some of the soldiers sang choruses. Harington returned to Constantinople in the *Carysfort*, saluted by the other British warships on the way.

Announcing the result to London the last two sentences of his telegram said, 'Am distinctly pleased. Can you suppress my name from papers as it is hateful to me.' The Prime Minister, however, had more pressing matters on his mind than the inexplicable susceptibilities of modest generals.

The Mudania convention was to come into force at midnight on 14/15th October. Only on the last day did the Greek government signify its assent, without ever having the heart to sign the document, so its operation was delayed for one day until midnight on October 15th.

The actual terms were simple. The hostilities between Greeks and Turks would cease. The Greek forces would retire to the left bank of the Maritza from its outlet in the Aegean to the point where it met the frontier of Bulgaria. The Allies would occupy the right bank of the Maritza. The Greek civil administration would then hand over to Allied military commissions. Seven Allied battalions would stay in Thrace for a maximum of thirty days to preserve law and order. In return the Turks at Chanak would retire fifteen kilometres from the coast and not increase the numbers of their troops. A similar provision applied to the Ismid peninsula. At Constantinople and in the Gallipoli peninsula the Allies would remain until the conclusion of a formal peace treaty. Until then also the Turks would not transport troops to eastern Thrace nor attempt to raise an army there. In a sense both sides could congratulate themselves. The Turks had gained all that they expected and the Allies had given nothing away for the moment. The only losers were the Greeks.

Immediately the armistice was announced the Greek population of eastern Thrace began its trek towards the banks of the Maritza. According to the League of Nations figures over a quarter of the population began to move. The population of eastern Thrace was a peasant population; its wealth was in its crops and its livestock. The crops and the dwellings had to be left behind; the livestock they endeavoured to move. Both Ernest Hemingway and Ward Price witnessed the exodus. Thousands of families, some walking, some with carts pulled by donkeys or oxen, moving along at a snail's pace shepherded by listless Greek cavalry-men. There were disputes, there was violence. Greeks attempted to denude the countryside before the Turks arrived. The British troops transferred from Chanak and Constantinople kept Greeks and Turks apart and became accustomed to scenes of viciousness, brutality and misery inexplicable to men brought up in the quiet and safety of English towns and villages.

Soon the kindest of hearts became indifferent. Greeks and Turks, with their hatreds and their incomprehensible languages, became merged, and from feelings of compassion the ordinary British soldier passed to one almost of contempt. With full stomachs, an ordered life and no fear it was easy to do. The crowds of refugees with their bundles on their backs and their children beside them stumbled on.

So ended Veniselos' dream of a Greek empire and Lloyd George's postwar foreign policy.

18

'*A dynamic force is a very terrible thing*'
Stanley Baldwin

In the *Daily Mail* Ward Price announced that 'General Sir Charles Harington has brought back peace with honour'. The phrase had been originally Disraeli's when he returned from the Congress of Berlin.

The triumph this time was a general's, not a Prime Minister's. For a moment, however, it looked as if Lloyd George might profit now that the danger of war was averted. One of Harington's staff, writing home to his parents, was of the opinion that 'the Chief had saved Lloyd George'.

In fact Chanak proved to be the last nail in the coffin of the Coalition government. The Conservative backbench M.P.s had always had a slight penchant for the Turks, as Lloyd George's secretary, Miss Stevenson, had noted. It went back in its origins to Disraeli's day. On the other hand Lloyd George's fervent espousal of the Greek cause had struck them as being an unfortunate relic of his own Liberal past. Even after the passage of more than forty years they were not happy to be saddled with a Gladstonian

319

policy. Now that policy had ended ignominiously. The Turks, as so many had predicted, were triumphant and Britain had been pushed to the brink of war. How near, of course, few of them knew. Nevertheless, even from the reports in the press and information that was public it was easy to draw a contrast between the moderation of Harington, the soldier-diplomat, and the reckless belligerence of the Prime Minister.

Out came the old grudges against Lloyd George: his slipperiness over the Coupon Election, his handling of Ireland, the 'Honours Scandal', his Garden Suburb method of government, his failure with Soviet Russia. Added to these now was the most dangerous of all, as it came to be labelled, 'the Chanak crisis'.

The hopes of the critics and the dissidents inevitably centred on Bonar Law. His letter to *The Times* and the *Daily Express* had brought him many expressions of agreement and pledges of support from Members of Parliament and Conservative laymen alike. Bonar Law was himself, apparently, restored to health and not tainted by recent service under Lloyd George. His only rival, Austen Chamberlain, his successor to the leadership of the Conservative party, was still unshakeably loyal to Lloyd George and the Coalition.

Outside Parliament the government was unpopular; by-elections, those pointers to popularity, had not gone well. The public, sick of war, had been thoroughly frightened by the imminence of another, without allies and for reasons which seemed either inadequate or incomprehensible. The press was almost unreservedly opposed to a continuance of the Coalition. The *Express*, which had, under Lord Beaverbrook's guidance, momentarily held its hand while Britain had been on the brink of hostilities, now came out firmly on Bonar Law's side. Lord Rothermere's *Daily Mail*, which had been so critical of the policy in the Near East as nearly to provoke government action, continued to praise Harington, blame Lloyd George by contrast, and began to support Bonar Law as an alternative. The influence of *The Times* was also brought to bear. Lord Northcliffe, its proprietor, had degenerated into insanity, ending in death. For a brief period the policy of the newspaper was in the hands of its powerful editor, Wickham Steed. *The Times* had certainly not been overkind to Lloyd George's foreign policy; its editor was now, in addition, convinced that the continuation of the Coalition would be positively detrimental to British political life. So the paper in public, and the editor in private, both urged Bonar Law to follow up his letter and make a stand against Lloyd George.

Among the inner circle of the Cabinet, Lloyd George, Churchill, Birkenhead, Balfour, Chamberlain, Worthington-Evans and Horne, the danger seems to have been ill comprehended or underestimated. They were not repentent over the part they had played in the recent crisis, rather the reverse, and its successful conclusion may even have persuaded them of their own ability to ride out another storm. The politician's disease, the delusion of thinking oneself irreplaceable in the favour of party and public, had entered into their systems and rotted their judgment. Alone among his colleagues Austen Chamberlain, perhaps more cautious, perhaps more modest than the rest, had some faint glimmerings of the force of the criticism about to be unleashed. Confidently, back in September, as the *Daily Express* had revealed, the Cabinet had planned a general election, designed to anticipate the Conservative Party Conference on November 15th. The crisis and the preparations for war had for the last month taken precedence. The crisis over, and ignoring or misinterpreting its effect, plans for an election were again put in train.

Now an election was precisely what many Conservatives ardently desired, but not so that they could again support a coalition led by Lloyd George. The Chief Whip and the party agents reported their misgivings to Austen Chamberlain, as leader of the party. He determined on a showdown with the critics to take place at a meeting of Conservative M.P.s. It was finally decided that it should be held on October 19th at the Carlton Club,[1] the stronghold of

[1] The origin of the present '1922 Committee', consisting of all Conservative Members of Parliament who are not Ministers, which meets weekly in the House of Commons during the sitting of Parliament. It

traditional Conservatism. At this stage he was still confident that the idea of continuing the Coalition would carry the vote. Some part of his confidence was no doubt due to the fact that apparently the Conservative party had no leader of substance other than himself.

For Bonar Law had not yet declared his hand. His personal dilemma was acute. He still retained a sense of past affection and loyalty towards Lloyd George, in whom once he had had so much confidence. He had misgivings about his own health and his general fitness for the task that lay ahead: the leadership of the Conservative party and the ranging of that party against some of the most powerful and skilled politicians of the day.

What final influence, whether person or principle, persuaded him, it is impossible to say. Convinced, however, that the prolongation of the dominance of Lloyd George would split and ruin his own party, at the last moment Bonar Law made his decision to speak at the Carlton Club meeting in favour of Conservatives fighting the election as an independent party.

The day before the meeting Bonar Law gained an unexpected and belated ally. Originally Lord Curzon had promised to throw in his lot with his colleagues of the government. Not that he had any reasons to be fond of Lloyd George, but perhaps because, with some justification, he thought of himself as the man most fitted to be Foreign Secretary. The habit of government was ingrained into his soul; he could not imagine himself being outside one. However, on October 14th Lloyd George made a speech in Manchester in which he aired all his old prejudices: hatred for the Turks, admiration for the Greeks and criticism of the French as allies. This at a time when the Mudania convention was not yet in effect; when it was still important not to offend the Turks and to hold on to the French. It proved too much for Curzon, who had laboured hard, without thanks, to preserve British foreign policy from the attentions and interference of the Prime Minister. So he saw Bonar Law

has an elected Chairman, Secretary and Treasurer, etc. Customarily abbreviated to '22 Committee.

and pledged himself to fight the Prime Minister, who had always thought of him as 'the gilded door-mat', incapable of that much courage.

Bonar Law had decided, Curzon had decided; so had the right wing of the Conservative party which had always been uneasy with Lloyd George, the ex-Liberal; so had a number of junior Ministers dissatisfied with the Prime Minister's methods of government and management. It still remained to convince the rank and file of the Conservative back-benchers. It seemed likely to be a considerable task; the odds were not good. Those who remained loyal to Lloyd George had all the prestige of seniority and office around them and the Conservative party has never been noteworthy for its revolutionary tendencies. Up until the morning of the Carlton Club meeting those Conservatives who stayed loyal to the Coalition government were confident of success and their opponents were apprehensive of failure. On the very morning the result of the Newport by-election was printed in the newspapers; in 1918 in the Coupon Election the results had been Coalition-Liberal, 14,080, Labour, 10,234, Independent, 647. This time there was no Coalition candidate but a Conservative, a Labour and a Liberal candidate. Everyone assumed that Labour would win. Reginald Clarry, the Conservative candidate, had campaigned openly against the Coalition, attacking it throughout the three weeks' election period, and defining his own position as an 'Independent' Conservative, that is in favour of Conservatives breaking free from the Coalition and standing on their own again as one party. It was, however, assumed that Labour would win the seat. Newport, like most of Wales, was traditionally Labour in its allegiance, with some regard still for the old Liberal party. The victory in 1918 had been won by a Liberal but, as in many other seats, in the immediate aftermath of the successful conclusion of the war. Everyone knew that the Coalition was now unpopular but it was difficult to apportion accurately the blame for its unpopularity. Disraeli had said that 'England does not love coalitions'. That was probably still true, but the vital calculation now was whether the odium of membership rubbed off on Liberals or Conservatives, or on both equally. The country might be dissatisfied with its present government, covered with their camouflage garments of coalition, but what would they think of them dressed again in their old party colours? Naturally the answer to this question was the one that most concerned Conservative M.P.s—without the wartime giants could their party stand alone and stand successfully?

The result of the by-election in Newport seemed to provide that answer. Before they went to their meeting at 11 a.m. on October 19th, Conservative M.P.s had read in their morning papers that Clarry had gained 13,515 votes, Bowen for the Labour party 11,425, Lyndon Moore the Liberal 8,841. On a very high poll for a by-election, 80 per cent of the electorate having voted, there had been a Conservative victory with a majority of 2,090.

Properly speaking the proceedings at the Carlton Club were private and confidential. The minutes taken at the meeting have been accidentally destroyed, but it hardly matters as it was one of those not untypical political gatherings where secrecy was enjoined and every word uttered immediately appeared set out verbatim in the newspapers. Two hundred and seventy-five members attended and when Bonar Law entered gave him a vociferous and enthusiastic welcome. Austen Chamberlain spoke first and on the principle that Balfour had enunciated in private the night before: 'this is a revolt and it should be crushed'. Chamberlain, consequently, made no concessions to Conservative feelings and so appeared to treat the members of his own party in a rather high-handed way. Back in July a group of Conservative junior Ministers had aired their complaints and grievances to the Cabinet Ministers and had been lashed by Birkenhead's contemptuous tongue. A similar speech, even if less cutting and arrogant, from Austen Chamberlain in October was too much to bear, and so the words of the leader of the party were received coldly and in almost dead silence. Thus Chamberlain, because of his devotion to Lloyd George, threw away the prize that could have been his: leadership of an independent party and the premiership of Great Britain.

324

The next speaker was Stanley Baldwin, President of the Board of Trade. Short and stocky, with a big ponderous head, he had been in office for only a few months, and had made no particular mark. A rich businessman by profession, he had brought with him into the Cabinet room a quality of sober commercial rectitude and apparently little else. With Curzon and Sir Arthur Griffith-Boscawen, the Minister of Agriculture, he had been opposed to the handling of the Chanak crisis, but he was not an expert on foreign affairs and had no reputation as an orator, unless dullness pursued as a positive virtue be considered oratory.

On this occasion he surprised his hearers. The root of the difficulty, he thought, was the position of the Prime Minister. 'The Prime Minister,' said Baldwin, 'was described this morning in *The Times* as a live-wire. He was described to me, and to others, in more stately language, by the Lord Chancellor as a dynamic force and I accept those very words. He is a dynamic force, and it is from that very fact that our troubles, in our opinion, arise. A dynamic force is a very terrible thing, it may crush you, but it is not necessarily right. It is owing to that dynamic force, and that remarkable personality, that the Liberal party, to which he formerly belonged, is smashed to pieces, and it is my firm conviction that, in time, the same thing will happen to our party. . . .'

Mr. Chamberlain was prepared to go into the wilderness if compelled to forsake the Prime Minister. 'I am prepared to go into the wilderness to avoid him. . . .'

Two M.P.s, Pretyman and Lane-Fox, proposed and seconded a motion in favour of the Conservatives fighting the general election as an independent party. Lane-Fox took up Baldwin's description, 'It is impossible for a coalition to have principles. They are only a sort of improvisation based on the brain-waves of a dynamic force. . . .'

There followed a few short speeches. Sir Henry Craik said, 'I feel we have been led on to a slippery, dangerous and doubtful path,' and then, as if by general consent, Bonar Law rose to address the meeting. He too had never been an inspiring speaker; indeed nearly all the great phrase-spinners of the day were collected together in the Lloyd George camp. He spoke slowly and almost hesitantly, and as always, with curious syntax.

'A coalition in any form is so alien to all our habits that the necessity for it, since the war was ended, we are bound to challenge.... I confess frankly that in the immediate crisis in front of us I do personally attach more importance to keeping our party a united body than to winning the next election. . . . This coalition is like a marriage without any law of God to interfere with your decision; it is like a marriage where one of the parties is determined to go away; and if so nothing that you can do can make it a real union. I am sorry that is the conclusion to which I have come.... I say today that whether it is Mr. Lloyd George's fault or the force of circumstances—and I think in the main it is the force of circumstances ... there is precisely the same feeling in our party today that it must end' [as with Asquith's wartime coalition] 'and for that reason there is no good trying to keep it alive.'

Finally, Bonar Law stated that he would vote for the motion. It was carried by 187 votes to 87.

The night before Lloyd George, Churchill, Birkenhead and Balfour had spent a convivial evening together. Informed of the decision of Bonar Law and Curzon to oppose them, they deplored Bonar Law's conduct but regarded Curzon's as dishonest to the point of treason. As Viceroy, in collision with Kitchener, then Commander-in-Chief in India, he had threatened resignation and been taken at his word. Those who knew him confidently assumed thereafter that he would never resign again. There was something about Curzon that brought out a cruel bullying streak in Lloyd George, and he had certainly given his Foreign Secretary ample provocation, personal and political. Yet Curzon had soldiered on. Now he had resigned. It could only be assumed that he thought he was leaving a sinking ship.

For the rest of the evening they talked. Lloyd George amused them with his witty parodies of Curzon's pomposity. Together they were rude and silly about L. S. Amery, the leader of the junior Ministers opposed to the Coalition.

Birkenhead, of whom Vansittart said 'he could no more keep off wit than spirits. Neither did him any good,' was at the top of his best coruscating form. Maybe they were whistling to keep their courage up. Curzon's defection had affected all of them more than they would have cared to admit.

The next morning, before lunch, Lloyd George walked from the Cabinet Room to the office next door where his two Civil Service secretaries, A. J. Sylvester and J. T. Davies, were working. Cheerfully he greeted them and asked if there was any news. Both Sylvester and Davies knew what he meant. There was none. Lloyd George remained standing, twisting his pince-nez round and round on their black silk ribbon. The telephone rang. Davies answered it and then told the Prime Minister of the result of the voting at the Carlton Club. 'That's the end,' said Lloyd George and walked out of the room.

At 5 p.m. the same afternoon he had an audience of the King and tendered his resignation as Prime Minister. Afterwards George V wrote in his diary, 'I am sorry he is going, but some day he will be Prime Minister again'; but the King was wrong and the Prime Minister was right. The next day *The Times* leader observed, 'The Coalition fell like an overripe pear, it was so rotten that the passer-by did not even stoop to examine it.'

The series of events which had been put in motion when some Greek troops had landed on the quayside at Smyrna and which had involved two Greek kings and a prime minister, a Turkish general, a British general who had saved his country from war, and thousands of dead Greeks and Turks, had now brought down the most renowned statesman in Europe. The Liberal H. A. L. Fisher, one of the Ministers carried away with Lloyd George, who subsequently achieved greater eminence as a scholar than as a politician, wrote in his *History of Europe*, somewhat inaccurately and bitterly, 'Providentially delivered from the ghost of Mr. Gladstone and the aeroplanes of Mr. Lloyd George, Musta-pha Kemal, beneficiary of the Carlton Club, quietly crossed the Dardanelles.'

On the same day as Lloyd George resigned Bonar Law was granted an audience by the King. In his own view he could not form a government until he had been elected leader of his party. This formality was carried out four days later at a meeting of Conservative peers, M.P.s and candidates. His proposer was Curzon, his seconder Stanley Baldwin. He went straight from the meeting, at the Hotel Cecil, to Buckingham Palace to be appointed Prime Minister. The next day the names of his Cabinet were announced. The former rebels received their rewards: Curzon remained as Foreign Secretary, Baldwin was Chancellor of the Exchequer, Griffith-Boscawen became Minister of Health, and L. S. Amery First Lord of the Admiralty. Outside the Cabinet Sir Samual Hoare, another leader of the back-bench revolt, became Secretary for Air. Perhaps the most surprising appointment was that of Neville Chamberlain (Lloyd George called him 'a pinhead') to the Office of Postmaster-General. Neville was Austen's brother. Winston Churchill, not without truth or bias, called it 'a government of the second eleven'. On October 26th Parliament, which had not met since August 4th, was dissolved, and Bonar Law announced that he would take his 'second eleven' and the Conservative party to the polls on November 15th.

The election campaign which followed was a bitter one. Lloyd George and Bonar Law tended to abstain from personal criticism of each other, but no such restraint was exercised by their lieutenants. Lloyd George regretted that Bonar Law's judgment had been overborne by diehard Tories, and talked of the Carlton Club decision as a 'crime against the nation'. Birkenhead laid about himself in fine style: the new Ministry was composed of 'second-class intellects' and 'their mediocrity frightened him'. But Birkenhead's tongue 'made him enemies as flies breed in summertime', as Churchill observed, and he had made too many by now for his criticisms to carry any political weight. Churchill himself had been stricken with gastro-enteritis on the night of October 18th and was admitted to hospital for an appendix operation. Consequently he was only able to get to his constituency of Dundee for the latter part of the campaign and then had to be carried in a chair to meetings. On October 28th, however, he sent a message to the Dundee Liberal Association. In it, among other things, he gave his views on the recent crisis in the Near East. It was good resounding stuff and there were no apologies.

'. . . I am very proud indeed to have taken part in the decisions and energetic action of the British Cabinet which prevented the Turks from carrying a new war into Europe. When I read the official reports of the massacres and burnings in Smyrna, when I read in the newspapers of the hundreds of thousands of Christians who are now fleeing from Thrace, I thank God that a voice went out from this land strong enough and clear enough to halt advancing armies and to cast a merciful shield between the hapless fugitives and their fierce pursuers. General Smuts, the great Liberal statesman of South Africa, has vindicated the action which we took. Australia and New Zealand have stood at our side. Throughout the United States you will find only gratitude and respect for what Britain has done and done alone and unaided by her Allies. So far from excusing the course we adopted, I regard my association with it as one of the greatest honours in my long political life.

'I have yet a word to say. In the political confusion that reigns, and with causes so precious to defend, I take my stand by Mr. Lloyd George. I was his friend before he was famous. I was with him when all were at his feet. And now today, when men who fawned upon him, who praised even his errors, who climbed into place in Parliament upon his shoulders, have cast him aside . . . I am still his friend and lieutenant. . . .'

Those of Lloyd George's Ministers who stayed bound to him were especially vicious in their attacks upon those such as Curzon whom they accused of treachery and disloyalty. Personal accusations and counter-accusations filled the air. To make things even more complicated it was a five-party fight, between Bonar Law's Conservatives, Lloyd George's Liberals and a dissident rump of Conservatives who stayed loyal to Lloyd George, Ramsay MacDonald's Labour party and Asquith's old Liberals. The conduct of affairs in the

Near East inevitably bulked large in nearly all the candidates' speeches. The Coalitionists like Churchill, who stood as a 'National Liberal', remained unrepentant, and their critics were not armed with their secret information. Nevertheless Bonar Law's watchwords of 'tranquillity and stability both at home and abroad' implied criticism of foreign adventures. Wittily, Violet Bonham Carter, speaking in support of her father Asquith, observed that Britain was being offered a choice between a Prime Minister suffering from sleeping sickness and one afflicted with St. Vitus' dance. Wittily, but hopelessly; for when the results were declared, despite the personal brilliance and expertise of its opponents, the party of tranquillity carried the day. Conservatives had won 344 seats, Labour 138, Asquith Liberals 60, Lloyd George Liberals 57. Bonar Law had a majority over all other parties combined of 77.

A number of Bonar Law's prominent opponents lost their seats. Sir Donald Maclean, who had led the Liberals in Asquith's absence from the House of Commons; Hamar Greenwood, who had first mentioned in Cabinet the approach to the Dominions for help against Turkey. In Dundee, which returned two Members, Winston Churchill gained 2,000 fewer votes than the other National-Liberal candidate, and was ejected from Parliament in favour of the only Prohibitionist ever elected to the House of Commons. Of the other ex-Ministers closely connected with Chanak, Horne, Mond, Greenwood and Lord Lee, apart from Lloyd George himself, were never to see office again.

Needless to say the world had not stood still while Britain had fought out a general election. Among the speeches, manifestos and the photographs of candidates, readers of the newspapers would have observed that, after a comic opera march on Rome, on October 31st an ex-Communist journalist called Benito Mussolini had become Prime Minister of Italy. Sforza, although invited, had refused to serve in his government. There were photographs and descriptions too of Greek refugees entering Greece from Thrace, and of Turkish cavalry, made more sinister by dust goggles, trotting in to take their place.

At Constantinople too the signing of the armistice at Mudania had its effect. There was now to be a full peace conference at Lausanne between Britain, France, Italy and Turkey and other concerned nations. Until then the Allied garrisons would remain but the situation was a curious one; Britain, France and Italy had signed an agreement with the new government of Turkey but in Constantinople it did not exist. There lingered Tewfik Pasha, the Grand Vizier, and the Sultan himself, presiding over a government which had outlawed Mustapha Kemal and condemned him to death.

It was a situation which concerned Kemal more than the Allies, for properly speaking it was no part of their function to differentiate between two rival governments. Kemal's problem was that he knew that a large number of Turks still held the Sultan and Caliph in high regard. They were a conservative people. Some of the older generation, incredible as it may seem, still resented the Young Turks' removal of Abdul Hamid. The three years which Kemal had employed to increase his own power were a short time in which to change the habit of centuries. To many Turks Kemal was still only a superbly successful general; the realities had not yet dawned upon them. Even among Kemal's own entourage there were men who confessed to an ineradicable sentimental regard for the office, if not the person, of the Sultan.

As it turned out the British, almost accidentally, solved Kemal's problem for him. Just as for the London Conference, so for Lausanne, invitations were sent not only to the Grand National Assembly in Ankara, but also to the Sublime Porte at Constantinople. Meanwhile Kemal had sent Refet Bey as military governor of Thrace to take up his headquarters in Constantinople. He had two tasks: to act as Kemal's representative in the capital and, as he later confessed to Harington, 'to make as much of a nuisance of himself as possible' to the Allies. Refet's reception by the delirious Turks in Constantinople surpassed all expectations, with flags, processions and cheering crowds. The Allies wisely stayed aloof while Refet happily acted out the part of popular hero.

There was now less doubt in Kemal's mind about the popularity of his own regime; if they had mobbed his deputy what would they not do for him? A brief interlude of negotiations, through Refet, with the Sultan, when the possibility of some form of constitutional monarchy was discussed, decided him. The Sultan, buried in the past, was either too stupid or proud to co-operate. The invitation to Lausanne provided Kemal's opportunity; the Nationalists were incensed, once more it appeared as if the Allies were trying to play off one set of Turks against the other. Resentment against the Constantinople government, which had contributed nothing save opposition to the glorious events of the last three years, increased, especially among the younger generation. Kemal steam-rollered a bill through the Assembly in Ankara separating the spiritual powers of the Caliphate from the temporal powers of the Sultanate. The latter office was abolished, retrospectively, back to the date of the Allied military occupation of Constantinople. As for the Caliphate, the occupant of that position would be chosen by the Assembly.

In Constantinople on November 4th Tewfik, the last Grand Vizier, surrendered the seals of office to the last Sultan. Refet informed Rumbold, Pellé and Garroni that he was now the representative of the new government of Turkey. The Allies stayed neutral, but had on their hands the embarrassment of an ex-Sultan. He, Mehmed Vahid ed Din, was now frightened for his life, the history of his House scarcely provided precedents to reassure him, and attempted to enlist the support of the British. Rumbold could only inform him that in future Britain would have to deal solely with the government in Ankara, but that the Sultan could rely on him for personal protection. Mehmed obviously feared arrest or worse at the hands of the Kemalists, but in reality he was probably perfectly safe. Kemal had no intention of causing a popular outcry by laying hands on a harmless but still respected old man. The one danger was the action of some fanatic or an enthusiast anxious to ingratiate himself with the new regime. Turkish history was not without previous examples.

On November 16th Harington received a message from the Sultan's bandmaster, father of one of the Sultan's wives, that the ex-monarch had been deserted by all save a few of his followers and had heard rumours that he was to be assassinated on his weekly Friday Selamlik, during his procession through the streets. He therefore threw himself on the protection of the British.

Rumbold was in Lausanne, so Harington asked for confirmation of the request. He received the following letter:

Sir,
 Considering my life in danger in Constantinople, I take refuge with the British government, and request my transfer as soon as possible from Constantinople to another place.

November 16th 1923,
Mehmed Vahid ed Din,
Caliph of the Mussulmans

The request made formal, Harington obviously enjoyed himself devising a John Buchan-like plan.

On the Thursday night before the morning of the Selamlik, the Sultan with his son, his chamberlain, the faithful bandmaster, a few servants and a couple of eunuchs, having previously announced their intention of spending the night in one of the kiosks in the Palace gardens, packed valuables and jewellery into trunks.

Before 6 a.m. on the Friday morning—'the rain was coming down in buckets'—the Palace was surrounded by British troops, all of whom seemed to have decided to take an early morning stroll. On street corners officers, armed with revolvers, lounged and talked. On the seafront by the Dolma Bagtche Palace a hundred armed blue-jackets had been landed to stretch their legs. In all the streets leading from the Sultan's palace to the quay, lorries containing machine-guns and their crews under the tarpaulins had unaccountably broken down. Perhaps the only part of the charade that occasioned little surprise, at least from the British, was the battalion of the Grenadiers solemnly carrying out punctilious arms drill on the square, within sight of the small back entrance to the Palace.

At 6 a.m. two army ambulances sped across the square and up to the gate. With umbrellas over their heads the Sultan and his suite left the Palace and climbed awkwardly aboard. At the naval yard Harington and Nevile Henderson awaited the Sultan. He arrived late in the second ambulance; despite the careful arrangements a tyre had blown and a wheel had had to be changed. Harington and Henderson breathed again, saluted the Sultan and escorted him to the Commander-in-Chief's launch, which soon took him to H.M.S. *Malaya*. In the launch, in Harington's words, 'I perhaps hoped that he might give me his cigarette case as a souvenir, instead he suddenly confided to me the care of his five wives.' On board *Malaya* Henderson asked the Sultan if Malta would be a suitable destination. The Sultan seemed to have no preference and agreed. So the British battleship steamed out across the Sea of Marmora, leaving Constantinople without a Sultan for the first time in 500 years.

'I think that the Nationalists were very glad when they found he had gone,' said Harington, and he was right. After a moment of surprise and annoyance Kemal accepted a situation which was to his own advantage. The Sultan had not been harmed nor converted into a martyr; he had slunk away, a pathetic figure, guarded against his former subjects by the British. The way was now open to approach Abdul Medjid, the fifty-four-year-old cousin of Mehmed, with the suggestion that he should become Caliph and confine himself to spiritual matters, leaving temporal power with the National Assembly and, of course, Kemal.

Vahid ed Din did not stay long at Malta, but soon settled down in a villa at San Remo. The British arranged the transfer of the bulk of his private wealth and he took no further active interest in the affairs of Turkey. Nor did any of his numerous descendants and relations. So ended, in comfortable obscurity, the house of Osman, once the most powerful dynasty in the world.

19

'With the British Union Jack flying high'
Lieutenant-General Sir Charles Harington

The last act of the old Turkey was played out at Lausanne. Turkey herself had changed, but Europe seemed not to have realised it. The overall object of the Conference was to re-define her relationship to her former conquerors and other concerned states, to settle the vexed question of the Straits, and to deal with a number of economic, commercial and legal subjects.

There was still something of the air of the old nineteenth century congresses about it all: the Great Powers were assembling to have yet another attempt at the Eastern Question and decide Turkey's place in the world. Therefore, although the Lausanne Conference had a long, if interrupted, run, it was not a very good play; at times it seemed to verge on tragedy, at others farce, and it had a number of touches of low comedy.

The cast was more interesting than the theme and there were a number of effects off-stage. The delegates assembled in Lausanne for November 20th. Needless to say, the

335

Marquess Curzon represented Britain, assisted by Sir Horace Rumbold, of whose abilities, curiously, Curzon had no very high opinion. Rumbold was now, officially, as well as High Commissioner, Ambassador to Turkey. Among Curzon's advisers was Harold Nicolson. France sent Barrère, her Ambassador to Italy, Maurice Bompard, and General Pellé, the High Commissioner in Constantinople. Garroni, the Italian High Commissioner, headed his country's delegation, although it was to be reinforced at times by the presence of Mussolini for purposes of prestige.

The United States was represented by Richard Child, the Ambassador to Rome, Joseph Grew, the Minister in Berne, and the unpopular Admiral Bristol, now described officially as High Commissioner at Constantinople. The Japanese, Romanians, Bulgarians, Yugoslavs and Belgians also sent delegations, and the Portugese their Minister at Berne. Of more interest than any of these was the Soviet delegation, led by Georgi Chicherin, a former Tsarist diplomat, with a meagre reddish beard and a particularly unpleasant high-pitched voice. It was he who had seduced the Germans away at Rapallo. There were shades of 1918 again in the presence of Veniselos as head of the Greek delegation, with Caclamanos, the Minister in London, who had supported him in *The Times*, as his second-in-command. It was, however, the Turkish delegation which provided the biggest surprise of all, because it was headed by Ismet Pasha. Now Ismet had few advantages as a diplomat. He had been thoroughly miserable at Mudania, he was a soldier by profession, he was deaf, he had hardly set foot in Europe all his life. He did speak French, despite Ernest Hemingway, but so did most educated Turks. He certainly did not want the task, but Kemal had created him Minister for Foreign Affairs specially so that he could fulfil it. Indeed Kemal had been forced to order him to do so, and there, simply, lay the reason for the choice. Ismet was a soldier, he obeyed orders, and he was at Lausanne to do just that: to obey orders from Kemal to give nothing away.

*   *   *

Rightfully, as he always received something less than justice, the Conference was Lord Curzon's. On three counts: for what he did achieve, which was considerable in the circumstances; for the sheer volume of his spoken words, which was stupendous; and for the number of anecdotes of which he was the subject, which were legion. With his erudition and eloquence and charm, not always wasted on his fellow-countrymen, his stiff, corseted back, immaculate dress, and alabaster countenance (the Foreign Office called it 'Alabasster' as the Marquess pronounced his a's short), he dominated the Conference.

Unfortunately this combination of qualities impressed everyone but the Turks. 'He treated us all like schoolboys,' said Ismet, but the schoolboys were not above giggling behind the headmaster's back. Like schoolboys they had their private jokes and Curzon's appearance, which put less well-dressed Europeans—and there were many—in awe, had the opposite effect on the Turks. Slatin Pasha, once an Austrian subject and a prisoner of the Mahdi's in the Sudan, confided to a British staff officer, 'With his smooth cheeks and frock coat he looks like a court eunuch; you should have sent a big man with a moustache in a Life Guard's uniform.' Of this, of course, Curzon was sublimely unconscious, as also of the reason behind a minor personal irritant. There existed in London at the time a Servants' 'Black List': a list of those houses in which domestic servants would not seek posts unless desperate. As Curzon paid as much attention to the layout of a table, the household accounts, or even the contents of the jam cupboard, as to an international treaty, his numerous establishments headed the list. In consequence, just before the Lausanne Conference, he had acquired, like so many heroes of fiction but less happily, a comic man-servant, who admitted that he was 'ambitious to get into the service of a famous man'.

To be fair, an early incident had rather tickled Curzon's fancy. The new valet was helping the crippled Foreign Secretary on with his socks when he stumbled and fell. 'You are either very ill or very drunk,' said Curzon. 'Both, my lord,' replied the man.

Later incidents were, at least to Curzon, but not to Nicolson or Vansittart who also knew the valet, less amusing.

At first the Conference had a delusive air of going very well indeed. Many of the divisions between British, French and Italians had been smoothed away. Curzon had worked hard to bring this about, and no doubt the disappearance of Lloyd George, at daggers drawn with Poincaré and in French eyes ridiculously pro-Greek, had helped him. Further, now that the French and Italians were seated comfortably round a conference table and were not liable to be asked to commit troops to battle, their mood was much more co-operative. Rumbold and Curzon were also much relieved that a rumour that Franklin Bouillon was to be the principal French delegate proved to be false. So the old Allies were able to present something of a united front.

With his sense of history and the interests of the British Empire well to the fore in his mind, Curzon concentrated, naturally enough, on the question of the Straits and Turkey's external boundaries. To the French and Italians, with their economic interests in Turkey and their colonies of business-men and merchants, he left those matters which would affect the future status of foreigners inside Turkey. Curzon's was the strategic approach, and inevitably he came into collision with the Russians, who, although they were now Communist at home, were still very Russian in their external diplomacy. Chicherin's interest in the exit to the Black Sea was just as obsessive as that of any of the Foreign Ministers of the Tsars. He had, however, he thought, an advantage over his predecessors in the relationship already established with the new revolutionary Turkey. Having given financial aid to Kemal, having settled the disputed Russo-Turkish border, and having co-operated in the final settlement of the Armenian problem, Russia adopted an almost paternalistic attitude to Turkey. In this Chicherin made just as big a mistake as Western diplomats in the past. Ismet was a Turk and he was proud and obstinate. He and his countrymen had driven out the Greeks and dealt on terms of military equality with Britain. He was not now going to be patronised by Russia. Curzon, although addicted

338

to paternalism himself, saw this, and cleverly drove a wedge between Turkey and Russia. Chicherin's voice became higher and higher and his protests about unfairness to Russia were positively spat out, but it was of no avail. The draft agreement with regard to the Straits was therefore eminently sane and reasonable, almost as if the fulminations of Lloyd George a month ago had never been. A matter which had vexed the Great Powers and Turkey for a century was at last settled.

In time of peace and of war, if Turkey were neutral, there was to be complete freedom for all merchant vessels. If Turkey were involved in a war, she was to be allowed to prevent enemy merchant ships from using the Straits. More important, though, was the question of warships. In time of peace the only restriction was that no one nation could send into the Black Sea a fleet more powerful than that of the most powerful fleet of the littoral powers. In time of a war in which Turkey was neutral, similar provisions were to apply, but with rather stricter regulations to protect the interests of the Black Sea powers, and with the additional provision that no hostilities were to be permitted actually within the Straits. Finally, if Turkey were at war, how she dealt with her enemies was her affair, but the rights of neutrals would still be preserved, providing that they observed more stringent rules for their own safety.

The next matter was the military dispositions on land adjoining the Straits; and again it seemed almost incredible that a month ago Britain had been prepared to go to war over this very issue. At Constantinople Turkey was allowed to maintain a garrison not exceeding 12,000 men, with an arsenal and a naval base. Throughout the whole of the coastline of the Straits a demilitarised zone was to be maintained, lying back some fifteen to twenty kilometres from the shore. Both Greek and Turkish islands in the area were also to be demilitarised, and the frontier zone along the Maritza.

A Straits Commission was to be formed, consisting of a Turkish president and representatives of the signatory powers at Lausanne. The Commission was to operate under the auspices of the League of Nations and to supervise the maintenance of the demilitarised areas. In the event of violations which imperilled the freedom of the Straits or the security of the demilitarised zones, France, Britain, Italy and Japan were to act in conjunction, under the control of the Council of the League of Nations.

The draft was simple as well as sensible, and it seemed unlikely that there would be violations of its provisions as at last Turkey was master in her own house, but with certain obligations to those using the waterway which passed through her territory.[1] So far Lord Curzon had every reason to feel pleased with himself despite the presence of his drunken valet, whom Lady Curzon called 'your horrid man'.

The next problem was the future relationship between Greece and Turkey. Here again the prospect for amicable settlement was hopeful. Veniselos seemed almost resigned to the complete defeat of all his grand designs and prepared to accept the realities of the situation. Some part of his public attitude may have been attributable to the news from Athens, which caused Curzon great concern. There, on November 13th, the trial by court martial had begun of Gounaris, the former Premier, Protopopadakis, the former Finance Minister, Theotokis, War Minister, Baltazzis, who had been Foreign Minister, Stratos, the Minister of the Interior, and Admiral Goudas, General Strategos and General Hajianestis. Rumours were in the press of further arrests and future trials. The new Plastiras regime was seemingly determined to place all the blame for the Anatolian disaster on the previous government. Presumably Veniselos agreed with this policy, for without any apparent twinges of conscience over the part he had played himself, he sat contentedly at Lausanne negotiating with the Turks.

Few difficulties arose. The frontier of eastern Thrace and Adrianople was agreed, following the lines drawn up at Mudania. The next decision was the wisest ever arrived at

[1] In 1936, after an international conference, the Montreux Convention was signed. Turkey re-occupied the demilitarised zones and the Straits Commission was abolished. The Turkish Republic, just like the Ottoman Empire, controlled the waterway which ran through its territory.

in the long history of Graeco-Turkish relations. To avoid sources of future conflict the two nations agreed that under the aegis of the League of Nations there should be an exchange of minority populations. Greeks in Turkey should go to Greece; Turks in Greece to Turkey. Of course there were hardships involved and many difficult personal decisions had to be made by the individuals concerned, but generally speaking the wholesale decision was acceptable. By this drastic piece of surgery a cancer was to be removed from both bodies politic. A few Turks were to remain in western Thrace and a few Greeks in eastern Thrace, and a sizable Greek minority in Constantinople, but otherwise the only potential battleground left between Greek and Turk was Cyprus. However, that island's troubles were in the future. It was the only sensible solution, but in two respects the Greeks were the losers, and it was one of the ironies of history that Veniselos was to be the negotiator and ultimately the signatory of the agreement. For in 1919 Greeks, although unredeemed, had extended their commercial and maritime influence throughout the littoral of the Aegean. Now, by a process begun by Veniselos, that influence, and profit, had disappeared. Thousands of lives had been sacrificed and whole populations uprooted, and Greece itself was flooded with poverty-stricken and jobless refugees, an unwelcome burden upon her already overstrained economy.

As the mechanics of the migration were discussed at Lausanne, the trials proceeded in Athens. Much of the evidence must have made unwelcome reading both at Lausanne and in London. Gounaris had contracted severe para-typhoid and so was unable to give evidence on his own behalf, but General Hajianestis, as might have been expected, put the blame for the military defeat on his predecessor, General Papoulas, and what he called 'the moral fatigue of the Army'. However Theotokis said that King Constantine had only been appointed Commander in-Chief in Anatolia because 'a friendly great Power' had given the government to understand that the moral force of the King ought to be used. General Strategos was even more specific, and said that Gounaris had received encouragement from Lloyd George and Curzon, and that Sir Robert Horne had written to Gounaris a letter promising financial assistance.

Curzon was troubled by the pattern the trials were taking and tried to persuade Veniselos to intervene, but the latter took refuge in the 'justice must run its course' argument, and with perhaps more honesty revealed his personal opinion that the accused deserved their fate. This was not the point that concerned Curzon, but the whole issue of trying politicians and generals by court martial for policies for which they were not entirely responsible but which had failed. Accordingly, on November 26th, the British government despatched a formal note to Athens urging clemency for the fallen Ministers and officers.

The appeal was ignored. On the 27th General Othonaios, the President of the Court and the only Greek general to have been wounded in Anatolia, read out the sentences in a 'noticeably tremulous voice'. Gounaris, Theotokis, Baltazzis, Stratos, Protopopadakis and Hajianestis were all sentenced to death, and Plastiras, now a General, signed the death warrants. The next morning all six were shot by firing squad. Gounaris was strapped to a chair, being unable to stand on account of his illness. General Hajianestis' medals were stripped off before he was shot. Stratos had time to hand his cigarette case to the officer in charge, requesting him to give it to his son with the advice never to enter politics. *The Times* reported that all six 'had faced death bravely'.

Admiral Goudas and General Strategos were both sentenced to life imprisonment. The British, with their traditions of fair trial by the civil courts, accompanied by the right of appeal, were especially horrified. Some part of Curzon's indignation must have penetrated to Veniselos, who did at this late and useless stage protest to his government, at least about the executions. The Revolutionary Committee in Athens, however, showed no signs of remorse; a spokesman even describing the British intervention as 'a great error', and adding that 'to encourage the Constantinists would be harmful to British interests'.

342

In disgust the British government broke off diplomatic relations with Greece, and the Minister was ordered to leave Athens. The execution of the six men had brought the British, government and people alike, to the point where they simply did not want to have anything more to do with the Greeks, whatever their political complexion. This spontaneous gesture of exasperation did probably have a beneficial effect. A large number of other generals had been arrested and were due for trial, including Prince Andrew, Papoulas, Dousmanis and Exadactylos. This 'second string' was dealt with much more leniently than their unfortunate predecessors. Even luckier was Stergiades, lately High Commissioner in Smyrna, who had left Greece and so was tried in his absence. Papoulas, who had once before been tried by a Veniselist court martial, was found to have acted fairly and honestly and was released. Exadactylos and others were released without formal trial. Prince Andrew, however, was tried by court martial. The trial was to a large extent merely an attempt to shift more of the blame for Greece's defeat onto the shoulders of the Royal Family and Constantine's Ministers and generals, and conversely to divert any blame from the members of the new ruling clique. Prince Andrew was charged with disobeying military orders in refusing to advance against the enemy in the late part of 1921. The Prince had certainly disagreed with G.H.Q. but then so, for that matter, had Colonel, now General, Plastiras. Similarly, Veniselos could have been charged with the same offence as Gounaris. General Papoulas gave evidence reluctantly and in fact almost provided Andrew's defence. Nevertheless the verdict was a foregone conclusion: Prince Andrew was found guilty, deprived of his military rank and his estates in Greece, and sentenced to be banished.

John Buchan's novels were very popular that year, and so King George V, concerned for the Prince's safety, managed with the help of a Commander Talbot, who had been a Naval Attaché in Athens, to get Prince Andrew and his wife and family quickly on board H.M.S. *Calypso* and away from Greece the night after the conclusion of the trial. The

Prince and his family, including his eighteen-month-old son, Prince Philip, settled in London.

Although producing a break-up in the Cabinet in Athens and an atmosphere of coldness between Curzon and Veniselos the trials in Greece did not seriously affect the progress of negotiations in Lausanne. Lady Curzon travelled out to join her husband, and 'was delighted to find George so well and happy'. She attended a gala banquet for Ismet and afterwards danced with the little general. Apparently she found him most difficult to talk to, 'as indeed George also found him—in Conference'. Lady Curzon also informed her husband, with some pleasure, that at a dinner in London she had 'merely shaken hands with Sir Robert Horne', but had cut Birkenhead and his wife in public. Mussolini was another less charming visitor to the Conference. Lady Curzon recorded that 'his conceit and vanity were beyond belief'. Her husband realised this, but was prepared to pander to the Italian demagogue's little stratagems, such as keeping everyone else waiting for his arrival. The French were irritated, but Curzon had his reward. Mussolini classified the Foreign Secretary as 'friendly', which was not everyone's judgment, and a little more cement was applied to the wall of Allied solidarity. Nicolson, often with a more snobbish and less realistic eye than his master, was merely struck by the dictator's lack of ease, constantly wriggling in badly fitting clothes.

Lord Curzon's apparent success was beginning to be noticed in the British press, and on November 28th he wrote a most revealing letter to his wife, who had now returned to England: 'I have suddenly been discovered at the age of sixty-three. I was discovered when I was Viceroy of India from thirty-nine to forty-six. Now I have been dug up and people seem to find merit in the corpse.'

Then, towards Christmas, the Conference began to slow down. Ismet was digging in his toes, with Britain so far as Mosul and the border with Iraq were concerned, and with France and Italy with regard to their demand for special internal concessions. Curzon had assumed that the French and Italians would be able to reach conclusions as quickly as the British, and he was wrong. Neither Kemal nor Ismet was prepared to give up their country's hard-earned independence. Curzon's letters record the deterioration from the rapid progress of the earlier days. 'The Turks are becoming impossible,' he wrote. 'We have made every conceivable concession but the Turks fight every point as though they were the conquerors of the world.'

Curzon was particularly irritated by the fact that although, with his great knowledge of Asia, he was able to demolish all Ismet's arguments on ethnic, religious and historical grounds, the Turks would still not give way. Even his sarcasm was of no avail. Mosul, occupied by the British, was important for its oil fields and its strategic position with regard to the frontier with Iraq; its population contained many more Kurds and Arabs than Turks. But 'one might just as well talk to the Duke of York's column', said Curzon. Eventually, however, perhaps because the mere volume of Curzon's arguments began to tell, Ismet agreed that the question, like that of the Christian minorities in Turkey, should be referred to the League of Nations. (In 1925 the League fully endorsed Curzon's arguments.)

The British Foreign Secretary, often by holding out membership of the League of Nations to the Turks, which they regarded as a status symbol, had achieved all that he really wanted. Now he became impatient of the French and Italian concern with financial and commercial matters; with details, as he saw them, of railways and banks, businesses and services. All these, dating from the days of the Capitulations which gave tax and customs concessions to foreigners, were in fact small independent empires within Turkey, and the French and Italians wanted to hold on to them. They had been the reason behind their desire to keep on friendly terms with Turkey before and during the Chanak crisis. Now, paradoxically, they had become the stumbling block to the signing of the treaty, for the Turks had no intention of remaining an economic vassal state. Unwisely, perhaps, Curzon recalled the success of Disraeli at the Congress of Berlin, achieved, it was said, by ordering his train to be ready to leave the capital at a publicised hour if

345

the treaty were not signed. Curzon decided to try the same approach. On January 31st a draft treaty was presented to Ismet. Ismet asked for time to consider and prepare his arguments and objections, but Curzon was growing increasingly impatient.

There were perhaps other reasons besides emulation of Disraeli why Lord Curzon should decide to vent his impatience on Ismet. Apart from the constant pain in his spine he was also troubled by phlebitis and recurring bouts of insomnia, both of which afflicted him when he was overworking. On December 3rd, as an aftermath of the trials in Greece, the *Sunday Express* had published a letter from Gounaris to Curzon, written on February 15th, 1922, in which the Greek Prime Minister had called attention to the declining strength of his own country and the increasing might of the Turks, and had said that unless arms and money could be made available by Britain, Greece would be forced out of Asia Minor. Gounaris had caused the letter to be produced at his trial in an effort to save himself from blame. Lloyd George, Worthington-Evans, Austen Chamberlain and Birkenhead denied having seen the letter, and suggested that Curzon had neglected to perform his duty and inform his Cabinet colleagues. They argued that if they had known those facts their subsequent actions would have been vastly different. Questions were asked in the Commons and the Lords, and Birkenhead mounted a full-scale attack on Curzon in the latter House. In the event the ex-Ministers all made fools of themselves. The letter had been circulated with the Cabinet papers and they had initialled their copies. Lloyd George wriggled dishonestly, but Birkenhead and Austen Chamberlain apologised handsomely. Curzon was vindicated but incensed, no doubt as much by the revelation of his ex-colleagues' dislike of him as by the suggestion of incompetence. On December 16th the *Daily Express* revealed some of Lloyd George's part in encouraging the Greeks to fight even after the fall of Smyrna, an accusation that Lloyd George never refuted. Curzon was mollified, but still hurt.

On a lower plane, his valet still added to his master's

problems. Chancing to walk down to the ballroom of his hotel with Nicolson, Curzon espied him dancing amorously with a much bejewelled American woman. Unfortunately, when he became aware of Curzon's eye upon him, the valet fell drunkenly between his partner's legs, bringing her down on top of him. 'I think he had better leave,' observed the Foreign Secretary, and leave he did, but on going, as a last gesture, hid all Curzon's trousers.

However, spurred on by whatever combination of motives, calculations, and quirks of temperament, Curzon decided to be high-handed with Ismet. He would leave Lausanne on February 4th. On February 3rd there were a series of last-minute meetings between Curzon and Ismet, assisted by the Italian, French and U.S. delegates. It was confidently expected that Ismet would yield, but he did not. Lord Curzon, unlike Disraeli, left on his ordered train. He did not return to Lausanne.

In retrospect it seems a pity that no one told Curzon of his effect on one of the delegates: Stambolisky, the Bulgarian, and leader of his country's Peasant Party, who was to meet a foul death at the hands of his enemies a few years later. At one stage in the Conference he had an audience, no other word applies, of the British Foreign Secretary. Curzon was superb, polite, aristocratic and charming. At the end of their conversation Curzon escorted his guest to the door, and in so doing placed his hand on his shoulder. The Bulgarian was much impressed by this condescension, a colleague reported later; '*ce geste là était rare pour un lord*,' he said.

Curzon would have liked that, but it would not have consoled him for a lost conference.

*   *   *

The breakdown at Lausanne had its effect at Constantinople. Throughout the period while the Conference had been sitting, the British had stayed in their positions at Chanak, Nagara Point and in the Ismid peninsula. As news had been telegraphed through of apparent successes or failures, the soldiers had been allowed to relax or ordered to be ready to repel possible Turkish incursions. The last drafts of troops in October had strengthened the British forces, but it was a trying time, not improved by the freezing cold of the Anatolian winter. The Highland Light Infantry were usually apprised of some hitch at Lausanne by the appearance among them of their fiery colonel, shouting at the top of his voice, 'it's war, bloody war'. It never was, however, and the pipe-major occupied some of his time in composing a slow retreat march entitled 'Nagara Point'.

The real crisis centre was now Constantinople. The British managed to preserve a calm imperial front. Sports were played, officers ran a pack of fox-hounds and hunted the local fox; there was some very good duck shooting. The presence of three battalions of the Foot Guards and the Rifle Brigade even permitted of a performance of the Eton Wall Game, not always comprehensible even to participants. At the centre of it all Harington remained his usual charming outwardly imperturbable self, caring for his troops and cosseting his allies, and keeping on friendly terms with the Turks. There was a great deal of entertaining. Lady Harington on one occasion surprised Mombelli, a stiff, dignified man, by sliding downstairs on a tea tray to a reception. Generally, the French and Italians were confirmed in their view of the strangeness of the English.

There always existed, however, the danger of a popular uprising in the city. Almost every day Harington, Charpy and Mombelli, or the High Commissioners, met with Refet; 'an aggravating little man with his highly polished manners and his gold pencil', was how one of the officers present described him. There were a hundred and one petty arguments, but the theme was always the same: the Allies maintaining that they were in Constantinople as of right, Refet arguing that he was the new Turkish government.

When the Conference did finally collapse, plans had once again to be made to defend the city, and once again the British garrison was put on a war footing. The breakdown also had its effect in Ankara. The deputies of the Grand National Assembly criticised Ismet, and more seriously

348

Kemal. As a foretaste of things to come Kemal finally dissolved the Assembly and elections were held throughout Turkey. There was in reality only one party: his own. The results confirmed him in power, and once more an attempt could be made to reach a settlement at Lausanne. In the event it was all rather an anti-climax. Curzon did not attend, sending Rumbold in his place. The other nations also merely sent their High Commissioners. Commercial realism triumphed over diplomatic protocol. Minister Grew of the U.S.A. was naturally concerned for the newly formed Chester Group, now establishing considerable interests in Turkey. The French and Italians had taken the hint; the old economic subservience of the Ottoman Empire had gone for ever.

The treaty was finally signed on July 24th, 1923. Rumbold alone wore a grey top hat to give the proceedings a bit of tone, and an era had closed.

In fact, of course, the British are as concerned with 'face' as much as any Oriental. The Allied Force of Occupation were to leave Turkey in October, and for ten weeks staff officers prepared embarkation schedules and loading programmes. A whole army had to be moved: men, horses, guns, vehicles, kitchens and field hospitals. Engineer and ordnance officers worked night and day. There still remained the non-warlike stores: tents, boats, ground sheets, and the thousands of items from tins of paint to pontoon bridges that an army collects in four years of static existence. Much was immovable; for example huts, 'temporary' barracks and store houses. Finally, a solution was arrived at, and the nightmare task of counting every nail and coil of rope was abandoned. Whole mountains of clothing and stores were sold to the Red Crescent—the Turkish Red Cross—at knock-down prices. Such was the hurry that one artillery unit spent its last nights in Anatolia sleeping in the open air, because its tents were dismantled ready to be sold to the Turks.

Presumably a large number of Turks, and not all members of the Red Crescent organisation, made a handsome profit. The British tax-payer made a fantastic loss. For £32,000 the

British Army sold something like £600,000 worth of equipment, including huts, lorries, light railways and boats. These matters disposed of, the British were now prepared to make their final exit from Turkey. The French and Italians may have been a trifle hesitant, but Harington was determined to leave, as he put it, 'with the British Union Jack flying high'. It is difficult to say he was wrong, for as well as persuading the Allies to participate in a final parade he roped the Turks in as well. When they pointed out that their soldiers were ill-equipped for such ceremonies the Coldstream Guards obligingly fitted out a whole regiment with a complete set of new boots.

On the morning of October 2nd, 1923, Constantinople was *en fête*. True, many of the restaurants and little tobacco shops were closed, as well as the establishments of dried fruit and carpet vendors. They had been owned by Greeks, and many Greeks had left. An enormous Turkish flag floated over the Tophane naval depot, which had been handed over the day before. Round the square at the Dolma Bagtche Palace a large crowd, kept back by Turkish gendarmerie, watched as guards of honour, French, British, Italian and Turkish, were assembled. With the characteristic high-pitched scream of the drill sergeants, the British contingent of the 3rd Grenadier and 2nd Coldstream Guards was dressed by the right. In the centre was the colour party of the Irish Guards, picked from the tallest soldiers of the Battalion, every man well over six feet tall. This was the finest drilled infantry in the world, and so it looked, towering over the French, Italians and stocky Turks.

At 11.30 a.m. the official party appeared: Harington and Lady Harington, Charpy and Mombelli, the Turkish commander, General Salahaddin Bey, and the High Commissioners—Nevile Henderson in immaculate morning coat and top hat. The guards were inspected and the colours saluted. When Harington saluted the Turkish flag the crowd pushed aside the not very efficient gendarmerie, and spilled out on to the parade ground. Harington was separated from his wife, and the other Allied generals had to fight their way through a mob of not unfriendly Turks.

The National Anthems were played in an attempt, perhaps, to restore order. As few people recognised the new Turkish national anthem the plan was not entirely successful. The guards began to march off towards the quay. The departure of the French and Italians was marked by silence, punctuated by a few shouts and whistles. The slow, steady tramp of the Brigade of Guards did, however, have its effect; and the Turks, who do not cheer in admiration, began to clap. It may have been some lingering respect for the British; it may simply have been the superb bearing of those tall impassive soldiers. Whatever the cause—and the Coldstream band played the popular Turkish tune, its refrain, 'Mustapha Kemal Pasha', as it left the square—the British were pleased with the compliment.

Soldiers and crowd all moved towards the quay. Harington and his wife were squeezed into a gateway to get them out of the way of the surging mob. The Italian High Commissioner had his pocket picked. The last troops began to embark on the transports. Henderson prepared to return to what was now the British Embassy. Almost the last soldier to embark was Harington himself. He had exchanged a number of friendly letters with Ismet, and had left a final message for him which included a soldierly reference to the service of both British and Turkish troops in the Crimea. The General had hoped to meet Mustapha Kemal, and had indeed made plans for a meeting on a warship in the Black Sea, but 'the Foreign Office had stopped it'. Harington stepped out of his official Rolls-Royce and it was left on the quay. The ship's sirens hooted and a naval band played 'Auld Lang Syne'.

The day after the British left, a mob broke into the British Crimean War cemetery and broke some of the headstones with crowbars. The awning in front of one of the largest hotels, being blue and white, the Greek colours, was destroyed; and Constantinople as a true Moslem city went dry, seals being placed on all the wine shops and cafés. Three days later, along streets covered in Turkish flags, interspersed with garlands of greenery on what had once been British tentpoles, the Turkish army marched into the city.

A Turkish newspaper commenting on the British withdrawal had this to say:

'At last they are gone, they are gone after having embarked their guns, their rifles and their soldiers under the scornful and despising looks of the noble Turkish people, and after having saluted with the deepest respect our glorious flag. They told us that they were bringing us to justice and civilisation, their justice consisted in knocking off pedestrians at street corners, in shots fired by drunken men on the peaceful population, in beating innocent folks with sticks. As for their civilisation, it consisted in debauching the civilised families of Pera, Pera which was already a university of dirt and filth, which became a house of ill-fame. It consisted in opening gambling houses all over the town and in transforming our seaside resorts into exhibitions of most repugnant scandals. We bear witness today to the superiority of Eastern civilisation and to its triumph over that of the West.'

Finale

The night before he left Constantinople General Harington destroyed nearly all his correspondence and papers. Although not meant as such, it turned out to be a symbolic gesture.

By his actions a disaster had been averted and most others directly concerned were anxious to turn the page. Nations and men went their separate ways. In the relations between Britain and the Dominions the Chanak crisis proved to be a lesson learned on both sides. Henceforth there were to be no more attempts to dictate foreign policy from London. Significantly, the first treaty between a Dominion and a foreign power (Canada and the U.S.A.) was signed in March, 1923.

For Mustapha Kemal the signing of the treaty at Lausanne was only the beginning. H. A. L. Fisher, who did not like the Turks, contemptuously described them as 'a nation of private soldiers'; yet private soldiers have qualities which can be put to good use. The soldier-statesman at the head of the Turks ordered them to march into the

353

twentieth century and they obeyed. That his methods were rough by the standards of Westminster was irrelevant.

Abdul Medjid proved to be the last Caliph. The office was soon abolished, and although most Turks are still Moslem, Turkey became a secular state, and thus divorced from the last vestige of connection with her former dominions in the Middle East. The fez disappeared by order; a statue of Kemal in full Western evening dress was erected in Smyrna, presumably to set an example, but the head-dress of Anatolia became a singularly unattractive cloth cap. The yashmak over the faces of the Turkish women also disappeared, as a sign of their new emancipation. In private Kemal may have said that the only quality he admired in women was availability, but publicly he brought Turkish women educationally and socially to equality. The process of modernisation was continued into the vital field of education. The Western alphabet was introduced and illiteracy drastically reduced by the provision of schools and a compulsory education system. As his detractors are quick to point out, Kemal was the first of modern dictators, but his dictatorship remained reasonably benevolent and his country stayed at peace. When he died on November 10th, 1938, he was truly, as entitled, Kemal Ataturk—father of the Turks. His successor as President of Turkey was Ismet, who, when Turks had acquired surnames, another sign of modernisation, had taken Inönü after his double victory. Ismet Inönü remained President until 1950, becoming in the process an ally of Britain in the latter part of the 1939–45 War. He and Churchill met amicably after the Yalta Conference.

Greece, until invaded by the Italians in 1940, also avoided war, but her internal politics were chaos. The memories, hatreds and rivalries bred by her Anatolian imperialism died hard. In the fourteen years after her defeat she experienced nineteen changes of government, three changes of the constitution and seven military *coups d'état*. In December 1923—it was the year in which his father Constantine died—King George II was compelled to leave Greece, and soon after a republic was proclaimed. Mr. Morgenthau, prematurely, was delighted. In June 1925 a Cabinet of generals was replaced by one general. He, Pangalos, saw himself as the strong man of Greece, and proved it by heavy censorship of the press and a decree with regard to the length of women's skirts. A year later, by another coup, he was dismissed in favour of General Kondylis, who had more merit in that he attempted to make way for an elected civilian government. However, the kaleidoscope continued to be shaken; fragmented parties and diverse personalities appeared in a variety of temporary attachments. Presidents, prime ministers and their deputies came and went. Generals Plastiras, Pangalos, Kondylis, Metaxas, Admirals Kondouriotis and Hadjikyriakos, and the odd embarrassed civilian[1]. At all times there were more generals and politicians in exile or prison than government.

In July 1928 Veniselos, who had made brief appearances before, was elected Prime Minister of Greece and received a letter of encouragement from his old friend Lloyd George. Sensibly, no doubt, Veniselos concentrated on external affairs and succeeding in improving considerably Greece's relations with her Balkan neighbours and with Turkey. In 1930 a final settlement was made with Turkey with regard to the property of emigrants and the status of non-exchanged minorities. In October of the same year Veniselos, braving a storm of criticism at home, visited Constantinople (by then renamed Istanbul) and Ankara. In the new Turkish capital he signed a treaty 'of neutrality, conciliation and arbitration', an agreement limiting naval re-armament and a commercial convention. In October 1931 Ismet Inönü, then Prime Minister, paid a return visit to Athens. In the same month Veniselos again courted domestic unpopularity by denying support to the Greek Cypriots, who were in a state of minor rebellion against British rule. Nothing, in the Prime Minister's view, 'must alienate British friendship for Greece'. A statue

---

[1] Metaxas was dictator, under the returned King George II, when the Italians invaded Greece. Plastiras emerged again as an influence in the civil war which followed the end of the German occupation. A meeting with Churchill at this time occasioned the comment: 'I hope that General Plastiras hasn't got feet of clay.'

of Canning was unveiled in Athens, and of Rupert Brooke on Skyros, for it was the 100th anniversary of the declaration of Greek independence.

In 1932, having failed to persuade the League of Nations to lend more to Greece than an offered £2 million, Veniselos resigned, and his career entered into a steep decline. In 1935 the monarchy was restored and George II returned to Greece from his exile in Britain. By then, however, Veniselos had been concerned with various unsuccessful military coups and he eventually took refuge on Rhodes as a somewhat discredited conspirator. He died in Paris on March 18th, 1936. Lloyd George's telegram of condolence to his widow called him 'the greatest Greek statesman since Pericles'. His body was returned to his native Crete, but not via Athens, for fear of disturbances. Vansittart, who had known him since the Peace Conference, wrote in 1958:

'The Cretan was the worst influence in Lloyd George's life, and in the end its undoing. He was a courteous fox, an affable barmecide of reason, the best foul weather friend we ever had, benign and transparent beneath a black skull cap. Invincible eyes glinted behind his glasses. I admired and distrusted him immensely.'

As an epitaph it will serve.

By 1936, when Veniselos died, a number of those closely concerned with Greece's tragic years had gone before. Bonar Law had resigned as Prime Minister on May 20th, 1923. His reason was his failing health, and he died on October 30th. On November 5th he was buried in Westminster Abbey, his coffin borne on the shoulders of sergeants of the battalion of the King's Own Scottish Borderers which had been at Chanak. Of his two sons lost in the war the younger had been killed with the regiment fighting the Turks at Gaza. To Asquith was attributed the remark: 'It is fitting that we should have buried the Unknown Prime Minister by the side of the Unknown Soldier.'

Bonar Law's resignation left the premiership and the leadership of the Conservative party open. Curzon confidently expected it, but the ultimate political prize was to be snatched away from him. Bonar Law, in his declining health, had been in no state to advise King George V as to a successor, but Balfour was consulted. Officially his argument against Curzon was that he was a peer and that the Prime Minister must be in the House of Commons. However, Balfour had never liked Curzon and had resented his going over to the rebels in 1922. When Balfour returned home to his house guests, among whom was Edwin Montagu and his wife, Lady Blessington asked, 'Will dear George be chosen?' There was a ring of satisfaction in Balfour's reply: 'No, dear George will not.' The new Prime Minister was Baldwin, 'a person of the utmost insignificance' in Curzon's view. After tears in private, Curzon accepted the situation, and continued to serve as Foreign Secretary. Eventually he had to relinquish the seals of that office to Austen Chamberlain and accept that of Lord President of the Council, a high-sounding demotion. In that post he died on March 20th, 1925. Churchill wrote: 'The morning had been golden, the noontide was bronze, and the evening lead. But all were solid, and each was polished until it shone after its fashion.' One of Curzon's doctors, on leaving the funeral service in Westminster Abbey, was less sonorous: 'He tried to teach us all our business,' he said.

Birkenhead, having been created an Earl in 1922, was an indifferent Secretary of State for India from 1924 to 1928. He died two years later. He left behind a store of sarcastic remarks and a smaller number of friends. Worthington-Evans, having been Postmaster-General from 1923 to 1924, died a year later. Balfour left the world he had always pretended to disdain in the same year as Birkenhead.

By 1930 Horace Rumbold had completed two years of his five-year term as Ambassador in Germany, and was finding that his warnings to London about developments there were receiving scant attention. Harington had been promoted full General in 1927, and was now G.O.C. Western Command in India. His part at Chanak was beginning to be forgotten. Cavan was succeeded in 1926 as Chief of the Imperial General Staff by General Sir George Milne, who occupied the post until 1933. In that year Harington finished his tour of duty as G.O.C. Aldershot Command, whence he had gone from India in 1931. Naturally enough he now wondered if the highest post in the Army might be his, with the eventual dignity of Field Marshal. At Chanak he had thought that his independence and disobedience to orders might prejudice future governments against him. Whether his prognostication was correct or not it is impossible to say. The post was, however, given to a lesser man, and many of Harington's friends thought that he had not received his due reward.

Disappointed, Harington accepted the post of Governor and Commander-in-Chief of Gibralter, which he held from 1933 to 1938. It was the period of the Civil War in Spain and there were numerous crises, but it was not an unpleasant way to round off an army career. Until his death on October 22nd, 1940, he frequently corresponded with Ismet, who signed himself 'your comrade at Mudania'.

In the same year Robert Horne died. Since his days as Chancellor of the Exchequer he had occupied himself in a welter of commercial activities, being a director of the Suez Canal Company and of Lloyd's Bank, and chairman of the Burmah Corporation and the Great Western Railway. Presumably for these services he had been created a Viscount in 1937. Rumbold died in 1941. The last ambassador in Berlin before the outbreak of war in 1939 was his former deputy in Constantinople, Nevile Henderson. Marden also died in 1941. After his command at Chanak he had held only one more post, as a major-general commanding the Welsh division until 1927, when he retired. He was knighted in 1924. Shuttleworth held a number of posts after 1923, all in India, progressing from Colonel to Major-General, and finally commanding the Kohat District from 1932 to 1936. He retired in that year and was created a Knight Commander of the Order of the Indian Empire. He died in 1948.

*　　　*　　　*

From 1929 to 1939 Winston Churchill was in the political wilderness but not in obscurity. Baldwin, still apprehensive of Lloyd George's influence, had separated him from his principal ally by offering Churchill the surprise appointment of Chancellor of the Exchequer in his second administration, from 1924 to 1929. Churchill had rejoined the Conservative party and come to rest in the secure parliamentary constituency of Epping. Thus when Baldwin's government fell in 1929 Churchill was a somewhat more 'respectable', if still rebellious, Cabinet colleague. He was a Conservative, his natural place in the political spectrum, he was an ex-Chancellor of the Exchequer in a Conservative administration, and he was still an M.P. with a platform in Parliament.

He devoted much of his vast energy to writing, producing during this period his life of his ancestor, the 1st Duke of Marlborough, and his history of the Great War and its aftermath. In the latter he put forward a highly personalised account of the Chanak crisis. He sent the proofs of the book to Lloyd George and on his treatment of that subject received by letter the following comment:

'French statesmen played a mean and treacherous game over Greece. The Italians were beneath contempt. Had Mussolini been there he would have stuck to Adalia and found an outlet for his surplus population in developing that derelict country. As you point out our active support of a Greek policy was rendered impossible by the fact that the Tory members of the Cabinet (except Balfour) were all pro-Turk.'

A year before Lloyd George had written to Veniselos: 'What an opportunity they [the Greeks] threw away of becoming the greatest power in South East Europe.'

In enforced retirement from government, though still a Member of Parliament, Lloyd George had seen no reasons to change his opinion or regret his actions.

Like Churchill in the period of the 1930's, Lloyd George was out of office, but unlike Churchill no particular cause captured his interest. Churchill was soon to be demanding rearmament and drawing attention to the German menace. Lloyd George, like many others, met Hitler and was not unimpressed. He was, of course, by now an elder statesman (he had celebrated his seventieth birthday in 1933), and

359

although still a devastating performer in the House of Commons, the chances of power again were fast receding. The personalities of his premiership were disappearing too. Beatty hastened his own death by insisting on marching in the funeral procession of his old friend, Jellicoe, in the winter of 1935, and then following the coffin of King George V in January 1936. Cavan's last command of troops was of those ceremonially employed at George VI's Coronation in May 1937. Trenchard, the other member of the triumvirate, was to live to inspect the air force which he had fostered in a previous war fighting in a second.

That war and the appointment of Churchill as Prime Minister brought home to Lloyd George the fact that his political course was run. Churchill was prepared to give him an appointment but sensibly Lloyd George refused. He was to die on March 27th, 1945, when victory was assured but not yet concluded. In 1941 his wife had died and in 1943 he married Miss Frances Stevenson, who had worried about the telegram to the Dominions in 1922. It was hardly a surprise. As she put it, 'our real marriage had taken place thirty years before'. Almost in his last year her husband accepted an earldom, becoming Earl Lloyd-George (the first use of the hyphen) of Dwyfor. His last public utterance was in Caernarvon at a dinner for the new mayor. Looking forward to a new peace settlement he had said by way of warning: 'Great men sometimes lose the reins and lose their heads.'

After Lloyd George's death there came to his widow a small bag of soil from the Acropolis, with the request that it should be sprinkled on his grave. The senders were the Pan-Hellenic Union of Reserve Officers, the survivors of the movement which had put Veniselos in power during the Great War.

*   *   *

On the morning of January 30th, 1965—it was one of the coldest days of the year—the Horse Artillery guns thudded from Hyde Park and the British prepared to bury their last hero. Winston Churchill, who in 1922, when writing to the Dundee Liberals, had spoken of 'my long political life'. The years between had been filled with adversities and triumphs. His active political life had spanned three generations; he had in his time filled almost every political office; he had been a member of two political parties; he had broken almost every rule for success and yet succeeded.

The bands of the great-coated regiments clanged out the Dead March from Handel's *Saul*. The Union Jack draped coffin on its gun-carriage was pulled steadily by blue-jackets through the London streets to St. Paul's Cathedral. There the stone faced guardsmen of the Inkerman Company of the Grenadiers lifted the heavy lead-lined coffin. Among the pall-bearers on both sides were Field Marshall Slim, who had fought the Turks at Gallipoli, Earl Attlee, who before taking to politics had commanded his infantry company in the same campaign, and Field Marshal Alexander, who had commanded the 1st Irish Guards in Constantinople in 1922.

After the funeral service the coffin was borne down the steps for its final journey and the mourners emerged from the cathedral to pay their last respects. Princess Marina, Duchess of Kent, daughter of Prince Nicholas of Greece; the Vice-President of Turkey; the young Constantine, King of the Hellenes, in his dark blue military cloak, great-grandson of that other Constantine who had twice lost his throne. At the Queen's side, standing to the salute in his uniform of Admiral of the Fleet, was Prince Philip, Duke of Edinburgh, son of Prince Andrew who had once commanded an Army Corps in Anatolia.

There only remained Ismet Inönü, living in retirement in Ankara.

Sources

Unpublished

The Records of the Cabinet Office, 1920, 1921, and 1922.
The Public Record Office, London.
By kind permission of H.M.S.O. (Crown-copyright records are quoted by permission of the Controller)
These were made available for inspection and photographic reproduction in December 1966. The records which are relevant to the Chanak crisis contain as well as the minutes of discussion within the Cabinet all communications to and from the Cabinet, e.g. Curzon's telegrams from Paris, the Cabinet's telegrams to Harington and Rumbold in Constantinople, and their replies. The records also contain all reports to the Cabinet, e.g. the military appreciations of the Chiefs of Staff and the War Office, the conclusions and recommendations of all Committees and Sub-Committees and personal reports such as that of Churchill and Wilson on their interview with Veniselos.

The Lloyd George papers.
The *Daily Express* Beaverbrook Library, London.
By kind permission of the Trustees.

This collection, opened to historians in 1967, contains, in addition to official documents and correspondence, Lloyd George's private letters and papers, for instance his letters to Churchill and Veniselos and their replies. Quotations are by permission of the Beaverbrook Newspapers Ltd.

The Dardanelles Sector Defence Force.
Report by Colonel Commandant D. I. Shuttleworth.
R.H.Q. the Queen's Regiment (Royal Sussex), Chichester.
By kind permission of Major J. F. Ainsworth.
This is a detailed and lengthy report prepared by Shuttleworth for Harington.

The Diary of Brigadier J. S. Omond.
The R.A.O.C. Museum, Camberley.
By kind permission of Lieutenant-Colonel W. H. J. Gillow.
Omond was an indefatigable diarist who typed a foolscap sheet a day describing his own part as an Ordnance Officer on both sides of the Straits in 1922 and 1923, as well as comments upon the military and political situation. He died while *The Chanak Affair* was in preparation.

The Records of Service, War Diaries, etc., of:
The 2nd Grenadier Guards
The 3rd Coldstream Guards
The 1st Irish Guards
(Wellington Barracks, London)
by kind permission of the Regimental Adjutants, Major C. J. Airey, Major P. R. Adair and Major A. B. Mainwaring-Burton.
The 1st King's Own Scottish Borderers
(Berwick upon Tweed)
by kind permission of Lieutenant-Colonel P. St. C. Harrison.
The 2nd Royal Sussex Regiment
(Chichester)
by kind permission of Major J. F. Ainsworth.
The 2nd Highland Light Infantry
(Glasgow)
by kind permission of Captain A. J. Wilson.
Units of the Corps of Royal Engineers
Royal Engineers Corps Library
(Chatham)
by kind permission of Brigadier J. H. S. Lacey and Lieutenant-Colonel F. T. Stear.

Lectures and essays delivered and presented at the R.A.F. Staff College.

Lent to the author by Air Commodore R. H. S. Spaight.

Correspondence with the following, who produced information from regimental records:
Major J. S. Sutherland (the 3rd Hussars), Major M. A. Urban-Smith (the 20th Hussars), Colonel H. R. Grace (1st Buffs), Major T. R. Stead (2nd Essex Regiment), Mr. J. Jeffrey (1st the Loyal Regiment), Captain R. Quayle (1st King's Regiment), Lieutenant-Colonel G. C. B. Sass (the Lancashire Regiment), Captain R. Fogg-Elliot (1st Gordon Highlanders), Major H. Butterworth (1st North Staffordshire Regiment) and the late Brigadier F. Stephens (the Rifle Brigade).

The author would also like to thank the following who were in either Greece or Turkey during the period 1919–23 and whose correspondence with him was of great assistance:
Brigadier L. Bootle-Wilbraham, Lieutenant-Colonel Sir Guy Shaw-Stewart, Lieutenant-Colonel J. H. Plumridge, Lieutenant-Colonel F. H. Thompson, Major J. L. Breeds, Major Y. A. Burges, Mr. A. T. Stoddart.

Published
Journals and Newspapers
The magazines and journals of the regiments, corps and units present in Greece and Turkey 1919–23 and, where such exist, the official regimental histories.

The Army Quarterly, in particular, for Brigadier van Cutsem's article 'Anatolia 1920' (1966), Mehmed Arif Bey's 'The Anatolian Revolt' (1926) and General Marden's articles 'With the British Army in Constantinople' (1933, 1933–4).

The Naval Review, in particular for the double article 'Smyrna and After' (1923) contributed by an anonymous eyewitness.

The Royal United Services Institution Journal (1920 and 1921) for an examination of the French campaign in Cilicia and an account of the events in Athens in December 1916.

History Today (1966) for Cyril Falls' 'The Greek Anatolian Adventure'.

The Survey of International Affairs, 1920–3, *The Times, Daily Telegraph, Daily Express, Daily Mail* and the *Manchester Guardian*, 1919–23.

Documents and Reports

Documents on British Foreign Policy, 1919–39
   First series, Vol. XIII 1920–21—HMSO 1963
       Vol. XV 1921—HMSO 1967

The Lausanne Conference—published as a Parliamentary paper—HMSO 1923.

Papers relating to the Foreign Relations of the United States 1922. Vol II—United States Department of State, 1938.

The League of Nations Report on the Operation of the Refugee Settlement Commission in Greece. Geneva 1924.

Official Journal of the League of Nations. Refugees from Asia Minor—Report by Dr. Fridtjof Nansen. Geneva 1923.

Bibliography

This is not an exhaustive list nor does it include all the works, particularly general histories, consulted by the author. Those works from which significant quotations have been made in the text are indicated by an asterisk and the author wishes to thank those authors and or publishers who have given him permission so to do.

Abbott, G. F., *Greece and the Allies* (Methuen, London 1922)
Aga Khan, the, *Memoirs* (Cassell, London 1954)
Alastos, D., *Veniselos* (Lund Humphries, London 1942)
Alexandra of Yugoslavia, Queen, *For a King's Love* (Odhams, London 1942)
Amery, L. S., *My Political Life* (Hutchinson, London 1953)
Andrew of Greece, Prince, *Towards Disaster, the Greek Army in Asia Minor, in 1921* (John Murray, London 1930)
Armstrong, A., *Turkey in Travail* (John Lane, London 1925)
Barker, A. J., *The Neglected War* (Faber, London 1967)
Barnett, Corelli, *The Sword Bearers* (Eyre & Spottiswoode, London 1963)
Beaverbrook, Lord, *Politicians and the Press* (Hutchinson, London 1925)

Beaverbrook, Lord, *The Decline and Fall of Lloyd George* (Collins, London 1963)

Bierstadt, E. H., *The Great Betrayal* (Hutchinson, London 1925)

Birkenhead, Earl of, *F.E. Life of F. E. Smith, 1st Earl Birkenhead* (Eyre & Spottiswoode, London 1959)

Blake, Robert, *The Unknown Prime Minister* (Eyre & Spottiswoode, London 1955)

*Bonham Carter, V., *Soldier True* (Muller, London 1963)

Boothby, Robert, *I fight to live* (Gollancz, London 1947)

Boyle, Andrew, *Trenchard* (Collins, London 1962)

Bujac, Colonel A., *Les campagnes de l'Armée hellenique 1918–1922* (Ch. Lavavzelle et Cie, Paris 1930)

*Callwell, Major-General Sir C. E., *F.M. Sir Henry Wilson, His life and diaries* (Cassell, London 1927)

Camp, William, *The Glittering Prizes, a biographical study of F. E. Smith* (MacGibbon & Kee, London 1960)

Chalmers, Rear Admiral W. S., *The Life and Letters of David Beatty* (Hodder & Stoughton, London 1951)

Chamberlain, Sir Austen, *Down the Years* (Cassell, London 1935)

Chester, S. B., *Life of Veniselos* (Constable, London 1921) by kind permission of The Hamlyn Publishing Group, London

*Churchill, Winston, *Great Contemporaries* (Macmillan, London 1937)

*Churchill, Winston, *The World Crisis* (Thornton Butterworth, London 1927) by kind permission of Charles Scribner's Sons, New York

Cosmetatos, S. P. P., *The Tragedy of Greece* (Kegan, Paul, London 1928)

Curzon, Marchioness, *Reminiscences* (Hutchinson, London 1955)

Dawson, R. MacGregor, *William Lyon Mackenzie King* (Methuen, London 1959)

Deville, Gabriel, *L'Entente, la Grèce, et la Bulgarie* (E. Figuiere et Cie, Paris 1921)

Domville, Admiral Sir Barry, *By and large* (Hutchinson, London 1936)

Edmonds, C. J., *Kurds, Turks and Arabs* (O.U.P., London 1957)

Falls, Cyril, *The First World War* (Longmans, London 1960)

Fenton, Charles A., *The Apprenticeship of Ernest Hemingway* (Farrar, Straus and Young, New York 1954)

Forster, E. S., *A Short History of Modern Greece 1821–1956* (revised edition Methuen, London 1958)

Fournet, Admiral Dartiges du, *Souvenirs de Guerre d'un Amiral* (Edition Plon, Paris 1930)

Gibbons, Herbert Adams, *Veniselos* (Fisher Unwin, London 1921)

367

Graves, Sir Robert Windham, *Storm Centres in the Near East 1879-1929* (Hutchinson, London 1923)

Grey of Fallodon, Viscount, *Twenty-five Years* (Hodder & Stoughton, London 1925)

Harington, General Sir Charles, *Plumer of Messines* (John Murray, London 1935)

*Harington, General, Sir Charles, *Tim Harington looks back* (John Murray, London 1940)

Hemingway, Ernest, *The Snows of Kilimanjaro* (Penguins, London 1963)

Hemingway, Ernest, *By-line: Ernest Hemingway*, ed. William White (Collins, London 1968)

Henderson, Sir Nevile, *Water under the Bridges* (Hodder & Stoughton, London 1945)

Jackson, Stanley, *Rufus Isaacs 1st Marquess of Reading* (Cassell, London 1936)

James, Robert Rhodes, *Gallipoli* (Batsford, London 1965)

Kinross, Lord, *Ataturk: The Rebirth of a Nation* (Weidenfeld and Nicolson, London 1964)

Kirkpatrick, Sir Ivone, *Mussolini: Study of a Demagogue* (Odhams, London 1964)

Knatchbull-Hugessen, Sir Hugh, *Diplomat in Peace and War* (John Murray, London 1949)

Korofilas, C., *Eleftherios Veniselos* (John Murray, London 1915)

Lloyd George D., *The Truth about the Peace Treaties* (Gollancz, London 1938)

*Lloyd George, Frances, *The Years that are Past* (Hutchinson, London 1967)

Mackenzie, Sir Compton, *Athenian Memories* (Cassell, London 1931)

Mackenzie, Sir Compton, *Greek Memories* (Chatto and Windus, London 1939)

Magnus, Sir Philip, *Kitchener* (John Murray, London 1958)

Mavrogordato, J., *Modern Greece, 1800–1931* (Macmillan, London 1931)

McCormick, Donald, *Pedlar of Death: The Life of Sir Basil Zaharoff* (Macdonald, London 1965)

Melas, G. M., *Ex-King Constantine and the War* (Hutchinson, London 1920)

Miller, W., *A History of the Greek People 1821–1921* (Methuen, London 1922)

Morgenthau, H., *Secrets of the Bosphorus* (Hutchinson, London 1918)

Morgenthau, H., *Ambassador Morgenthau's Story* (Hodder & Stoughton, London 1928)

Nicolson, Harold, *Some People* (Constable, London 1927)

368

Nicolson, Harold, *Curzon: The Last Phase* (Constable, London 1934)

*Nicolson, Harold, *King George V* (Constable, London 1952)

*Nicolson, Harold, *Peacemaking* (Constable, London 1933) by kind permission of Nigel Nicolson, Esq.

Owen, Frank, *The Tempestuous Journey: Lloyd George, His Life and Times* (Hutchinson, London 1954)

Pallis, A. A., *Greece's Anatolian Adventure—and after* (Methuen, London 1937)

Palmer, Alan, *The Gardeners of Salonika* (Andre Deutsch, London 1965)

Price, J. Ward, *Extra-special Correspondent* (Harrap, London 1957)

Rawlinson, A., *Adventures in the Middle East* (Andrew Melrose, London 1923)

Reading, Marquess of, *Rufus Isaacs, First Marquess of Reading* (Hutchinson, London 1945)

Robertson, Field Marshal Sir William, *Soldiers and Statesmen* (Cassell, London 1926)

Ronaldshay, Earl of, *Life of Lord Curzon* (Ernest Benn, London 1928)

Sforza, Count Carlo, *Makers of Modern Europe* (Elkin, Mathews and Marrot, London 1930)

Spender, J. A. and Asquith C., *Asquith* (Hutchinson, London 1932)

Sylvester, A. J., *The Real Lloyd George* (Cassell, London 1947)

Thomson, Malcolm, *David Lloyd George* (Hutchinson, London 1948)

Toynbee, A. J., *The Western Question in Greece and Turkey* (Constable, London 1922)

Toynbee, A. J., *The World after the Peace Conference* (Milford, London 1925)

Toynbee, A. J. and Kirkwood, K. P., *Turkey* (Ernest Benn, London 1926)

Trevelyan, G. M., *Grey of Fallodon* (Longman's, Green, London 1937)

Tuchman, Barbara W., *August 1914* (Constable, London 1962)

*Vansittart, Lord, *The Mist Procession* (Hutchinson, London 1958)

Waley, E. D., *Edwin Montagu* (Asia Publishing House, London 1964)

Wheeler-Bennett, Sir J. W., *A Wreath to Clio* (Macmillan, London 1967)

*Windsor, the Duke of, *A King's Story* (Cassell, London 1951) by kind permission of Fulton, Walter & Duncombe, New York

Woodrooffe, Commander T., *Naval Odyssey* (Jonathan Cape, London 1936)

Young, G. M., *Baldwin* (Rupert Hart Davis, London 1952)

Young, Kenneth, *Arthur James Balfour* (G. Bell, London 1963)

Index

equipment, etc., 129–32; *see also* Regiments. French—withdraws from Chanak, 222. *See also* Regiments. Greek—purges in, 96–7; advances into Anatolia, 98; state of, 105–6; fights first battle of Inönü, 115; Harington's opinion of, 140; Harington's reports on, 146; M. Gounaris and M. Theotokis visit, 148; retreats to Smyrna, 170–1; casualties after Smyrna, 179; evacuation from Anatolia, 191; Marden's opinion of, 194–6; character of its officers, 265–6; evacuates E. Thrace, 318. Indian—composition of, 158; effect of Turkish propaganda on, 159; battalions withdraw from Constantinople, 186. Italian—withdraws from Chanak, 222. Turkish—retreats beyond Sakarya river, 150; approaches Chanak, 203; strength at Chanak, 210; condition of, 221; enters neutral zone, 242; description of cavalry, 243; advance on Chanak, 259; disposition of troops, 261; description of, 270–1; occupies E. Thrace, 318

Artillery, at Chanak, 252

Aspasia Manos: marriage to King Alexander, 85; birth of daughter to, note, 87

Asquith, H. H.: ousted by Lloyd George, 51, loses seat, 62; epitaph on Bonar Law, 356

Ataturk; *see* Kemal, Mustapha

Australia; *see* Dominions

Baghdad Railway, 23

Baldwin, Stanley: comment on House of Commons, 1918, 62; attends Cabinet, 299; speaks at Carlton Club, 325; becomes Chancellor of Exchequer, 328; becomes Prime Minister, 357; appoints Churchill as Chancellor, 358

Balfour, A. J.: elder statesman, 63; leaves for Washington

Conference, 156; supports Lloyd George, 191; speech at Geneva, 281; attitude before Carlton Club meeting, 326; consulted by King George V, 357; dies, 357

Baltazzis, Greek Foreign Minister, 340–2

Barrère, French Ambassador to Italy, 336

Beatty, Admiral of the Fleet Lord: character and career, 222–3; at Paris talks, 232; member of Committee of Ministers, 248; cannot prevent invasion of Constantinople, 260; death, 360

Beaverbrook, Lord: seeking new Prime Minister, 114; reports from Athens, 183; reaction to Veniselos' visit, 267–8; uses *Express* to support Bonar Law, 320

Beckwith, Colonel A.T., 251

Bekir Sami Bey, 116

Berkeley Milne, Admiral Sir Archibald, *see* Milne

Bevin, Ernest, 135

Birkenhead, Lord: character, 63; supports Lloyd George, 191; responsibility for ultimatum, 287–9; attitude before Carlton Club meeting, 326; denies seeing Gounaris letter, 346; Secretary of State, India, and death, 357

Blessington, Lady, 357

Blunt, Lieutenant J. S., 305

Bompard, Maurice, 336

Bondfield, Margaret, 239–40

Bonham Carter, Violet, 330

Briand, Aristide: Ribot replaces, 51; at London Conference, 118; Curzon visits, 149; at Cannes Conference, 162; falls from power, 162

Bristol, Admiral, U.S.N., 133, 174, 176, 336

Brock, Admiral Sir Osmond: prepares to defend Constantinople, 167; agrees to defend Chanak, 193; seeks instructions, 254; describes situation in Constantinople, 275

Brockway, Fenner, 238

Brooke, Rupert, 42

Harington, Lady, 111, 348, 350, 351
Harington, Lieutenant-General
Sir Charles: takes over military
command, Constantinople, 106;
career and character, 125-7;
attitude to his men, 132; opinion
of Greek army, 140; reports on
Greek army, 146; approaches
Kemal, 164; decides to defend
Constantinople, 167-8; War Office
instructions to, 181; decides to
defend Chanak, 193; orders to
Shuttleworth, 245; views on
Kemal's intentions, 245-6;
Kemal's estimate of him, 247;
concerned for defence of
Constantinople, 250; request for
more troops, 252; ordered to
warn Kemal again, 254; gives
Marden permission to fire if
attacked, 259; cables
suggestions to avoid war, 261-2;
restrains Marden at Chanak, 271;
negotiates with Kemal, 274;
disagrees with Cabinet, 278;
receives further instructions,
279; receives Cabinet's ultimatum,
281-2; in touch with Kemal,
289-90; reply to Cabinet, 296-7;
Chiefs of Staff consider conduct
of, 298; arranges meeting with
Kemal at Mudania, 299; receives
instructions for, 299-300;
conducts Mudania negotiations,
303-18; smuggles Sultan out of
Constantinople, 333-4; negotiates
with Turks in Constantinople,
348; leaves Constantinople,
350-1; destroys his papers, 353;
subsequent career and death,
357-8
Harmsworth, Cecil, 90
Hemingway, Ernest, 120, 318
Henderson, Nevile: deputy High
Commissioner, Constantinople,
130; opinion of Harington, 132;
opinion of High Commissioners,
133; decides to defend
Constantinople, 167-8; helps
Sultan leave Constantinople,
334; becomes Ambassador to
Turkey, 351
Hepburn, Captain, U.S.N., 171, 177

Heywood, Major T. G. G. (later
Colonel), 194, 305
Hoare, Sir Samuel, 328
Horne, Sir Robert, 113, 330, 358
Horton, Mr., 173
Hughes, Lieutenant-Colonel, 208
Hussein Kamal, 30

Inönü: first battle of, 115; second
battle of, 120
Inönü, Ismet; see Ismet Pasha
Ireland: Easter Rebellion, 108;
terrorism in, 122; truce signed
with, 135; Government of
Ireland Act, 136; troubles
continue, 237
Isaacs, Rufus; see Reading, Marquis
of
Istanbul; see Constantinople

Jellicoe, Admiral Lord, 21, 253, 360
Johnston, Major M. A. B., 194
Jonnart, Charles, 51

Kaiser Wilhelm II, 23, 34, 53
Kalogeropoulos, Greek Prime
Minister, 116, 229
Karaburun, 47
Karagatch, 313
Kars, 85
Kelly, Rear-Admiral, 98, 209, 244
Kemal, Mustapha (Kemal Ataturk):
reputation at Gallipoli, 42;
without a job, 58; in Anatolia,
74; dismissed by Sultan, 75;
reputation grows, 76; establishes
H.Q. in Ankara, 79; agreement
with Russia, 85; denounced by
Sultan, 99; Turkish opinion turns
to, 100; position in 1920, 103;
character, 103; British consider
offers to, 141; at battle of
Sakarya river, 152-4; entitled
Ghazi, 154; enters Smyrna, 175;
his peace terms, 182; attitude to
neutral zone, 220-1; talks to
Pellé, 231; Allied Note to, 242;
his intentions, 246-7; delays
reply to Note, 248; military odds
lengthened against, 252; increases
pressure at Chanak, 269-70;
negotiates with Harrington, 274;
in contact with Harington,

375